T0178233

Lecture Notes in Computer Science 11656

Ying Tan · Yuhui Shi · Ben Niu (Eds.)

Advances in Swarm Intelligence

10th International Conference, ICSI 2019
Chiang Mai, Thailand, July 26–30, 2019
Proceedings, Part II

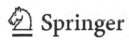 Springer

Editors
Ying Tan
Peking University
Beijing, China

Ben Niu
Shenzhen University
Shenzhen, China

Yuhui Shi
Southern University of Science
and Technology
Shenzhen, China

ISSN 0302-9743   ISSN 1611-3349 (electronic)
Lecture Notes in Computer Science
ISBN 978-3-030-26353-9   ISBN 978-3-030-26354-6 (eBook)
https://doi.org/10.1007/978-3-030-26354-6

LNCS Sublibrary: SL1 – Theoretical Computer Science and General Issues

This Springer imprint is published by the registered company Springer Nature Switzerland AG
The registered company address is: Gewerbestrasse 11, 6330 Cham, Switzerland

Preface

This book and its companion volumes, LNCS vols. 11655 and 11656, constitute the proceedings of the 10th International Conference on Swarm Intelligence (ICSI 2019) held during July 26–30, 2019, in Chiang Mai, Thailand.

The theme of ICSI 2019 was "Serving Life with Intelligence Science." ICSI 2019 provided an excellent opportunity and/or an academic forum for academics and practitioners to present and discuss the latest scientific results and methods, innovative ideas, and advantages in theories, technologies, and applications in swarm intelligence. The technical program covered most of the aspects of swarm intelligence and its related areas.

ICSI 2019 was the tenth international gathering in the world for researchers working on most of the aspects of swarm intelligence, following successful events in Shanghai (ICSI 2018), Fukuoka (ICSI 2017), Bali (ICSI 2016), Beijing (ICSI-CCI 2015), Hefei (ICSI 2014), Harbin (ICSI 2013), Shenzhen (ICSI 2012), Chongqing (ICSI 2011), and Beijing (ICSI 2010), which provided a high-level academic forum for participants to disseminate their new research findings and discuss emerging areas of research. It also created a stimulating environment for participants to interact and exchange information on future challenges and opportunities in the field of swarm intelligence research. ICSI 2019 was held in conjunction with the 4th International Conference on Data Mining and Big Data (DMBD 2019) held in Chiang Mai, Thailand, for sharing common mutual ideas, promoting transverse fusion, and stimulating innovation.

The ICSI 2019 was held in Chiang Mai, Thailand, which was founded in 1296 as the capital of the ancient Lanna Kingdom, located 700 km north of Bangkok in a verdant valley on the banks of the Ping River. Chiang Mai is a land of misty mountains and colorful hill tribes, a playground for seasoned travelers, a paradise for shoppers, and a delight for adventurers. Chiang Mai can expand visitors' horizons with Thai massage, cooking courses, variety of handicrafts, and antiques. Despite its relatively small size, Chiang Mai truly has it all. Today it is a place where past and the present seamlessly merge with modern buildings standing side by side with venerable temples.

ICSI 2019 took place at the Duangtawan Hotel in Chiang Mai, Thailand, which is located in the center of Night Bazaar, one of the famous shopping areas in downtown Chiang Mai. Surrounded by a night market where there is an ideal district for shopping, sightseeing, meeting, and commercial business, the hotel is only 15 minutes away from Chiang Mai International Airport, the main railway station, and Chiang Mai bus station. Guests can easily access the weekend walking streets, historical attractions, and traditional temples, while indulging in fascinating northern eateries, original handicrafts, souvenirs, and local entertainment. The hotel offers comfortable and convenient guestrooms overlooking Chiang Mai's vibrant city view, and a plentiful service of TAI-style restaurants and bars, as well as a complete service of MICE events towards a selection of our function rooms. Guests can enjoy the wide-panoramic view of an outdoor swimming pool, fully-equipped fitness center, and well-being Varee Spa.

ICSI 2019 received 179 submissions and invited submissions from about 429 authors in 30 countries and regions (Algeria, Australia, Austria, Bangladesh, Brazil, China, Colombia, Finland, Germany, Chinese Hong Kong, India, Iraq, Italy, Japan, Malaysia, Mexico, New Zealand, Norway, Portugal, Romania, Russia, Serbia, Singapore, South Africa, Spain, Sweden, Chinese Taiwan, Thailand, United Kingdom, United States of America) across 6 continents (Asia, Europe, North America, South America, Africa, and Oceania). Each submission was reviewed by at least two reviewers, and on average 2.6 reviewers. Based on rigorous reviews by the Program Committee members and reviewers, 82 high-quality papers were selected for publication in this proceedings volume with an acceptance rate of 45.81%. The papers are organized into 13 cohesive sections covering major topics of swarm intelligence research and its development and applications.

On behalf of the Organizing Committee of ICSI 2019, we would like to express our sincere thanks to Peking University, Southern University of Science and Technology, and Mae Fah Luang University for their sponsorship, and to Computational Intelligence Laboratory of Peking University, School of Information Technology of Mae Fah Luang University, and IEEE Beijing Chapter for its technical co-sponsorship, as well as to our supporters of International Neural Network Society, World Federation on Soft Computing, Beijing Xinghui Hi-Tech Co., and Springer Nature.

We would also like to thank the members of the Advisory Committee for their guidance, the members of the international Program Committee and additional reviewers for reviewing the papers, and the members of the Publications Committee for checking the accepted papers in a short period of time. We are particularly grateful to the proceedings publisher Springer for publishing the proceedings in the prestigious series of Lecture Notes in Computer Science. Moreover, we wish to express our heartfelt appreciation to the plenary speakers, session chairs, and student helpers. In addition, there are still many more colleagues, associates, friends, and supporters who helped us in immeasurable ways; we express our sincere gratitude to them all. Last but not the least, we would like to thank all the speakers, authors, and participants for their great contributions that made ICSI 2019 successful and all the hard work worthwhile.

June 2019

Ying Tan
Yuhui Shi
Ben Niu

Organization

General Co-chairs

Ying Tan   Peking University, China
Russell C. Eberhart   IUPUI, USA

Programme Committee Chair

Yuhui Shi   Southern University of Science and Technology, China

Advisory Committee Chairs

Xingui He   Peking University, China
Gary G. Yen   Oklahoma State University, USA
Benjamin W. Wah   Chinese University of Hong Kong, SAR China

Technical Committee Co-chairs

Haibo He   University of Rhode Island Kingston, USA
Kay Chen Tan   City University of Hong Kong, SAR China
Nikola Kasabov   Aukland University of Technology, New Zealand
Ponnuthurai Nagaratnam   Nanyang Technological University, Singapore
  Suganthan
Xiaodong Li   RMIT University, Australia
Hideyuki Takagi   Kyushu University, Japan
M. Middendorf   University of Leipzig, Germany
Mengjie Zhang   Victoria University of Wellington, New Zealand
Qirong Tang   Tongji University, China

Plenary Session Co-chairs

Andreas Engelbrecht   University of Pretoria, South Africa
Chaoming Luo   University of Mississippi, USA

Invited Session Co-chairs

Andres Iglesias   University of Cantabria, Spain
Haibin Duan   Beihang University, China
Junfeng Chen   Hohai University, China

Special Sessions Chairs

Ben Niu	Shenzhen University, China
Yan Pei	University of Aizu, Japan
Yinan Guo	China University of Mining and Technology, China

Tutorial Co-chairs

Milan Tuba	Singidunum University, Serbia
Junqi Zhang	Tongji University, China
Shi Cheng	Shanxi Normal University, China

Publications Co-chairs

Swagatam Das	Indian Statistical Institute, India
Radu-Emil Precup	Politehnica University of Timisoara, Romania

Publicity Co-chairs

Yew-Soon Ong	Nanyang Technological University, Singapore
Carlos Coello	CINVESTAV-IPN, Mexico
Yaochu Jin	University of Surrey, UK
Rossi Kamal	GERIOT, Bangladesh
Dongbin Zhao	Institute of Automation, CAS, China

Finance and Registration Chairs

Andreas Janecek	University of Vienna, Austria
Suicheng Gu	Google Corporation, USA

Local Arrangement Chair

Tossapon Boongoen	Mae Fah Luang University, Thailand

Conference Secretariat

Renlong Chen	Peking University, China
Xiangyu Liu	Peking University, China

Program Committee

Rafael Alcala	University of Granada, Spain
Esther Andrés	INTA, Spain
Sabri Arik	Istanbul University, Turkey
Carmelo J. A. Bastos Filho	University of Pernambuco, Brazil
Sujin Bureerat	Khon Kaen University, Thailand

Boyang Qu	Zhongyuan University of Technology, China
Guangchen Ruan	Indiana University Bloomington, USA
Kevin Seppi	Brigham Young University, USA
Ponnuthurai Suganthan	Nanyang Technological University, Singapore
Jianyong Sun	University of Nottingham, UK
Ying Tan	Peking University, China
Mario Ventresca	Purdue University, USA
Guoyin Wang	Chongqing University of Posts and Telecommunications, China
Yan Wang	The Ohio State University, USA
Ning Xiong	Mälardalen University, Sweden
Benlian Xu	Changshu Institute of Technology, China
Yingjie Yang	De Montfort University, UK
Peng-Yeng Yin	National Chi Nan University, Taiwan
Zhi-Hui Zhan	South China University of Technology, China
Chenggang Zhang	Tsinghua University, China
Jie Zhang	Newcastle University, UK
Junqi Zhang	Tongji University, China
Qieshi Zhang	Shenzhen Institutes of Advanced Technology, Chinese Academy of Sciences, China
Xingyi Zhang	Anhui University, China
Zili Zhang	Deakin University, Australia
Qiangfu Zhao	The University of Aizu, Japan
Xinchao Zhao	Beijing University of Posts and Telecommunications, China

Additional Reviewers

Chai, Zhengyi
Deng, Xiaodan
Fan, Zhun
Gao, Chao
Li, Li
Liu, Xiaoxi
Liu, Yuxin
Lu, Yu
Luo, Juanjuan
Mahmoud, Mohammed

Nguyen, Kieu Anh
Sun, Xiaoxuan
Thomas, Kent
Tian, Yanlling
Wang, Chunxia
Wang, Hongfeng
Wang, Jue
Xiao, Fuyuan
Zhang, Peng
Zhou, Kang

Contents – Part II

Identification and Recognition

Social Computing and Knowledge Graph

Service Quality and Energy Management

Contents – Part I

Ant Colony Optimization

Fireworks Algorithms and Brain Storm Optimization

Swarm Intelligence Algorithms and Improvements

Genetic Algorithm and Differential Evolution

Swarm Robotics

Multi-agent System

Multi-robot Cooperation Strategy in a Partially Observable Markov Game Using Enhanced Deep Deterministic Policy Gradient

Qirong Tang[✉], Jingtao Zhang, Fangchao Yu, Pengjie Xu,
and Zhongqun Zhang

Laboratory of Robotics and Multibody System,
School of Mechanical Engineering, Tongji University,
No. 4800, Cao An Rd., Shanghai 201804, People's Republic of China
qirong.tang@outlook.com

Abstract. Deep reinforcement learning (DRL) has been applied to solve challenging problems in robotic domains. However, since non-stationary of the environment and the difficulty of long-term interaction between robots, traditional DRL is poorly suitable for multi-robot. Thus, an enhanced deep deterministic policy gradient algorithm is proposed in this study to explore the application of DRL in multi-robot domains. The algorithm ensures a cooperation strategy for multi-robot, which merely uses partially observed state of each robot, named a partially observable Markov game, realize global optimality in executing process. It is achieved by eliminating non-stationary of the environment in training process and a centralized critic for decentralized multi-robot. Simulations with increasingly complex environments are performed to validate the effectiveness of the proposed algorithm.

Keywords: Enhanced deep deterministic policy gradient ·
Multi-robot · Cooperation strategy ·
Partially observable Markov game · Deep reinforcement learning

1 Introduction

In recent years, due to high efficiency and robustness, multi-robot are profoundly potential and have been increasingly applied, such as service multi-robot [1], SLAM multi-robot [2], and so on. Using multi-robot can reduce the completion time and improve robustness considering the failure of a single robot [3]. To accomplish these tasks, multi-robot should have the basic ability for cooperation. Traditional methods guarantee multi-robot cooperation via some communication interaction [4]. However, it is not always feasible to make decisions relying on communication interaction. In other words, the most reliable information is local observations of each robot, called a partially observable Markov game, which will be introduced next.

© Springer Nature Switzerland AG 2019
Y. Tan et al. (Eds.): ICSI 2019, LNCS 11656, pp. 3–10, 2019.
https://doi.org/10.1007/978-3-030-26354-6_1

Deep reinforcement learning (DRL) has been applied to solve challenging problems in robotic domains [5]. Compared to non-learning methods, robots can make optimal decisions online using their learned policies without considering computational complexity when dealing with complex scenarios. But most successes of DRL appear in single robot cases, or single agent domains. There still are barriers and challenges to be further addressed when applied in multi-agent domains. A simple approach is to use independently-learning agents, i.e., regarding other agents as a part of the environment. It was attempted with Q-learning in [6], but doesn't perform well in practice [7]. Identically, independently-learning policy gradient methods also perform poorly [8]. The reason is that changing policy of each agent leads to non-stationary of the environment when using experience replay in training process. To solve this problem, research [9] shares policies parameters to cooperate, but this requires homogeneous agent capabilities and special communication guarantee practically. Therefore, multi-robot cooperation strategy using DRL remains as a challenge, especially in a partially observable Markov game.

Thus, this study aims at using DRL to train multi-robot to cooperate in a partially observable Markov game without any special communication guarantee. Specifically, the contributions are summarized as follows.

- A general environment with continuous observation space and continuous action space based on *pyglet* is built.
- An enhance deep deterministic policy gradient (EDDPG) algorithm for multi-robot learning cooperation strategy in a partially observable Markov game is designed.
- Simulations with increasingly complex environments are performed and the results show the effectiveness of EDDPG.

The rest of this article is organized as follows. Section 2 details the proposed EDDPG algorithm for multi-robot. In Sect. 3, simulations are performed in the proposed continuous environment and results are analysed. Section 4 gives the conclusions.

2   The Enhanced Deep Deterministic Policy Gradient Algorithm for Multi-robot

2.1   Assumptions and Definitions

In practice, it is difficult to guarantee that communication is always connected and the sensing of a robot has a certain range. Therefore, in this study, no advanced methods of special communication guarantee is assumed, and only self-observed information is reliable, i.e., the learned policies of multi-robot only use local information, called a partially observable Markov game, which will be detailed in the following section.

Definitions are shown as follows to better demonstrate the EDDPG algorithm for multi-robot.

- S_i represents the local state of robot i, which is called a partially observable state in Markov games,

- S represents a set of all S_i, i.e. S is the global state,
- a_i represents the action of robot i in a step,
- a represents a set of actions of all robots in a step,
- r_i represents the reward of the action a_i in this step,
- S_i' represents the local state of robot i after performing the action a_i,
- S' represents the global state after all robots performing all actions,
- R_i represents the discount reward in an episode.,
- μ_{θ_i} represents the current, or trained, continuous policy with parameters θ_i of robot i, and μ_{θ_i}' represents target policy with delayed parameters θ_i',
- $Q_i^{\mu'}$ represents the action-value function,
- M represents the experience replay buffer.

2.2 Problem Description

In this study, multi-robot is considered as an extension of Markov decision processes called partially observable Markov games [12], because multi-robot cannot always get global observation.

Value-based reinforcement learning methods, such as Q-Learning, Sarsa, was directly applied to multi-robot by letting each robot i learn an independently optimal function Q_i [11]. However, because robots independently update their policy when learning, the environment appears non-stationary from the view of each robot, violating Markov assumptions for convergence [10], and [13] proposed that the experience replay buffer in such situation cannot be used since probability of next state $P(S'|S, a, \pi_1, \cdots, \pi_N) \neq P(S'|S, a, \pi_1', \cdots, \pi_N')$ when any $\pi_i \neq \pi_i'$. This is a category of deep reinforcement learning for discrete environments. As for continuous environment, policy based reinforcement learning methods, such as policy gradient(PG), deterministic policy gradient(DPG), deep deterministic policy gradient(DDPG), still have this problem, and turning discrete policies π_i into continuous policies μ_{θ_i} can get the result, i.e., $P(S'|S, a, \mu_{\theta_1}, \cdots, \mu_{\theta_N}) \neq P(S'|S, a, \mu_{\theta_1}', \cdots, \mu_{\theta_N}')$ when any $\mu_{\theta_i} \neq \mu_{\theta_i}'$.

In summary, the problem of using DRL to train multi-robot to cooperate is non-stationary of the environment and a partially observable state without special communication guarantee.

2.3 EDDPG

DDPG is a variant of deep neural network where the policy and critic are approximated with deep neural network [14]. It samples trajectories from a replay buffer of experiences that are stored throughout training. The tricks like soft replacement, prioritized sample, make DDPG a great success in continuous environments for one robot. Actor produces action according to observed state, and critic evaluates the action and guide the robot to produce a better action. However, due to non-stationary of the environment, DDPG is hard to convergence if directly deployed in multi-robot.

Therefore, an enhanced DDPG is proposed to overcome these problems while preserving the advantages of DDPG. Key point of the EDDPG is that each robot has a centralized critic which has global information in training process, and only uses partially observed information produce actions in executing process i.e., the input of the robot is partially observed state, but the loss to minimize is given by the critic, whose inputs are global state and actions of all robots. Thus, a partially observable Markov game with N robots in a continuous environment with continuous policy μ_{θ_i} is considered.

In training process, the gradient of the expected return for robot i, $J(\theta_i) = E(R_i)$, can be calculated by

$$\nabla_{\theta_i} J(\mu_{\theta_i}) = E_{S,a \to M}[\nabla_{\theta_i}\mu_{\theta_i}(a_i|S_i)\nabla_{a_i}Q_i^{\mu}(S,a_1,...,a_i,...,a_N)|_{a_i=\mu_i(S_i)}], \quad (1)$$

where M records $(S_1, \cdots, S_N, a_1, \cdots, a_N, r_1, \cdots, r_N, S'_1, \cdots, S'_N)$. The centralized action-value function Q_i^{μ} is updated to calculate the loss, such that

$$\pounds(\theta_i) = E_{s,a,r,s' \to M}(y_i - Q_i^{\mu}(S,a_1,...,a_i,...,a_N))^2, \quad (2)$$

$$\text{s.t. } y_i = r_i + \gamma Q_i^{\mu'}(S',a'_1,...,a'_i,...,a'_N)|_{a'_j=\mu'_j(s'_j)}, \quad (3)$$

where $\mu' = \{\mu_{\theta'_1}, \cdots, \mu_{\theta'_N}\}$ is the set of target policies with delayed parameters θ'_i. Algorithm 1 shows the training process.

Algorithm 1. EDDPG for multiple robots.

1: **for** episode = 1 to 15000 **do**
2:    initialize a random process $\mathbb{N}$ for action exploration
3:    receive initial state $\{S, S_1, \cdots, S_N\}$
4:    **for** t = 1 to 100 **do**
5:       for robot i, choose an action $a_i = \mu(S_i)$ using the current policy
6:       execute actions $a = \{a_1, ..., a_N\}$ and obtain reward $\{r_1, \cdots, r_N\}$ and new state $\{S', S'_1, \cdots, S'_N\}$
7:       store $\{S_1, \cdots, S_N, a_1, \cdots, a_N, r_1, \cdots, r_N, S'_1, \cdots, S'_N\}$ in replay buffer M
8:       update state $\{S_1, \cdots, S_N\} \leftarrow \{S'_1, \cdots, S'_N\}$
9:       **if** replay buffer M is full **then**
10:          **for** robot i = 1 to N **do**
11:             sample a minibatch $\{S_1^j, \cdots, S_N^j, a_1^j, \cdots, a_N^j, r_1^j, \cdots, r_N^j, S'^j_1, \cdots, S'^j_N\}$ of m samples randomly from replay buffer M
12:             set $y^j = r_i^j + \gamma Q_i^{\mu'}(S'^j, a'_1, ...a'_N)|_{a'_k=\mu'_k(S'_k)}$
13:             update critic by minimizing the loss
14:             $\pounds(\theta_i) = \frac{1}{m}\sum_j(y^j - Q_i^{\mu}(S^j, a_1^j, ..., a_i^j, ..., a_N^j)|_{a_i=\mu_i(S_i)})^2$
15:             update actor using the sampled policy gradient
16:             $\nabla_{\theta_i}J \approx \frac{1}{m}\sum_j \nabla_{\theta_i}\mu_i(S_i^j)\nabla_{a_i}Q_i^{\mu}(S^j, a_1^j, ..., a_i^j, ..., a_N^j)|_{a_i=\mu_i(S_i^j)}$
17:          **end for**
18:       **end if**
19:       update target network parameters for each robot i using soft replacement
20:          $\theta'_i \leftarrow \tau\theta_i + (1-\tau)\theta_i$
21:    **end for**
22: **end for**

In executing process, robot i uses learned policy μ_{θ_i} choose an action by

$$a_i = \mu_{\theta i}(S_i). \tag{4}$$

Note that, if the actions of all robots are known, the environment is stationary even the policies change, since

$$
\begin{aligned}
P(S'|S, a_1, \cdots, a_N) &= P(S'|S, a_1, \cdots, a_N, \mu_{\theta_1}, \cdots, \mu_{\theta_N}) \\
&= P(S'|S, a_1, \cdots, a_N, \mu'_{\theta_1}, \cdots, \mu'_{\theta_N})
\end{aligned}
\tag{5}
$$

for any $\mu_{\theta_i} \neq \mu'_{\theta_i}$.

3 Simulations in Continuous Environments

In this simulation, the algorithm of EDDPG for multi-robot is compared with original DDPG in increasingly complex environments to validate the effectiveness.

Figure 1 shows three kinds of continuous environments with different complexity. Figure 1(a) includes three robots and three targets. Figures 1(b) and (c) have 1 more static obstacles and dynamic obstacles, respectively. A robot has learned speeds ranging from 0 to 120 in any direction. A static obstacle has a random position in an episode. A dynamic obstacle has random speeds ranging from 0 to 20 in any direction. The fresh rate is 0.1.

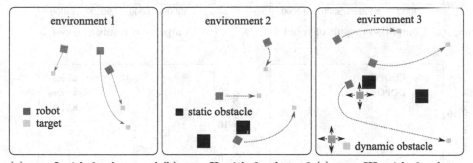

(a) env. I with 3 robots and 3 targets (b) env. II with 3 robots, 3 targets and 2 static obstacles (c) env. III with 3 robots, 3 targets, 2 static obstacles and 2 dynamic obstacles

Fig. 1. Overview of three continuous environments

The simulations are performed with multi-robot multi-target path planning, which is effective to validate the cooperation strategy [9]. Multi-robot is trained in the first environment using EDDPG and DDPG, respectively, and runs the trained model in all three environments to validate the robustness.

The parameters in the simulation are shown as follows. Number of robots is 3, dimension of partially observed state is 9, dimension of all state is 24, dimension of a robot's action is 2, learning rate of policy network is 0.001, learning rate of policy network is 0.002, soft replacement rate is 0.01, memory capacity is 100000, batch size is 512, episode is 15000, and maximal step in a episode is 100. Specifically, partially observed state includes positions of targets, distance to other robots, its own positions and speeds.

Figure 2 shows different convergence performances of EDDPG and DDPG. The training process using EDDPG can converge within a reasonable number of steps, while original DDPG diverges after a certain number of training steps. Figure 2(a)–(c) show the convergence of deep network of robot 1, robot 2 and robot 3, respectively. Figure 2(d) shows the comparison of all robots using EDDPG. The light and thick areas are raw data produced in training process. The dark and thin lines are smoothed to show the results better. The horizontal axis is episodes, and vertical axis is loss.

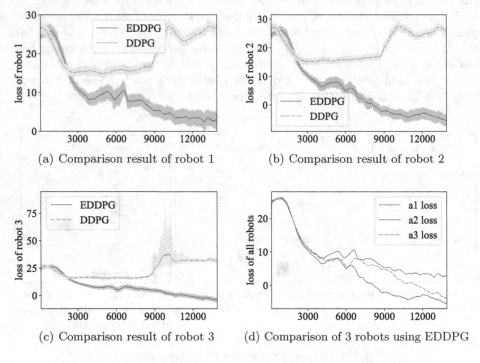

(a) Comparison result of robot 1

(b) Comparison result of robot 2

(c) Comparison result of robot 3

(d) Comparison of 3 robots using EDDPG

Fig. 2. Comparison of convergence with EDDPG and DDPG

Table 1 shows the success rate in 15000 episodes, which illustrates the robustness of the algorithm. For traditional DDPG, each robot regards others as parts of the environment, so the changing policy of each robot leads to non-stationary of the environment when using experience replay, which results in still diverging after enough training episodes. However, EDDPG uses a centralized critic in training process. It let the trainer know all the changing policies of multiple robots, which means the non-stationary of the environment is eliminated. So the results converge after enough training episodes.

In training process, since the basic ability of multi-robot multi-target path planning is trained only in environment I, the success rate in environment II and environment III is zero. The success rate of DDPG is relatively low and can be regarded as invalid. For EDDPG, the success rate of environment I is 89.8%. With the increasing of the environmental complexity, i.e., environment II and environment III, the success rates are 68.4% and 41.48%, respectively. It proves that the EDDPG is relatively robust. Each data is the average of 10 runs.

Table 1. Success rate in 15000 episodes

	Enhanced DDPG			Original DDPG		
	env. I	env. II	env. III	env. I	env. II	env. III
Training process	45.88%	/	/	6.82%	/	/
Executing process	89.80%	68.40%	41.48%	9.84%	1.38%	0.5%

In summary, multi-robot cooperation by EDDPG achieves global optimization using only the information itself observes. It gets rid of the limitations of getting the global information using communication or something else. What's more, there will be a physical obstacle avoidance module on the actual robot, which will change the predetermined trajectory. Thus, simulations with environment II and environment III validate the robustness of EDDPG.

4   Conclusions

This study proposes an enhanced deep deterministic policy gradient (EDDPG) algorithm for exploring in multi-robot domains. The algorithm aims at eliminating non-stationary of the environment in training process and only using partially observed state achieve global optimality, which facilitates the application of multi-robot using deep reinforcement learning in practice. Note that the cooperation strategy is just the first step, applying the algorithm to complete more complex tasks and perform experiments is currently under doing.

Acknowledgements. This work is supported by the projects of National Natural Science Foundation of China(No. 61603277, No. 61873192), the Key Pre-Research Project of the 13th-Five-Year-Plan on Common Technology (No. 41412050101), and Field Fund (No. 61403120407). Meanwhile, this work is also partially supported by the Fundamental Research Funds for the Central Universities, and the Youth 1000 program project. It is also partially sponsored by the Key Basic Research Project of Shanghai Science and Technology Innovation Plan (No. 15JC1403300), as well as the projects supported by China Academy of Space Technology, and Launch Vehicle Technology. All these supports are highly appreciated.

References

1. Nuovo, A.D., et al.: The multi-modal interface of robot-era multi-robot services tailored for the elderly. Intell. Serv. Rob. **11**(1), 109–126 (2018)
2. Schmuck, P., Chli, M.: Multi-UAV collaborative monocular SLAM. In: International Conference on Robotics and Automation, pp. 3863–3870. Singapore (2017)
3. Luo, W., Tang, Q., Fu, C., Eberhard, P.: Deep-sarsa based multi-UAV path planning and obstacle avoidance in a dynamic environment. In: Tan, Y., Shi, Y., Tang, Q. (eds.) ICSI 2018. LNCS, vol. 10942, pp. 102–111. Springer, Cham (2018). https://doi.org/10.1007/978-3-319-93818-9_10
4. Milad, N., Esmaeel, K., Samira, D.: Multi-objective multi-robot path planning in continuous environment using an enhanced genetic algorithm. Expert Syst. Appl. **115**, 106–120 (2019)
5. Levine, S., Finn, C., Darrell, T., Abbeel, P.: End-to-end training of deep visuomotor policies. J. Mach. Learn. Res. **17**(1), 1334–1373 (2015)
6. Tan, M.: Multi-agent reinforcement learning: independent vs. cooperative agents. In: International Conference on Machine Learning, Amherst, USA, pp. 330–337 (1993)
7. Matignon, L., Laurent, G.J., Fort-Piat, N.L.: Independent reinforcement learners in cooperative Markov games: a survey regarding coordination problems. Knowl. Eng. Rev. **27**(1), 1–31 (2012)
8. Hao, J., Huang, D., Yi, C., Leung, H.F.: The dynamics of reinforcement social learning in networked cooperative multiagent systems. Eng. Appl. Artif. Intell. **58**, 111–122 (2017)
9. Gupta, J.K., Egorov, M., Kochenderfer, M.: Cooperative multi-agent control using deep reinforcement learning. In: Sukthankar, G., Rodriguez-Aguilar, J.A. (eds.) AAMAS 2017. LNCS (LNAI), vol. 10642, pp. 66–83. Springer, Cham (2017). https://doi.org/10.1007/978-3-319-71682-4_5
10. Fan, B., Pan, Q., Zhang, H.C.: A multi-agent coordination method based on Markov game and application to robot soccer. Robotics **182**(4), 357–366 (2005)
11. Foerster, J.N., Assael, Y.M., Freitas, N.D., Whiteson, S.: Learning to communicate with deep multi-agent reinforcement learning. In: International Conference on Neural Information Processing Systems, Barcelo, Spain, pp. 2137–2145 (2016)
12. Olsder, G.J., Papavassilopoulos, G.P.: A Markov chain game with dynamic information. J. Optim. Theor. Appl. **59**(3), 467–486 (1988)
13. Foerster, J., Nardelli, N., Farquhar, G., Torr, P.H.S., Kohli, P., Whiteson, S.: Stabilising experience replay for deep multi-agent reinforcement learning. In: International Conference on Machine Learning, pp. 1146–1155. PMLR, Singapore (2017)
14. Silver, D., Lever, G., Heess, N., Degris, T., Wierstra, D., Riedmiller, M.: Deterministic policy gradient algorithms. J. Mach. Learn. Res. **32**, 387–395 (2014)

Research on the Construction of Underwater Platform Combat Deduction System Based on Service-Oriented and Multi-agent Technology

Yuxiang Sun[✉], Xianzhong Zhou, and Dongpo Li

School of Management and Engineering,
Nanjing University, Nanjing 210093, China
sunyuxiangsun@126.com

Abstract. Object-Oriented intelligent modeling, model management, et al., are difficult problems in the designing and development of underwater platform combat deduction system. The command and control description model based on OODA loop depicted the business process of underwater platform combat deduction, using service oriented and Agent modeling technology, established an underwater platforms deduction system architecture based on service oriented and multi-Agent, effectively solve the problem of intelligence, reusing and extensibility in combat deduction modeling, and established program framework. The paper has reference value in the designing and development of underwater platforms deduction system.

Keywords: Underwater platform · Combat deduction · Service-oriented · Multi-agent

1 Introduction

Combat deduction refers to: "Imitation of combat processes according to known or intended situations and data. Including the simulation of actual military exercises and computer combat simulation. It is usually used to research and test the combat plan, evaluate the effectiveness of combat equipment, and explore new combat theories. By means of combat deduction, both the rationality and feasibility of combat strategies and combat plans can be verified, the ability of commanders to analyze problems and deal with incidents can be trained, and new tactics can be explored in the context of combat scenarios. Therefore, research and build an underwater platform combat deduction system that is close to actual combat, model intelligence, reasonable structure and flexible use, and carry out combat plan exercises for underwater platforms such as underwater unmanned vehicles and submarines, plays an important role in optimizing the underwater platform combat plan and training the commander's combat ability.

Based on the OODA ring command and control description model, this paper briefly describes the business process of underwater platform combat deduction, combines service-oriented technology and Agent modeling technology, and builds an architecture of underwater platform combat deduction system based on service-oriented

Y. Tan et al. (Eds.): ICSI 2019, LNCS 11656, pp. 11–22, 2019.
https://doi.org/10.1007/978-3-030-26354-6_2

and multi-Agent, and discusses the implementation method of agent modeling technology.

2   Definition of Combat Deduction Function of Underwater Platform

The definition of the underwater platform combat deduction function is the basis for constructing the underwater platform combat deduction system. At present, different types and uses of combat deduction systems have been developed and applied domestic and abroad [3–10]. Among them, the Joint Warfare System (JWARS) is a simulation system supported by the US military to support joint combat operations, mainly including the problem domain, simulation domain and platform domain. The problem domain provides software for analysis purposes and describing combat functions; the simulation domain provides "engine" that drives the simulation run; and the platform domain provides system hardware and human-computer interaction interface [1, 2]. With the function definition method of the joint war system, the typical OODA ring command and control description model [11, 12] is adopted for the underwater platform combat process and its characteristics. The business process analysis of the underwater platform combat process is carried out, and the underwater platform combat deduction function is described.

The general working process of the underwater platform combat system is as follows: the intelligence sub-system collects the battlefield information, completes the comprehensive processing of intelligence, and forms a unified tactical situation; the command sub-system carries out underwater acoustic environment and tactical situation analysis, assists the commander to complete the offensive and defensive decision-making, and clarifies the attack and defense plan. That is to determine the type of attack and defense weapons, channels, platform occupying maneuver schemes, etc.; weapon subsystems launch for shooting solution, launch control, complete weapons attack and integrated defense and other combat activities.

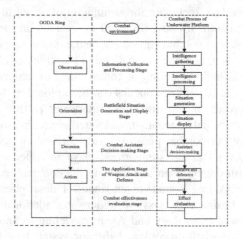

Fig. 1. Combat process model of underwater platform

Taking the underwater platform as an example, according to the Observation (O) - Orientation (O) - Decision (D) - Action (A) process [13], the operation process of the underwater platform is mainly divided into the following stages: information collection and processing, battlefield situation generation and display, combat assistant decision-making, weapon attack and defense application, and combat effectiveness evaluation [14], as shown in Fig. 1.

3 Structure Construction of Underwater Platform Combat Deduction System

3.1 Basic Composition of Combat Deduction System for Underwater Platform

According to the function definition, the underwater platform combat deduction system is mainly composed of guidance and control subsystem, underwater platform model simulation subsystem, environment and force simulation subsystem, combat deduction workbench and deduction resource database. The connection relationship of each part is established by simulation service bus (SSB), as shown in Fig. 2.

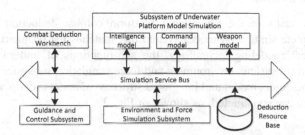

Fig. 2. Composition of combat deduction system for underwater platform

The guidance and control subsystem is the management and control center of the underwater platform combat deduction system. It mainly includes such functional components as scenario editing and generation, simulation operation control, deduction event generation and management, deduction effect evaluation, deduction process recording and playback, battlefield situation display, deduction data management and so on. It is used for the control and management of the whole underwater platform combat deduction by the guidance and control personnel. The simulation subsystem of underwater platform model is the core component of underwater platform combat deduction system. It mainly consists of three parts: intelligence model, command model and weapon model. It includes sonar, radar, navigation, information fusion processing, tactical situation and parameter display, assistant decision-making, target motion element solution, weapon (torpedo, missile, sonar reactance, etc.) launching and controlling and other functional components. It is used to complete the combat function simulation of underwater platform combat system.

The environment and force simulation subsystem is the basis of the underwater platform combat deduction system. It is used to generate and maintain battlefield environment and combat entities, and to provide static and dynamic information such as geographical environment and main entities of combat area.

Combat deduction workbench is a human-computer interaction interface of underwater platform combat deduction system. It is mainly used for commanders to monitor the combat situation of underwater platform in real time, and use deduction aided tools to complete command and control activities in the process of deduction.

The deduction resource base is the data and model management center of the underwater platform combat deduction system. It mainly includes environment database, combat model database, combat scenario database, protocol service library, etc. It provides data and model services for combat deduction.

Simulated Service Bus (SSB) is the interconnection and interworking part of each component of the underwater platform combat deduction system. It provides a standardized communication infrastructure for service requesters and service providers. It has the ability of discovery, routing, matching and selection, and supports dynamic interaction between services.

3.2 Agent Model Composition of Underwater Platform Combat Deduction System

One of the key tasks of the underwater platform combat deduction system is to establish a complete simulation model system that matches the problem solving [16]. Using multi-agent modeling technology, the sub-functions of underwater platform model simulation subsystem, environment and force simulation subsystem are modeled by Agent, and the object model and integrated structure of underwater platform combat deduction system are constructed, as shown in Fig. 3.

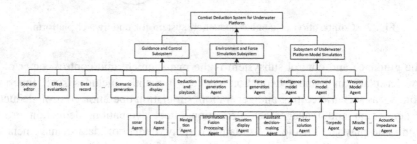

Fig. 3. The agent model of underwater platform combat deduction system

The environment and force simulation subsystem mainly simulate all the geographical environment, marine environment, meteorological environment and electromagnetic environment in the combat area. It also models the main combat entities and event entities in the combat area, and accurately simulates the battlefield environment and the counterforce behavior.

The simulation subsystem of underwater platform model includes intelligence model agent, command model agent and weapon model agent. Among them, intelligence model agent mainly collects combat information, provides basic data for estimating and analyzing combat situation, and provides information basis for combat decision-making, including sonar agent, radar agent and navigation agent, etc. Command model agent is the core component of the system, which has the ability of obtaining information from outside and certain decision-making ability, and can change its own state, and with others. Entities interact to complete the related command and control activities, including information fusion processing agent, tactical situation and parameter display agent, assistant decision-making agent, target motion element solving agent, etc. Weapon model agent cooperates with torpedo agent, missile agent, acoustic countermeasure agent to complete torpedo attack, missile attack, mine deployment and countermeasure according to the instructions issued by combat command model agent. Anti-defense and other combat processes.

Guidance and control subsystem is used to control and manage the whole underwater platform combat deduction. It is the management and control center of the underwater platform combat deduction system. Service-oriented is used to model it.

3.3 Architecture Establishment of Combat Deduction System for Underwater Platform

As a technical design tool of simulation model service system, service-oriented has good encapsulation, reusability and high integration across platforms. Literature [15] proposes a framework of underwater platform combat simulation platform based on Web service, which divides different types of subsystems into modules and integrates them with Web service technology, which improves the reusability of the model. However, in essence, the integration process is based on the order of service execution provided by the process and the data transmission relationship between them. As a static application, Web service technology can only passively wait for the call, but cannot actively provide services, so it is difficult to adapt to the requirements of the underwater platform combat deduction system. Agent technology has the characteristics of autonomy, adaptability and responsiveness due to the introduction of artificial intelligence. It combines with service-oriented to form a multi-agent system based on Web service, which can complement each other.

Therefore, based on the underwater platform combat deduction model system, making full use of the advantages of service-oriented and multi-agent modeling, a service-oriented and intelligent underwater platform combat deduction system architecture is constructed, as shown in Fig. 4.

The system structure adopts a five-layer architecture including working layer, service process layer, agent processing layer, Web service layer and resource layer. Through hierarchical processing, the coupling of each module in the system is weakened and the system has stronger adaptability.

(1) Working layer: This layer is mainly composed of combat deduction workbench and guidance and control subsystem. It mainly provides the human-computer interaction of trainees to the combat deduction system of underwater platform and the

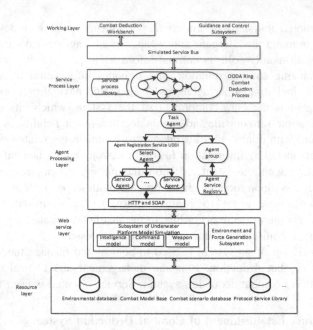

Fig. 4. Architecture of underwater platform combat deduction system

control and management of the combat deduction system of underwater platform for trainees.

(2) Service process layer: This layer provides OODA loop operation process for underwater platform combat deduction system, and stores it through service process description library. The function is to ensure that the user sends a deduction instruction to the task agent to assign tasks according to the OODA loop operation process, and then finds the Web service that is most suitable for the combat task in the Agent processing layer and feeds back to the task agent. Task Agent sends selected Web service information to service process template, and combines these service information according to the order of service process to construct new applications to meet the needs of trainees.

(3) Agent Processing Layer: This layer is in the middle layer, which is the key part of service integration intellectualization. There are four main aspects of work: first, responsible for the communication between Web service and Agents, registering corresponding Web service for each service agent; second, publishing tasks according to the functional requirements in the service process; third, selecting the most matching services according to certain needs evaluation; fourth, selecting the best service according to certain needs evaluation; and third, selecting the best service. Good service information is bound to the process to form a new application that can meet business needs.

(4) Web service Layer: It is the executor of service integration system, mainly for encapsulating existing functional components and forming Web service. The encapsulation of services can not only reduce development costs and improve reusability, but also improve the flexibility of the system and facilitate the construction of new

application systems. Each service in the Web service Layer is registered in the Agent Registry by a corresponding Service Agent. Instead of communicating directly between each Web service, the corresponding Service Agent is responsible for it.

(5) Resource layer: This layer includes environment database, battle model database, battle scenario database, protocol service library, etc. It provides data support and persistent service for underwater platform combat deduction system.

3.4 Service Agent Management Process

Service Agents mainly include "command model agent", "intelligence model agent", "weapon model agent", "environment generation agent" and "force model agent". The management includes registration and call.

(1) Service Agent Registration Process
The registration process of the service agent is shown in Fig. 5. The UDDI central node is the core position in the entire Agent service integration architecture, providing a unified discovery, service description and integration platform for the realization of the collaborative work functions of each service agent. Each service agent sends a SOAP request to the UDDI central node of Agent service. The SOAP server of the registration center receives the UDDI SOAP message and processes it, registers the service agent that issued the SOAP request in the Agent service registration database, and then returns the SOAP response to the SOAP server. The service agent that issued the SOAP request. Each of the above service agents can publish its own basic information to the UDDI central node, or look up other related registered service agents from the UDDI as needed, and finally call the bound service to form an integrated architecture for collaborative work.

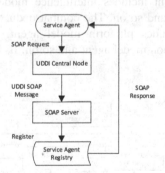

Fig. 5. Registration flow chart of service agent

(2) Service Agent Call Process
The flow chart of calling Agent service is shown in Fig. 6. In this structure, the trainee can find the corresponding service flow in the service process library by inputting the demand, and send the service type required by the process to the task agent to allocate the task. After receiving the service type, the task agent goes to the UDDI center. The selection agent of the node sends a message, and the selection agent in the agent service

library selects the service that best meets the user's requirement in the current service library according to the user's needs, and the task agent sends the Web service information corresponding to the selected service agent to the task agent. Service process templates, combined with service information in the order of service processes, to build new applications that meet user needs.

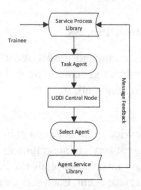

Fig. 6. Call flow chart of service agent

4 An Agent Design Example of Underwater Platform Combat Deduction Business Model

4.1 Relations and Structures of Main Business Model Agents

Business function class agent includes intelligence model agent, command model agent, weapon model agent and so on. The combat deduction model agent of underwater platform mainly includes platform model agent, intelligence model agent, command model agent, weapon model agent and so on. Its basic relationship is shown in Fig. 7.

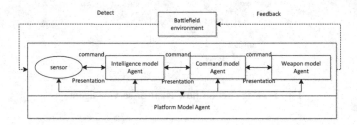

Fig. 7. Basic business model agent

4.2 Design Example of Platform Model Agent

Taking the platform model Agent as an example, the platform model Agent is established based on the establishment of the related entity equipment model and according to the steps of business model construction. Platform model Agent is mainly composed of perception module, decision module and action module. Its structure description is shown in Fig. 8.

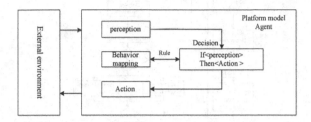

Fig. 8. Platform model agent structure description

5 The Simulation Process of Underwater Platform Combat Deduction System Based on MAXSim

5.1 Operation Flow of Combat Deduction System of Underwater Platform

Based on the MAXSim underwater platform combat deduction system architecture, and on the basis of the logical description model of business model Agent and the functional model of equipment, an underwater platform combat deduction system composed of guidance control, deduction workbench, general data blackboard, simulation model package, CGF and database is constructed, which has both automatic and semi-automatic operation modes. The system is simulated. The actual operation process is shown in Fig. 9.

(1) Preparatory stage of simulation: Start up Manager, GBB space and distributed server, load combat scenario and generate underwater platform model.

(2) Simulation operation stage: underwater platform intelligence model Agent real-time observation of sea conditions, organization and configuration of sensors to implement target reconnaissance and search of sea areas. The command model Agent of underwater platform deals with information acquired by sensors, identifies targets, judges threats and so on, and generates battlefield tactical situation. The command decision model gives corresponding combat instructions according to the current situation. Weapon model agent organizes weapon channels according to combat instructions, keeps track of targets, outputs weapon firing data, or uses underwater acoustic countermeasure equipment for defense.

(3) Effectiveness evaluation stage: After the simulation operation, the deduction effect evaluation information is given according to the combat deduction evaluation model of underwater platform, and the related information is archived.

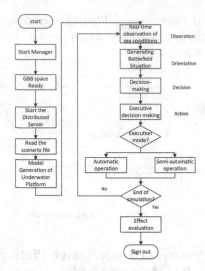

Fig. 9. Simulation flow of submarine combat system

5.2 Verification of the Simulation Process of the Combat Deduction System for Underwater Platforms

Operation Scenario Description of Underwater Platforms

In order to realize the combat deduction of underwater platforms, and verify the models and systems established by the models mentioned above, a simple combat scenario of underwater platforms is designed. Through this scenario, we can deduce the purpose, situation and development of both sides of the battle, and guide the whole battle deduction. The details are described as follows:

Red team and Blue team are XXX underwater platform with several torpedoes on board. They swim in a certain sea area. The Blue team underwater platform moves from distant sea to a reserved sea area. Red team underwater platform encounters Blue team underwater platform swimming in the sea area during its combat readiness patrol mission. According to the relevant rules, Red team underwater platform carries out tactical evacuation of Blue team underwater platform, and blue team underwater platform decides to leave.

Operation Simulation Process of Underwater Platform Combat Deduction

In the process of battle deduction simulation, according to the battle scenario, the Red team underwater platform and the Blue team underwater platform carry out tactical confrontation deduction. Each business model agent is an autonomous agent. The whole battle process is simulated based on Agent, and through GBB, the two sides of the confrontation form interactive perception.

In the course of tactical confrontation deduction, the Red team underwater platform expels the Blue team underwater platform which intrudes into a certain sea area. After sensing by its sensors, the Blue team underwater platform turns its course and accelerates its departure from a certain sea area, as shown in Fig. 10.

Fig. 10. The red underwater platform away from blue underwater platform situation map (Color figure online)

6 Conclusions

Based on the description model of OODA ring command and control, this paper analyses the business process and function of underwater platform combat deduction, and constructs an underwater platform combat deduction system based on service-oriented and Agent modeling technology. Compared with the framework of the combat simulation platform based on service-oriented, the framework of the system is characterized by the organic combination of service-oriented and Agent modeling technology, and the establishment of a service-oriented and intelligent underwater platform combat deduction system structure. It has the advantages of intelligence, reusability and scalability of the combat deduction model. The simulation process of the underwater platform combat deduction system is given and the underwater level is realized. The process simulation of the platform combat deduction system verifies the rationality of the system structure and business model Agent. It provides a feasible technical approach for the construction of intelligent and flexible underwater platform combat deduction system, and has important reference value for the agent modeling of the underwater platform combat deduction system.

References

1. Huang, C., Wei, J.: Preliminary Strictness: Military Chess Deduction and Its Application. Aviation Industry Press, Beijing (2015)
2. Li, N., Yi, W., Sun, M., Gong, G.: Development and application of intelligent system modeling and simulation platform. Simul. Model. Pract. Theory **29**, 149–162 (2012)
3. Bello, P.: Theoretical Foundations for Rational Agency in Third Generation Wargames. US Air Force Research Lab, USA (2006)
4. Wei, Y., Sub Song, K., Kim, D.-S.: Message oriented management and analysis tool for naval combat systems. IFAC Proc. Vol. **47**, 10524–10528 (2014)
5. Jin, T., Liu, Z.-W., Zhou, H., Guan, Z.-H., Qin, Y., Yonghong, W.: Robust average formation tracking for multi-agent systems with multiple leaders. IFAC-PapersOnLine **50**, 2427–2432 (2017)

6. Alexander, R., Kelly, T.: Supporting systems of systems hazard analysis using multi-agent simulation. Saf. Sci. **51**, 302–318 (2013)
7. Tavcar, A., Gams, M.: Surrogate-agent modeling for improved training. Eng. Appl. Artif. Intell. **74**(12), 280–293 (2018)
8. Hu, X., Si, G., Wu, L.: SDS2000: a qualitative and quantitative integrated research and simulation environment for strategic decision. J. Syst. Simul. **1**(6), 595–599 (2000)
9. Yan, B., Zhang, S., Sun, J.: A service-oriented air combat simulation system. In: Asia Simulation Conference the 7th International Conference on System Simulation and Scientific Computing (ICSC 2008) (2008)
10. Zhao, Z.G., Zhang, S.G., Sun, J.B., et al.: Service-oriented air combat simulation architecture. J. Beijing Inst. Technol. **21**(3), 408–414 (2012)
11. Guanhua, P.: Principle of Integrated Command and Control System for Ships. Northwest Industrial Press, Xi'an (2015)
12. Fusano, A., Sato, H., Namatame, A.: Multi-agent based combat simulation from OODA and network perspective. In: Uksim International Conference on Modelling & Simulation. IEEE Computer Society (2011)
13. Jiang, Z., Wei, C., Hua, X.: Combat simulation experiment based on OODA command and control loop. Command Control Simul. **37**(3), 112–115 (2015)
14. Li, M.: Research on Deductive Evaluation of Underwater Countermeasure Effectiveness Based on Monte Carlo Method. China Ship Research Institute, Beijing (2014)
15. Wu, H., Li, H., Xiao, R., Liu, J.: Modeling and simulation of dynamic ant colony's labor division for task allocation of UAV swarm. Stat. Mech. Appl. **491**, 127–141 (2018)
16. Yang, A.: A networked multi-agent combat model: emergence explained (2007)

Context-Aware Layered Learning for Argumentation Based Multiagent Collaborative Recognition

Zhi-yong Hao[1,2], Tingting Liu[1], Chen Yang[1(✉)], and Xiaohong Chen[1(✉)]

[1] College of Management, Shenzhen University, Shenzhen, China
yangc@szu.edu.cn, lrene.hong@foxmail.com
[2] School of Finance and Economics,
Shenzhen Institute of Information Technology, Shenzhen, China

Abstract. Multiagent recognition based on argumentation is highly concerned with the utilization of the advantages offered by argument games for the purpose of justifying and explaining the decision results of intelligent systems. However, arguing agents for collaborative recognition tasks are often encountered with disagreement due to different abstract levels of object categories. To cope with this category level inconsistent problem in argumentation based multiagent recognition, we propose CALL, a context-aware layered learning method for conflict resolution among multiple agents. Context-awareness is explored, in this paper, to investigate how structured contextual knowledge can facilitate dynamic arguments constructing in argumentation. The main contribution provided by the proposed method is that it not only can achieve natural conflict resolution in multiagent collaborative recognition systems, but also give consistent explanations with easily assimilated reasoning of multi-party argument games. Preliminary experimental results demonstrate the effectiveness of our method with significant improvements over state-of-the-art, especially in presence of noise.

Keywords: Multiagent systems · Computational argumentation · Context-aware · Ensemble learning

1 Introduction

Ensemble classifier systems have been considered as an effective means to improve classification performance in pattern recognition applications, e.g. biometric identification [1], traffic flow prediction [2], and etc. In fact, it is well known that combination of different individual classifiers could achieve the purpose of group optimization, through making full use of their complementary information. Hence, ensemble classifiers are gaining continuous attention of researchers from academia and industry [3]. One of the main concerned issues is how to efficiently combine multiple classifiers in a way that is easy for humans to assimilate, which poses a big challenge to machine intelligence and pattern recognition community.

© Springer Nature Switzerland AG 2019
Y. Tan et al. (Eds.): ICSI 2019, LNCS 11656, pp. 23–32, 2019.
https://doi.org/10.1007/978-3-030-26354-6_3

Recently, approaches to combine classifiers even take the perspective of human deliberation into account, and make use of the computational argumentation, which is a popular approach to commonsense reasoning [4]. It is noted that argumentation provides a natural means of justifying an agent's point views that greatly resemble the way in which humans evaluate alternatives to make decisions. Thus, multiagent argumentation based recognition techniques received a large number of research attention, due to its interpretability [5, 6]. Our previous work has shown that argumentation-based multiagent collaboration classification could be implemented by combining several modular rule classifiers, i.e. Arguing Prism [7].

However, in the task of multiagent collaborative recognition, different levels often exist in categories of objects (a.k.a. class labels), which may confuse the multiagent discrimination. Considering space object recognition, its core task is to recognize the objects (e.g. satellites, debris and rockets) in complex space environments. Since the categories (e.g. satellite, early warning satellite) of objects in the training phrase of classifiers are labelled at different levels, these classifier agents may have conflict recognition assertions, due to their different abstract levels of cognition [8]. Thus it is likely to have disagreements of categorizing objects in argumentation based multiagent recognition.

This paper presents a Context-Aware Layered Learning method (CALL), for argumentation based multiagent recognition. The aim of the CALL method is to cope with the problem of category level inconsistency encountered by classifier agents, and further improve the performance of multiagent collaborative recognition systems. It is noted that each agent performing collaborative recognition tasks has the ability to learn modular classification rules with Prism algorithms, which is a noise-tolerant alternative to TDIDT (Top Down Induction of Decision Trees) [9]. Thus our key idea is to construct arguments for multiagent collaborative recognition tasks with the help of context-aware layered learning according to real-time needs in argumentation process. The empirical evaluation shows that that better performance can be obtained by exploiting CALL method in argumentation based multiagent collaborative recognition.

The remainder of this paper is organized as follows. Section 2 briefly reviews related studies. In Sect. 3, we propose the context-aware layered learning method. Section 4 presents the comparative evaluation of our method, through preliminary experiments. Finally, this study is concluded in Sect. 5.

2 Related Work

Concerning explainable ensemble classifiers, the idea that not only good classification performance is needed, but also the reasons behind the results are very important to human decision makers. Basically, in the area of machine intelligence and pattern recognition, there is a series of different approaches to categorize new observations by using a classifier learnt from already labeled examples, from decision trees to deep convolutional neural networks (DCNN). For providing human-interpretable classification recognition within intelligent systems, in this paper, our method relates to the following two fields.

On one hand, computational argumentation has been deemed an effective technique used by intelligent agents to give explanations for classification results with justification [4]. The main idea about this approach is that argumentation based classification could show why arguments for categories are preferred to counterarguments through dialectical reasoning. Fan et al. [10] proposed an argumentation based framework that incorporates low level sensor data classifiers with high level activity recognition rules, which represented by arguments. This explanatory power of argumentation [11] for classification offers significant advantages that not only the category of the object is given, but also the reasons behind it are provided to human users in an interpretable form. To deal with the inconsistent in ensemble learning, an argumentation based conflict resolution method [5] is proposed to increase transparency, comparing with vote-based methods. The experiments on remote sensing crop data showed that their method could increase classification accuracy significantly over the voting conflict resolution. Wardeh et al. [12] presented an argumentation framework that allows multiple agents to argue about the categories of objects with fixed assertion. They used associate rules mining algorithms to construct arguments, rather than modular classification rule learning.

On the other hand, hierarchical classification is a basic approach to recognize object categories, using predefined semantic taxonomies [8]. As the opposite of a flat classification, the hierarchical taxonomies defined "Is-A" relationship from the most abstract categories to the most specific ones. In Liu et al.'s work [13], Hierarchical Classification Rules (HCRs) are obtained from semantic attributes of object categories guided by Ontology, which is typically a kind of taxonomy. Built by these HCRs, the classifiers were constructed for object classification at different abstract levels. For example, A hierarchical category taxonomy is built for the typical dataset "Animals with Attributes" [14]. This hierarchy can be used to learn HCRs for object classification tasks. To take advantage of Ontology for representing different kinds of knowledge, there are a number of works on Ontology based classifiers [15], which organize knowledge hierarchically to integrate classification rules. It is noted that the hierarchical relations in Ontology between concepts can be used to make generalization over semantic attributes, and construct a semantic attribute-value tree (SAT), which is proved to be effective for generating classification rules at different abstract levels [16].

Our method in this paper adopts a multiagent argumentation based approach for the reason that it could better simulate the scenario, in which multiple people make decisions together. In this method each agent could flexibly hold alterable recognition assertion for dynamic open data environments, with respect to existing works. In addition, we propose a context-aware layered learning method, by exploring the hierarchical information in object categories, for constructing recognition arguments according to real-time needs in argumentation process. In this paper, the rich contextual knowledge of categories are concerned dynamically, aiming to discriminate the objects at different abstract levels.

3 Arguing to Recognize Objects with the Context-Aware Layered Learning Method

In this section, we show how to exploit structured contextual knowledge for argumentation based multiagent collaborative recognition, in order to cope with the category level inconsistent problem among multiple classifier agents. Particularly, we assume that each classifier agent has the ability to learn context-aware classification rules for constructing arguments according to real-time needs. In general, given object instance to be classified, the system provides recognition results with explanations and corresponding underlying reasoning process through multi-party argument games among agents. Thus it is noted that this collaborative recognition task can be performed through arguing among multiple agents. In particular, we use the context-aware layered method to improve the process of arguing to recognize objects In what follows, our argumentation model for multiagent collaborative recognition is firstly presented in Subsect. 3.1. Then, in Subsect. 3.2, we describe how to construct arguments hierarchically with context-aware classification rules learned by agents, to reaching agreement in argumentation based multiagent collaborative recognition.

3.1 Multiagent Recognition Based on the Collaborative Argumentation Model

As indicated previously, in the task of multiagent recognition, a collection of classifier agents try to come to consensus about the category of a particular object. Here each agent could learn from different training datasets of their own, and give the predicted category of an object instance. We focus on multiagent collaborative recognition, which defined formally as follows.

Definition 1 (Multiagent Collaborative Recognition, MaCR). Given a multiagent system $Ag = \{Ag_1, \cdots, Ag_n\}$, the example space $\mathcal{X}$ and the shared category concept space $\mathcal{C}$, each agent has its individual set of training data, $\mathcal{T}_1, \cdots, \mathcal{T}_n$. For an arbitrary object instance x ($x \in \mathcal{X}$), the task of multiagent collaborative recognition is to find the category of x, such that it is consistent with each agent's learned classifier.

Argumentation has been considered as an effective technique for conflicts resolution through multi-party argument game. Based on this intuition, we exploit a collaborative argumentation model to reach agreement in multiagent recognition, by extending Yao et al.'s Arena [17]. Our argumentation model uses recognition arguments differing from Dung's abstract framework [18] in that the arguments are constructed for a given argumentation topic to be deliberated.

Definition 2 (Collaborative Argumentation Model, CAM). The collaborative argumentation model is formally defined as CAM $= < \mathcal{R}ef, \mathcal{T}c, \mathcal{P}ar, \mathcal{O}, \mathcal{R}oles, \mathcal{A}Rules, \mathcal{Q}, \mathcal{R} >$, where: (i) $\mathcal{R}ef$ is the referee agent; (ii) $\mathcal{T}c$ is the topic for arguing; (iii) $\mathcal{P}ar \subseteq \mathcal{A}g$, is the set of all participant agents in argumentation; (iv) $\mathcal{O}$ is the common knowledge shared by all participant agents; (v) $\mathcal{R}oles = \{Master, Challenger, Spectator\}$, is the set of roles played by participating agents, and it consists of masters, challengers and spectators respectively; (vi) $\mathcal{ARules}$ is the set of argumentative rules abided by all participant agents; (vii) $\mathcal{Q}$ is the set of arguments; (viii) $\mathcal{R}$ is the set of attack relations, namely $\mathcal{R} = \mathcal{Q} \times \mathcal{Q}$.

The CAM is used here to allow a number of agents to argue about the recognition of a particular object instance collaboratively. Recognition arguments for or against a particular assertion are constructed via learning from an agent's local training dataset. Specifically, it is defined formally as follows.

Definition 3 (recognition argument). A recognition argument $Arg = \langle Ag, x, con, s, \vartheta \rangle$, where: (i) $Ag \in \mathcal{Par}$ is the proponent agent; (ii) $x \in \mathcal{Tc}$, is the object instance to be recognized; (iii) $con \in \mathcal{C}$, is the conclusion; (iv) s is the reasons of con; (v) $\vartheta \in [0, 1]$ is the strength of Ag's argument, noted as $stren^{Ag}(Arg)$.

It is noted that the strength of a recognition argument is calculated depending on the learning algorithms used. Without loss of generality, recognition arguments, in this study, are constructed using Prism inductive rule learning algorithms, which mentioned in the first section, due to its easy assimilation by humans. In general, three different kinds of recognition arguments are used for MaCR, namely advocating argument, rebutting argument and undercutting argument.

The details of the realization of CAM will no longer be demonstrated here due to the limited space. The researchers who are interested in this part can refer to our previous research literature [7, 16]. Once the dialogue game process has terminated, the status of the argument game tree will indicate the recognition result and its corresponding reasons in form of arguments.

3.2 Constructing Arguments Hierarchically with Context-Aware Classification Rules

Having indicated the multiagent collaborative argumentation model, this subsection presents the construction of recognition arguments used in dialogue games for MaCR. In what follows, we will describe the proposed context-aware classification rule learning algorithm. Therefore, the system realized with Prism induction, called CAL +Arguing Prism, exploits context-aware layered learning for argumentation based collaborative recognition, following our previous work of Arguing Prism.

Most of previously research in pattern recognition and machine learning communities focused on recognition tasks in the "flat" structure of category set, without considerations on different levels of class labels. In fact, a number of important realistic object recognition applications naturally consist of hierarchical structures of categories, i.e. the categories of objects are organized into a taxonomy, which confuse different arguing agents in MaCR. To cope with this problem, we attempt to learn context-aware classification rules for constructing arguments coordinately. First, the definition of context-aware classification rule is described as follows.

Definition 4 (Context-Aware Classification Rule, CACR). A context-aware classification rule $cacr$ is defined in the form: $IF\ class = sub\_c_k \bigwedge \mathbb{A}_i\ rel_i\ v_{ix} \bigwedge \cdots \bigwedge, \mathbb{A}_j\ rel_j\ v_{jx} \cdots THEN\ class = c_k$ where $\mathbb{A}_i, ..., \mathbb{A}_j \in \mathcal{A}$, are attributes and $rel_i, \cdots, rel_j \in \{=, \neq, <, >, \leq, \geq\}$ are relational operators, $v_{ix}, \cdots, v_{jx}$ are attribute values, and sub_c_k is the direct subclass of c_k in the category taxonomy $\mathcal{Ta}$.

Clearly, the antecedent of CACR, noted as *ante* (*cacr*), is a logical conjunction of a category annotation and attribute-value pairs, and the consequent, noted as *cons(mgcr)* is a category annotation. As seen from the above definition, to obtain the specific category of a given object, we need to use the context-aware classification rules gradually in the top-down manner. Supposing if $cacr_1, cacr_2, \cdots cacr_\eta$ are a series of CACRs used for recognition at different levels, then $cons(cacr_i) \in ante(cacr_{i+1})$ $(1 < i \leq \eta + 1)$. In this case, our context-aware classification rules can give the categories of objects at different abstract levels required by arguing agents in MaCR.

In general, CACRs can be learned hierarchically from the training datasets, referring to the category taxonomy $\mathfrak{Ta}$, which obtained from domain Ontology. Our proposed algorithm for learning context-aware classification rules is described in Table 1.

Table 1. Learning context-aware classification rules for hierarchical arguments

Algorithm 1. CACR_Learning ($\mathcal{T}, \mathfrak{Ta}, c_k$)
input: a training dataset $\mathcal{T}$ with attribute set $\mathcal{A}$, category taxonomy $\mathfrak{Ta}$, target category c_k
output: a set of context-aware classification rules $\mathcal{CR}$

01	$\mathcal{T}' := \mathcal{T}$
02	$sub_c_k := $ getSubClass(c_k)
03	**for each** $exa \in \mathcal{T}'$ **do**
04	$\quad$ $cate\_set := sub\_c_k \cap$ getSuperClasses($\mathcal{T}$, cateOf(exa))
05	$\quad$ **if** $cate\_set \neq \emptyset$ **then**
06	$\quad\quad$ $exa\_cate :=$ getOneElement($cate\_set$)
07	$\quad$ **else**
08	$\quad\quad$ $\mathcal{T}' := \mathcal{T}' - \{exa\}$
09	$\quad$ **end if**
10	**end for**
11	$attr\_set := \emptyset$
12	$rul\_set := \emptyset$
13	**repeat**
14	$\quad$ $attr\_set := attr\_set \cup$ attributeUsed(rul_set)
15	$\quad$ $rul\_set :=$ Prism_Learning($\mathcal{T}', \mathcal{A} - attr\_set$)
16	**until** $rul\_set = \emptyset$
17	**for each** $rul \in rul\_set$ **do**
18	$\quad$ $ca\_rul :=$ genNewRul(rul, c_k)
19	$\quad$ $\mathcal{CR} := \mathcal{CR} \cup \{ca\_rul\}$
20	**end for**
21	$\mathcal{T}'' := \mathcal{T}$
22	**for each** $sub\_cate \in sub\_c_k$ **do**
23	$\quad$ $\mathcal{CR} := \mathcal{CR} \cup$ CACR_Learning ($\mathcal{T}'', \mathfrak{Ta}, c_k$)
24	**end for**
25	**return** $\mathcal{CR}$

In Algorithm 1, the context-aware classification rules for a particular category c_k are learned through mapping the target categories in training dataset $\mathcal{T}$ to the direct subclass of c_k in taxonomy $\mathfrak{Ta}$. First of all, the categories in $\mathcal{T}$ are changed, leaving only the data labeled by the subclass of c_k (line 03 to 10). Then learning Prism classification rules with different attribute sets, where each rule is derived from the dataset of the direct subclass of c_k (line 13 to 16). It is worth noting that although several rules may have the same consequent, their antecedents consist of different attribute-value pairs. Correspondingly, the given target category c_k is added to CACRs that are transformed (line 17 to 20). Finally, the CACR_Learning algorithm executes recursively until the rules for every subclass of c_k are learned (line 21 to 24).

4   Experimental Evaluation

This section presents the experimental evaluation of the CALL method proposed in our paper. To this end, 5 benchmark datasets from the UCI Machine Learning Repository[1], and a space object recognition practical dataset, called SOR dataset, were used in our experiments, which are shown in Table 2. These datasets vary in their numbers of examples and category levels. Thus all these datasets meet the desired structured contextual knowledge of categories, shared by each individual arguing agent for collaborative recognition tasks.. As indicated in the last section, using Prism, we designed the comparative experiments of CAL+Arguing Prism and Arguing Prism [7], to evaluate the effectiveness of our proposed method. The comparison to other methods, in which other base algorithms similar to Prism are used to construct arguments for collaborative recognition, is beyond the scope of this study. We will further extend the method presented here in further research, and carry out comparative experiments with the related multi-classifier fusion method.

Table 2. Datasets used for our experimental evaluation

No	Datasets	#examples	#categories	#category levels
D1	*Nursery*	12960	5	3
D2	*Soybean*	307	19	3
D3	*Poker hand*	1025010	10	2
D4	*Audiology*	226	24	4
D5	*Dermatology*	366	6	3
D6	SOR	9099	23	3

For each dataset used in our experiments, the results presented in this section are estimated using Ten-fold Cross-Validation (TCV). The experimental system has been implemented with WEKA machine leaning workbench[2] combining with Java Agent

---

[1] http://www.ics.uci.edu/mlearn/MLRepository.html.

[2] https://www.cs.waikato.ac.nz/ml/weka/.

DEvelopment framework (JADE)[3]. In what follows, we first describe the evaluation of hierarchical recognition performance, and then investigate CAL+Arguing Prism's tolerance to noise.

Firstly, we present experiments conducted to compare the hierarchical recognition performance of the two methods, using the datasets in Table 2. For each of the compared methods, three common hierarchical recognition metrics, following Silla et al.'s work [10], were estimated for each dataset: (i) hierarchical precision $\left(hP = \sum_{k=1}^{N}\left|\widehat{P_k} \cap \widehat{T_k}\right| \middle/ \sum_{k=1}^{N}\left|\widehat{P_k}\right|\right)$; (ii) hierarchical recall $\left(hR = \sum_{k=1}^{N}\left|\widehat{P_k} \cap \widehat{T_k}\right| \middle/ \sum_{k=1}^{N}\left|\widehat{T_k}\right|\right)$; (iii) hierarchical f-measure $(hF = 2 * hP * hR/(hP + hR))$. Where N is total number of test instances, $\widehat{P_k}$ is the set, which consists of the most specific categories predicted for the k th test instance, and all their ancestor categories; and $\widehat{T_k}$ is the set, which consists of the true most specific categories for the k th test instance, and all their ancestor categories. Clearly, it is seen that hF is a synthesized indicator for evaluation of hierarchical recognition performance.

Table 3. Hierarchical recognition performance obtained using different methods

#	hP		hR		hF	
	Arguing Prism	CAL +Arguing Prism	Arguing Prism	CAL +Arguing Prism	Arguing Prism	CAL +Arguing Prism
D1	0.92	**0.97**	0.90	**0.95**	0.909	**0.960**
D2	**0.78**	0.77	0.72	**0.79**	0.749	**0.780**
D3	0.76	**0.80**	0.79	**0.83**	0.775	**0.815**
D4	0.70	**0.74**	**0.81**	0.78	0.751	**0.759**
D5	**0.96**	0.94	0.87	**0.90**	0.912	**0.919**
D6	0.72	**0.82**	0.69	**0.76**	0.705	**0.789**

The results of hierarchical recognition performance are described in Table 3, comparing the operation of Arguing Prism and CAL+Arguing Prism, with respect to hP, hR and hF. First, it can be seen that, in context of hP, CAL+Arguing Prism produces the best results in 4 of 6 datasets tested, performing slightly worse than the other method only on two datasets (D2 and D5). Second, although the proposed method performs poorly on the dataset D4 with respect to hR, it obtains better performance with 5 other test datasets. Finally, concerned hF, it is noted that CAL +Arguing Prism performs best in all the 6 datasets compared to Arguing Prism. This is a strong evidence indicating the superiority of the proposed method in this paper.

To investigate CAL+Arguing Prism's tolerance to noise in multiagent recognition tasks, we explore to conduct experiments with noisy data. Hence, several version of the six datasets were generated by introducing different rates of noise. A noisy value is any

---

[3] http://jade.tilab.com/.

valid value for this category, varying from its original value. For each rate of noise (0.05, 0.1, 0.15, 0.2, 0.25, 0.3), the operations of the two methods were induced using the same setting described above.

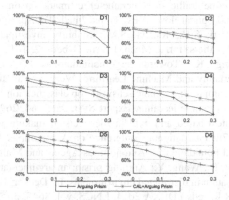

Fig. 1. Accuracy obtained when introducing different rates of noise

The results are presented in Fig. 1, where the horizontal axe represents the noisy rate and the vertical axe represents the accuracy. Obviously, it can be observed that, for all the two argumentation based recognition methods, the accuracy decreases with the increasing rates of noise in all the six investigated datasets. But it is noted that, CAL +Arguing Prism out-performs the other method with presence of noisy data, in 5 out of 6 datasets, with the exception of dataset D2. This robust characteristic for noisy data maybe offered by our CALL method in argumentation based multiagent collaborative recognition.

5 Conclusion

A context-aware layered learning method, namely CALL, has been proposed for argumentation based multiagent recognition. We improve arguing agents' hierarchical recognition performance by exploiting structured contextual knowledge of categories according to real-time needs in argumentation processes. Thus the category level inconsistent problem of objects among different classifier agents can be coped with multilevel information consists in category taxonomies. The experimental study establishes that the proposed method performs better than state-of-the-art methods, especially for noisy data. In future research, we would like to harness the power of group cognitive context knowledge for coming to semantic consensus dynamically.

Acknowledgements. This work is supported by Postdoctoral Science Foundation of China (Grant No. 2018M643187), National Natural Science Foundation of China (Project No 71701134), The Humanity and Social Science Youth Foundation of Ministry of Education of China (Project No. 16YJC630153).

References

1. Rida, I., et al.: Palmprint recognition with an efficient data driven ensemble classifier. Pattern Recognit. Lett., 1–10 (2018)
2. Ke, R., et al.: Real-time traffic flow parameter estimation from UAV video based on ensemble classifier and optical flow. IEEE Trans. Intell. Transp. Syst. **20**, 1–11 (2018)
3. Pourtaheri, Z.K., Zahiri, S.H., Razavi, S.M.: Stability investigation of multi-objective heuristic ensemble classifiers. Int. J. Mach. Learn. Cybern. **2**, 1–13 (2018)
4. Thimm, M., Kersting, K.: Towards argumentation-based classification. In: Logical Foundations of Uncertainty and Machine Learning, Workshop at IJCAI, vol. 17 (2017)
5. Conţiu, Ş., Groza, A.: Improving remote sensing crop classification by argumentation-based conflict resolution in ensemble learning. Expert Syst. Appl. **64**, 269–286 (2016)
6. Zeng, Z., et al.: Context-based and explainable decision making with argumentation. In: Proceedings of the 17th International Conference on Autonomous Agents and MultiAgent Systems. International Foundation for Autonomous Agents and Multi-agent Systems (2018)
7. Hao, Z., Yao, L., Liu, B., Wang, Y.: Arguing prism: an argumentation based approach for collaborative classification in distributed environments. In: Decker, H., Lhotská, L., Link, S., Spies, M., Wagner, R.R. (eds.) DEXA 2014. LNCS, vol. 8645, pp. 34–41. Springer, Cham (2014). https://doi.org/10.1007/978-3-319-10085-2_3
8. Silla, C.N., Freitas, A.A.: A survey of hierarchical classification across different application domains. Data Min. Knowl. Disc. **22**(1-2), 31–72 (2011)
9. Le, T., et al.: On expressiveness and uncertainty awareness in rule-based classification for data streams. Neurocomputing **265**, 127–141 (2017)
10. Fan, X., et al.: A first step towards explained activity recognition with computational abstract argumentation. In: 2016 IEEE International Conference on Multisensor Fusion and Integration for Intelligent Systems (MFI). IEEE (2016)
11. Zeng, Z., et al.: Building more explainable artificial intelligence with argumentation. In: Thirty-Second AAAI Conference on Artificial Intelligence (2018)
12. Wardeh, M., Coenen, F., Capon, T.B.: PISA: a framework for multiagent classification using argumentation. Data Knowl. Eng. **78**, 34–57 (2012)
13. Liu, B., et al.: Combining ontology and reinforcement learning for zero-shot classification. Knowl.-Based Syst. **144**, 42–50 (2018)
14. Lampert, C.H., Nickisch, H., Harmeling, S.: Attribute-based classification for zero-shot visual object categorization. IEEE Trans. Pattern Anal. Mach. Intell. **36**, 453–465 (2014)
15. Noor, M.H.M., et al.: Enhancing ontological reasoning with uncertainty handling for activity recognition. Knowl.-Based Syst. **114**, 47–60 (2016)
16. Hao, Z., Liu, B., Wu, J., Yao, J.: Exploiting ontological reasoning in argumentation based multi-agent collaborative classification. In: Nguyen, N.T., Trawiński, B., Kosala, R. (eds.) ACIIDS 2015. LNCS (LNAI), vol. 9011, pp. 23–33. Springer, Cham (2015). https://doi.org/10.1007/978-3-319-15702-3_3
17. Yao, L., et al.: Evaluating the valuable rules from different experience using multiparty argument games. In: Proceedings of the 2012 IEEE/WIC/ACM International Joint Conferences on Web Intelligence and Intelligent Agent Technology, vol. 02. IEEE Computer Society (2012)
18. Dung, P.M.: On the acceptability of arguments and its fundamental role in nonmonotonic reasoning, logic programming and n-person games. Artif. Intell. **77**(2), 321–358 (1995)

TH-GRN Model Based Collective Tracking in Confined Environment

Yutong Yuan[1,3], Zhun Fan[1], Xiaomin Zhu[2,3](✉), Meng Wu[3], Li Ma[3], Taosheng Fang[3], Zhaojun Wang[1], Weidong Bao[3], Yun Zhou[3], Huangke Chen[3], Yugen You[1], and Wenji Li[1]

[1] Department of Electronic Engineering, Shantou University, Shantou 515063, China
{17ytyuan,17zjwang,12ygyou}@stu.edu.cn, {zhun_fan,wenji_li}@126.com
[2] State Key Laboratory of High Performance Computing, Changsha, China
[3] College of Systems Engineering, National University of Defence Technology, Changsha 410073, China
{xmzhu,wumeng15,mali10,wdbao,zhouyun007,hkchen}@nudt.edu.cn,
fts1787353511@163.com

Abstract. Collective task in swarm robots has been studied widely because of the ability limitation of a single robot. Collective tracking is an important ability for swarm, and many of previous tracking tasks are based on leader-follower model. Unfortunately, simple following behavior brings much tracking uncertainty in constrained environment and difficulty for a convergence tracking pattern. To address this issue, we propose a new model for tracking by combining tracking-based hierarchical gene regulatory network with leader-follower model named (TH-GRN) for swarm robots. The TH-GRN model simulates the process that proteins are generated and diffused to control swarm activities. The concentration diffusion forms a tracking pattern and guides swarm robots to designated pattern. In order to be adaptive to confined environment, some flexible strategies are devised and integrated into our proposed TH-GRN model to achieve better performance. Besides, the TH-GRN model is also used to generate dynamic and complex environment. In our experiments, we design three obstacle scenarios, i.e., fixed obstacles, mobile (dynamic) obstacles, and hybrid obstacles. We conduct some simulation to validate the effectiveness of tracking-based TH-GRN model, and the experiment results demonstrate the superiority of our model.

Keywords: Collective tracking · Self-organization · Pattern formation · Swarm robots

1 Introduction

Swarm intelligence stands for the progress of intelligence and cooperation for accomplishing more complex tasks. Simple, flexible, and modular structured interacting robots will replace those single complex systems [1]. Swarm robots are able to finish some complex tasks which are negative for a single robot, with

© Springer Nature Switzerland AG 2019
Y. Tan et al. (Eds.): ICSI 2019, LNCS 11656, pp. 33–43, 2019.
https://doi.org/10.1007/978-3-030-26354-6_4

cooperation and local communication [2,3]. Some bio-inspired algorithms reveal that nature has competence for accomplishing some complex collective tasks, such as bird flocking [4]. All of collective phenomenon in nature urge collective tasks developed in multi-robot system.

The multi-robot tracking is one of collective tasks for directly tracking the target through specific distance and angle, or generating an effective and appropriate tracking pattern or alignment relying on the target, which hints the pattern formation can be used. One of classic control methods is the leader-follower model in which the leaders carry primitive information and the followers follow the leaders with an expected pattern [5,6]. These methods belongs to macroscopic genre.

In microscopic realm, morphogen-diffusion, reaction-diffusion, gene regulatory network and chemotaxis represent microscopic genre [4], where gene regulatory network exhibits systematic and functional framework as the tissue works. Guo et al. [7,8] proposed a metaphor between robot system and mechanism between DNA and cell. Then, the hierarchical gene regulatory network (H-GRN) is utilized to express the robot system, which succeeds in controlling pattern formation and extracting the pattern with B-spline [9]. The entrapment function has been achieved well by the concentration diffusion model. Oh et al. [10] improved H-GRN in replacing point control with segment control via partitioning the pattern into pieces, then respectively making every pieces same curvature. Oh et al. [11] added description about avoidance and revised the H-GRN model. Peng et al. [12] replaced B-spline with interpolating implicit function (IIF) methods to control pattern formation adaptive to environment and considered the situation that robots enclosing a target pass through a tunnel. Zhang et al. [13] replaced B-spline with Radial Basis Implicit Function (RBIF) to accomplish multi-target entrapment. The tracking function based on light source tracking and concentration gradient following has ever been made [14].

The contributions of this paper are as follows: First, we propose a novel model based on tracking-based hierarchical gene regulatory network (TH-GRN) to achieve tracking function and enhance the accuracy and robustness of process of tracking. Then, we test the availability of the algorithm in constrained environment and obtain the experiment results. The overall paper is organized as follows. Section 1 mainly introduces related work about GRN model. Section 2 elaborates TH-GRN model including four parts:upper layer, lower layer, additional layer, avoidance strategy. Section 3 describes the experiment setting in three scenarios including fixed, dynamic and hybrid obstacles, effectiveness analysis and summary of the experiments. Section 4 conducts conclusions and future work.

2   TH-GRN Model

TH-GRN model is a hybrid of H-GRN model and leader-follower model. The H-GRN model processes advantage in systematicness and structural integrity, and the entrapment effect between robots and targets performs well. Leader-follower model utilizes simple control between angle and distance to achieve tracking behaviors with high flexibility. However, leader-follower has disadvantage in great reliance on leader and uneasy tracking pattern; As for H-GRN, H-GRN supplies accurate predictive position for robots in pattern formation, but the pattern generation is vulnerable in confined environment, which leads to weak performance on collective task. Therefore, TH-GRN is proposed to extend H-GRN capacity and enhance H-GRN performance in confined environment via specific angle control to achieve tracking function and taking advantage of concentration diffusion from obstacles for avoidance.

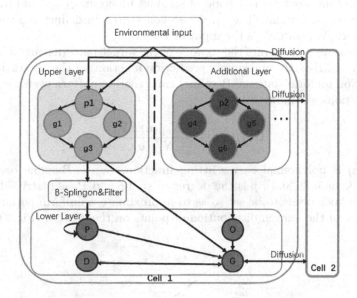

Fig. 1. The framework of TH-GRN model.

2.1 Upper Layer: Target Tracking Pattern Generation

For generation of target tracking pattern, each organizing robots will utilize the following gene regulatory dynamics to generate the concentrations:

$$\frac{dp_j}{dt} = -p_j + \triangledown^2 p_j + \gamma_j, \tag{1}$$

$$p = \sum_{j=1}^{n_t} p_j, \tag{2}$$

$$\frac{dg_1}{dt} = -g_1 + sig(p, \theta_1, k), \tag{3}$$

$$\frac{dg_2}{dt} = -g_2 + [1 - sig(p, \theta_2, k)], \tag{4}$$

$$\frac{dg_3}{dt} = -g_3 + sig(g1 + g2, \theta_3, k), \tag{5}$$

$$sig(x, z, k) = \frac{1}{1 + e^{-k(x-z)}}, \tag{6}$$

where p_j, an internal state, denotes the protein concentration produced by the j_{th} target. $\bigtriangledown^2$, a Laplacian operator, which is defined as the second-order derivative of p_j in the spatial domain and can be treated as the diffusion process in the biological system. p denotes the sum of concentrations from all n_t targets. k, a positive constant, controls the slope of sigmoid function. g_1, g_2 and g_3 denote the protein concentrations. The g_3, whose concentration defines the contour of target pattern, is regarded as the input of B-spline.

B-Spline is used to extract the contour of the target pattern generated by the upper layer of TH-GRN, and supply prediction function for the agents' location. NURBS (Non-uniform Rational B-spline) can generate pattern evenly according to the equations as follow:

$$\mathbf{C}(u) = \frac{\sum_{i=0}^{n} N_{i,p}(u)\omega_i \mathbf{P}_i}{\sum_{i=0}^{n} N_{i,p}(u)\omega_i}, \tag{7}$$

where $\mathbf{C}(u)$ is polynomial curves fitting function, $N_{i,p}$ is B-spline basis functions with knot $u \in [0,1]$, p is the degree of spline and $\mathbf{P}_i$ is matrix of control points. The knot needs to be set so as to approximate a uniform parameterization because of the uneven distribution of points on the pattern (Fig. 2).

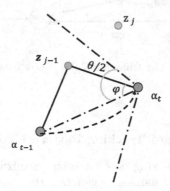

Fig. 2. Angle-based control for tracking pattern. (The yellow circles denote the target with different moments. Blue and red circles denote different extracted points of the pattern) (Color figure online)

Then, according to the vectors from the pattern extracted by NURBS model to the target, the tracking vector can be expressed explicitly. The angle between the tracking vector and the moving direction of the target will control overall tracking pattern. Therefore, the angle θ is set to control the tracking pattern so that the pattern can reflect a desired result. If the angle is more than θ, the excess of pattern will not satisfy the tracking need, then the excessive part will be abandoned. If the angle is less than or equal to θ, the pattern will be retained and combined with the lower layer to guide robots.

$$\varphi = arcCos(\frac{dis(\alpha_t, z_j)^2 + dis(\alpha_t, \alpha_{t-1})^2 - dis(\alpha_{t-1}, z_j)^2}{2 * dis(\alpha_t, z_j) * dis(\alpha_t, \alpha_{t-1})}), \qquad (8)$$

where $dis(,)$ is the distance between two points, α_t is position of target with moment t, z_j is the position of the j_{th} point from pattern. We set θ to control the angle of tracking pattern and φ is calculated to obtain the angle between predictive position and target. Owing to the symmetry between control angle and the moving direction of target, the $\frac{\theta}{2}$ is the threshold corresponding to φ. When φ is less than or equal to $\frac{\theta}{2}$, the predictive position will preserve to use. Otherwise, the predictive position will be deleted.

2.2   Lower Layer: Tracking Strategy Control

The lower layer of the TH-GRN takes responsibilities for guiding all agents into the desired region generated by the upper layer and gives competence for avoidance when the pattern is invalid. Four factors will be considered: 1. minimum avoidance distance, 2. the direction to the pattern, 3. density of neighbor, 4. concentration of obstacles. All factors generate possible movement vector with unitization.

$$G_i = aA + bP_i + cD + d\beta(t)O, \qquad (9)$$

$$\beta(t) = \begin{cases} 1, & when \ avoiding \ obstacle \\ 0, & else \end{cases} \qquad (10)$$

where A is the factor of avoiding neighbors, P_i is the factor of direction to pattern, including z_i and α_t in Fig. 1. D is neighbor density factor (guiding i_{th} robot to low density), O is the factor to keep away from obstacles and D is the factor pointing to low density within neighbor. $\beta(t)$ is a switching function to control avoiding mode. G_i is final sum of all direction factors. The coefficient a, b, c, d are positive constant, where d goes beyond another three.

2.3   Additional Layer: Obstacle Generation

The additional layer is to capture the obstacles in the environment. The fixed and dynamic (mobile) obstacles are chosen to establish the obstacle environment. For dynamic obstacles, we use the upper layer to simulating the people zone (or stream). The shape can change slightly and finally split to two zones independently. The fixed obstacles will be directly generated in the test zone. They can be arbitrary geometric figure. The additional layer is kept separate from upper layer, which is helpful to package all obstacle setting and easier to be embedded into map.

2.4 Avoidance Strategy

The concentration of obstacles can be detected by robots. Once a robot goes into and detect concentration field, it will prepare for avoidance, even though the pattern is trapped into internal obstacles. The avoidance will be triggered after the robot compares both concentration of obstacles within a unit step with expected quantitative deflection angle. Therefore, when the robot observes the avoiding moment coming, the switching function β in Eqs. (9), (10) will activate O in Eq. (9) to greatly influence the movement direction of robots. γ decides on whether robots can avoid obstacles.

3 Experiments and Analysis

3.1 Experiment Setting

The experiment is set to $25 * 25$ m^2 and left bottom corner $(2 * 2$ m$^2)$ is the base of robots, where robots will be randomly generated in this region. The number of target and robots is 1 and 16, respectively. The target is generated in left bottom corner with bigger ordinate and abscissa values than robots but smaller than all obstacles. The velocity of robots is 0.25 m/s and the velocity of the target is slightly lower than robots. The detective field is 10 m. The safety distance between robots and target is 0.25 m (their own size) and 1.5 m respectively. The avoidance distance is 1.5 m. The deflection angle γ is 40°. The direction of movement is set to top right and the route is set to going through all obstacle in the test zone. The test termination condition is no robots' tracking or when the target touches right or top boundary of the test zone.

The target and robots keep the condition: the target ignoring the obstacles goes through the zone from left to right (encountering all obstacles) and agents have to keep avoiding the obstacle zone, but still track the target. In both two scenarios, it is possible for the pattern to walk to the internal obstacles (the limited region). The target ignoring terrain will bring great difficulties to robots, therefore, the effectiveness of the model for avoidance is key to accomplish tracking task and TH-GRN will help robots recover the tracking pattern after bypassing the obstacles. The two stages of experiments are corresponding to both conditions above.

For verifying the effectiveness of TH-GRN, there are three scenarios for the test as follows: 1. fixed obstacles, 2. dynamic (mobile) obstacles, 3. hybrid obstacles.

3.2 Fixed Obstacles

The scene is set to fixed obstacles (shown in Fig. 3). The target and agents have to go through a $2 * 2$ square and a $2 * 4$ rectangle. It is easier for the target to avoid the obstacles for the reason that the scale of tracking pattern is larger than target, the agents have to overcome the difficulties the environment brings, so as to accomplish the tracking task. The square and rectangle process obvious sharp corner, which brings greater disturbance than those shapes with smooth curve. The result of experiment shows the robots avoid sharp corner well and recover tracking pattern swiftly.

The red points stands for robots and blue circle stands for the target. The green points means the pattern generated in upper layer with maximum safety tracking angle and real tracking angle is controlled by η. The green rectangles are the obstacles generated in test map to verify the effectiveness of tracking and avoidance.

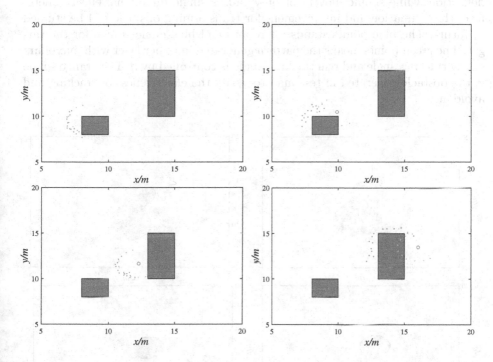

Fig. 3. Four stages evolving with time in tracking task with fixed obstacle. (From left to right then from top to bottom) (Color figure online)

3.3 Dynamic Obstacles

The scene is set to a dynamic obstacle (shown in Fig. 4). The upper layer of TH-GRN can also be used to generate dynamic moving and transforming obstacle. Also, it seems like crowds of people for density estimation or monitoring. The distribution of density can be mapped into the distribution of diffusion concentration and the center of density is mapped into the target. When the density apex has been known, the upper layer can be used to simulate and estimate the scale of surrounding. The result of experiment reveals the robots will be trapped into a corner when the target is going through the obstacle. Some robots choose to bypass the obstacle by moving up along the contour of obstacle, while others choose to stay at the corner. Then, the obstacle zone splits into two zones, so those waiting start to get through the tunnel.

In general, the basic tracking and avoidance are completed, but the performance is arduous. Apparently, when dynamic obstacle does not move and transform faster than robots, the robots can avoid the obstacle. The transforming influences the avoidance performance greater because the transforming causes multidirectional effect, especially on those avoidance methods based on angular deflection, while simple movement only causes single directional effect. Therefore, the estimation and improvement for transforming obstacle will be studied in future. The blue points stands for robots and blue circle stands for the target. The green points means the pattern generated in upper layer with maximum safety tracking angle and real tracking angle is controlled by η. The orange shape is the obstacle generated in test map to verify the effectiveness of tracking and avoidance.

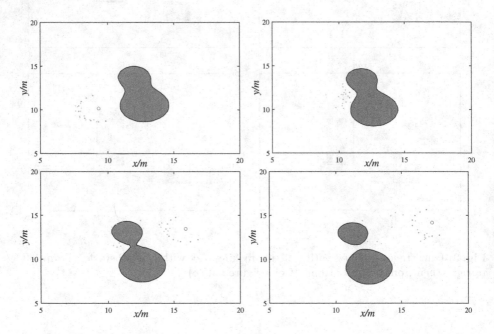

Fig. 4. Four stages evolving with time in tracking task with dynamic obstacle. (From left to right then from top to bottom) (Color figure online)

3.4 Hybrid Obstacles

Hybrid obstacles (shown in Fig. 5) imply the fixed and dynamic obstacles are generated simultaneously. Hybrid obstacles are closer to the obstacles in reality.

With the obstacles obstructing, the agents will encounter greater difficulty in trading off tracking and avoiding. Therefore, when tracking pattern is trapped into obstacles, the agents dispatched have to conceal the dependence of pattern and use avoidance strategy to avoid. The result of experiment reveals all robots undergo from tracking to avoidance repeatedly and perform well.

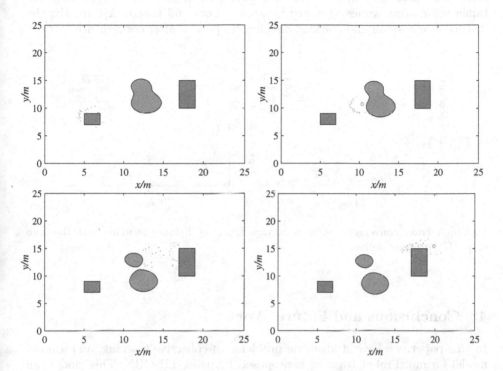

Fig. 5. Four stages evolving with time in tracking task with hybrid obstacles. (From left to right then from top to bottom)

The Fig. 6 shows average convergence error within three different scenarios. The convergence error is calculated by average distance between robots and tracking pattern. The blue line (fixed scenario) reflects two obvious peaks corresponding to two avoidance process for two fixed obstacles. The green line (dynamic scenario) illustrates the first descending stage that robots accomplish tracking pattern generation and first ascending stage that all robots are trapped into corner while the target goes through the obstacle which accounts for tracking pattern farther away from robots. Then, some robots bypass the obstacle and the other robots finally gather and get close to pattern, causing the second descending stage until tracking pattern converge. The red line (hybrid scenario) shows tracking and avoidance process within three obstacles, as a combination between blue one and green one. It is interesting that the red one only expresses two obvious peak rather than three because the position of robots after avoiding the second dynamic obstacle is similar as the top boundary of the third obstacle, which causes robots avoid the third obstacle easier. Therefore, the third peak is not obvious. In general, the disturbance is not small and there is possibility of improvement in stability.

The average tracking distance intuitively reflects the effectiveness of TH-GRN with average distance between robots and target. Average tracking distance means the average distance between robots and target. Apparently, the disturbance is small and tracking distance keeps well after convergence.

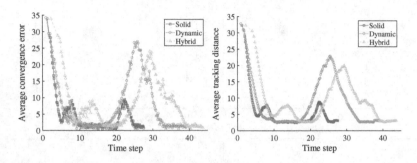

Fig. 6. Average convergence error & average tracking distance evolving with the time step. (Color figure online)

4   Conclusions and Future Work

In this paper, we have studied the problems of collective tracking, and a novel model for multi-robot tracking is proposed by using TH-GRN. This model can generate initial tracking pattern for robots, supply an avoidance strategy when tracking pattern is invalid and generate fixed or dynamic obstacles. The result of experiments reflects good performance and effectiveness on tracking tasks with obstacles. Although the model can control accurate pattern formation, yet, the uncertainty in environment and some disturbance in controlling still greatly influence the tracking process. As for some complex environments, the robots need to spend more time in avoidance, let alone tracking. There is no doubt that addressing effectiveness of avoidance can greatly enhance the ratio of prompt and successful tracking. Besides, the scale of target is smaller than swarm robots, so the routine the target chooses also affects global development.

In the future, the number of targets can be increased. The behavior pattern of target can be more complex, such as reversing immediately and anti-tracking, including standing by or moving in circle, and the agents can be more intelligent to hide or track. The obstacles can be more complex, such as steep non-convex shapes, which is easier to take agents to dead end. The reinforcement learning has gained excellent performance in avoiding different obstacles, but there may be a better method to combine learning or expertise system in TH-GRN. Besides, some meaningful comparative experiments and multi-target tracking will be done in future work.

Acknowledgements. This research work was supported by Guangdong Key Laboratory of Digital Signal and Image Processing, and the National Defense Technology Innovation Special Zone Projects.

References

1. Mastellone, S., Stipanovic, D.M., Spong, M.W.: Remote formation control and collision avoidance for multi-agent nonholonomic systems. In: Proceedings of the 2007 IEEE International Conference on Robotics and Automation, pp. 1062–1067 (2007)
2. Franks, N.R., Richardson, T.: Teaching in tandem-running ants. Nature **439**(7073), 153 (2006)
3. Krieger, M.J.B., Billeter, J.-B., Keller, L.: Ant-like task allocation and recruitment in cooperative robots. Nature **406**(6799), 992 (2000)
4. Oh, H., et al.: Bio-inspired self-organising multi-robot pattern formation: a review. Robot. Auton. Syst. **91**, 83–100 (2017)
5. Oh, H., et al.: Decentralised standoff tracking of moving targets using adaptive sliding mode control for UAVs. J. Intell. Robot. Syst. **76**(1), 169–183 (2014)
6. Chen, X., et al.: Formation control of mobile robots with input constraints: an elliptic approximation approach. In: 2011 11th International Conference on Control, Automation and Systems, pp. 186–191 (2011)
7. Guo, H., Meng, Y., Jin, Y.: A cellular mechanism for multi-robot construction via evolutionary multi-objective optimization of a gene regulatory network. BioSystems **98**(3), 193–203 (2009)
8. Guo, H., Meng, Y., Jin, Y.: Swarm robot pattern formation using a morphogenetic multi-cellular based self-organizing algorithm. In: 2011 IEEE International Conference on Robotics and Automation, pp. 3205–3210 (2011)
9. Piegl, L., Tiller, W.: The NURBS Book, pp. 117–139 (1997)
10. Oh, H., Jin, Y.: Adaptive swarm robot region coverage using gene regulatory networks. In: Mistry, M., Leonardis, A., Witkowski, M., Melhuish, C. (eds.) TAROS 2014. LNCS (LNAI), vol. 8717, pp. 197–208. Springer, Cham (2014). https://doi.org/10.1007/978-3-319-10401-0_18
11. Oh, H., Jin, Y.: Evolving hierarchical gene regulatory networks for morphogenetic pattern formation of swarm robots. In: 2014 IEEE Congress on Evolutionary Computation (CEC). IEEE (2014)
12. Peng, X., Zhang, S., Huang, Y.: Pattern formation in constrained environments: a swarm robot target trapping method. In: 2016 International Conference on Advanced Robotics and Mechatronics (ICARM), pp. 455–460 (2016)
13. Zhang, S., et al.: Multi-target trapping with swarm robots based on pattern formation. Robot. Auton. Syst. **106**, 1–13 (2018)
14. Oh, H., Shiraz, A.R., Jin, Y.: Morphogen diffusion algorithms for tracking and herding using a swarm of kilobots. Soft Comput. **22**(6), 1833–1844 (2018)

Multi-objective Optimization

Multi-objective Optimization of a Steering Linkage Using Alternative Objective Functions

Suwin Sleesongsom[1(✉)] and Sujin Bureerat[2]

[1] Department of Aeronautical Engineering,
International Academy of Aviation Industry,
King Mongkut's Institute of Technology Ladkrabang, Bangkok 10520, Thailand
suwin.se@kmitl.ac.th
[2] Sustainable and Infrastructure Development Center,
Department of Mechanical Engineering, Faculty of Engineering,
KhonKaen University, Khonkaen 40002, Thailand

Abstract. This paper proposes comparing objective functions in multi-objective optimization of a rack-and-pinion steering linkage in which the optimum results can be affected by the types of objective functions especially when using evolutionary algorithms. The optimization of a steering linkage in the past studied minimizing a steering error and/or a turning radius which can be formulated as a single or multi-objective optimization problem. Steering error usually defines as the different angle between actual angle of steering wheels and the theoretical angle of the wheels according to the Ackerman's principal. Alternatively, the steering error can be rearranged in form of a deviation of instantaneous center based on the same principal, but it still needs to clarify the advantage of using different steering error measures. As a result, it is our attention to study the effect of objective functions to the optimum results on multi-objective optimization of a rack-and-pinion steering linkage. The objective functions are assigned to simultaneously minimize a steering error (dimensionless angle or length) and a turning radius. The design variables are linkage dimensions. The design problem is solved by improving the hybridization of real-code population-based incremental learning and differential evolution (RPBIL-DE). The comparison shows that the alternative objective function can compare with the traditional objective, which leads to effective design of rack-and-pinion steering linkages.

Keywords: Rack-and-pinion steering linkage · Steering error · Turning radius · Multi-objective optimization · Population-based incremental learning

1 Introduction

The advantages of rack-and-pinion steering are simple to construct, economical to manufacture, and compact and easy to operate, which cause this linkage to be commonly used in small cars. The simplicity is due to this mechanism consisting of two steering arms, two tie rods, and rack-and-pinion as shown in Fig. 1(a). The mechanisms are classified as being used with manual or power operations. Normally, the

© Springer Nature Switzerland AG 2019
Y. Tan et al. (Eds.): ICSI 2019, LNCS 11656, pp. 47–58, 2019.
https://doi.org/10.1007/978-3-030-26354-6_5

linkage has two types as central take-off (CTO) and side take-off (STO), which can be divided as trailing or leading configurations upon the arrangement to fit it into the front chassis of the car [1]. Exceptional design of this linkage can reduce the skidding and wear of the tires if it can follow the Ackermann principle. Such a principle states all lines pass the knuckle axle of the front wheels should meet at a point (instantaneous center) on a line pass the rear axle when a car turning as shown in Fig. 1(b). The Ackerman principle is used to relate the outer front wheel angle θ_{OA}, and the inner wheel angle, θ_I as shown by the following equation

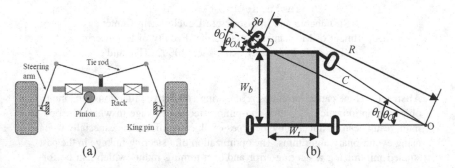

Fig. 1. (a) Rack-and-pinion steering linkage schemes in case of Central take-off (CTO), (b) Ackermann principle, radius of turning and steering error.

$$\theta_{OA}(\theta_I) = \tan^{-1}\frac{1}{\cot\theta_I + W_t/W_b}.\tag{1}$$

where W_b is the wheel base, and W_t is the wheel track. In practical design, the four-bar (old car) and six-bar (new car) linkages for the steering linkage cannot follow the Ackermann principal at every turning angle, but the expectation is to minimize the difference of the theoretical and practical as much as possible. This is the reason why researchers still focus on improving the design process of the steering linkage. From the review of literature, the optimum synthesis of four-bar linkage is proposed by Simionescu and Beale [2] by using the gradient based optimizer, while steering error is an objective function. Steering error (STE) was defined as the deviation between the desired and the real turning angle provided to the wheels by the steering linkage as shown as following equation

$$\delta\theta_O(\theta_I) = |\theta_O(\theta_I) - \theta_{OA}(\theta_I)|.\tag{2}$$

where θ_O is the actual angle made by the outer front wheel during turning and θ_{OA} is the correct angle for the same wheel based on the Ackermann principle.

The formulation of the actual angle and the correct angle can be seen in reference [2]. Later, this function is a traditional objective function for synthesizing the steering mechanism, while improving the technique of optimizers are expected to improve the result. Due to a common four-bar linkage cannot follow the Ackermann principle at all turning angles [3], the six-bar linkage has been proposed to be the steering linkage [4–8]. There is expectation of the optimist that the six-bar steering linkages can satisfy the Ackermann principle [9–15]. As mentioned previously, there is no one linkage can completely follow the Ackermann principle. To increase the design performance of steering linkage synthesis, the McPherson suspension is proposed to be integrated with the steering linkage to make it more realizable in practice [11, 13, 16]. Recent works added the reliability analysis into steering linkage synthesize to make the steering linkage more precise [17], while three coupling systems of an electric-wheel vehicle, comprising differential assisted steering, hub motor driving, and semi-active suspension systems are integrated to study enhancing the performance of the integrated chassis system [18].

In the past, it is found that the objective is used in most work while performing single-objective optimization of a steering error [2, 3, 5, 6, 10–14] or link-length sensitivity [1, 2, 4]. Some work extended the previous single objective function [1, 13] to be bi-objective optimization using a weighted sum method with the exception of [13] which combines the steering error and the change of toe-in angle during wheel jumping [13]. Most if not all of them defined the steering error in form of the deviation of angles. Only a few works defined the steering error in the form of deviation distance from the instantaneous center, which can measure the difference of actual angle and one computed by the Ackermann principal [19]. Furthermore, most optimization techniques used for solving this task are gradient-based [1, 4, 14] and evolutionary techniques [2, 3, 5, 13]. It has only one work which employed a multi-objective evolutionary algorithm (MOEA), which can find a set of Pareto optimal solutions within one of optimization run [15]. The work showed that the performance of MOEAs is a better choice of optimizers to accomplish a traditional steering error and turning radius.

From the review of literature, the comparison of using different steering error objective functions is interesting and worth to investigate. In this study, design objectives are the steering error, and the turning radius. These are two conflicting criteria since reduced steering error results in an increase of a turning radius. The design problem is solved by adaptive hybrid multi-objective real-code population-based incremental learning and differential evolution (RPBIL-DE) [20]. The best constraint handling scheme is selected from the previous study [15].

The rest of this paper is organized as follows. Section 2 derives kinematic analysis, the steering errors and the turning radius of a six-bar linkage while the optimization problem is formulated. The adaptive RPBIL-DE (aRPBIL-DE) is detailed in Sect. 3. A numerical experiment is given in Sect. 4 while the design results are in Sect. 5. The conclusions and discussion of the study are finally drawn in Sect. 6.

2   Kinematic Analysis and an Optimization Problem

A new kinematic analysis of the six-bar linkage used in this research has been proposed in our previous work [15]. The model of this linkage is a leading type of the STO configuration as shown in Fig. 2. The idea is from a drawing technique when using a divider to find a connected point of two lines with known lengths. Consider the first half of STO as drawn with solid lines in Fig. 2. The positions of C and O_2 are known and, by using the technique of drawing, the position of B can be obtained from the intersection of two circles that have the centers at C and O_2. Every rack movements cause the position C changing, thus, a mathematical technique can be used to formulate the shape changing of the linkage given all link dimensions. The normal components of a six-bar planar rack-and-pinion steering linkage compose of two types of linkage that are the twin and the single components. The twin components are steering arms (2, 6) with the length of L_a, and tie rods (3, 5) with length L_t. Single components are a rack (4) and a frame (1). The displacement of rack length L_r is b, as well as the distance from the front wheel axle to the steering rack axis is H. For the details of formulation, see [15].

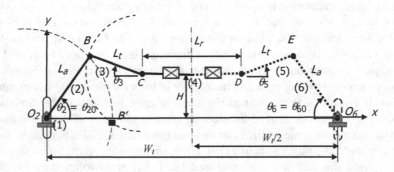

Fig. 2. Six-bar planar rack-and-pinion steering linkage for the STO configuration.

To perform kinematic analysis, start with defining the coordinate of point C as $(C_{x2}, C_{y2}) = (W_t/2 - L_b, H)$ where $L_b = L_r/2 - b$ in cases of turning right and b is the displacement of the rack to the positive right-hand side. This L_b value will be used for computing θ_2 and θ_3 while, to compute θ_5 and θ_6, L_b is set to be $L_r/2 + b$. The positions of points B and B' are the intersection points of the two circles:

$$x^2 + y^2 = L_a^2. \tag{3}$$

And

$$(x - C_{x2})^2 + (y - C_{y2})^2 = L_t^2. \tag{4}$$

Back substituting $x = (L_a^2 - y^2)^{1/2}$ into (3) and rearranging to quadratic equation,

$$a_2 y^2 + a_1 y + a_0 = 0. \tag{5}$$

where $a_2 = 1 - B^2$, $a_1 = -2CB$, $a_0 = C^2 - L_a^2$, $C = \frac{(L_a^2 - L_t^2 + C_{x2}^2 + C_{y2}^2)}{2C_{x2}}$, and $B = \frac{C_{y2}}{C_{x2}}$.
The solutions of (5) are

$$y_1 = (-a_1 + \sqrt{a_1^2 - 4a_2 a_0})/2a_2 \tag{6}$$

and

$$y_2 = (-a_1 - \sqrt{a_1^2 - 4a_2a_0})/2a_2. \tag{7}$$

Equation (3) is used to compute x_1 and x_2 from y_1 and y_2 respectively.

The value y_1 and y_2 is chosen from comparing their values while the highest positive value between them is chosen; thus, the preferable root for a leading mechanism is y_1. The initial angle on the left arm $\theta_2 = \theta_{20}$ is equal to the initial angle on the right arm $\theta_6 = \theta_{60}$ when the car goes straight. For leading type STO, the trigonometric relations, θ_2, θ_3, θ_5 and θ_6 are shown as follows:

$$\theta_2 \text{ or } \theta_6 = \tan^{-1}\left(\frac{y_1}{x_1}\right). \tag{8}$$

and

$$\theta_3 \text{ or } \theta_5 = \tan^{-1}\left(\frac{y_1 - H}{W_t/2 - L_r - x_1}\right). \tag{9}$$

where $L_b = L_r/2 - b$ for computing θ_2 and θ_3, and $L_b = L_r/2 + b$ for θ_5 and θ_6.

Then the inner front wheel angle is $\theta_I = \theta_6 - \theta_{60} = \theta_6 - \theta_{20}$, while the outer front wheel angle is $\theta_O = \theta_{20} - \theta_2$. The traditional steering error in (2) can be assigned to be the first objective function that will be detailed in the next subsection.

Limiting position of this kind of mechanism is in our consideration to protect our design optimization from having disadvantages. The limiting position is detailed in our previous work [15].

2.1   Turning Radius

Turning radius is a very important characteristic of vehicles used in big cities, which has problems of traffic jam. The less turning radius is more preferable since it makes the car having a nimble drive in a narrow way. The smallest turning radius can be derived from Fig. 1(a) as

$$R_{min} = D + C = D + W_b/\sin\theta_{O,max}. \tag{10}$$

where C is the distance from the instantaneous center of turning to the kingpin, D is a kingpin length, and $\theta_{O,max}$ is the maximum angle of outer front wheel during full turning.

2.2   Unconventional Steering Error

Another way to define the steering error is from the definition of Ackermann principal which states that all lines pass the knuckle axle of the front wheels should meet at a point (instantaneous center) on a line pass the rear axle when a car is turning. The actual steering mechanism normally causes the different instantaneous centers in form of different length by the line passing the knuckle axle of outer and inner front wheels on the line passing the rear axle as shown in Fig. 3.

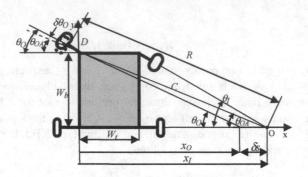

Fig. 3. Ackermann principle, turning radius (R) and steering error (δs).

From the trigonometric relation in Fig. 3, one can have:

$$x_O = \frac{W_b/W_b}{\tan \theta_O} = \frac{1}{\tan \theta_O}. \tag{11}$$

$$x_I = \frac{W_b/W_b + W_t/W_b \tan \theta_I}{\tan \theta_I} = \frac{1}{\tan \theta_I} + \frac{W_t}{W_b}. \tag{12}$$

Then, the unconventional steering error is defined as

$$\delta s = x_O - x_I = \frac{1}{\tan \theta_O} - \frac{1}{\tan \theta_I} - \frac{W_t}{W_b}. \tag{13}$$

when x_O and x_I are dimensionless.

If θ_I and θ_O in Eq. (13) are equal, the subtraction of the first and second terms is zero but the steering error is hardly zero and the value is equal to W_t/W_b. It means two lines passing the front knuckle axle never meet at the same point (instantaneous center) on a line passing the rear axle when a car turning. The W_t/W_b is a car geometric ratio, which depends on the geometry of a car. Normally this value is smaller than 1. In this research, one expectation is to find the best scaling factor (k) that scales a car geometric ratio to minimize the steering error, where k is less than 1.

$$\delta s = x_O - x_I = \frac{1}{\tan \theta_O} - \frac{1}{\tan \theta_I} - k\left(\frac{W_t}{W_b}\right). \tag{14}$$

2.3   Optimization Problems

The multi-objective optimization problem is assigned to minimize two alternatives of the steering error and turning radius, which can be expressed as:

Optimization problem 1 (OP1):

$$\text{Min} \left\{ \begin{array}{l} f_1(\mathbf{x}) = \max|\delta\theta_O(\theta_I)| \; ; \theta_I \in [0°, 40°] \\ f_2(\mathbf{x}) = R_{\min} \end{array} \right\}. \tag{15}$$

Subject to $\theta_{6,\max} - \theta_{60} \geq 40°$.

$f_1 \leq 0.75°$

$f_2 \leq 5$ m

$L_a + L_t < L_0 = \sqrt{H^2 + (W_t/2 - L_r/2)^2}$, $L_a \geq L_t + L_0$, $L_t \geq L_a + L_0$, and $\{0.1, 0, 0\}^T \leq \mathbf{x} \leq \{0.3, 0.3, 0.3\}^T$ m

Optimization problem 2 (OP2):

$$\text{Min} \begin{cases} f_1(\mathbf{x}) = \max|\delta s(\theta_I)| \; ; \theta_I \in [0°, 40°] \\ f_2(\mathbf{x}) = R_{\min} \end{cases}. \tag{16}$$

Subject to $\theta_{6,\max} - \theta_{60} \geq 40°$

$$f_1 \leq k(W_t/W_b)$$

$$f_2 \leq 5 \text{ m}$$

$L_a + L_t < L_0 = \sqrt{H^2 + (W_t/2 - L_r/2)^2}$, $L_a \geq L_t + L_0$, $L_t \geq L_a + L_0$, and $\{0.1, 0, 0\}^T \leq \mathbf{x} \leq \{0.3, 0.3, 0.3\}^T$ m

where $\mathbf{x} = \{L_a, L_t, H\}^T$. The steering errors f_1 of problems OP1 and OP2 are computed in the range of $\theta_I \in [0°, 40°]$. The constraints are set for usability. The problems OP1 and OP2 define constraints of steering error smaller than or equal to $0.75°$ and $k(W_t/W_b)$ respectively. The steering error of the problem 2 assigns $k \in \{0.1, 0.2, 0.3, 0.4, 0.5\}$. For both problems, the constraint of turning radius must be smaller than or equal to 5 m to give the car more nimble.

3   The aRPBIL-DE

The hybridization of real-code population-based incremental learning and differential evolution (RPBIL-DE) has been proposed for solving the multi-objective optimization of steering linkage [15]. The results show that RPBIL-DE using the DE/best/2/bin in combination with the relaxation scheme is an efficient technique for solving the narrow feasible region. It is therefore selected for this study. The present algorithm is based on the opposition-based concept of our previous study [15]. The mutation operator is based on DE/best/2/bin where the mutated offspring $\mathbf{c}$ can be calculated using the following equation.

$$\mathbf{c} = \mathbf{p} + F(\mathbf{q}_1 - \mathbf{r}_1) + F(\mathbf{q}_2 - \mathbf{r}_2). \tag{17}$$

where F is a uniform random number sampling a new in the interval [0.25, 0.75]. $\mathbf{q}_1$, $\mathbf{r}_1$, $\mathbf{q}_2$, and $\mathbf{r}_2$ are chosen from the current real code population at random.

Furthermore, we propose to update probability matrix with the learning rate and the opposite learning rate where such an idea has been proposed in [21]. The generation of the learning rate or the opposite learning rate is in accordance with binomial probability. More details of the procedure are given in Algorithm 1, where p_c is a DE crossover probability, and CR is the crossover ratio of an element of an offspring c in the binomial crossover. For more details of the original RPBIL-DE, see Pholdee and Bureerat [20].

For increasing the searching performance as with our previous study, the relaxation scheme as shown in Fig. 4(a) has been proposed [15]. The relaxing scheme starts with the initial tolerance as $10°$ and linearly reduces to $0.75°$ at iteration 30 and becomes constant afterwards. This technique is an efficient technique for tackling the constraints of the multi-objective optimization problem. This scheme is used for the first optimization problem, while the second problem has an adaptation as show in Fig. 4(b). The scheme starts with a initial tolerance as a car geometric ratio W_t/W_b as 0.5586 and linearly reduces to $k(W_t/W_b)$ at iteration 30 and becomes constant afterwards.

Algorithm 1. aRPBIL-DE

Input: N_G, N_P, n_l, N_T, objective function name (*fun*), Pareto archive size (N_A)
Output: x^{best}, f^{best}
Initialization: $P_{ij}= 1/n_l$ for each tray
Main steps
: Generate a real code population X from the probability trays and find $f = fun(X)$
: Find a Pareto archive A
1: For i = 1 to N_G
2: Separate the non-dominated solutions into N_T groups using a clustering technique, and find the centroid r_G of each group
3: Update each tray P_{ij} based on r_G
4: Generate a real code population X from the probability trays
5: For j = 1 to N_P recombine X and A using DE operators
5.1: Select p from A randomly
5.2: Select q and r from X randomly, $q \neq r$
5.3: Calculate $c = p + F(q_1-r_1) + F(q_2-r_2)$ (DE/best/2/bin)
5.4: Set c_i into its bound constraints.
5.5: If $rand < p_c$, perform crossover
5.5.1: For k = 1 to n
5.5.2: If $rand < CR$, $y_k= c_k$
5.5.3: Otherwise, $y_{j,k}= p_k$
5.5.4: End
6: End
7: New real-code population is $Y = \{y_1, ...,y_j, ..., y_{NP}\}$ and find $f = fun(Y)$
8: Find non-dominated solutions from $Y \cup A$ and replace the members in A with these solutions
9: If the number of archive members is larger than N_A, remove some of the members using a clustering technique
10: End

4 Numerical Experiment

The objectives of this research are to compare the objective functions for multi-objective optimization of steering linkage and find the optimal dimensions of a rack-and-pinion steering linkage while minimizing the steering error and the minimizing the turning radius. All important dimensions of the car are W_b = 2175 mm, W_t =1215 mm, L_r = 678 mm, and D = 300 mm. The aRPBIL-DE is applied to solve the problems with the population size of 50 and the number of iterations being 80. The external Pareto archive size is set to be 100. Other parameters are assigned as n_I = 40 where each probability tray produces five design solutions. The crossover rate and CR are set as p_c = 0.7 and CR = 0.5 respectively. The initial learning rate used for the updating matrix is 0.25. It should be noted that those are default values used in the previous studies [15]. The procedure is terminated when reaching the maximum generation number. The adaptive RPBIL-DE is proposed to tackle the problems for 30 runs in order to compare the alternative objective functions and find the best k, where $k \in \{0.1, 0.2, 0.3, 0.4, 0.5\}$.

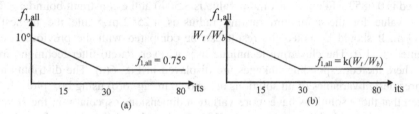

Fig. 4. Constraint handling schemes

5 Design Results

Having performed 30 runs for all multi-objective design problems, the obtained results are shown in Table 1. This table shows the hypervolume (HV) of a Pareto front explored from the proposed problem where the reference point used for computing the hypervolume indicator is $\{f_1, f_2\} = \{1°, 5.0 \text{ m}\}$. The higher hypervolume means the better Pareto front. The data in Table 1 is based on the averaged hypervolumes from 30 runs, the Pareto front of OP2 is changed to OP1 to make possible to compare with the OP1 and reduce the number of Pareto solutions to 50 for all cases. The technique used for clustering selection is from our previous work [22]. The optimizer gives the best convergence rate (highest mean hypervolume) is where k = 0.4 (darker highlighted value) whereas the second best is k = 0.5 (lighter highlighted value). In terms of consistency (lowest standard deviation of hypervolumes), the best and second best are still k = 0.4 and k = 0.5 respectively. When considering only the best max (maximum hypervolume), it is found OP1 gives the best maximum, while the second is k – 0.4. This implies that using k = 0.4 is more powerful. The constraint relaxation scheme can adapt to a new objective function leading to the best results.

Table 1. Performance comparison based on a hypervolume.

Hypervolume	Mean	STD	Max	Min
OP1	0.2562	0.1121	0.3651	0.0717
OP2(k=0.5)	0.2784	0.0838	0.3489	0.0753
OP2(k=0.4)	0.3066	0.0630	0.3561	0.1006
OP2(k=0.3)	0.2705	0.0972	0.3554	0.0923
OP2(k=0.2)	0.2427	0.1179	0.3552	0.1663
OP2(k=0.1)	0.1733	0.1294	0.3393	0.0781

Figure 5(a) shows the best front obtained from all problems. From the result the newly proposed objective function is comparable with the traditional objective, but the new one can lead to a variety of design solutions than the traditional one, which causes it having higher hypervolume. The best front and some selected solutions are obtained from the best result with k = 0.4 and shown in Fig. 5(b). The minimum steering error obtained is 0.0852 while the maximum value is 3.5040 at the constraint boundary. The lowest value for the minimum turning radius is 4.2552 m while the highest is 4.7289 m. It should be noted the result can be compared with the previous results presented in [15]. The clustering technique uses an even Pareto filter technique from [22] where the corresponding linkages are displayed in Fig. 6(a). The distribution of the three design variables of all solutions are shown in Fig. 6(b) using box-plots. It can be seen that those solutions have more variation dimensions especially in the *H* value when comparing with the previous study [15]. That is why the new objective function should be used for steering linkage design.

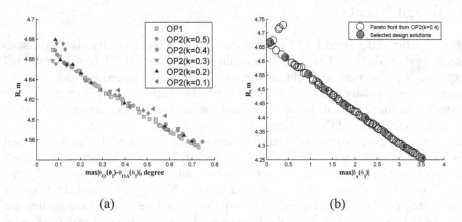

(a)   (b)

Fig. 5. (a) Best Pareto front of all problems and (b) the best Pareto front from OP2 (k = 0.4)

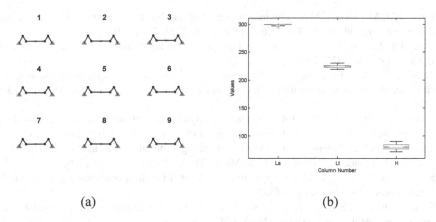

(a)   (b)

Fig. 6. (a) Linkages corresponding to the Pareto front in Fig. 5(b), (b) Distribution of link dimensions

6   Conclusions

This paper proposes comparing of two objective functions for the steering linkages synthesizing, which is the steering error. The traditional steering error is normally indicated in form of angular, while the new one is the deviation length from theoretical instantaneous center with respect to the Ackermann principal. The design problem has two conflicting objectives of the steering error and turning radius. The design variables are a steering arm length, a tie rod length, and a distance from the front wheel axis to the rack axis. The adaptive optimizer used to solve the multi-objective optimization problem is aRPBIL-DE which is extended from the original one. The results show the newly proposed steering error give good results as those obtained from using the traditional steering error while the new objective has overall higher HV as it can increase diversity of the design variables. With the proposed technique, acceptable steering linkages with various minimum turning radii are obtained for decision making within one optimization run.

Our future work is extension of the proposed technique to design the steering mechanism of a tri-wheel motorcycle to make it more efficiency. At the present the new motorcycle has been developed to have a similar steering system to the car.

Acknowledgement. The authors are grateful for the financial support provided by King Mongkut's Institute of Technology Ladkrabang, the Thailand Research Fund (RTA6180010), and the Post-doctoral Program from Research Affairs, Graduate School, KhonKaen University (58225).

References

1. Hanzaki, A.R., Rao, P.V.M., Saha, S.K.: Kinematic and sensitivity analysis and optimization of planar rack-and-pinion steering linkages. Mech. Mach. Theory **44**, 42 56 (2009)
2. Simionescu, P.A., Beale, D.: Optimum synthesis of the four-bar function generator in its symmetric embodiment: the Ackermann steering linkage. Mech. Mach. Theory **37**, 1487–1504 (2002)

3. EttefaghM, M., Javash, M.S.: Optimal synthesis of four-bar steering mechanism using AIS and genetic algorithms. J. Mech. Sci. Technol. **28**, 2351–2362 (2014)
4. Zhao, J.S., Liu, X., Feng, Z.J., Dai, J.S.: Design of an Ackermann-type steering mechanism. J. Mech. Eng. Sci. **227**, 2549–2562 (2013)
5. Peñuñuri, F., Peón-Escalante, R., Villanueva, C., Pech-Oy, D.: Synthesis of mechanisms for single and hybrid tasks using differential evolution. Mech. Mach. Theory **46**(10), 1335–1349 (2011)
6. Simionescu, P.A., Smith, M.R., Tempea, I.: Synthesis and analysis of the two loop translational input steering mechanism. Mech. Mach. Theory **35**(7), 927–943 (2000)
7. Carcaterra, A.: D'Ambrogio: a function generating differential mechanism for an exact solution of the steering problem. Mech. Mach. Theory **33**(5), 535–549 (1998)
8. Simionescu, P.A., Smith, M.R.: Applications of Watt II function generator cognates. Mech. Mach. Theory **35**, 1535–1549 (2000)
9. Simionescu, P.A., Smith, M.R.: Four- and six-bar function cognates and over constrained mechanism. Mech. Mach. Theory **36**, 913–924 (2001)
10. Zarak, C.E., Townsend, M.A.: Optimal design of rack-and-pinion steering linkages. J. Mech. Des. **105**, 220–226 (1983)
11. Felzien, M.L., Cronin, D.L.: Steering error optimization of the McPherson strut automotive front suspension. Mech. Mach. Theory **20**, 17–26 (1985)
12. Simionescu, P.A., Smith, M.R.: Initial estimates in the design of rack-and-pinion steering linkages. J. Mech. Des. **122**, 194–200 (2000)
13. Zhou, B., Li, D., Yang, F.: Optimization design of steering linkage in independent suspension based on genetic algorithm. In: Proceedings of Computer-Aided Industrial Design & Conceptual Design, Wenzhou, China, pp. 45–48 (2009)
14. Kim, S.I., Kim, Y.Y.: Topology optimization of planar linkage mechanisms. Int. J. Numer. Methods Eng. **98**, 265–286 (2014)
15. Sleesongsom, S., Bureerat, S.: Multiobjective optimization of a steering linkage. J. Mech. Sci. Technol. **30**, 3681–3691 (2016)
16. Sleesongsom, S., Bureerat, S.: Optimization of steering linkage including the effect of McPherson strut front suspension. In: Tan, Y., Shi, Y., Tang, Q. (eds.) ICSI 2018. LNCS, vol. 10941, pp. 612–623. Springer, Cham (2018). https://doi.org/10.1007/978-3-319-93815-8_58
17. Wang, L., Zhang, X., Zhou, Y.: An effective approach for kinematic reliability analysis of steering mechanisms. Reliab. Eng. Syst. Safe. **180**, 62–76 (2018)
18. Zhao, W.Z., Wang, Y.Q., Wang, C.Y.: Multidisciplinary optimization of electric-wheel vehicle integrated chassis system based on steady endurance performance. J. Clean. Prod. **186**, 640–651 (2018)
19. Showers, A., Lee, H.H.: Design of the steering system of an SELU Mini Baja car. Int. J. Eng. Res. Tech. **2**(10), 2396–2400 (2013)
20. Pholdee, N., Bureerat, S.: Hybridisation of real-code population-based incremental learning and differential evolution for multiobjective design of trusses. Inform. Sci. **223**, 136–152 (2013)
21. Sleesongsom, S., Bureerat, S.: Topology optimisation using MPBILs and multi-grid ground element. Appl. Sci. **8**, 271 (2018)
22. Sleesongsom, S.: Multiobjective optimization with even Pareto filter. In: Proceedings of Natural Computation, Jinan, China, pp. 92–96 (2008)

Using Two Reproduction Operators for Balancing Convergence and Diversity in MOEA/D

Liang Chen[1,2]([✉]) [iD], Hongwei Li[1], Jingjing Wen[2], Lei Fu[1], Ming Lu[1],
Jingbo Bai[1], and Lin Cao[1]

[1] Army Engineering University of PLA, Nanjing 210007, Jiangsu, China
Chenbb0708@163.com
[2] Army Military Transportation University, Bengbu 233011, Anhui, China

Abstract. Reproduction operator is an important component used in multi-objective evolutionary based on decomposition (MOEA/D). This paper proposes two reproduction operators with different characteristics and studies how to employ these two operators to balance the convergence and the diversity in MOEA/D. One of the reproduction operators is a Lévy flights crossover and improved polynomial mutation, and the other one is orthogonal crossover operator. We come up with a scheme to incorporate these two reproduction operators in MOEA/D and propose a new algorithm, i.e., MOEA/D–FL&OX, and compares the proposed algorithm with MOEA/D-DE on the test instances. The experimental results show that MOEA/D-FL&OX could significantly outperform the compared algorithms. It suggests that the proposed algorithm is an effective and competitive candidate for multi-objective optimization.

Keywords: Multi-objective · MOEA/D · Reproduction · Convergence · Diversity

1 Introduction

A multi-objective optimization problem (MOP) can be stated as follows:

$$\begin{aligned}\text{minimize} \quad & F(x) = (f_1(x), \cdots, f_m(x)) \\ \text{subject to} \quad & x \in \Omega\end{aligned} \tag{1}$$

Where Ω define the decision (variable) space, R^m is the objective space, and $f_1(x), \cdots, f_m(x)$ are the m objective functions. Let $u = (u_1, \cdots, u_m) \in \Omega$, $v = (v_1, \cdots, v_m) \in R^m$ be two vectors, u is said to dominate v if $u_i \leq v_i$ for all $i \in \{1, \cdots, m\}$ and $u_j < v_j$ for at least one $j \in \{1, \cdots, m\}$. The set of trade-off optimal solutions in objective variable space is called the *Pareto front* (*PF*) in respect to the concept of Pareto dominance, and the corresponding set in the decision space is called the pareto set (*PS*). Multi-objective evolutionary optimization algorithms (MOEAs) aim to find the Pareto optimal set to approximate the whole true *PF*.

© Springer Nature Switzerland AG 2019
Y. Tan et al. (Eds.): ICSI 2019, LNCS 11656, pp. 59–68, 2019.
https://doi.org/10.1007/978-3-030-26354-6_6

How to balance the convergence and the diversity is the key to design high-performance MOEA/D algorithm. In MOEA/D, many components and operations are closely related to convergence and diversity. For example, the matching of subproblems and solutions [1, 2], the distribution of direction vectors [3, 4] and the selection of scalarizing methods [5, 6] are all have effect on convergence and diversity.

However, replacement and reproduction are the two most important components to control convergence and diversity. Replacement determines which solutions will be replaced by a new one, thus updating the population. The neighborhood size was studied in [7]. That the maximal number of solutions replaced by a child solution is bounded by a smaller number was discussed in [8]. To find the most suitable neighboring subproblems, a global replacement strategy is proposed in [9]. Reproduction mainly involves reproduction operator. Simulated binary crossover(SBX) [10] and differential evolution (DE) [8] were suggested as reproduction operators. Afterwards, a strategy of combining two reproduction operators is proposed in [11]. In recently, adaptive selection reproduction operators have been used in MOEA/D [12, 13].

Obviously, the application of efficient reproduction operators to MOEA/D is always one of the most basic and effective methods to improve the performance of algorithm. In this paper, we study two production operators with different search characteristics, one is Lévy flights crossover and improved polynomial mutation, the other is orthogonal crossover operator. Based on MOEA/D framework, the major contributions of this paper are as follows:

(1) Two reproduction operators, i.e., Lévy flights crossover and improved polynomial mutation (denoted as FL), and orthogonal crossover (denoted as OX), are employed.
(2) We analyze the search characteristics of two operators proposed and a scheme proposed to incorporate the two operators into MOEA/D. A new variant of MOEA/D, called MOEA/D-FL&OX is proposed.
(3) Experiments on some test instances have been conducted to verify the effectiveness of MOEA/D-FL&OX.

The remainder of the paper is organized as follow. In Sect. 2, we briefly review MOEA/D. In Sect. 3, we give the details of the reproduction operators and propose MOEA/D-FL&OX algorithm. In Sect. 4, we show the results of our comparative experiments. Finally, in Sect. 5 we give our conclusion and future work.

2 Related Works

2.1 Framework

MOEA/D applies a decomposition approach for transforming MOP (Eq. (1)) into a number of scalar subproblems and optimizes them in a collaborative manner.

MOEA/D framework can be briefly stated as follows:

Step (1) Initialize. Generate N solutions $x^1, \cdots, x^N$ randomly, where x^i is the corresponding solution to subproblem i. For each subproblem i, generate a neighborhood containing T solutions (denoted by $B(i)$) of the subproblems in T-neighborhood of subproblems i. Initialize the ideal reference point z^*.

Step (2) Update: For each subproblem i, randomly select parent solutions from $B(i)$, and then perform the reproduction operator on them to generate new solution y. Computer $F(y)$ and update the reference point z^*. Then, for each index $j \in B(i)$, if $g^{te}(y|\lambda^j, z^*) \leq g^{te}(x_j|\lambda^j, z^*)$, then set $x_j = y$, and $F^j = F(y)$. In the end, update the external population.

Step (3) Terminate. If stopping criteria is satisfied, then terminate and output the result. Otherwise, go to Step 2.

2.2 Decomposition

There are several decomposition approaches to decompose MOP into a number of single objective problems [5]. In our paper, we adopt Tchebycheff decomposition approach. With the Tchebycheff decomposition approach, each subproblem can be stated as:

$$\text{minimize } g^{te}(x|\lambda, z^*) = \max_{1 \leq i \leq m} \left\{ \lambda_i |f_i(x) - z_i^*| \right\}$$
$$\text{subject to} \qquad x \in \Omega \tag{2}$$

Where $\lambda = (\lambda_1, \cdots, \lambda_m)^T$ is a weight vector satisfying $\lambda_i \geq 0 (i = 1, \cdots, m)$ and $\sum_{i=1}^m \lambda_i = 1$. $z^* = (z_1^*, \cdots, z_m^*)^T$ is ideal reference point. The direction vector for this subproblem is $\left(\frac{\frac{1}{\lambda_1}}{\sum_{i=1}^m \frac{1}{\lambda_i}}, \frac{\frac{1}{\lambda_2}}{\sum_{i=1}^m \frac{1}{\lambda_i}}, \cdots, \frac{\frac{1}{\lambda_m}}{\sum_{i=1}^m \frac{1}{\lambda_i}} \right)^T$.

To balance the convergence and diversity of MOEA/D, adaptive decomposition methods are come up with to balance the diversity and convergence according to the characteristics of the estimated Pareto front [5, 6].

2.3 Reproduction Operator

Using the reproduction operator, parent solutions generate child solutions. Reproduction operator plays a key role in respect of the convergence and diversity of MOEA/D. Different reproduction operators have different characteristics, some are good at exploration, some are good at exploitation and some are both. Therefore, searching for efficient reproduction operators is the most basic approach to improve the performance of MOEA.

In original MOEA/D [10], simulated binary crossover (SBX) and polynomial mutation operator are adopted as reproduction operator called MOEA/D-SBX. While MOEA/D-SBX is not suitable for some multi-objective optimization problems with complicated Pareto Sets (PS), then a new reproduction operator with a differential evolution (DE) operator and a polynomial mutation operator are proposed [8], called MOEA/D-DE. Two different reproduction operators are proposed to balance the convergence and diversity [11]. Two novel mutation operators are developed in [14], and the hybrid cross-generation mutation operation achieves good exploration-exploitation balance. Adaptive operator selection (AOS) is a new trend to make use of reproduction operators in MOEA/D. A bandit-based AOS method is used in [12] and significantly improve the performance of MOEA/D. Credit assignment strategies which is used in AOS are effective in elevating the generality of a multi-objective evolutionary algorithm in outperforming a random operator selector [15].

3   MOEA/D-FL&OX

To search more efficient reproduction operators for MOEA, in this paper, we introduce two reproduction operator and incorporate them into MOEA/D. The first one is the Lévy flights operator and improved polynomial mutation operator (denoted as LX). The other one is the orthogonal crossover operator (denoted as OX). In the following, we introduce the details of these two operators.

3.1   LX

Lévy flights operator has infinite mean and variance and can generate larger jumps than the Brownian motion and thereby explore search space more broadly. In this paper, inspired by the model in cuckoo search algorithm proposed by Yang and Deb [16], we can easily extend it to be a reproduction operator. For each subproblem i, choose its current solution x^i as the first mating parent, and randomly select another different mating parent x^j from the mating neighborhood. In the LX operator, an intermediate solution $\bar{y}^i = (\bar{y}^i_1 \cdots, \bar{y}^i_n)$ is first generated by:

$$\bar{y}^i = x^i + (x^j - x^i) \otimes \alpha_0 \times \frac{\phi \times \mu}{|v|^{1/\beta}} \tag{3}$$

$$\phi = \left\{ \frac{\Gamma(1+\beta)\sin(\pi \times \beta/2)}{\Gamma(1+\beta/2)\beta \times 2^{(\beta-1)/2}} \right\}^{1/\beta} \tag{4}$$

Where $\otimes$ denotes entry-wise multiplications, $\alpha_0 > 0$ is the step size scaling factor, β is Lévy flights exponent. μ and v have standard normal distribution. Γ is the standard Gamma function.

As a simple case and without loss of the generality, the search directions of Lévy flights operator in a 2D search space are presented in Fig. 1(a). Sine Lévy flights can generate large jumps, $x^i + (x^j - x^i) \otimes r$ can explore new solutions in all the whole search space as showing in Fig. 1(a). LX can well maintain the diversity for MOEA/D.

The polynomial mutation (PLM) was proposed in [17], and this operator was later improved in [18]. In our proposed algorithm, we use the improved polynomial mutation (IPLM) to mutate for the intermediate solution $\bar{y}^i$. By applying the improved polynomial mutation new solution, $y^i = (y^i_1, \cdots, y^i_n)$ is generated in the following way:

$$y^i_k = \begin{cases} \bar{y}^i_k + \delta(b_k - a_k) & \text{if } rand \leq p_m \\ \bar{y}^i_k & \text{otherwise} \end{cases} \tag{5}$$

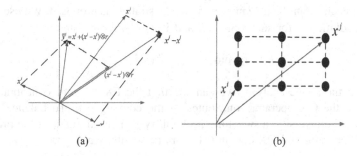

Fig. 1. Search space of the FL operator and the OX operator.

With

$$
\delta =
\begin{cases}
\left[2u + (1 - 2u)\left(1 - \frac{\bar{y}_k^i - a_k}{b_k - a_k}\right)^{\eta+1} \right]^{\frac{1}{\eta+1}} - 1 & \text{if } \quad rand < 0.5 \\
1 - \left[2(1 - u) + 2(u - 0.5)\left(1 - \frac{b_k - \bar{y}_k^i}{b_h - a_k}\right)^{\eta+1} \right]^{\frac{1}{\eta+1}} & \text{otherwise}
\end{cases}
\tag{6}
$$

Where a_k and b_k are the lower and upper bounds of the k-th decision variable. Where the distribution index η and the mutation rate p_m are controlling parameter in polynomial mutation. *rand* is a uniform random number from $[0,1]$.

3.2 OX

Inspired by the orthogonal design, Leung and Wang [19] have incorporated a quantization technique into orthogonal crossover (OX) and have proposed quantization orthogonal crossover (QOX). For more details about QOX, refer to [19]. In this paper, we will employ QOX as a reproduction operator, termed OX reproduction operator. For each subproblem i, choose its current solution x^i as the first mating parent, and randomly select another different mating parent x^j from the mating pool. With these two solutions, we can get Q^2 new solutions as follows: $\left[y^1, \cdots, y^{Q^2}\right] = \text{OX}\,(x^i, x^j, K, Q)$.

Where K represents the number of factors, Q represents the number of levels. In Fig. 1(b), the black solid circle points represent the new solutions obtained by OX. We can easily see that the search space is between x^i and x^j. The search domain is strictly restricted. It is distinctly different from the FX. The OX operator could perform better than LX in convergence.

3.3 Some Other Improvements

(1) As mentioned above, for subproblem i, orthogonal crossover operator can obtain Q^2 new solutions $\left[y^1, \cdots, y^{Q^2}\right]$. In order to make full use of the information of the

solution, for each subproblems j in $B(i)$, a greedy strategy is proposed. We use the most appropriate solution y^l for subproblems j and it can be represented as:

$$l = \arg\min_{1 \leq k \leq Q^2} g^{te}\left(y^k | \lambda^j, z^*\right).$$

(2) From the above analysis, we can see that the FX operator contributes to the diversity and the OX operator contributes to the convergence. To balance the convergence and the diversity, a switching probability p_o is used to adjust the probability of using FL operator and OX operator. For more details, see Algorithm 1.

Algorithm 1: MOEA/D-FL&OX
1   Input: MOP, a stopping criterion, N.
2   Output: external archive (EA)
3   Initialize a set of weight vectors $\lambda = (\lambda^1, \cdots, \lambda^N)^T$, the population $P \leftarrow x^1, \cdots, x^N$, $z^* = min\{f_i(x) | x \in \Omega\}$, set $B(i) = \{i^1, \cdots, i^T\}$ are the T closest weight vectors to λ^i.
4   While the stopping criterion is not satisfied do
5   for i=1 to N do
6   if rand $>= p_o$
7   Generate a new solution y^i by applying the FL reproduction operator. Repair y^i.
8   Get $F(y^i)$, and $nEFS = nEFS + 1$.
9   For each $j = 1, \cdots, m$, if $F_j(y^i) < z_j^*$, then $z_j^* = F_j(y^i)$.
10   For each index $j \in B(i)$, if $g^{te}(y^i | \lambda^j, z^*) < g^{te}(x_j | \lambda^j, z^*)$, then set $x_j = y^i$, and $F^j = F(y^i)$.
11   else
12   Generate a set of new solutions $[y^1, \cdots, y^{Q^2}]$ by applying the OX reproduction operator. Apply a problem-specific repair on $[y^1, \cdots, y^{Q^2}]$.
13   Get $F(y^k), k = 1, \cdots Q^2$, and $nEFS = nEFS + Q^2$.
14               $l = \underset{1 \leq k \leq Q^2}{\text{argmin}}\ g^{te}(y^k | \lambda^j, z^*)$
15   For each index $j \in B(i)$, if $g^{te}(y^l | \lambda^j, z^*) < g^{te}(x_j | \lambda^j, z^*)$, then set $x_j = y^l$, and $F^j = F(y^l)$.
16   end
17   Update external archive (EA)
18   end
19 end

4   Experiments

4.1   Test Problems

To assess the performance of the proposed approach, we compare its results with those obtained by the state-of-the-art MOEA/D-DE [8]. We adopt two suits of test instances: ZDT (except for ZDT5, which is a binary problem) and UF. The PS shapes of ZDT test instances are often strikingly simple. The UF test instances with arbitrary prescribed PS shapes, which could be used for dealing with complicated PS shapes [8]. UF8, UF9, UF10 are there-objective problems, the other test instances are two-objective problems. We use 30 decision variables for ZDT1 ~ ZDT3, ZDT6 and UF1 ~ UF10. ZDT4 is a test instance using 10 decision variables.

4.2 Performance Metric

The inverted generational distance (IGD) [20] is used to assess the performance of the algorithms in our experiment. Let P^* be a set of uniformly distributed points in the objective space along the PF. Let P be an approximation to the PF, the inverted generational distance from P^* to P is defined as follows.

$$IGD(P^*, P) = \frac{\sum_{v \in P^*} d(v, P)}{|P^*|} \qquad (7)$$

Where $d(v, P)$ is the minimum Euclidean distance between v and the points in P. IGD metric could measure both the diversity and convergence of P.

4.3 Parameter Settings

MOEA/D-DE and MOEA/D-FL&OX have been implemented in MATLAB. We use the same method as in [8] to obtained uniform spread weight vectors $\lambda = (\lambda^1, \cdots, \lambda^N)^T$. Therefore, the number of weight vectors (i.e., the population size) N is set 100 for the 2-objective instances and 91 for the 3-objective instances. Moreover, we select 1000 evenly distributed points in PF and let these points be P^* for each test instance with two objectives, and 990 points for each test instance with three objectives. The other parameter settings are given in Table 1.

Table 1. Parameter setting in experiments

Parameters	Values
Max External archive size and max function evaluation number	200, 2.5e+4
Number of runs for each instance	20
T: Neighborhood size	15
Parameter CR and F of DE	1, 0.5
Parameter p_m of polynomial mutation	$1/N$
Distribution index η of simulated binary crossover and polynomial mutation	20
Parameter α_0, β and p_o of FL	1, 1.5, $1/N$
Parameter K and Q of OX	4, 3

4.4 Discussion of Results

Table 2 shows the mean and standard deviation of IGD values obtained by the studied algorithms in 20 runs. In order to test whether there is a statistical difference between

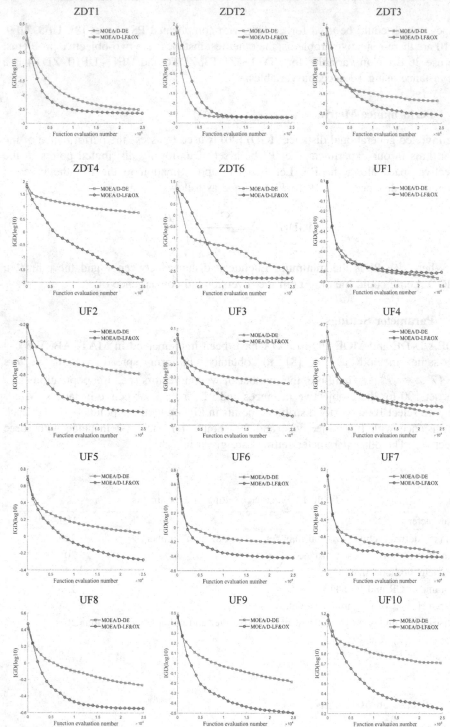

Fig. 2. Evolution of the mean of IGD values versus the number of function evaluation number.

the performance of these two approaches, Wilcoxon's rank sum test at 0.05 significance level has been adopted. In Table 2, ‡, † and ≈ denote that the performance of MOEA/D-FL&OX is better, worst or equal to MOEA/D-DE's. Figure 2 shows the evolutions of the mean of IGD values with the number of function evaluation of the two algorithms. As shown in Table 2 and Fig. 2, MOEA/D-FL&OX significantly outperforms MOEA/D-DE in most of the test instance except UF4. The above experimental results verify that the MOEA/D-FL&OX algorithm is a competitive candidate for global optimization problems.

Table 2. Mean and standard deviation of IGD values

Inst.	MOEA/D-DE mean error±std dev	MOEA/ D-FL&OX mean error±std dev	Inst.	MOEA/D-DE mean error±std dev	MOEA/ D-FL&OX mean error±std dev
ZDT1	2.96E-03± 4.57E-04	2.23E-03± 7.51E-05‡	UF4	5.80E-02± 2.40E-03	6.39E-02± 4.57E-03†
ZDT2	1.93E-03± 7.22E-05	1.94E-03± 1.63E-05≈	UF5	1.09E+00± 1.49E-01	5.22E-01± 1.03E-01‡
ZDT3	1.34E-02± 1.24E-02	2.55E-03± 8.99E-04‡	UF6	6.00E-01± 5.23E-02	3.77E-01+ 8.65E-02‡
ZDT4	5.67E+00± 2.63E+00	1.23E-02± 1.83E-02‡	UF7	1.61E-01± 6.40E-02	1.43E-01± 1.32E-01≈
ZDT6	2.14E-03± 1.58E-03	1.54E-03± 2.21E-05†	UF8	5.42E-01± 8.16E-02	2.85E-01± 2.50E-02‡
UF1	1.35E-01± 3.68E-02	1.53E-01± 6.50E-02≈	UF9	6.51E-01± 1.30E-01	3.19E-01± 7.76E-02‡
UF2	1.60E-01± 1.79E-02	5.58E-02± 1.18E-02‡	UF10	5.12E+00± 6.19E-01	1.76E+00± 3.50E-01‡
UF3	4.39E-01± 7.09E-02	2.37E-01± 3.47E-02‡			

5 Conclusion

We have presented two reproduction operators with different characteristics to balance convergence and diversity. Lévy flights production operator and orthogonal crossover production operator were simply analyzed. A switch parameter was proposed to adjust exploration and exploitation. A greedy strategy was adopted to make use of the solutions generated by orthogonal crossover production operator. Based on this strategy, we have proposed MOEA/D-FL&OX. The experimental results demonstrate our proposed algorithm is superior to MOEA/D-DE on most of test instances. As a part of our future work, we plan to adaptively use the two operators in MOEA/D-FL&OX and compare with other MOEAs on other test instances.

References

1. Li, K., et al.: Stable matching based selection in evolutionary multiobjective optimization. IEEE Trans. Evol. Comput. **18**(6), 909–923 (2014)
2. Wu, M.Y., et al.: Matching-based selection with incomplete lists for decomposition multiobjective optimization. IEEE Trans. Evol. Comput. **21**(4), 554–568 (2017)
3. Qi, Y., et al.: MOEA/D with adaptive weight adjustment. Evol. Comput. **22**(2), 231–264 (2014)
4. Gu, F.Q., Cheung, Y.M.: Self-organizing map-based weight design for decomposition-based many-objective evolutionary algorithm. IEEE Trans. Evol. Comput. **22**(2), 211–225 (2018)
5. Jiang, S., et al.: Scalarizing functions in decomposition-based multiobjective evolutionary algorithms. IEEE Trans. Evol. Comput. **22**(2), 296–313 (2018)
6. Wu, M., et al.: Learning to decompose: a paradigm for decomposition-based multiobjective optimization. IEEE Trans. Evol. Comput. **PP**(99), 1 (2018)
7. Ishibuchi, H., Akedo, N., Nojima, Y.: Relation between neighborhood size and MOEA/D performance on many-objective problems (2013)
8. Li, H., Zhang, Q.: Multiobjective optimization problems with complicated Pareto sets, MOEA/D and NSGA-II. IEEE Trans. Evol. Comput. **13**(2), 284–302 (2009)
9. Wang, Z., et al.: Adaptive replacement strategies for MOEA/D. IEEE Trans. Cybern. **46**(2), 474–486 (2015)
10. Zhang, Q.F., Li, H.: MOEA/D: a multiobjective evolutionary algorithm based on decomposition. IEEE Trans. Evol. Comput. **11**(6), 712–731 (2007)
11. Wang, Z., Zhang, Q., Li, H.: Balancing convergence and diversity by using two different reproduction operators in MOEA/D: some preliminary work. In: IEEE International Conference on Systems, Man, and Cybernetics (2015)
12. Li, K., et al.: Adaptive operator selection with bandits for a multiobjective evolutionary algorithm based on decomposition. IEEE Trans. Evol. Comput. **18**(1), 114–130 (2014)
13. Gonçalves, R.A., Almeida, C.P., Pozo, A.: Upper Confidence Bound (UCB) algorithms for adaptive operator selection in MOEA/D. In: Gaspar-Cunha, A., Henggeler Antunes, C., Coello, C.C. (eds.) EMO 2015, Part I. LNCS, vol. 9018, pp. 411–425. Springer, Cham (2015). https://doi.org/10.1007/978-3-319-15934-8_28
14. Qiu, X., et al.: Adaptive cross-generation differential evolution operators for multiobjective optimization. IEEE Trans. Evol. Comput. **20**(2), 232–244 (2016)
15. Hitomi, N., Selva, D.: A classification and comparison of credit assignment strategies in multiobjective adaptive operator selection. IEEE Trans. Evol. Comput. **21**(2), 294–314 (2017)
16. Yang, X.-S., Deb, S.: Cuckoo search via Levey flights. In: Abraham, A., et al. (eds.) 2009 World Congress on Nature & Biologically Inspired Computing, p. 210 (2009)
17. Deb, K., Agrawal, R.B.: Simulated binary crossover for continuous search space. Complex Syst. **9**(3), 115–148 (1995)
18. Debab, K.: Omni-optimizer: a generic evolutionary algorithm for single and multi-objective optimization. Eur. J. Oper. Res. **185**(3), 1062–1087 (2008)
19. Leung, Y.W., Wang, Y.: An orthogonal genetic algorithm with quantization for global numerical optimization. IEEE Trans. Evol. Comput. **5**(1), 41–53 (2002)
20. Zitzler, E., et al.: Performance assessment of multiobjective optimizers: an analysis and review. IEEE Trans. Evol. Comput. **7**(2), 117–132 (2003)

A Surrogate-Assisted Improved Many-Objective Evolutionary Algorithm

Bin Cao$^{(\boxtimes)}$, Yi Su , and Shanshan Fan

Hebei University of Technology, Tianjin 300401, China
caobin@scse.hebut.edu.cn
201622102025@stu.hebut.edu.cn

Abstract. The many-objective evolutionary algorithm is an effective method to tackle many-objective optimization problems. We improve the two-archive2 algorithm (Two_Arch2) by adopting the Levy distribution and opposition-based learning strategy. In addition, we propose a hybrid adaptive strategy of the surrogate models. The criterion for evaluating the model quality is developed. In model management, selection of individuals is based on the criterion named angle penalized distance (APD). In the experiments, we make comparisons of the IGD among our algorithm and the other algorithms on the DTLZ and MaF test suites, which exhibits the superiority of the improved algorithm.

Keywords: Evolutionary algorithm · Surrogate model · Hybrid adaptive strategy · Many-objective optimization

1 Introduction

In real life, many complex optimization problems can be solved by evolutionary algorithms [1–3]. With the increasing complexity of optimization problems, many-objective optimization problems (MaOPs) with more than three objectives are emerging [4]. Traditional multi-objective evolutionary algorithms (MOEAs) used to deal with multi-objective optimization problems (MOPs) can not be directly adapted to solve MaOPs, so new optimization methods need to be designed. A novel dominance relation-based evolutionary algorithm has been applied for solving MaOPs [5]. From another perspective, reference vector guided evolutionary algorithm (RVEA) was used to address MaOPs [6]. In addition, following NSGA-II framework [7], Deb et al. [8] proposed a many-objective evolutionary algorithm (MaOEA) based on reference points, which emphasizes the nondominated population members and those close to a set of supplied reference

---

Supported by organization in part by the Opening Project of Guangdong Province Key Laboratory of Computational Science at the Sun Yat-sen University under Grant 2018002, in part by the Foundation of Key Laboratory of Machine Intelligence and Advanced Computing of the Ministry of Education under Grant No. MSC-201602A.

Y. Tan et al. (Eds.): ICSI 2019, LNCS 11656, pp. 69–78, 2019.
https://doi.org/10.1007/978-3-030-26354-6_7

points. However, the evolutionary process requires a lot of calculation of function evaluations and environmental selection, taking a long time; therefore, the method based on surrogate model will be beneficial.

Surrogate model [9] can reduce the computational cost. To reduce the computation time, the neural network (NN) was used to evaluate fitness [10]. In the search of memetic evolution, diverse surrogate models were unified to solve MOPs [11]. ParEGO [12] adopted surrogate model to comprehend the search landscape and updated the surrogate model along with function evaluation. The Gaussian process model of each subproblem was built in the work of [13]. However, most of surrogate-assisted evolutionary algorithms (SAEAs) aim at single-objective optimization or multi-objective optimization based on fitness approximation. While the work of [14] presented a surrogate-assisted reference vector-guided EA to solve MaOPs, and the computational cost could be reduced by using the Kriging model to approximate each objective function. To solve expensive MaOPs, Pan et al. [15] proposed a SAEA, the dominance relationship was predicted between candidate solutions and reference solutions by an artificial NN.

An improved two-archive (Two_Arch2) algorithm [16] was used to address MaOPs. Two_Arch2 integrated strategies of convergence and diversity simultaneously. Experimental results have shown that Two_Arch2 performed well. However, the algorithm still has some disadvantages. In this paper, Levy distribution strategy and opposition-based learning mechanism are introduced to enhance global search ability. Furthermore, in the work of [17], the heterogeneous ensemble consisting of a least square support vector machine (LSSVM) and two radial basis function (RBF) networks was introduced to tackle MOPs. In addition, RVEA integrated strategies of reference vectors and angle penalized distance (APD)-based selection to manage both convergence and diversity [6]. Therefore, those advantages of algorithms above enable us to propose a better algorithm. We adopt the hybrid adaptive strategy of the surrogate models, and the selection method of the individuals is based on APD in model management for solving MaOPs. A surrogate-assisted improved many-objective evolutionary algorithm (SAIMaOEA) is proposed.

The remainder of this paper is organized as follows. Section 2 introduces the relevant background knowledge. We describe our algorithm in Sect. 3. Experimental study is provided in Sect. 4. Finally, we draw the conclusion of this paper in Sect. 5.

2   Surrogate-Assisted Optimization

Surrogate model [11,15] is often utilized to approximate the objective function or fitness function of candidate solutions in SAEAs, expressed as follows:

$$F(x) = F(x)^* + e(x) \tag{1}$$

where $F(x)$ denotes the objective value calculated using the real fitness function, $F(x)^*$ is the approximated value of the surrogate model, and $e(x)$ is the error function and reflects the uncertainty of surrogate model approximation [11].

3 Improved Many-Objective Evolutionary Algorithm Based on Surrogate

3.1 The Improved Two_Arch2

Two_Arch2 algorithm [16] has the advantage of setting up both convergence archive (CA) and diversity archive (DA). Crossover and mutation are two separate processes, and the mutation probability is a fixed value. This paper proposes a MaOEA with Levy mutation strategy and opposition-based learning mechanism. To improve the diversity of the population and the global search ability of the algorithm, the random number obeying Levy distribution is used to mutate the population individuals. In addition, Two_Arch2 performs crossover between CA and DA while mutation only on CA. The opposition-based learning can effectively maintain the population diversity and avoid falling into local optima during the optimization process. After all, our algorithm combines the advantages of the Levy mutation strategy, the opposition-based learning and the Two_Arch2 algorithm.

Evolution Process Based on Levy Mutation Strategy. Two_Arch2 performs mutation only on CA. As the role of CA is for convergence, it does not in charge of diversity maintenance. In the evolution process, the mutation of individuals in CA is performed as follows [16]:

$$x_{i,j}(g+1) = \begin{cases} v_{i,j}(g+1), & if\ rand <= PM[i] \\ x_{i,j}, & otherwise \end{cases} \tag{2}$$

where $PM[i]$ is the mutation probability for individual i. The mutation probability of each individual i satisfies the Levy distribution [18,19], whose probability density function is as follows:

$$L_{\alpha,\gamma}(z) = \frac{1}{\pi} \int_0^\infty \exp(-\gamma q^\alpha) cos(qz), \mathrm{d}q \tag{3}$$

where α and γ are two characteristic parameters of Levy distribution, specifically, α controls the sharpness of Levy distribution within $(0, 2]$, and γ controls the scale of distribution within $(0, \infty)$. Levy mutation mechanism is used to improve the diversity of the population, which ensures that the population searches in the surrounding areas in detail and has exploration ability at the same time. Convergence and diversity are alternately performed to achieve adequate traversal, contributing to improving the exploitation and exploration abilities of the algorithm.

Opposition-Based Learning Mechanism. Opposition-based learning (OBL) [20] generally evaluates the current individuals and the opposition-based individuals at the same time, and selects better individuals as the next generation. The generalized OBL is proposed in the work of [21]. In the strategy of the OBL, for the populations $C_i(g)$ after the crossover and $X_i(g)$ after the mutation, the opposition-based populations $\breve{C}_i(g)$ and $\breve{X}_i(g)$ are obtained separately, utilizing the following formula:

$$\breve{x}_{i,j} = (a_j + b_j) - x_{i,j} \tag{4}$$

where $i = 1, \ldots, N$, here, N is the population size, $j = 1, \ldots, D$, here, D is the dimension of the individual, and $x_{i,j}$ is the jth dimensional value of the ith individual within the range of $[a_j, b_j]$.

Afterwards, the populations of $C_i(g)$, $X_i(g)$, $\breve{C}_i(g)$ and $\breve{X}_i(g)$ are combined, where non-dominated individuals are selected. In the work of [16], the quality indicator $I_{\varepsilon+}$ in IBEA [22] was chosen as the selection principle for CA, while a selection criterion of the L_p-norm-based distance was used for DA. In this paper, we adopt the two strategies above to improve the diversity of the population and avoid the algorithm falling into local optima.

3.2   The Hybrid Adaptive Strategy of the Surrogate Models

In this paper, the hybrid adaptive strategy of the surrogate models is proposed. The double surrogate models are used during the evolution process, namely, LSSVM and Kriging model. To avoid excessive sample aggregation, we initialize the population utilizing the Latin hypercube sampling method [23]. The objective values of individuals are calculated by the real fitness functions in the initial population, and the individuals and objective values are utilized as samples for training surrogate models.

In the work of [14], Kriging, also known as the Gaussian process is used to approximate each objective function. To apply the Kriging model [14], we utilize the following criterion:

$$F(x^i) = \begin{cases} f_r(x^i), & f^*(x^i) > O_{ts} \text{ or } e_r^*(x^i) > E \\ f_s(x^i), & otherwise \end{cases} \tag{5}$$

where $f^*(x^i)$ is objective value evaluated by surrogate model, O_{ts} is the minimum value of each objective in the non-updated training samples, $e_r^*(x^i)$ is the error of surrogate model, E is the maximum error in all evaluated results, $f_r(x^i)$ and $f_s(x^i)$ are the real fitness vector and that approximated by the surrogate, respectively, and $F(x^i)$ represents the final result. The solutions that satisfy the above conditions will be selected to be evaluated using the real fitness function; otherwise, the result obtained by surrogate models is accepted. This strategy can avoid the influence of inaccurate evaluation by surrogate models to some extent. We adopt the two kinds of surrogate models in this paper. In the early stage of evolution, LSSVM-based surrogate is used for evaluating the objectives, which may reduce computation time because of complete replacement. In the later stage, Kriging models adaptively replace the real fitness functions based on the criterion aforementioned. By combining the surrogate models and the criterion, the hybrid adaptive strategy can reduce the time of solving complex optimization problems and enhance the effectiveness of the algorithm.

In model management, selection of individuals is based on the APD [6] to retrain the surrogate models. The selected individuals are representative in terms of convergence and diversity. APD [6] is formulated as follows:

$$D^i = (1 + P(\theta^i)) \|\bar{d}^i\| \tag{6}$$

$$P(\theta^i) = k(\frac{g}{g_{max}})^\alpha \frac{\theta^i}{\gamma^v} \tag{7}$$

where θ^i represents the angle between the ith individual and reference vector, γ^v represents the angle between two neighboring reference vectors, and $\alpha = 2$ is a parameter.

4   Experiments

4.1   Experimental Setup

In the experiments, the number of individuals that are evaluated using the real fitness functions is $11D - 1$ in the initialization phase; the number of the decision variables is 10; the maximum number of function evaluations is 500; the generation number of updating the surrogate models is 20; the number of the independent runs is 20. In addition, to compare our algorithm with CPS-MOEA [24] and K-RVEA [14], the size of population is 50 and the maximum number of function evaluations is 300. For the algorithm parameters, we refer to the most recommended parameter settings of Two_Arch2. To compare different algorithms, inverted generational distance (IGD) [14,15] is used as the performance measure.

4.2   Comparison Experiments

We evaluate the performance of our algorithm and the Two_Arch2 algorithm for tackling MaOPs. We consider two cases of objective numbers, which are 8 and 10, respectively. Table 1 illustrates the experimental results obtained by our algorithm and Two_Arch2 algorithm. As listed in Table 1, it can be seen that our algorithm performs better than the Two_Arch2 algorithm on most of the tested instances. SAIMaOEA achieves the best results over most test cases, except on DTLZ6 with 8 objectives, as well as DTLZ5 and DTLZ6 with 10 objectives. DTLZ1 and DTLZ3 are hard-to-converge problems. SAIMaOEA tries to keep a well-distributed set of solutions, and the convergence rate of SAIMaOEA is relatively faster than Two_Arch2 on these problems by using surrogate models.

Figure 1 depicts the non-dominated front achieved by our algorithm and Two_Arch2 algorithm when the number of objectives is 4 on DTLZ1. Each line represents the objective values of each individual on all objectives. It can be seen from Fig. 1, the values of objectives in Two_Arch2 are higher than our algorithm. The result indicates that more function evaluations may be better to solve such problems for Two_Arch2. That is to say, the convergence of SAIMaOEA algorithm for MaOPs is superior to Two_Arch2.

Table 1. IGD test results of SAIMaOEA and TWO_ARCH2.

Pro.	m	TWO_ARCH2	SAIMaOEA	m	TWO_ARCH2	SAIMaOEA
DTLZ1	8	1.10e+1(3.73e+0)	5.12e+0(2.40e+0)	10	4.39e-1(1.16e-1)	3.89e-1(8.02e-2)
DTLZ2	8	5.79e-1(2.01e-2)	5.45e-1(1.37e-2)	10	6.44e-1(2.09e-2)	5.94e-1(1.83e-2)
DTLZ3	8	2.33e+1(6.56e+0)	2.15e+1(7.24e+0)	10	1.32e+0(3.38e-1)	1.26e+0(3.31e-1)
DTLZ4	8	7.27e-1(5.11e-2)	6.96e-1(2.53e-2)	10	7.42e-1(3.19e-2)	7.03e-1(1.51e-2)
DTLZ5	8	6.96e-2(1.68e-2)	6.59e-2(6.45e-3)	10	2.08e-2(4.89e-3)	2.51e-2(4.15e-3)
DTLZ6	8	2.09e+0(2.67e-1)	2.38e+0(7.91e-2)	10	5.50e-1(2.07e-1)	6.89e-1(4.40e-2)
DTLZ7	8	6.52e+0(2.33e+0)	5.34e+0(1.47e+0)	10	2.02e+0(2.90e-1)	1.78e+0(1.26e-1)

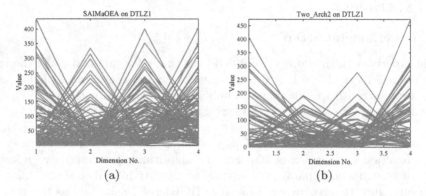

(a)   (b)

Fig. 1. The non-dominated front obtained by SAIMaOEA and Two_Arch2.

We compare SAIMaOEA with CPS-MOEA, K-RVEA and Two_Arch2. CPS-MOEA and K-RVEA are surrogate-assisted MaOEAs. The experimental results are shown in Table 2, with the best values highlighted. As shown in Table 2, SAIMaOEA obtains the best performance on 11 cases, while CPS-MOEA and K-RVEA are the best on 5 and 2 cases, respectively. Owing to the fact that, Two_Arch2 is the algorithm without the surrogate models, it converges slowly to the Pareto front with limited function evaluations. On the contrary, SAIMaOEA with surrogates has more advantages. The hybrid adaptive strategy of the surrogate models and the method of selecting individuals based on the APD can improve the optimization performance of the algorithm.

The results of Two_Arch2, CPS-MOEA, K-RVEA and SAIMaOEA on the MaF1-5 problems with 10 objectives are shown in Table 3. MaF benchmark functions can well represent various real-world scenarios. As shown in Table 3, SAIMaOEA achieves the best results on MaF1, MaF3 and MaF4. While K-RVEA is the best-performing algorithm on MaF5, and SAIMaOEA has slightly worse IGD values than CPS-MOEA on MaF2. Compared with other algorithms, SAIMaOEA adopts the scheme of maintaining diversity and convergence, and designs the strategy of using two surrogate models to achieve as accurate an assessment as possible.

Table 2. IGD test results of TWO_ARCH2, CPS-MOEA, K-RVEA and SAIMaOEA on DTLZ.

Pro.	m	TWO_ARCH2	CPS-MOEA	K-RVEA	SAIMaOEA
DTLZ1	4	6.69e+1(2.02e+1)	5.68e+1(1.24e+1)	8.08e+1(2.01e+1)	5.56e+1(3.56e+0)
	8	9.56e+0(4.56e+0)	1.17e+1(2.89e+0)	1.51e+1(4.33e+0)	7.65e+0(1.96e+0)
	10	4.55e-1(1.65e-1)	5.16e-1(3.83e-1)	4.71e-1(1.96e-1)	4.35e-1(1.15e-1)
DTLZ2	4	3.80e-1(2.60e-2)	4.51e-1(4.06e-2)	3.69e-1(3.41e-2)	3.49e-1(2.43e-2)
	8	6.02e-1(2.75e-2)	6.70e-1(2.77e-2)	6.11e-1(2.85e-2)	5.94e-1(3.29e-2)
	10	6.68e-1(3.21e-2)	6.85e-1(2.77e-2)	6.71e-1(3.92e-2)	6.29e-1(6.35e-3)
DTLZ3	4	1.81e+2(5.39e+1)	1.59e+2(2.94e+1)	2.57e+2(5.26e+1)	1.47e+2(3.03e+1)
	8	2.85e+1(1.42e+1)	5.02e+1(1.29e+1)	3.22c+1(1.98e+1)	2.76e+1(8.92e+0)
	10	1.87e+0(1.19e+0)	7.29e+0(6.48e+0)	1.84e+0(5.65e-1)	1.28e+0(2.59e-1)
DTLZ4	4	8.13e-1(1.78e-1)	6.23e-1(2.75e-2)	6.43e-1(1.08e-1)	6.02e-1(2.71e-2)
	8	8.24e-1(8.97e-2)	6.61e-1(1.82e-2)	7.43e-1(3.64e-2)	6.98e-1(2.53e-2)
	10	8.08e-1(4.82e-2)	6.46e-1(7.00e-3)	7.12e-1(3.77e-2)	7.15e-1(1.10e-2)
DTLZ5	4	2.04e-1(2.97e-2)	2.12e-1(5.22e-2)	2.21e-1(2.52e-2)	1.71e-1(2.28e-2)
	8	9.25e-2(1.86e-2)	1.25e-1(2.88e-2)	7.78e-2(1.09e-2)	9.48e-2(1.74e-2)
	10	3.59e-2(8.10e-3)	5.79e-2(1.20e-2)	2.00e-2(0.00e+0)	5.32e-2(8.68e-3)
DTLZ6	4	5.46e+0(3.29e-1)	3.21e+0(6.92e-1)	5.16e+0(5.19c-1)	4.20e+0(1.52e+0)
	8	2.27e+0(2.28e-1)	1.18e+0(4.80e-1)	1.91e+0(2.51e-1)	2.56e+0(7.49e-2)
	10	7.08e-1(1.84e-1)	1.82e-1(1.11e-1)	4.58e-1(2.27e-1)	7.92e-1(3.75e-2)

Table 3. IGD test results of TWO_ARCH2, CPS-MOEA, K-RVEA and SAIMaOEA on MaF.

Pro.	m	TWO_ARCH2	CPS-MOEA	K-RVEA	SAIMaOEA
MaF1	10	3.99e-1(3.17e-2)	4.26e-1(2.40e-2)	4.61e-1(1.88e-2)	3.62e-1(1.09e-2)
MaF2	10	3.23e-1(3.79e-2)	2.69e-1(1.58e-2)	2.77e-1(1.64e-2)	3.01e-1(2.45e-2)
MaF3	10	9.35e+0(3.38e+1)	2.52e+2(2.68e+2)	2.02e+0(1.94e+0)	1.97e+0(1.06e+0)
MaF4	10	5.88e+2(4.88e+2)	3.65e+2(1.01e+2)	2.35e+2(6.35e+1)	2.31e+2(4.22e+1)
MaF5	10	1.45e+2(1.93e+1)	1.14e+2(1.51e+1)	8.43e+1(1.08e+1)	1.52e+2(1.32e+1)

In addition, we also compare the five cases of objective numbers which are 3, 4, 6, 8, and 10 on DTLZ2, respectively. Figure 2 presents the IGD test results calculated by SAIMaOEA algorithm, Two_arch2 algorithm, CPS-MOEA algorithm and K-RVEA algorithm. As shown in Fig. 2, the difference of test results of the four algorithms is evident. Therefore, SAIMaOEA algorithm is significantly better than other algorithms among the tested objectives.

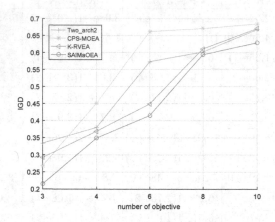

Fig. 2. IGD test results obtained by SAIMaOEA, K-RVEA, CPS-MOEA and TWO_ARCH2 for various objective numbers on DTLZ2.

5   Conclusion

In this paper, we apply the surrogate models to the improved evolutionary algorithm for tackling MaOPs. In our algorithm, we adopt the Levy distribution and opposition-based learning strategy. And we use the surrogate models to approximate the objective functions. The criterion for evaluating the model quality is developed. In addition, to retrain surrogate models, we use the angle penalized distance for selecting individuals. We compare the proposed algorithm with Two_Arch2, CPS-MOEA and K-RVEA, and our algorithm performs better than the other algorithms. In future work, we can try to further improve the algorithm, use different surrogate models and design more model management methods and so on.

References

1. Segredo, E., Luque, G., Segura, C., Alba, E.: Optimising real-world traffic cycle programs by using evolutionary computation. IEEE Access **7**, 43915–43932 (2019)
2. Herrero, J.G., Berlanga, A., Lopez, J.M.M.: Effective evolutionary algorithms for many-specifications attainment: application to air traffic control tracking filters. IEEE Tran. Evol. Comput. **13**(1), 151–168 (2009)
3. Liu, C., Zhao, Q., Yan, B., Elsayed, S., Ray, T., Sarker, R.: Adaptive sorting-based evolutionary algorithm for many-objective optimization. IEEE Trans. Evol. Comput. **23**, 247–257 (2019)

4. Fleming, P.J., Purshouse, R.C., Lygoe, R.J.: Many-objective optimization: an engineering design perspective. In: Coello Coello, C.A., Hernández Aguirre, A., Zitzler, E. (eds.) EMO 2005. LNCS, vol. 3410, pp. 14–32. Springer, Heidelberg (2005). https://doi.org/10.1007/978-3-540-31880-4_2
5. Yuan, Y., Xu, H., Wang, B., Yao, X.: A new dominance relation-based evolutionary algorithm for many-objective optimization. IEEE Trans. Evol. Comput. **20**(1), 16–37 (2016)
6. Cheng, R., Jin, Y., Olhofer, M., Sendhoff, B.: A reference vector guided evolutionary algorithm for many-objective optimization. IEEE Trans. Evol. Comput. **20**(5), 773–791 (2016)
7. Deb, K., Pratap, A., Agarwal, S., Meyarivan, T.: A fast and elitist multiobjective genetic algorithm: NSGA-II. IEEE Trans. Evol. Comput. **6**, 182–197 (2002)
8. Deb, K., Jain, H.: An evolutionary many-objective optimization algorithm using reference-point-based nondominated sorting approach, part i: solving problems with box constraints. IEEE Trans. Evol. Comput. **18**(4), 577–601 (2014)
9. Jin, Y.: Surrogate-assisted evolutionary computation: recent advances and future challenges. Swarm Evol. Comput. **1**(2), 61–70 (2011)
10. Ohno, M., Yoshimatsu, A., Kobayashi, M., Watanabe, S.: A framework for evolutionary optimization with approximate fitness functions. IEEE Trans. Evol. Comput. **6**(5), 481–494 (2002)
11. Lim, D., Jin, Y., Ong, Y.S., Sendhoff, B.: Generalizing surrogate-assisted evolutionary computation. IEEE Trans. Evol. Comput. **14**(3), 329–355 (2010)
12. Knowles, J.: ParEGO: a hybrid algorithm with on-line landscape approximation for expensive multiobjective optimization problems. IEEE Trans. Evol. Comput. **10**(1), 50–66 (2006)
13. Zhang, Q., Liu, W., Tsang, E., Virginas, B.: Expensive multiobjective optimization by MOEA/D with Gaussian process model. IEEE Trans. Evol. Comput. **14**(3), 456–474 (2010)
14. Chugh, T., Jin, Y., Miettinen, K., Hakanen, J., Sindhya, K.: A surrogate-assisted reference vector guided evolutionary algorithm for computationally expensive many-objective optimization. IEEE Trans. Evol. Comput. **22**(1), 129–142 (2018)
15. Pan, L., He, C., Tian, Y., Wang, H., Zhang, X., Jin, Y.: A classification-based surrogate-assisted evolutionary algorithm for expensive many-objective optimization. IEEE Trans. Evol. Comput. **23**, 74–88 (2019)
16. Wang, H., Jiao, L., Yao, X.: Two_arch2: an improved two-archive algorithm for many-objective optimization. IEEE Trans. Evol. Comput. **19**(4), 524–541 (2015)
17. Guo, D., Jin, Y., Ding, J., Chai, T.: Heterogeneous ensemble-based infill criterion for evolutionary multiobjective optimization of expensive problems. IEEE Trans. Cybern. **PP**(99), 1–14 (2018)
18. Reynolds, A.: Liberating lévy walk research from the shackles of optimal foraging. Phys. Life Rev. **14**, 59–83 (2015)
19. Schroeder, A., Ramakrishnan, S., Kumar, M., Trease, B.: Efficient spatial coverage by a robot swarm based on an ant foraging model and the lévy distribution. Swarm Intell. **11**(1), 39–69 (2017)
20. Al-Qunaieer, F.S., Tizhoosh, H.R., Rahnamayan, S.: Opposition based computing — a survey. In: The 2010 International Joint Conference on Neural Networks (IJCNN), pp. 1–7, July 2010
21. Wang, H., Wu, Z., Rahnamayan, S., Liu, Y., Ventresca, M.: Enhancing particle swarm optimization using generalized opposition-based learning. Inf. Sci. **181**(20), 4699–4714 (2011)

22. Zitzler, E., Künzli, S.: Indicator-based selection in multiobjective search. In: Yao, X., et al. (eds.) PPSN 2004. LNCS, vol. 3242, pp. 832–842. Springer, Heidelberg (2004). https://doi.org/10.1007/978-3-540-30217-9_84

23. Zolan, A.J., Hasenbein, J.J., Morton, D.P.: Optimizing the design of a Latin hypercube sampling estimator. In: 2017 Winter Simulation Conference (WSC), pp. 1832–1843, December 2017

24. Zhang, J., Zhou, A., Zhang, G.: A classification and pareto domination based multiobjective evolutionary algorithm. In: 2015 IEEE Congress on Evolutionary Computation (CEC), pp. 2883–2890, May 2015

Research of Multi-objective Personalized Recommendation Algorithm Based on Multi-thread Concurrency

Xiaoyan Shi[1], Wei Fang[1(✉)], Guizhu Zhang[1], Shi Cheng[2], and Quan Wang[3]

[1] College of Engineering the Internet of Things, Jiangnan University, Wuxi, China
fangwei@jiangnan.edu.cn
[2] School of Computer Science, Shaanxi Normal University, Xi'an, China
[3] Wuxi SensingNet Industrialization Research Institute, Wuxi, China

Abstract. In order to strengthen the recommendation system's ability to mine user preferences and unpopular products, a recommendation model based on three goals is proposed and the MOEA-PGMA algorithm was designed. Aiming at the large computation time of MOEA-PGMA based on this model because of the computation scale, the multi-thread concurrent execution framework Executor is introduced into the multi-core environment to achieve multi-task concurrent execution. The scheme refactors MOEA-PGMA to make it more suitable for multi-threaded environments. The experimental results show that the scheme can be effectively improve operational efficiency.

Keywords: Personalized Recommendation Algorithm · Thread · Concurrency · Execution Framework

1 Introduction

With the rapid development of information network technology, the e-commerce system has penetrated into every aspect of life. Through a variety of online sales platforms, people can complete the shopping and trading of goods without leaving their homes, which saves a lot of purchase time. However, the ever-expanding e-commerce system has also caused some problems. For example, users may need to spend a lot of time and energy to find the part they are interested in from the massive commodity information. As a technology based on information collection and knowledge discovery, recommendation systems has been increasingly applied in the e-commerce systems. The recommendation system can help users to find the products they need quickly by simulating the function of offline shopping guides who provide users with shopping information and suggestions. It should be noted that as people's needs become more and more abundant, it is far from enough to simply pursue the accuracy of recommendations. In order to meet the personalized needs of users, some new performance indicators, such as diversity and novelty, should be added into the traditional recommendation technology. At present, the mainstream of personalized

© Springer Nature Switzerland AG 2019
Y. Tan et al. (Eds.): ICSI 2019, LNCS 11656, pp. 79–91, 2019.
https://doi.org/10.1007/978-3-030-26354-6_8

recommendation algorithm based on multi-objective optimization usually takes accuracy and diversity as dual goals [1–3]. Compared with traditional algorithms, this algorithm can provide users with more abundant products. However, due to the high popularity of recommended products, this multi-objective recommendation algorithm is not conducive to mining the potential user preferences and cold products. In the long run, this is also not conducive to improve the purchase rate of the system. In order to overcome the shortcomings of the recommendation system, a personalized recommendation algorithm based on three objectives (MOEA-PGMA) is proposed in this paper. By introducing novelty as the third objective, we can increase the ability of mining the potential interest of users and improve the recommendation probability of unpopular products.

By abstracting the item recommendation problem into a multi-objective optimization problem, the MOEA-PGMA algorithm can provide users with multiple sets of recommendations with high accuracy, diversity and novelty at one time. In order to provide recommendation for multiple users at the same time, MOEA-PGMA codes all the recommendation solutions into one individual, which makes the calculation scale of personalized recommendation problem reach 1000 dimensions. With the number of users in the system increasing, the calculation scale of this algorithm will be further expanded. At the same time, as the number of objective functions increases, the complexity of the personalized recommendation problem becomes larger. Especially, when solving the frontier of Pareto [4], a lot of computation time will be consumed. In response to this problem, we try to introduce multi-threaded concurrency [5] technology under multi-core conditions to improve operational efficiency. Firstly, the related knowledge of three-objective personalized recommendation algorithm (MOEA-PGMA) based on multi-thread concurrency is introduced. Then we use multithreading concurrency technology to improve the above shortcomings of the algorithm. The simulation results show that the speed of the MOEA-PGMA algorithm based on multi-threaded concurrency is significantly improved compared with the traditional personalized recommendation algorithm.

2   Design of Three-Objective Personalized Recommendation Model

Combined with the current research status in the recommendation field, it can be found that accuracy, diversity and novelty are important performance indicators for measuring the quality of recommendations. In this section, these three indicators are introduced in detail at first, and then the MOEA-PGMA algorithm flow based on the model is described.

2.1   Design of the Three-Objective Function

Considering all the optimization directions of current recommendation systems, MOEA-PGMA algorithm uses three objective functions to achieve multi-objective optimization, in which the first objective is used to evaluate the accuracy of the recommendation scheme. It should be noted that the real accuracy of the recommended scheme can only be obtained during the validation phase, so the prediction score is used to represent the accuracy at first. In order to compute the first objective function, a simple and effective recommendation algorithm needs to be determined. The material diffusion algorithm [3] (ProbS) is suitable for processing binary data. That is to say, users can get the predicted score of an unselected item by making a favorite and dislike evaluation of selected items. In summary, the prediction results of the ProbS algorithm are used to calculate the accuracy of the recommendation scheme, and the coverage and average popularity are used to measure the diversity and novelty of recommendation schemes respectively.

(1) Accuracy

In the item recommendation phase, the item with a higher predicted score will be recommended to the user based on the rating list of the items that the user has not selected. Assuming that the predicted score of user i for item α is $pr_{i\alpha}$, the number of items recommended by the system to the user at one time is L, and the scores of all users belonging to the same system S are calculated as the formula (1).

$$PR = \frac{\sum_{i \in S} \sum_{\alpha=1}^{L} pr_{i\alpha}}{|S| \times L} \tag{1}$$

where $|S|$ is the number of users in the system S.

(2) Diversity

Generally speaking, recommendation systems should recommend different objects to users according to their preferences. If a system only recommends popular objects to the user and ignores the user's own characteristics, it will lack the personalized features. Therefore, the recommendation system should have different recommend results for different users. Based on above analysis, this paper applies diversity to the recommendation system. Coverage refers to the proportion of items in the recommended scheme to all items. The higher the coverage rate of the recommended scheme gets, the more diverse items will be recommended to users. The coverage formula is generally used to predict the diversity of the recommended scheme and the calculation formula is shown in (2).

$$Coverage = \frac{|\cup_{u \in U} R(u)|}{I} \tag{2}$$

where U represents the total user set of the recommendation system, $R(u)$ represents a set of recommendation schemes of length N provided by the recommendation system to the current user, and I represents the total number of items in the recommendation system.

(3) Novelty

Novelty is also an important indicator to measure the recommendation ability, which is generally used to detect the system's ability to recommend non-hot items. The simplest way to generate relatively novel recommendation schemes is to filter out items which users have not acted on. For example, on an online shopping platform, some products that have not been added to the shopping carts, collected or purchased will be recommended to users. Inevitably, there are some products that users have not heard from the current shopping platform, but may have been bought by other means. Therefore, the value of novelty is low when the system only uses the user's behavior records to filter out items that may not have been touched.

In order to make the recommendation scheme more novel, the average popularity of the items in the recommendation results should be reduced. Because the less popular items indicate the fewer users who purchase it and the less likely a user is exposed to the item. Users will feel more novel when the system launches the item to them. Based on the above analysis, the novelty of the recommended scheme is predicted by the average popularity. The calculation of the average popularity is shown in formula (3).

$$Popularity\_avg = \frac{\sum_u \sum_{i \in R(u)} \log(1 + item\_pop(i))}{\sum_u \sum_{i \in R(u)} 1} \tag{3}$$

where $R(u)$ represents a recommendation scheme obtained by the current user, which is usually displayed to the user in the form of a list, and $item\_pop(i)$ represents the popularity of the item i.

2.2 Personalized Recommendation Algorithm Based on Three Objectives

In order to build a recommendation model based on the above three objectives, the basic algorithm MOEA-PGMA takes NSGA-II [6–8] as the main framework, and uses fitness selection, crossover and mutation [7] and elite retention strategies to realize the process of multi-objective optimization. The evaluation of candidate solution is to rank fitness values from high to low and select individuals with high fitness to breed and produce offspring. The running process of MOEA-PGMA algorithm is described as follows.

Step 1: The predicted score is calculated in conjunction with the ProbS algorithm based on the user's score record.

Step 2: Execute the NSGA-II algorithm and initialize the parent population T, with population size taken as N_0.

Step 3: The transitional progeny population EPOP is generated by the selection operator and the crossover operator.

Step 4: Calculate the fitness (the three objectives in Sect. 2.1) of the transitional progeny population EPOP. Perform the mutation operation on the same individual with different mutation rates according to the curve P_m [9] to generate the next generation population.

Step 5: Determine whether the stop condition is met. If the condition is met, go to step 6. Otherwise, go to step 3 and continue.

Step 6: Return the current set of optimal solutions to the user in the form of a recommendation list.

It has been verified that the MOEA-PGMA algorithm can provide all users with recommendation solutions with high accuracy and diversity in one operation. Compared with the traditional recommendation algorithm, it has a better effect in mining user's potential preferences and unpopular products. It should be noted that with the increase of the objective function, the complexity for solving the problem also increases, so the algorithm will take a long time to complete the process of recommendation. How to improve the efficiency of the algorithm will be the problem to be solved in this paper.

3 MOEA-PGMA Algorithm Based on Multi-threaded Concurrency

In order to solve the shortcomings of the MOEA-PGMA algorithm that due to the large computational scale, the algorithm has a high time complexity and the program runs slowly. This paper attempts to improve the algorithm's speed by using multi-threaded concurrency technology based on multi-core hardware.

In this section, we first introduce the multi-threaded concurrency technology. Next, we describe the details of concurrent implementation of MOEA-PGMA algorithm, including the concurrent idea and execution process of the algorithm, etc.

3.1 Characteristics of Thread Pool

In many applications, systems often need to process large amounts of data or perform high-intensity calculations during the same time period. However, in a single-core and single-threaded environment, the extra overhead of the huge operating system scheduling core switch makes the application less efficient and slower. In this context, multi-threaded concurrent programming technology emerges as the times require. With the continuous development of hardware, the price of multi-processor platforms is relatively cheap. More and more scholars are beginning to adopt multi-processor and multi-threaded forms to accelerate the implementation of algorithms and obtain better experimental results.

A thread is a single-order execution flow in a process, and multi-threaded concurrency refers to multiple execution flows in the same program while performing their own tasks. Therefore, multi-thread concurrency is also called multi-task concurrency.

Generally speaking, a program is usually divided into multiple tasks which will be uploaded to multiple threads for execution, and one task corresponds to one thread. The cycle of the thread is accompanied by the start and end of the task. In the preprocessing stage of the program, the system creates a thread for each task. When the corresponding task is completed, the thread must be revoked to release the resources occupied by the current thread, such as memory and processor. For example, in the same period of time, multiple threads may be waiting for CPU resources. If the thread that has completed the task continues to occupy the CPU without releasing it, which will cause other threads to remain in the waiting state. The program cannot be executed successfully, thus the algorithm loses the meaning of multi-threaded concurrency. However, there are obvious deficiencies in undoing threads. On the one hand, it takes a certain amount of time to create a thread, when a program needs to create and undo threads multiple times, it will obviously increase the overhead of the system. On the other hand, when the number of processors is less than the number of threads the program needed, there will be competition among threads, and some threads will be blocked by preempting processor resources for many times. At the same time, the memory of these threads may not be released, which will increase the pressure of memory allocation. The thread pool technology provides a good solution for solving thread scheduling problems and alleviating memory pressure. Its main ideas are described as follows: When a task requests a thread resource, a thread in the pool will be quickly assigned to the task if it is available. Once the task is completed, the system will reclaim the thread instead of immediately undoing the thread, so that it can also serve other tasks, which avoids creating threads multiple times and adding additional system overhead. If there are no free threads in the pool, the task will remain in a waiting state until an idle thread occurs. When a new request arrives, the system can immediately schedule the thread to perform the task if it is spare, thus greatly improving the system's response performance.

3.2   Thread Pool Implementation Mechanism

Java provides feature-rich multi-threaded programming at the language level, and JDK 1.5 began to introduce the Executor thread pool framework. In this framework, the thread pool will automatically manage the execution of tasks without the developer having to define too much. Executor framework not only realizes the function of establishing and managing thread pool, but also provides a general interface for task description and execution. Before JDK 1.5, the Executor framework used Runnable as the basic description of the tasks it accepted. The interface did not return the results of task execution, so it would not be applicable when some complex calculations were made and the task results needed to be collected. Therefore, later versions of JDK 1.5 provide a Callable interface that specifies the type of the return parameter when called: V call() throws Exception. JDK 1.5 and later provides a Future interface that can obtain asynchronous calculation results, and the interface provides the isDown method and the get method. The isDown method is used to query whether the thread has been calculated, and the get method is used to get the thread execution results. It should be noted that if the task thread has not completed the calculation, the thread that calls the get method will be automatically blocked until the task thread returns the calculation result. The Executor framework execution process is shown in Fig. 1.

Executor is a simple invocation interface, but it provides some basic components that can help users easily complete multithreaded operations, including ThreadPool Executor class and Scheduled ThreadPool Executor class.

The newCachedThreadPool() is used to create a new thread pool, and the thread pool supports thread caching. On the one hand, when there is a new task requesting thread, Executor first checks whether there is an idle thread in the pool, and if there is no reusable thread at this time, Executor will create a new thread to respond to the current task request, and this method has no limit on the size of the pool. On the other hand, in order to avoid excessive system resources occupied by idle threads in the pool for a long time, Executor will periodically recycle threads that have idle time of more

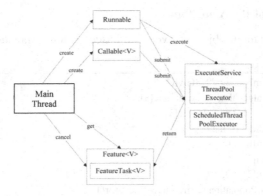

Fig. 1. Executor framework execution flowchart

than 60 s. When the program needs to execute a large number of short asynchronous tasks, the recovery mechanism of the thread pool can accelerate the operating efficiency of the system.

The newFixedThreadPool(int nThreads) is used to generate a fixed length thread pool. The user controls the maximum number of concurrent threads by setting nThreads. Executor assigns a thread to each task without exceeding the limit value of nThreads. When the number reaches nThreads, it will not continue to allocate threads for the task. At this time, the thread pool length will also reach the maximum and will not change afterwards.

The length of the thread pool created by the newScheduledThreadPool(int nThreads) is also fixed. It can perform tasks that require regular or periodic execution.

3.3   Concurrent Thought of the Algorithm

By analyzing the evolution process of NSGA-II algorithm, it is found that using multi-threaded concurrency to improve the efficiency of algorithm execution has certain feasibility. Each individual in the genetic construction phase is initialized based on predicted score data, and no information interaction is required between individuals, so multi-threaded concurrency can be used at this stage to reduce population initialization time. Since the length of the individual code increases rapidly as the number of users increases, calculating the target value of the individual will take more time. It should be noted that the individuals in the process are also independent of each other. Based on the above analysis, this paper attempts to improve the execution efficiency of the current recommendation model by using multi-threaded concurrency technology in the evolution process. First, a fixed number of threads pool is created by using new-FixedThreadPool to prevent the manager from creating new threads indefinitely and consuming system resources. Then, a shared unbounded queue is used to complete thread scheduling. When there are no idle threads in the thread pool, new tasks must wait in the queue until available threads appear. If a thread aborts task during execution, the manager will schedule a new thread instead of completing the subsequent task.

3.4   Pseudocode of the Algorithm

The pseudocode for multi-objective evolution based on multi-threaded concurrency is described as follows.

```
1.  String algorithmName = "NSGAII";
2.  double[] eval_algorithm = new double[3];
3.  double[] eval_aver = new double[3] ;
4.   for int iter=0;iter<10;iter++
5.  eval_algorithm[0] = 0;
6.  eval_algorithm[1] = 0;
7.  eval_algorithm[2] = 0;
8.  NondominatedPopulation result = new Executor()
9.  .withProblemClass(Recommend.class, input)
10. .withAlgorithm(algorithmName)
11. .withMaxEvaluations(50000)
12. .distributeOnAllCores().run();
13. for int i = 0; i < result.size(); i++
14.  eval_algorithm[0] /= result.size();eval_algorithm[1] /= result.size();
15.  eval_algorithm[2] /= result.size();
16.  end for
17. eval_aver[0] += eval_algorithm[0]; eval_aver[1] += eval_algorithm[1];
18. eval_aver[2] += eval_algorithm [2];
20. eval_aver[0] /= 10;  eval_aver[1] /= 10; eval_aver[2] /= 10;
21. end for
22. distributeOn(Runtime.getRuntime().availableProcessors());
23. problem.evaluate(solution);
24.  if solution instanceof FutureSolution
25. FutureSolution futureSolution = (FutureSolution)solution;
26. Future<Solution> future = executor.submit(new ProblemEvaluator(innerProblem, futureSolution));
27.  end if
28. futureSolution.setFuture(future);
29. Solution solution = future.get();
30. setObjectives(solution.getObjectives());
32. setConstraints(solution.getConstraints());
33. executor = Executors.newFixedThreadPool(numberOfThreads);
33. problem = new DistributedProblem(problem, executorService);
```

4   Simulation Experiment and Result Analysis

4.1   Data Preprocessing

This paper uses the classic benchmark problem test set to evaluate the performance of Movielens algorithm. As shown in Table 1, the dataset contains 943 users, 1682 movies, and related rating data. It should be noted that Movielens has always adopted the 5-point scoring rule, and the scoring prediction algorithm ProbS used in this paper is only applicable to the 0–1 rating system. Therefore, the training set must be processed as follows before predicting the score.

Table 1. Characteristics of the test dataset

Dataset	Number of users	Number of items	Sparsity
Movielens	943	6728	0.158

Set the rating of the movie with a score of 3 and above to 1; set the rating of the movie with a rating of less than 3 to 0; and set the rating of the movie that the user did not collect to −1. At the same time, 80% of the data is randomly selected as the training sample to complete the model construction, and the remaining data sets will be used as test samples to verify the effectiveness of the algorithm. Table 1 also shows the sparsity characteristics of Movielens. The sparsity is defined as the ratio of the number of non-empty elements in the matrix to the size of the matrix. For example, for a 4 × 4 scoring matrix, if there are only 5 non-null values, then the scoring data has a sparsity of 5/16. Therefore, the lower the sparsity of the dataset gets, which means the less the user's rating data on the item, and the higher the corresponding modeling requirements.

4.2 Experimental Results and Analysis

In this paper, a multi-objective evolution-based personalized recommendation algorithm runs on a 6-core 12-thread computer with a CPU frequency of 3.30 GHz, a memory of 8 G and different thread pool sizes (nThreads). In this experiment, the dimension of each individual is set at 1000, and the algorithm are measured for 10 times, then we take the average value as the experimental results. Table 2 shows the running time of the MOEA-PGMA with different thread number, and Fig. 2 shows the running time in a line chart. Besides that, in order to illustrate the effectiveness of multi-threaded concurrency in solving multi-objective personalized recommendation problems, we will compare the multi-threaded MOEA-PGMA with MOEA-ProbS [1], CB [21], CF [22] algorithms in the highest speed of 10 threads, and use accuracy [23], diversity [24] and novelty [25] to indicate the performance of the multi-threaded MOEA-PGMA. It should be noted that the accuracy of the recommendation algorithm is measured by the hit rate, and the diversity and novelty is measured by the formula (2) and formula (3), both of which is applied in the evolution stage. The calculation method of accuracy is show in formula (4):

$$hit\ rate = hit\ counts/the\ length\ of\ the\ recommendation\ list \qquad (4)$$

wherein, if the recommendation algorithm recommends the object O_j to the user U_i and the user U_i in the test set actually selects the object O_j in the validation phase, the algorithm is said to hit $U_i - O_j$.

Evaluation results of the above four algorithms are shown in Tables 3 and 4, and the comparison charts of the corresponding result are shown in Figs. 3 and 4.

Table 2. The running time of the MOEA-PGMA with different threads number

nThreads	averageTime
1	242
2	203
4	180
6	158
8	134
10	126
12	130
14	137

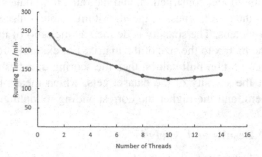

Fig. 2. The effect of the number of concurrent threads on the execution time of the algorithm

According to Table 2 and Fig. 2, when the number of nThreads is set as 1, which means only one thread is executing the task in the thread pool, the running efficiency of the processor is greatly reduced with nearly 4 hours' running time. When the number of nThreads is greater than or equal to 2, each task gets longer processor execution time on average under multithreading condition than single thread, so the execution efficiency is improved gradually with the increasing number of cores. When the number of nThreads is greater than 10, due to additional time cost caused by problems such as thread scheduling and resource contention, the running time is slightly increased before the number of threads reaching the maximum number of threads available in the system. Above all, multi-thread technology can maximize the processing ability of multi-core processors and significantly shorten the execution time. In addition, multi-thread concurrent execution also needs to ensure that the algorithm has high recommendation performance. As shown in Figs. 3 and 4, when nThreads is equal to 10, the pareto frontier formed by the optimal solution set generated by the MOEA-PGMA which is based on multi-threading technology basically covers the pareto frontier of MOEA-Probs in both accuracy - diversity and accuracy - novelty, which proves that the improved MOEA-PGMA can achieve better recommendation results than MOEA - ProbS. At the same time, we also compared the object algorithm with the traditional recommendation algorithm to demonstrate the effectiveness of the scheme. As shown in Tables 3 and 4, a group of recommendations generated by the MOEA-PGMA have multiple better solutions on three objectives than CF. Compared with CF,

Table 3. Comparison of MOEA-PGMA and MOEA-ProbS in the three indicators

MOEA-PGMA			MOEA-ProbS		
Accuracy	Diversity	Novelty	Accuracy	Diversity	Novelty
0.103687	0.704488	0.795051	0.114441	0.442789	0.679226
0.104821	0.711395	0.794211	0.129458	0.441478	0.653144
0.110134	0.694268	0.785946	0.134936	0.433083	0.649143
0.119275	0.687087	0.775376	0.138007	0.427569	0.64159
0.12554	0.672239	0.771476	0.143265	0.420899	0.632119
0.133947	0.659343	0.752005	0.146259	0.412526	0.629484
0.137248	0.649306	0.745431	0.156351	0.399361	0.6216
0.14877	0.627032	0.727823	0.162578	0.38092	0.610848
0.158086	0.612602	0.721525	0.170647	0.368844	0.593075
0.159058	0.608477	0.720409	0.177951	0.363602	0.587477
0.16414	0.602732	0.714334	0.188278	0.352177	0.57307
0.174795	0.573032	0.690232	0.193565	0.340761	0.562921
0.176587	0.568731	0.686492	0.203564	0.325873	0.547747
0.191119	0.531162	0.649544	0.210268	0.304206	0.523294
0.200575	0.513974	0.622556	0.218657	0.267174	0.505231
0.216997	0.445668	0.60727	0.219742	0.260283	0.504422
0.225186	0.405563	0.55977	0.229708	0.245695	0.483339
0.239256	0.337388	0.528917	0.234544	0.231983	0.45125
0.243316	0.28491	0.508082	0.241384	0.205452	0.420805
0.248273	0.253774	0.491033	0.248453	0.188372	0.401944
0.251618	0.228407	0.479212	0.251876	0.179013	0.379193
0.252337	0.219657	0.478055	0.255279	0.165602	0.369738
0.255118	0.18851	0.450807	0.261585	0.148484	0.347063
0.260194	0.156786	0.432574	0.264857	0.136313	0.333542
0.271023	0.103496	0.385576	0.265282	0.136107	0.326336
0.275869	0.065681	0.35904	0.268373	0.10269	0.302838

Table 4. Comparison of CB and CF in the three indicators

	Accuracy	Diversity	Novelty
CB	0.260207	0.052186	0.120063
CF	0.231092	0.135301	0.225817

the MOEA-PGMA can not only provide high-quality recommendation solutions, but also generate a set of candidate optimal solutions for users to choose. It should be noted that the initial purpose of the personalized recommendation algorithm based on multi-objective is to get good recommendations for diversity and novelty and guarantee a certain degree of accuracy. If the single-objective optimization is blindly pursued, the multi-objective recommendation problem will degenerate into a single-objective solution problem, and the result will not meet the practical requirements. From what

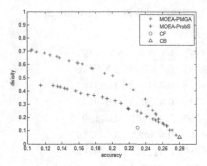 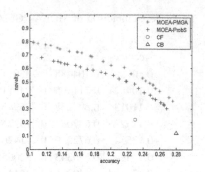

Fig. 3. Results of the four comparison algorithms in terms of accuracy and diversity

Fig. 4. Results of the four comparison algorithms in terms of accuracy and novelty

has been discussed above, MOEA-ProbS based on multi-thread technology can significantly shorten the running time of the algorithm and greatly improve the execution efficiency without losing the quality of multi-objective recommendation.

5 Conclusions

In this paper, a multi-objective recommendation algorithm based on multi-threaded concurrency is proposed by combing multi-objective recommendation algorithm with Executor framework. The experimental results show that under multi-core hardware conditions, multi-thread concurrency technology can significantly improve the execution efficiency of the algorithm. On the one hand, multi-core processors provide accelerated hardware conditions for multi-threaded concurrent programs, which assign more CPU processing time to each sub-task; on the other hand, the multi-threaded Executor framework manages threads by thread pools which can be reused, and let them handle the transferred Runnable task, rather than repeatedly creating and destroying threads. In practical scenario, if there are lots of threads to be created, the threading mechanism of Executor can effectively improve the concurrent processing capability of the system.

Acknowledgment. This work was partially supported by the National Key R&D Program of China (Project Nos. 2017YFC1601800, 2017YFC1601000), National Natural Science foundation of China (Grant No. 61673194), Key Research and Development Program of Jiangsu Province, China (Grant No. BE2017630), the Postdoctoral Science Foundation of China (Grant No. 2014M560390), and Blue Project of Jiangsu Province.

References

1. Zuo, Y., Gong, M., Zeng, J., et al.: Personalized recommendation based on evolutionary multi-objective optimization [Research frontier]. IEEE Comput. Intell. Mag. **10**(1), 52–62 (2015)

2. Tao, Z., Zoltán, K., Jian-Guo, L., et al.: Solving the apparent diversity-accuracy dilemma of recommender systems. Proc. Natl. Acad. Sci. U. S. A. **107**(10), 4511–4515 (2010)
3. Zhou, T., Jiang, L.L., Su, R.Q., et al.: Effect of initial configuration on network-based recommendation. Physics **81**(5), 58004 (2008)
4. Berg, V.D., Ewout, F., et al.: Probing the Pareto frontier for basis pursuit solutions. SIAM J. Sci. Comput. **31**(2), 890–912 (2008)
5. The art of concurrent programming in Java (2015)
6. Hamdani, T.M., Won, J.M., Alimi, A.M., Karray, F.: Multi-objective feature selection with NSGA II. In: Beliczynski, B., Dzielinski, A., Iwanowski, M., Ribeiro, B. (eds.) ICANNGA 2007, Part I. LNCS, vol. 4431, pp. 240–247. Springer, Heidelberg (2007). https://doi.org/10. 1007/978-3-540-71618-1_27
7. Mishra, A., Shukla, A.: A new insight into the schema survival after crossover and mutation for genetic algorithms having distributed population set. Int. J. Inf. Technol. **10**(2), 165–168 (2018)
8. Deb, K., Pratap, A., Agarwal, S., et al.: A fast and elitist multiobjective genetic algorithm: NSGA-II. IEEE Trans. Evol. Comput. **6**(2), 182–197 (2002)
9. Xiong, J., Gao, D., Dustin, et al.: Genetic algorithms with adaptive variation rate and population number. J. Southeast Univ. (Nat. Sci. Ed.) **34**(4), 553–556 (2004)
10. Wu, Y., Liu, M., Zhu, J.: Research on concurrency technology based on Java Executor (2), 11–13 (2009)
11. Wang, H., Ma, L., Gu, M.: Research and application of thread pool technology. Comput. Appl. Res. **22**(11), 141–142 (2005)
12. JDK Class 1.5 Library (2005)
13. Vecchiola, C., Pandey, S., Buyya, R.: High-performance cloud computing: a view of scientific applications. In: International Symposium on Pervasive Systems (2009)
14. Lea, D., Scott, M.L.: Scalable synchronous queues. Commun. ACM **52**(5), 100 (2009)
15. Core methods and frameworks for Java concurrent programming (2016)
16. Ansaloni, D., Binder, W., Villazón, A., et al.: Parallel dynamic analysis on multicores with aspect-oriented programming. In: International Conference on Aspect-Oriented Software Development (2010)
17. Emmerich, W.: Distributed component technologies and their software engineering implications (2002)
18. Ansaloni, D., Binder, W., Moret, P.: Parallel dynamic analysis on multicores with aspect-oriented programming. In: International Conference on Aspect-Oriented Software Development (2010)
19. Chen, C., Wang, N.: Adaptive method and mechanism of crossover and mutation probability selection in genetic algorithm. Control Theory Appl. **19**(1), 41–43 (2002)
20. Harper, F.M., Konstan, J.A.: The MovieLens Datasets: History and Context (2015)
21. Smeulders, A.W.M., Worring, M., Santini, S., et al.: Content-based image retrieval at the end of the early years. IEEE Trans. Pattern Anal. Mach. Intell. **22**(12), 1349–1380 (2000)
22. Schafer, J.B., Frankowski, D., Herlocker, J., et al.: Collaborative filtering recommender systems. ACM Trans. Inf. Syst. **22**(1), 5–53 (2004)
23. Gunawardana, A., Shani, G.: A survey of accuracy evaluation metrics of recommendation tasks (2009)
24. Ziegler, C.N., Mcnee, S.M., Konstan, J.A., et al.: Improving recommendation lists through topic diversification. In: International Conference on World Wide Web (2005)
25. Hurley, N., Mi, Z.: Novelty and diversity in Top N recommendation – analysis and evaluation. ACM Trans. Internet Technol. **10**(4), 1–30 (2011)

Multi-criteria Recommender Systems Based on Multi-objective Hydrologic Cycle Optimization

Shuang Geng, Churong Zhang, Xuesen Yang, and Ben Niu$^{(\boxtimes)}$

College of Management, Shenzhen University, Shenzhen, China
drniuben@gmail.com

Abstract. Traditional recommendation systems always consider precision as the unique evaluation standard. However, diversity and user tendency are also important for recommendation system performance. The implementation of multiple performance factors can be expressed as a multi-objective optimization problem (MOP). This paper attempts to combine multi-objective optimization algorithm with recommendation algorithm to solve this multi-objective recommendation problem. A novel multi-objective heuristic algorithm called Multi-objective Hydrologic Cycle Optimization (MOHCO) is proposed. MOHCO simulates the water flow, infiltration, evaporation and precipitation processes in nature, and aims to find a set of Pareto optimal solutions. Experimental tests on Grouplens – MovieLens 100K movie recommendation dataset demonstrate that MOHCO outperforms other heuristic algorithms including MOEAD, NSGAII, NSGAIII, MOPSO.

Keywords: Multi-objective problem · Hydrologic cycle optimization · Pareto optimal solutions · Recommender systems

1 Introduction

The information overload problem in this digital age makes it very difficult for consumers to discover the products they are interested in out of many commodities. For retailers, it is also very difficult to make their products stand out from the large amount of products in order to attract users' attention. Recommender system (RS) can help users find valuable products, and recommend commodities that users may like. RS collects various information to provide users with recommendations [1]. But many recommendation algorithms only care about the accuracy of recommendation results. However, customers not only want accurate recommendations of items but also want the results that are more diverse and novel items. To fulfill the multiple requirements of customers, the recommendation process can be modeled as a multi-objective problem solving process.

Many meta-heuristic algorithms are invented to solve the multi-objective problems in the last decade. The method based on pareto dominance is the most commonly used method among various multi-objective evolutionary algorithms. This type of algorithms use Pareto frontier to select the non-dominated set of solutions. Researchers

© Springer Nature Switzerland AG 2019
Y. Tan et al. (Eds.): ICSI 2019, LNCS 11656, pp. 92–102, 2019.
https://doi.org/10.1007/978-3-030-26354-6_9

have proposed a variety of multi-objective evolutionary algorithms. Some typical algorithms are NSGA-II, MOPSO, MOEA/D, and their variants. Deb et al. [2] proposed a fast, non-dominance sorting genetic algorithm with a parameterless niche operator, named NSGA-II. Coello et al. [3] developed a multi-objective particle swarm optimization algorithm with external archive and grid division. Zhang and Li [4] proposed a multi-objective evolutionary algorithm, named MOEA/D, based on decomposition which performs very well in solving the three-objective optimization problems.

Hydrologic Cycle Optimization (HCO) is a swarm intelligent algorithm proposed by Yan and Niu [5]. HCO was inspired by the processes of water flow, infiltration, evaporation and precipitation in nature. HCO exhibits better global search and enhance algorithm diversity than conventional swarm intelligent algorithms [5]. Based on HCO, this study proposed a multi-objective evolutionary algorithm, called Multi-objective Hydrologic Cycle Optimization (MOHCO). Then, we integrate MOHCO with collaborative filtering algorithm (CF) to solve the problem of multi-objective recommendation.

The remainder of this article is structured as follows: Sect. 2 presents a brief introduction of collaborative filtering. In Sect. 3, we describe Hydrologic Cycle Optimization algorithm and the proposed MOHCO in detail. Section 4 presents the MOHCO based collaborative filtering algorithm. The experimental results are discussed in Sect. 5. We conclude this paper in Sect. 6.

2   Related Work

2.1   Multi-objective Recommender System

Collaborative filtering algorithm (CF) is a popular recommendation algorithm with wide scope of applications. Currently, CF algorithm faces two challenges, which are cold start problem and sparsity of rating matrix. To solve these difficulties, Melville et al. [6] proposed a Content-Boosted Collaborative Filtering (CBCF) algorithm. The CBCF algorithm predicts the score of unspecified items first, and fill in the original matrix to generate a complete pseudo-scoring matrix. The complete matrix is then used to recommend items to users.

As for multi-objective recommendation methods, many scholars have applied it to different recommendation scenarios. Geng et al. [7] combined the Nondominated Neighbor Immune Algorithm (NNIA) and CF to settle multi-objective recommendation problems. Cui et al. [8] presented a novel mutiobjective heuristic algorithm (PMOEA) to solve recommend problems, which can coordinate the relationship between accuracy and diversity.

2.2   Hydrologic Cycle Optimization

Hydrologic Cycle Optimization (HCO) was novel heuristic algorithm, performing well both on the benchmark test problems and on the nurse scheduling problem (NSP) [8]. Recently, Niu et al. [9] proposed a hybrid data clustering approach based on

Hydrologic Cycle Optimization and K-means, which obtains relatively better clustering results. HCO proves to be able to search globally and escape from the local optimal trap.

Despite that some researchers have studied the multi-objective recommendation problems, we proposed to integrate MOHCO with collaborating filtering algorithm considering the good performance of HCO. The proposed MOHCO based collaborating filtering is adopted to solve the multi-objective movie recommendation problem.

3   Collaborative Filtering

The CF method is one of the earliest and successful algorithms for recommender system. It employs the nearest neighbor method, in with the user's historical preference information is first collected to calculate the distance between users. Since the scores of the nearest neighbor users are analogous to the target users, the target users' scores on the unrated items can be estimated by the nearest neighbors [10]. The CF calculates the weighted average of the nearest user's nearest neighbors to predict the user preference for items. According to predicted preference, the system recommends items to the target user. Two common CF methods are User-based Collaborative Filtering (User_CF) and Item-based Collaborative Filtering (Item_CF).

3.1   Similarity Measurement

The neighborhood similarity measurement is the most important step in collaborative filtering algorithm. In User-based Collaborative Filtering (User_CF) algorithm, one assumption is that different users can have similar interests. Based on the preference of users, User_CF finds some similar neighbors, and then predicts the user's score of these items based on those neighbors. There are two common similarity measurement methods, which are cosine similarity and pearson similarity.

- Cosine similarity:

$$sim(u, v) = \cos(r_u, r_v) = \frac{r_u \times r_v}{|r_u| \times |r_v|} \tag{1}$$

- Pearson similarity:

$$sim(u, v) = PearsonSim(r_u, r_v) = \frac{\sum_{i=1}^{t} (r_{ui} - \bar{r}_u) * (r_{vi} - \bar{r}_v)}{\sqrt{\sum_{i=1}^{t} (r_{ui} - \bar{r}_u)^2 * \sum_{i=1}^{m} (r_{vi} - \bar{r}_v)^2}} \tag{2}$$

where r_u is user u's rating vector, and r_v is user v' rating vector, $sim(u, v)$ means calculating the similar between user u and user v.

Item_CF algorithm works likewise. The difference between Item_CF and User_CF is that Item_CF calculates the item similarity instead of the users.

4 Multi-objective Hydrologic Cycle Optimization

4.1 Hydrologic Cycle Optimization

HCO is composed of three operators, such as flow, infiltration, evaporation and precipitation [5, 8]. The steps of HCO are described as follows:

Flow
The flow operator plays a critical part in the water cycle, which simulates the process that water flows to downstream in nature. This step lets each individual of drop flow to another position that has better fitness. Once the novel position is better than its original position, the individual will flow to the new position. Otherwise, the individual drop stays still. If the new fitness becomes worse or the total flow time reaches maximum, the individual stops flowing. The flow operator is formulated as follow:

$$X_{flow} = X_i + (X_j - X_i). * rand(1, Dimension) \qquad (3)$$

where X_{flow} is the position of the individual after flow. X_i is i individual's position. X_j is j individual's position in the direction of flow.

Infiltration
In the infiltration step, every individual randomly selects another individual as its neighbor and uses the formula (6) to infiltrate. Although the process of infiltration may make the position become worse, it can increase the diversity of the population.

$$X_{Infiltration} = X_{i,SD} + (X_{i,SD} - X_{j,SD}). * 2 * (rand(1, SD) - 0.5) \qquad (4)$$

where $X_{Infiltration}$ is the position of the individual after infiltration. $X_{i,SD}$ is the position of i individual on the dimension of SD. $X_{j,SD}$ is the position of j individual on the dimension of SD in the infiltration.

Evaporation and Precipitation
If the evaporation probability (P_{eva}) is reached, the individual will randomly evaporate and precipitate to another position. In the precipitation process, the individual will either randomly choose a direction to precipitate or create a new position by a Gaussian distribution.

4.2 Multi-objective Hydrologic Cycle Optimization

The traditional way of solving MOP is to use the weighting method to turn the MOP into a single-objective problem. However, the disadvantage of this method is that the weightings of the objective functions are uncertain and hard to determine. Therefore, multi-objective evolutionary algorithms are invented and employed by many researchers.

In this paper, inspired by the external repository method proposed in [3], we proposed a Multi-objective Hydrologic Cycle Optimization (MOHCO) which utilizes external archive and adaptive grid method for saving and updating non-dominated solutions. In the process of natural water flow, water drops can possibly infiltrate or evaporate and precipitate. Therefore, in this paper, we adopt a dynamic selection probability to select operators (infiltration or evaporation and precipitation).

External Repository

External repository is first proposed by Coello [4] which is the space used to store the non-dominant solutions after each computation of the dominant relationships. In the initialization, if the external file is empty, the current set of optimal solutions is saved. As the iteration time increases, the new non-dominant solutions are also saved into the external file. The adaptive grid helps to divide the target space into grid regions when the number of solutions stored in external file is greater than the predefined capacity. The small grids with more solutions are selected.

Dynamic Selection Probability

In HCO, water drops either permeates or evaporates and precipitates during the flow process. We select the operator through a dynamic selection probability mechanism. As iteration time increases, the probability of selecting infiltration becomes smaller. On the contrary, the probability of selecting evaporation and precipitation will increase gradually.

$$P_c = \max\_P_C - (max\_P_C - min\_P_C) * \frac{iter}{max\_iter} \tag{5}$$

where P_c is dynamic selection probability, max_P_C is the maximum value of dynamic selection probability, min_P_C is the minimum value of dynamic selection probability, $iter$ is the current number of iterations, max_iter is the maximum number of iterations.

The MOHCO algorithm' flow chart is shown in Fig. 1.

5 MOHCO for Recommender System

5.1 The Multi-objective Hybrid Recommendation Algorithm

In this paper, the content enhanced collaborative filtering algorithm is combined with MOHCO. MOHCO is embedded to adjust the weightings of user characteristics for calculating the similarity. In the traditional CF, the similarity is computed by user's rating matrix. This study also considers other users' characteristics, such as age, gender and occupation, and designs a similarity calculation method of multiple features. The content-boosted CF calculates the similarity between items according to the Item_CF first, and then predicts the rating items of unknown users, so as to generate a complete set of pseudo-rating matrix. Based on complete matrix, the User_CF is used to obtain the recommendation list for the target users. This hybrid algorithm is applied in the Movielens movie recommendation problem, and the application process is illustrated in Fig. 2.

5.2 Multi-objective Functions for Recommender System

In the multi-objective recommendation problem, the multiple objective functions determine the quality of the recommendation results. Extant research on multi-objective

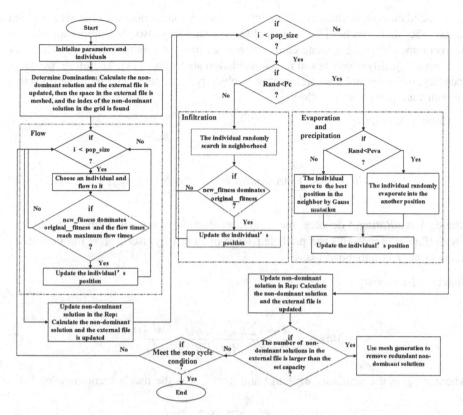

Fig. 1. MOHCO algorithm' flow chart

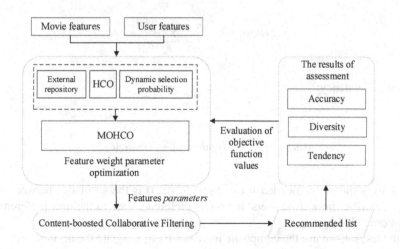

Fig. 2. MOHCO for recommender system

recommendation algorithms focus mainly on two recommendation objectives, which are accuracy and diversity [7, 8]. In real life, user tendency also plays important roles in the recommender system. Geng et al. adopted accuracy, diversity and user tendency as the multiple quality objectives in recommendation algorithms [14]. Therefore, we adopt accuracy, diversity and user preferences as objective functions. The multiple objective functions are presented as follows:

Function 1-Accuracy:

$$Min f_1 = \frac{1}{T} \sum_{i,j=1}^{N,K} \left| ActualRating_{ij} - PredictRating_{ij} \right| \tag{6}$$

where $ActualRating_{ij}$ denotes the actual evaluation score of item j by user i, $PredictRating_{ij}$ represents the predicted score of item j by user i, T is the number of items in the recommended list.

Function 2-Diversity:

$$Max f_2 = \frac{1}{U} \sum_{u \in U} \frac{\sum_{i,j \in R(u), i \neq j}(1 - s(i,j))}{|R(u)|(|R(u)| - 1)} \tag{7}$$

where $s(i, j)$ is the similarity of item i and item j, R is the user's recommended list.

$$Tendency1 = \sum_{i \in R(u)} \sum_{j \in R(u)} \frac{s(i,j)}{|R(u)|^2} \tag{8}$$

$$Tendency2 = \sum_{i \in R} \sum_{j \in R_u^1} \frac{s(i,j)}{|R_u^1|^2} \tag{9}$$

Function 3-Tendency:

$$Min f_3 = \frac{1}{N} \sum_{j=1}^{N} |Tendency1 - Tendency2| \tag{10}$$

where $R(u)$ is the recommended list of user(u), $s(i, j)$ is the similarity between item i and j. f_3 describes how close users' historical preferences are to the user preferences of the recommended list.

In the test set, we use the composite indicator F1 to evaluate the accuracy rate, F1 is calculated as follows:

$$\text{Precision} = \frac{\#true\,positive}{\#true\,positive + \#false\,positive} \tag{11}$$

$$\text{Recall} = \frac{\#true\,positive}{\#true\,positive + \#false\,negative} \tag{12}$$

$$\text{F1} = \frac{2PR}{P+R} \tag{13}$$

where #*true positive* refers to the proportion of recommendations accepted by the user, #*false positive* refers to the recommendations not accepted by the user. #false negative refers to the item accepted by the user not in the list of recommendations.

6 Experiments and Results

6.1 Experimental Data

In the recommendation experiments, we choose 100K dataset of Movielens, which is often used for recommendation system research, to test our proposed algorithm. This movielens dataset contains 100000 ratings from 943 users on 1682 movies, movie metadata and user attributes.

6.2 Experimental Parameter Settings

The parameters of recommendation experiments are described as follow. MOHCO is test together with four multi-objective optimization algorithms, including MOEAD, NSGAII, NSGAIII, MOPSO. Ref [8], in MOHCO, the population size is 100, the max flow time is 3, the probability of evaporation and precipitation is 0.1, the probability of selecting infiltration or evaporation and precipitation P_c is within the range of 0.1–0.8. P_c is determined by experimental results on a multi-objective test function. The parameter settings of other algorithms use the default setting of the multi-objective optimization algorithm platform (PlatEMO) [12].

The parameters setting is described as follow in the CF, Ref [11], the number of users in training process is 50, the amount of nearest user neighbors is 30, the amount of movies that selected by ranking is 10. The weighting of movie name similarity is 0.01. The weighting of movie time similarity is 0.1. The weighting of movie genre similarity is 0.1. The weighting of movie genre similarity is 0.8.

6.3 Results and Analyses

To evaluate the performance of MOHCO, its performance results for F1, Diversity and Tendency are compared with other algorithms. The four indicators, including "Ave", "Pre", "Div" and "Ten" [11] are adopted to validate the effectiveness of the pareto solution in the recommendation results. Experiment results are shown in Table 1.

Table 1 shows that MOEAD_CF have a good performance on precision. While accuracy describes the portion of correct results in recommendation results, the recall rate describes the portion of correct recommendation result that displayed among all the correct recommendations. These two measures are contradictory. Therefore, F1 is put forward as a comprehensive indicator to evaluate the accuracy. The experiment results demonstrate that the performance of MOHCO is superior than other algorithms in F1, which confirms the competitive performance of MOHCO. In terms of "Div" and "Ten", results of MOHCO_CF are slightly less diverse than content-boosted collaborative filtering algorithm. But MOHCO_CF has better tendency than other algorithms. Compared with the traditional content-boosted collaborative filtering algorithm, the hybrid multi-objective collaborative filtering algorithm considers multiple features, thus effectively improves recommendation's accuracy while maintaining diversity and tendency.

Table 1. Experimental result on 100k dataset

Algorithm		Precision	Recall	F1	Diversity	Tendency
Content-boosted CF		57.937	46.001	50.969	**82.049**	18.464
MOEAD_CF	Ave	**71.298**	57.325	63.076	81.946	17.418
	Pre	**70.875**	56.801	62.595	81.961	17.390
	Div	**71.420**	57.783	63.369	81.984	17.130
	Ten	**71.390**	57.778	63.352	81.979	17.130
NSGAII_CF	Ave	70.332	57.580	62.815	81.957	16.851
	Pre	70.657	56.372	62.243	81.923	17.811
	Div	70.742	57.179	62.770	81.948	17.236
	Ten	70.669	57.059	62.656	81.959	17.201
NSGAIII_CF	Ave	71.094	56.907	62.775	81.985	17.850
	Pre	70.450	56.139	62.015	81.942	17.808
	Div	71.116	56.843	62.742	81.965	17.578
	Ten	71.116	56.843	62.742	81.964	17.578
MOPSO_CF	Ave	71.371	57.859	63.368	82.009	17.153
	Pre	71.338	57.904	63.390	82.006	16.998
	Div	71.371	57.859	63.368	82.009	17.153
	Ten	71.371	57.859	63.368	82.009	17.153
MOHCO_CF	Ave	69.874	**60.058**	**64.225**	**82.101**	**15.423**
	Pre	70.597	**58.369**	**63.486**	**82.051**	**16.209**
	Div	71.273	**58.993**	**64.019**	82.012	**15.921**
	Ten	71.197	**58.992**	**63.980**	82.004	**15.921**

"Ave": the average of all points of each objective function in the results of each user.
"Pre": the point at which the most accurate measure is selected for each user's results.
"Div": the best point of choice for diversity's function in each user's results.
"Ten": the best point to select the tendency's function on the results of each user.

7 Conclusion

Solving multi-objective problems, a novel multi-objective heuristic algorithm is proposed, named Multi-objective Hydrologic Cycle Optimization (MOHCO). MOHCO adopts a dynamic probability operator for operator selection (infiltration or evaporation and precipitation). MOHCO is then integrated with content-enhanced collaborative filtering to solve multi-objective recommendation problems. In the comparative experiments, MOHCO-CF was compared with MOEAD-CF, NSGAII-CF, NSGAIII-CF and MOPSO-CF in solving the movie recommendation problem. MOHCO-CF proved to outperform other algorithms in terms of all the evaluation factors and obtained good balance between the multiple quality objectives.

In future research, it is planned to apply MOHCO_CF to other large-scale data sets, such as MoiveLens 1M data set. Other recommendation problems, such as music, jokes and other recommendation problems, are to be utilized to demonstrate the algorithm validity. The performance of MOHCO on more benchmark functions will be also be tested and improved.

Acknowledgement. This work is partially supported by the Natural Science Foundation of Guangdong Province (2016A030310074), Project supported by Innovation and Entrepreneurship Research Center of Guangdong University Student (2018A073825).

References

1. Bohadilla, J., Ortega, F., Hernando, A., Gutiérrez, A.: Recommender systems survey. Knowl. Based Syst. **46**(1), 109–132 (2013)
2. Deb, K., Pratap, A., Agarwal, S., Meyarivan, T.: A fast and elitist multiobjective genetic algorithm: NSGA-II. IEEE Trans. Evol. Comput. **6**(2), 182–197 (2002)
3. Coello, C.A.C., Pulido, G.T., Lechuga, M.S.: Handling multiple objectives with particle swarm optimization. IEEE Trans. Evol. Comput. **8**(3), 256–279 (2004)
4. Zhang, Q., Hui, L.: MOEA/D: A multiobjective evolutionary algorithm based on decomposition. IEEE Trans. Evol. Comput. **11**(6), 712–731 (2007)
5. Yan, X., Niu, B.: Hydrologic cycle optimization Part I: background and theory. In: Tan, Y., Shi, Y., Tang, Q. (eds.) ICSI 2018, Part I. LNCS, vol. 10941, pp. 341–349. Springer, Cham (2018). https://doi.org/10.1007/978-3-319-93815-8_33
6. Melville, P., Mooney, R.J., Nagarajan, R.: Content-boosted collaborative filtering for improved recommendations. In: AAAI/IAAI, vol. 23, pp. 187–192 (2002)
7. Geng, B., Li, L., Jiao, L., et al.: NNIA-RS: a multi-objective optimization based recommender system. Phys. A Stat. Mech. Appl. **424**, 383–397 (2015)
8. Cui, L., Ou, P., Fu, X., et al.: A novel multi-objective evolutionary algorithm for recommendation systems. J. Parallel Distrib. Comput. **103**, 53–63 (2017)
9. Niu, B., Liu, H., Liu, L., Wang, H.: A hybrid data clustering approach based on hydrologic cycle optimization and k-means. In: Qiao, J., et al. (eds.) BIC-TA 2018, Part II. CCIS, vol. 952, pp. 328–337. Springer, Singapore (2018). https://doi.org/10.1007/978-981-13-2829-9_30
10. Sarwar, B., Karypis, G., Konstan, J., Riedl, J.: Analysis of recommendation algorithms for e-commerce. In: Proceedings of ACM on E-Commerce, pp. 158–167. ACM Press (2000)

11. Shuang Geng, L.T., Wang, H., Xiao, L., Kris, K.M.: Law: a hypercube fast searching multi-objective bacterial foraging algorithm for collaborative filtering with multiple quality factors. Knowl. Based Syst. (2019). (Submitting: KNOSYS-D-19-00862)
12. Ye, T., Ran, C., Zhang, X., Jin, Y.: PlatEmo: a Matlab platform for evolutionary multi-objective optimization. IEEE Comput. Intell. Mag. **12**(4), 73–87 (2017)

Neural Networks

Convolutional Neural Network Inception-v3: A Machine Learning Approach for Leveling Short-Range Rainfall Forecast Model from Satellite Image

Kitinan Boonyuen[1], Phisan Kaewprapha[1(✉)], Uruya Weesakul[2(✉)], and Patchanok Srivihok[3(✉)]

[1] Department of Electrical and Computer Engineering,
Thammasat University Rangsit Campus, Khlong Nueng, Pathum Thani, Thailand
kitinanbooyuen@gmail.com, kphisan@engr.tu.ac.th
[2] Faculty of Engineering, Thammasat University Rangsit Campus,
Khlong Nueng, Pathum Thani, Thailand
wuruya@engr.tu.ac.th
[3] Innovation Institute, PTT Public Company Limited,
Wangnoi 13170, Ayuttaya, Thailand
patchanok.s@pttplc.com

Abstract. In this paper, we investigated the capability of artificial intelligence using one of the advanced convolutional neural networks (CNN) called inception-v3 model to forecast leveling of daily rainfall. The input of this model were the satellite images from areas in Thailand and neighboring areas. The output of the model was leveling of daily rainfall prediction. The training from scratch of inception-v3 model with the areas of satellite image got highest accuracy from our previous work. We improved the model in such way that the model outperformed our previous model by giving the information about the movement of the cloud, air mass and weather with a batch satellite. Klong Yai rain station in Rayong province of eastern region of Thailand was selected as our case study. The dataset contains satellite images of July, August, September and October 2017. 75% of the data was used for training and 25% was used as testing data. The result of forecasting reveal that the models were able to predict leveling of 1 day ahead rainfall, 2 days ahead rainfall and 3 days ahead rainfall successfully.

Keywords: Rainfall forecast · Convolutional neural networks (CNN) · Satellite image · Inception-v3

1 Introduction

Artificially Intelligent computers are machines can learn by themselves. Due to the advancement of the technology in these recent years, the computer's hardware power and storage capacity has increased too, because of which artificial intelligence are now being used in a lot of different areas in real life, from self-driving cars to medical image segmentation. Deep learning is one of the most efficient sub-filed of machine learning

Y. Tan et al. (Eds.): ICSI 2019, LNCS 11656, pp. 105–115, 2019.
https://doi.org/10.1007/978-3-030-26354-6_10

as it out performs the others. Since 2012, Deep learning has become famous because of their use of Convolutional Neural Network (CNN) [1] technique in the computer vision field that can easily classify images on a very large image database successfully. The examples of deep learning are Artificial Neural Network (ANN) [2] and Convolutional Neural Network. Artificial Neural Network mimics the way human brain work while Convolutional Neural Network mimics the human vision and it is most effective in image classification.

The objective of this study is to investigate the capability of advance technique of Convolutional Neural Network [1] in forecasting the leveling of daily rainfall from satellite images. For forecasting task, the satellite image normally used is the composition of the weather variable to forecast rainfall which is then interpreted by the expert who has the knowledge about the field. But the artificial intelligence that we developed will look for a relationship between satellite images as input and leveling of daily rainfall data as output without requiring the professionals to interpret the satellite images. The artificial intelligence for satellite images developed by using advance technique of convolutional neural network which is Inception-v3 model which has never been used in forecasting task on satellite images. The above study was done for the Klong Yai rain station in Rayong province, in eastern region of Thailand.

1.1   Motivation

In the recent years, the disasters in Thailand such as flood and drought has affected the natural habitat, assets, economic and life. The disasters have reoccurred frequently and have increased the damages by making bigger impact each time they strike because of the consequences of high variation of rainfall in Thailand due to the global climate change. A high accurate and reliable short-range rainfall forecast (up until 3 days) plays a crucial role as a support data in analyzing the water situation and watershed management in order to avoid the water disasters by providing them with the proper surveillance and warnings. The efficient planning and operation of the water resources will also lead to better efficient watershed management for agriculture, industry, resident consumption. Not many studies have investigated the crucial and challenging rainfall forecasting problem from the machine learning perspective which is very hard to capture the uncertainty of the rainfall due to the high variation of rainfall both in time and space. Since 2012, convolutional neural network became famous because for their use the in classifying images on ImageNet which is very large image database. The convolutional neural network can process image directly and performs features extracting automatically without requiring any handcrafted feature selection. Our study aims to investigate whether the leveling short-range rainfall forecasting model from satellite image using advance convolutional neural network is applicable for the daily rainfall forecast or not.

2   Literature Review

There are research papers that have been published on the machine learning perspective for forecasting rainfall such as Klein et al. [3], they used Dynamic Convolutional Layer model to predict a new satellite image. The normal convolutional layer's weight is random but Dynamic Convolutional uses the input image that has already went through Convolutional Network as a filter. The Dynamic Convolutional will find the lowest loss quicker. Their input consisted of 3 satellite images and the output produced was the new satellite image. They captured the satellite image every 10 min. Shi et al. [4] used Convolutional LSTM Network to predict nowcasting rainfall by using Convolutional and Recurrent neural network. Their input was a set of satellite images that contained 5 images. They captured an image every 6 min and their output was 'rain' or 'not rain' for the next 90 min. If the result consists rain of more than 0.5 mm/hour that means it was likely to rain. Their accuracy was 90.8%. In our previous research, Boonyuen et al. [5], The advance convolutional neural network which is inception-v3 was selected to predict daily rainfall from 1 day ahead up to 3 days ahead. Our input was satellite image from satellite called "Himawari-8" [6] that captured image of Asia area and the output was 'rain' or 'not rain'. The 3 set of images were chosen as input the first one contained the images that were not cropped, the second one contained the cropped images of Thailand and its neighboring areas and the last one contained the cropped images of Thailand as shown in Fig. 1. The two methods were used for training are transfer learning on Inception-v3 model and the trained Inception-v3 model from scratch. We found out that the best result came from training from scratch on image

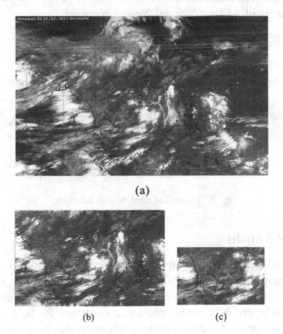

Fig. 1. Satellite images from previous work: (a) original image, (b) cropped Thailand and neighboring areas and (c) cropped Thailand

that contained cropped images of Thailand and its neighboring area with accuracy around 70%. Unlike other research and our previous paper, this paper predicts 4 classes of rainfall: 'not rain', 'light rain', 'moderate rain' and 'heavy rain' in short-rage rainfall forecast (up until 3 days) by using advance convolutional neural network which has never been used in forecasting task on satellite image. In this paper, we propose technique to pre-process for specific task on this type of data.

3   Methodology

3.1   Convolutional Neural Network

Currently as technology advances, the computer's hardware power and storage capacity increases, they have the capability to handle large size of data set and are able to train with large network such as convolutional neural network [1]. The important property of convolutional neural network (CNN) is that the network can process image directly and perform features extracting automatically without requiring any hand-crafted feature selection. To reduce the number of weights and extract features, convolutional neural network uses the combination of weights called filter instead of individual weights. After Convolution, it will apply the activation function called ReLU (Rectified Linear Unit). This output of ReLU is called as the filter map. In convolutional neural network, The CNN also have a Pooling layer, which is used to reduce the input by sub-sampling the input. The very last layer will be the fully connected layer to get the output value out of the filter map and use the same back-propagation method as artificial neural network to minimize the error. The Fig. 2 below shows different layers of a Convolutional Neural Network.

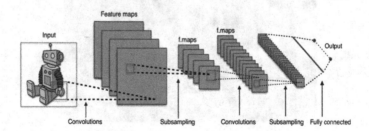

Fig. 2. Convolutional neural network

3.2   Inception V-3 Model

Inception-v3 model is an advance convolutional neural network which was recently invented by Szegedy et al. [7] from the Google. There are many sizes of filter or convolutional layer such as 7×7, 5×5, 3×3 and 1×1. Inception models use many convolutional layers at the same time and concatenate the layers called inception layer. Inception also uses 1×1 convolutional before normal convolutional. The 1×1

convolutional layer helped in reducing the size of the input in depth and makes the model deeper. The inception-v3 model accuracy rate when testing with ImageNet Top-1 was found to be 82.8% and with Top-5 was 96.42% which outperforms the human level or around 94.9%. The ImageNet is an image database that contains 14,000,000 images with 22,000 categories. The model was selected because of its accuracy and its layers (parameters). If we compare the inception-v3 model to the other CNN models, the accuracy rate of the inception-v3 model is 96.42%, it consists of 48 layers, nearly 25 million parameters and around 12 Giga Operations per second (G-Ops) which is capable to train along with the medium size server. The other CNN model's accuracy rate is lower than the inception-v3 model except for Inception-v4 and Inception-ResNet-v2 model [7] whose accuracy rate is more than the inception-v3 around 0.5% with 467 layers, nearly 55 million parameters and around 18 G-Ops. Because of that it needs a very large server and more time to train the model.

3.3 Pre-processing Satellite Images

We downloaded the satellite images from the website of the Meteorological Department of Thailand [9] which captures from satellite Himawari-8 [6]. We saw the potential of rainfall forecasting using the satellite image S4 [6], which is white area corresponds to the high-level clouds. Green and yellow areas are indicative of a warm airmass. Purple regions indicate a cold airmass. Red features in the images are associated with the Jetstream and a high potential vorticity. Satellite image S4 is the only image that contains RGB image (each pixel has 3 different variables), which has more variables than the gray scale image (1 pixel contains 1 variable).

Firstly, we collected satellite images from 4 July 2017 to 31 October 2017. The incomplete images were removed because it would have affected the model while training. Second, we cropped images of Thailand and its neighboring area which in the previous work [5] was the best result as the input. To decide the input of the model to predict leveling of rainfall, the trial and error method was used to find out which one of the images give the best result, single image or batch image. Batch image was used because we want to give information of the movement of the cloud, airmass and weather to the models to do better at the prediction task. The larger image may get low accuracy because the image has too much information and we predict a small part of the image which models can get confuse and can cause it to lose the focus. Batch images generate 2 steps. First, random 3 images from the images of 00.00 AM to 7.59 AM, 8.00 AM to 3.59 PM and 4.00 PM to 11.59 PM. Second, concatenate those 3 images to form new images. The images are shown in the Fig. 3 below.

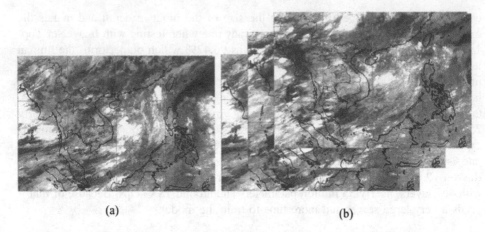

(a)   (b)

Fig. 3. Satellite images for training and testing: (a) single image and (b) batch image

We got the daily rainfall data of Klong Yai rainfall station from the Innovation Institute of Petroleum Authority of Thailand (PTT) Public company limited and compared images with daily rainfall data to get 4 classifications: 'not rain' which is when rain is 0 mm, 'light rain' which is when the rain is between 0.1 to 10 mm, 'moderate rain' when the rain is between 10.1 to 50 mm, 'heavy rain' when the rain is more than 50.1 mm.

3.4   Training and Testing

For training, Inception-v3 model was selected to build the rainfall forecasting model, which is an advance technique in convolutional neural networks. The inception-v3 model got very high accuracy on the ImageNet database. We used training from scratch on inception-v3 model. The inception-v3 model will backpropagate all the layers of the model. The model will learn to extract features and predict output on this specific type of data which is satellite image.

For testing the dataset of inception-v3 model, the test data around 25% was chosen from our dataset for each of 3 days for training and 1 days for testing in each class (training 75%). The prediction per day of inception-v3 model was done by calculating the maximum of the prediction class in each day where each image on the day had its own output or predict result. To calculate accuracy, we have used confusion matrix and formula as shown in formula (1), (2) and (3). Hits means the prediction for rainfall got the correct class. Misses means the prediction for rainfall got the class below the observed rainfall. False alarm means the predicted rainfall got the rainfall class more than that observed rainfall.

$$\text{Probability of detection: } POD = \frac{\text{Hits}}{\text{Hits} + \text{Misses}} \qquad (1)$$

$$\text{False alarm ratio: } FAR = \frac{\text{False alarms}}{Hits + \text{False alarms}} \qquad (2)$$

$$\text{Overall accuracy} = \frac{Hits}{Hits + Misses + \text{False alarms}} x100\% \qquad (3)$$

4   Results and Discussion

4.1   Result of Pre-processing Satellite Images

After downloading the satellite images from Meteorological Department of Thailand's website [9], we removed the incomplete images and cropped images. We then compared those images with our daily rainfall data to get 4 classification output calls, 'not rain', 'light rain', 'moderate rain' and 'heavy rain'. Around 8,514 images or 89 days for training (46 days for 'not rain', 29 days for 'light rain', 13 days for 'moderate rain' and 1 day for 'heavy rain') and around 2,817 images or 31 days for testing (14 days for 'not rain', 10 days for 'light rain', 6 days for 'moderate rain' and 1 day for 'heavy rain').

For batch satellite image, we pre-processed the image by taking 3 random images and then concatenating them into new 95 images per day because the number of images in the dataset is 11,311 images, which average to 94.42 images per day (around 8,455 images or 89 days for training and around 2,945 images or 31 days for testing).

4.2   Result of Inception-v3 with Satellite Images

We use the inception model by training it from scratch and trained the model from 20,000 to 50,000 training steps. We chose the training step that got us the highest overall accuracy. The test result is given through Figs. 4 and 5.

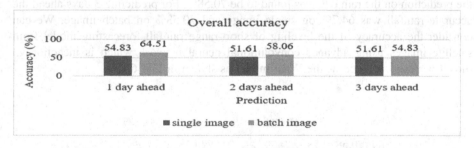

Fig. 4. Overall accuracy of inception-v3 from satellite image

If the training data set is enough for the model to find the relationship between satellite images and leveling of daily rainfall data, the model will get high accuracy. The result shows that the model can find the relationship because the single satellite image and the batch image also got high accuracy but the batch satellite image got the

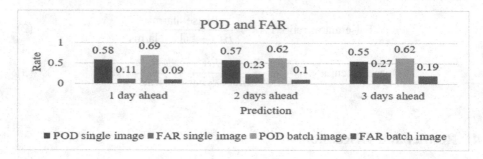

Fig. 5. Probability of detection and False alarm ratio of inception-v3 from satellite image

better accuracy than single satellite image because we gave information about the movement of the cloud, airmass and weather through the day. The models were able to find a relationship between batch satellite images and daily rainfall data. For example, to predict 1 day ahead rainfall, batch images got overall accuracy of 64.51% but overall accuracy of single image was 54.83%. The evaluated overall accuracy, POD and FAR rate result shows that with the training from scratch method, the batch satellite images used in predicting 1 day, 2 day and 3 day ahead leveling rainfall got better overall accuracy, POD and FAR rate than the single image. The higher POD rate means better for prediction. If the POD rate equal to 1, it means that the predicted rainfall is according to the one observed. The lower FAR rate means better for prediction. If the FAR rate equal to 0, it means that the predicted rainfall is more than the rainfall that actually occurred.

To compare with WRF model [10], we evaluated the model only on the rain day (rain more than 0 mm). WRF models had predicted 3 classes of leveling rainfall (light rain, moderate rain and heavy rain) but we had predicted 4 classes of leveling rainfall. So, we combine class 'not rain' and 'light rain' together on the rain day to be able to make it 3 class in order to compare to the WRF model. So, for 1 day and 2 days ahead the prediction on the rain day was found to be 70.58%. For predicting 3 days ahead the accurate rainfall was 64.7% on single image and 70.58% on batch image. We can consider the accuracy of the leveling of short-range rainfall forecasting model from satellite images using advance convolutional neural network which is inception-v3 model performs as good as the WRF model as shown in Fig. 6.

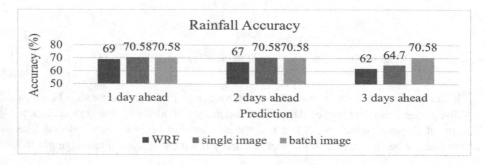

Fig. 6. Overall accuracy of inception-v3 from satellite image only rain date

4.3   Error

There were some errors that we got during our training and testing. These errors are shown through a confusion matrix as shown in Table 1.

Table 1. The confusion matrix for evaluation.

Observe rainfall (days)				
Predicted rainfall (days) **64.51% or 20 days**	Not rain (45.16%)	Light rain (32.25%)	Moderate rain (19.35%)	Heavy rain (3.22%)
Not rain	**41.93% Hits**	16.12% Misses	6.45% Misses	3.22% Misses
Light rain	0% False alarms	**12.9% Hits**	3.22% Misses	0% Misses
Moderate rain	3.22% False alarms	3.22% False alarms	**9.67% Hits**	0% Misses
Heavy rain	0% False alarms	0% False alarms	0% False alarms	**0% Hits**

We recorded the prediction result and compared that to the observe data. We made the confusion matrix for evaluation. The error occurred because of the images were misjudged into each other's category as they looked alike as described through Fig. 7 and their uncertainty is hard to capture due to the high variation of rainfall both in time and space. So, it was very hard for a computer to tell the difference.

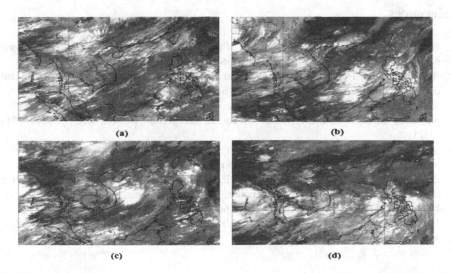

(a)   (b)

(c)   (d)

Fig. 7. Image of each class: (a) not rain, (b) light rain, (c) moderate rain and (d) heavy rain

5 Conclusion

This research is regarding developed Artificial Intelligence that was able to find the relationship between satellite images and leveling of the daily rainfall data by using advance convolutional neural network which is inception-v3. We have tried to use single satellite image and batch satellite image to predict 1 day, 2 days and 3 days ahead leveling of the daily rainfall by training the inception model from scratch which was the best result we got from our previous work [5].

The result of inception-v3 showed that the batch satellite image got better accuracy than the single image for predicting 1 day ahead, where the accuracy was 64.51%, for predicting 2 days ahead we got 58.06% and for predicting 3 days ahead the accuracy was found to be 54.83% because we gave the information about the movement of the cloud and weather and the model was then able to find the relationship with it. To compare with WRF model [10], we also evaluated the model only on rain day (rain more than 0 mm). For predicted 1 day, 2 days and 3 days ahead the accuracy on rain day was 70.58%.

For our future work, we aim to predict from 3 to up to 10 days ahead (Medium-range Forecast) by using batch images on a previous week rather than batch of 1 day. We want to predict the rainfall for different stations in various regions of Thailand by comparing it to the daily rainfall data of the other stations.

Acknowledgments. We are thankful to the Petroleum Authority of Thailand for providing us with the daily rainfall data and to Meteorological Department of Thailand's for providing us with the satellite images and daily temperature data. We would also like to thank miss Vishakha Singh for her help with this work.

References

1. Hinton, G.E., Krizhevsky, A., Sutskever, I.: ImageNet classification with deep convolutional neural networks. Adv. Neural. Inf. Process. Syst. **25**, 1106–1114 (2012)
2. Rosenblatt, F.: The perceptron: a probabilistic model for information storage and organization in the brain. Psychol. Rev. **65**(6), 386 (1958)
3. Klein, B., Wolf, L., Afek, Y.: A dynamic convolutional layer for short range weather prediction. In: IEEE Computer Vision and Pattern Recognition, Boston, MA, pp. 4840–4848 (2015)
4. Shi, X., Chen, Z., Wang, H., Yeung, D.Y.: Convolutional LSTM network: a machine learning approach for precipitation nowcasting. In: CS.CV, June 2015
5. Boonyuen, K., Kaewprapha, P., Srivihok, P.: Daily rainfall forecast model from satellite image using convolution neural network. In: The 3rd International Conference on Information Technology, 24–25 October, Khon Kaen, Thailand (2018)
6. Japan Meteorological Agency.: Introduction to Himawari-8. In: Sigmet workshop, Tokyo Japan, 27–30 June 2016

7. Szegedy, C., Vanhoucke, V., Ioffe, S., Shlens, J., Wojna, Z.: Rethinking the -inception architecture for computer vision. In: IEEE CVPR, Las Vegas, pp. 2818–2826 (2016)
8. Szegedy, C., Ioffe, S., Vanhoucke, V., Alemi, A.: Inception-v4, inception-ResNet and the impact of residual connections on learning. In: Computer Vision and Pattern Recognition (2016)
9. Satellite images from the meteorological department of Thailand's website page. http://www.sattmet.tmd.go.th/satmet/data/satdata.html. Accessed 01 Dec 2017
10. Thodsang, T., Chankarn, A., Kitiraj, S., Sinonpakorn, K., Boonyaarunneth, S.: Analysis and accuracy of the weather research and forecasting model (WRF) for climate change prediction in Thailand. In: 19th NCCE, 14–16 May, Khon Kaen, Thailand (2014)

Application of Convolutional Neural Network in Object Recognition of Remote Sensing Image

Yufang Feng[1,2], Jianchao Fei[1], Liang Chen[1,3], Jingbo Bai[1], Lin Cao[1], and Hong Yin[1(✉)]

[1] Army Engineering University of PLA, Nanjing 210007, Jiangsu, China
nanjingyh@126.com
[2] The Troops of 71375, Harbin 150038, Heilongjiang, China
[3] Army Military Transportation University, Bengbu 233011, Anhui, China

Abstract. Object recognition of remote sensing image is of great theoretical significance and application value in many fields. Faster and more effective object recognition methods are the hot and difficult point in the field of image research. Aiming at the problems of object recognition of remote sensing image, in this paper, the convolutional neural network with inter-class constraint (ICNN) is applied to object recognition of remote sensing image. This method replaces the softmax loss function of traditional convolutional neural network with the inter-loss function to obtain smaller intra-class distance and larger inter-class distance. This method significantly improves the effectiveness of image feature classification. Experiments are conducted on the US Land Use Classification Data Set 21(UCM_LandUse_21), and the experimental results showed that the proposed method can realize the fast and accurate recognition of remote sensing image and has a good promotion significance.

Keywords: Object recognition · Convolutional neural network · Inter-class constraint · Feature classification

1 Introduction

With the constantly improvement of resolution of satellite remote sensing images and aerial remote sensing images, people can obtain more useful data and information from remote sensing images. And the specific object of remote sensing images and its type and location can be gained by object recognition, which plays a very important role in applications of intelligent transportation, wisdom city, public safety, and military war. Therefore, the study of object recognition of remote sensing image is of great significance [1, 2].

In fact, the object recognition of remote sensing image is to classify specific object. The common recognition technologies are sliding window algorithm [3], the method based on image analysis [4], the BOW(bag-of Words) feature-based object recognition

Y. Tan et al. (Eds.): ICSI 2019, LNCS 11656, pp. 116–121, 2019.
https://doi.org/10.1007/978-3-030-26354-6_11

algorithm [5] and the HOG(Histogram of Oriented Gradients) feature-based object recognition algorithm [6]. But the features extracted by these methods are all from the underlying visual features of the object, which cannot express the abstract semantic features of the object. So the accuracy of object recognition is poor. In recent years, the models of deep learning have shown strong learning ability in the field of image recognition. The convolutional neural network has been widely applied in various fields of image recognition, such as face recognition [7], behavior recognition [8], medical image recognition [9]. The traditional convolutional neural network uses the softmax classifier, but the classification results are dissatisfaction. However, the Inter loss function can constrain the inter-class distance, which can reduce the within-class scatter while increase the distance between samples of different classes. This method can improve the effectiveness of classification. Therefore, this paper applies the convolutional neural network model with inter-class constraint to object recognition of remote sensing image. This model replaces the softmax loss function with the inter-class constraint loss function, which significantly improves the accuracy of image feature classification.

2   Related Work

In general, the study of the methods of object detection and recognition of remote sensing image has tended to be mature and perfect in recent years. However, there are few researches on object recognition of remote sensing image using the convolutional neural network, and most of them focus on the scene classification of remote sensing image. For examples, Castelluccio et al. [10] applied GoogLeNet network to the data sets of UCM_LandUse_21 using the method of transfer learning. This method achieved better classification results. Othman et al. [11] preprocessed remote sensing images using the sparse self-coding model, and then classified them by the CNN network. For the study on object recognition of remote sensing image, it is common to directly use the deep learning model of natural scene, such as AlexNet network [12], GoogLeNet network [13], etc. These deep learning networks can extract deep semantic features, and their classification performance is higher than the traditional middle-level and lower-level features. However, the differences between different remote sensing objects not only contain semantic information, but also contain some subtle feature differences. So this paper replaces the softmax loss function with the inter-class constraint loss function to highlight the subtle differences between classes. Experimental results show that the proposed method has better classification effect.

3   CNN with Inter-class Constraint

The inter-class constraint loss function [18] can be expressed as

$$J_{\text{inter}} = \frac{1}{2} \sum_{i=1}^{m} \sum_{j=1}^{n} \sum_{k=1}^{m} \left\| x_i^j - M_k \right\|_2^2$$

$$M_k = \frac{\sum_{k}^{q} x_k^p}{q}, \; i \neq k$$

(1)

where n is training sample size, m is the number of classes, q is the number of samples in class k, x_i^j is the ith deep feature in sample j, M_k is the center of class k.

In practical application, combining the formula (1) with the softmax loss function formula, the final loss function is defined as

$$J_{loss} = J_{softmax} + \alpha \frac{1}{J_{\text{inter}}}$$

(2)

where $J_{softmax}$ is the softmax loss function, α is a scalar to balance softmax loss function and inter-class constraint loss function.

The gradient of neurons z_i using the inter-class constraint loss function as follows

$$
\begin{aligned}
\delta_{\text{inter}} &= \frac{\partial J_{\text{inter}}}{\partial z_i^j} \\
&= \frac{1}{2} \sum_{i=1}^{m} \sum_{j=1}^{n} \sum_{k=1}^{m} \frac{\partial \left\| x_i^j - M_k \right\|_2^2}{\partial z_i^j} \\
&= \sum_{i=1}^{m} \sum_{j=1}^{n} \sum_{k=1}^{m} (x_i^j - M_k) \cdot [(x_i^j)' - (M_k)'] \\
&= \sum_{i=1}^{m} \sum_{j=1}^{n} \sum_{k=1}^{m} (x_i^j - M_k) \cdot (F'(z_i^j)), \; j \neq k
\end{aligned}
$$

(3)

where z_i^j is the ith neuron in sample j, $F(\cdot)$ is the activation function.

The training process of inter-class constraint loss function is followed in Table 1.

Table 1. The training process of inter-class constraint loss function

Algorithm: the training process of inter-class constraint loss function
input: the size of input sample x: {x1...n}
class identification number: m
set parameter: α
output:
while training number do
While n do
calculate the softmax loss function: $J_{soft\,max}$
calculate the center of class: M_k
calculate the inter-class constraint loss function: $J_{inter} = \dfrac{1}{2}\sum\limits_{i=1}^{m}\sum\limits_{j=1}^{n}\sum\limits_{k=1}^{m}\left\|x_i^j - M_k\right\|_2^2$
calculate the gradient of inter-class constraint loss function:
$$\delta_{inter} = \sum\limits_{i=1}^{m}\sum\limits_{j=1}^{n}\sum\limits_{k=1}^{m}(x_i^j - M_k)\bullet(F'(z_i^j))$$
calculate the total loss: $J_{loss} = J_{soft\,max} + \alpha\dfrac{1}{J_{inter}}$
calculate the gradient of loss: $\delta_{loss} = \delta_{soft\,max} + \delta_{inter}$
end while

4 Experiments

4.1 Data Set of Experiment

UCM_LandUse_21 is the US Land Use Classification Data Set, which contains 21 types of scene images. There are 100 scene images with size of 256 * 256 * 3 in each type (see Fig. 1). In the experiment, 80% of the scene images are randomly selected as training data, and the rest of images as test data.

Fig. 1. Remote sensing image examples of UCM_Land Use_21

4.2   Experiments and Analysis

To verify the advantages of classification of this method, the ICNN is compared with several representative methods in recent years, such as Spatial BOVW [14], Pyramid of spatial relations [15], MNCC [16], ConvNet [17]. The classification results are shown in Table 2.

Table 2. Comparison of recognition accuracy between different models

Algorithms	Accuracy/%
Spatial Bovw	80.61 ± 1.29
Pyramid of spatial relations	83.71 ± 0.97
MNCC	88.12 ± 1.85
ConvNet	89.39 ± 0.63
ICNN	91.54 ± 1.92

From Table 2, it can be seen that the classification accuracy of the algorithm based on neural network is relatively higher, but the classification accuracy of the ICNN is significantly higher than other models. The recognition accuracy of ICNN model achieved 89.62%–93.46%. Therefore, the model in this paper significantly improves its image classification ability.

5   Conclusion

In this paper, the deep learning method is applied to the object recognition of remote sensing images to propose object recognition method of remote sensing image based on the convolutional neural network method with inter-class constraint. Experiments are conducted on the US Land Use Classification Data Set 21(UCM_LandUse_21), this paper studies and analyzes the rapid and accurate identification of remote sensing image by the convolutional neural network with inter-class constraint. The proposed model is compared with the models of Spatial BOVW, Pyramid of spatial relations, MNCC, ConvNet. The experimental results show that the proposed method significantly improves the accuracy of feature classification of image. The proposed model has a good promotion significance.

References

1. Wang, Y.Q., Ma, L., Tian, Y.: State-of-the-art of ship detection and recognition in optical remotely sensed imagery. Acta Automatica Sinica **37**(9), 1029–1039 (2011)
2. Liu, Y., Fu, Z.Y., Zheng, F.B.: Review on high resolution remote sensing image classification and recognition. J. Geo-information Sci. **17**(9), 1080–1091 (2015)
3. Li, H.: Statistical Learning Methods. Tsinghua University Press, Beijing (2012).

4. Baatz, M.: Multiresolution segmentation: an optimization approach for high quality multi-scale image segmentation. Angewandte geographische informationsverarbeitung, pp. 12–23 (2000)
5. Zhang, D., Han, J., Cheng, G., et al.: Weakly supervised learning for target detection in remote sensing images. IEEE Geosci. Remote Sens. Lett. **12**(4), 701–705 (2015)
6. Mckeown, D.M., Denlinger, J.L.: Cooperative methods for road tracking in aerial imagery. In: Computer Society Conference on Computer Vision and Pattern Recognition, Proceedings CVPR, pp. 662–672. IEEE (1988)
7. Ma, Y., He, J., Wu, L., Qi, W.: An effective face verification algorithm to fuse complete features in convolutional neural network. In: Tian, Q., Sebe, N., Qi, G.-J., Huet, B., Hong, R., Liu, X. (eds.) MMM 2016. LNCS, vol. 9517, pp. 39–46. Springer, Cham (2016). https://doi.org/10.1007/978-3-319-27674-8_4
8. Ijjina, E.P., Mohan, C.K.: Human action recognition based on motion capture information using fuzzy convolution neural networks. In: International Conference on Machine Learning and Applications, pp. 159–164. IEEE (2015)
9. Ciompi, F., De, H.B., van Riel, S.J., et al.: Automatic classification of pulmonary peri-fissural nodules in computed tomography using an ensemble of 2D views and a convolutional neural network out-of-the-box. Med. Image Anal. **26**(1), 195–202 (2015)
10. Castelluccio, M., Poggi, G., Sansone, C., et al.: Land use classification in remote sensing images by convolutional neural networks. arXiv preprint arXiv:1508.00092 (2015)
11. Othman, E., Bazi, Y., Alajlan, N., et al.: Using convolutional features and a sparse autoencoder for land-use scene classification. Int. J. Remote Sens. **37**(10), 2149–2167 (2016)
12. Krizhevsky, A., Sutskever, I., Hinton, G.E.: Imagenet classification with deep convolutional neural networks. In: Advances in Neural Information Processing Systems, pp. 1097–1105 (2012)
13. Szegedy, C., Liu, W., Jia, Y., et al.: Going deeper with convolutions. In: Proceedings of the IEEE Conference on Computer Vision and Pattern Recognition, pp. 1–9 (2015)
14. Yang, Y., Newsam, S.: Bag-of-visual-words and spatial extensions for land-use classification. In: GIS 2010: Proceedings of the 18th SIGSPATIAL International Conference on Advances in Geographic Information Systems, pp. 270–279. ACM, New York (2010)
15. Lu, F.X., Huang, J.: Beyond bag of latent topics: spatial pyramid matching for scene category recognition. Front. Inf. Technol. Electron. Eng. **16**(10), 817–829 (2015)
16. Liu, Y., Fu, Z.Y., Zheng, F.B.: Scene classification of high-resolution remote sensing image based on multimedia neural cognitive computing. Syst. Eng. Electron. **37**(11), 2623–2633 (2015)
17. Nogueira, K., Miranda, W.O., Santos, J.A.D.: Improving spatial feature representation from aerial scenes by using convolutional networks. In: Proceedings of the 2015 28th SIBGRAPI Conference on Graphics, Patterns and Images, pp. 289–296. IEEE, Piscataway (2015)
18. Fei, J.C., Rui, T., Song, X.N., et al.: More discriminative convolutional neural network with inter-class constraint for classification. Comput. Electr. Eng. **68**, 484–489 (2018)

Paragraph Coherence Detection Model Based on Recurrent Neural Networks

Yihe Pang[1], Jie Liu[1,2(✉)], Jianshe Zhou[2], and Kai Zhang[2]

[1] Department of Information Engineering, Capital Normal University,
Beijing, China
{2171002020,liujie}@cnu.edu.cn
[2] Research Center for Language Intelligence, Capital Normal University,
Beijing, China
zhoujianshe@solcnu.net, irs_zhangkai@163.com

Abstract. Paragraph coherence detection which is to evaluate the semantic correlation and structure coherence between paragraphs in text. Most of previous studies are based on English text, and only few studies are based on Chinese composition. The Chinese compositions emphasize rich expressions and complex transformed sentence structures, these cause the difficulties in Chinese text level analysis. A good paragraph coherence is a reflection of a qualified composition, which it is also important criterion for automatic scoring for compositions. In this paper, we focus on the paragraph coherence detection based on Chinese composition. We propose a paragraph coherence detection model based on recurrent neural networks (RNNs) to detect the coherence between two paragraphs, and then we extended the model to the whole composition. The experimental results show that our model achieves remarkable results with 80% accuracy, for automatically detecting the paragraph coherence of Chinese composition.

Keywords: Coherence detection · Chinese composition · RNNs

1 Introduction

There is a close semantic relationship between paragraphs in a composition, and paragraphs of a good composition must be compact and coherent. Coherence between paragraphs are more difficult to judge than mistakes in grammar, vocabulary, and syntax. In addition, the coherence between paragraphs is an important indicator of composition evaluation. Therefore, it is important for the automatic evaluation of the semantic coherence between compositions' paragraphs, and it is also helpful to automatic score for compositions. The following two examples show paragraphs coherence and paragraphs inconsistency.

Example 1: ① *My father is very fat.* ② *He likes to watch TV and drink beer, but doesn't like doing sports.* ③ *Therefore, I think he should take more physical exercise.*

Example 2: ① *My dad is a happy man.* ② *He often prepares lots of presents for me.* ③ *Therefore, I think he should take more physical exercise.*

© Springer Nature Switzerland AG 2019
Y. Tan et al. (Eds.): ICSI 2019, LNCS 11656, pp. 122–131, 2019.
https://doi.org/10.1007/978-3-030-26354-6_12

The Example 1 shows the three paragraphs are coherent, because all the three paragraphs are the related description of one's dad's obesity. The first paragraph shows the topic, the second and the third paragraph show the reason and reasonable suggestion. But in Example 2, three paragraphs are incoherent. Although they all describe one's dad, the content between each paragraph is irrelevant. Especially the first two paragraphs are not the reason for the third paragraph.

Most of the previous coherence detection studies are based on English text, while only small amount of studies are Chinese coherence studies. Because Chinese compositions emphasize rich expressions and complex transformed sentence structures, which also causes the difficulties in Chinese text level analysis. In this article, we focus on Chinese compositions paragraph coherence detection which is to evaluate whether the semantic between paragraphs is correlated and structure is coherence. Due to the significant results of deep neural network for text processing, and recurrent neural networks (RNNs) have widely applied in the field of Natural Language Processing (NLP), such as speech recognition [1], automatic text generation [2, 3], neural machine translation [4, 5].

Therefore, we propose a paragraph coherence detection model based on recurrent neural networks for Chinese coherence detection. Our model can not only detect the coherence between two paragraphs in the composition, but also can detect the coherence of all paragraphs for the whole composition. Besides, in order to verify the performance of our model, we collected lots of the Chinese compositions of primary and secondary school students and manually labeled them to construct an experimental dataset. The verification results on the dataset show that our model achieves significant results with 80% accuracy.

2 Related Work

Previous paragraph coherence detection studies can divided into manual features methods and automatic features methods based on deep learning. The manual features methods mainly extract text features by hand that can reflect the paragraph coherence, such as paragraph potential semantics, syntactic dependencies, rhetorical relations between paragraphs and so on. The manual features methods rely heavily on a large number of manual operations and cause high complexity. For example, Barzilay *et al.* [6] proposed a text coherence detection method based on Hidden Markov Model (HMM), which manually extract the topic features of text to analyze the content coherence. This method has poor scalability and is not suitable for open field consistency detection. Foltz *et al.* [7] extract the latent semantic features (latent semantic analysis, LSA) of the text and model the text coherence, but the features extracted by this method will lose important information during processing, and the potential deep features of the text cannot well be extracted. Besides, some of text coherence studies based on entity graph modeling method, which predict the coherence by modeling the entities in the text as the graph structure [8–10]. They define the entities as nodes in the graph, and the semantic association with the entities in the text is defined as the edges between nodes. Then the text coherence is performed through the entity graph. Although this method can achieve significant results, but complex manual operations are required when constructing the entity graph model. And with the increase of the number of entities, the model complexity is higher.

Recently, significant results were achieved with deep neural networks in the field of natural language processing for its automatic feature extraction ability, such as neural machine translation [4, 5], automatic text generation [2, 3], speech recognition [1], and so on. Li *et al.* [11] first use the recurrent neural networks (RNNs) to get a distributed representation of the sentences in the text for the coherence detection. Different from above studies, we can achieve coherence detecting between paragraphs throughout the Chinese compositions of primary and secondary school students. Similar to Li *et al.* [11], we also employ the recurrent neural networks (RNNs) to automatically extract features.

3   Coherence Detection Model

In this section, we introduce the coherence detection model, which is composed with two parts. For the first part, we introduce the consecutive paragraphs coherence detection model. Then in the second part, we introduce the extended model for detecting the coherence of the whole composition.

3.1   Consecutive Paragraphs Coherence Detection Model

The consecutive paragraphs means two paragraphs appeared next to each other in the composition. The consecutive paragraphs coherence detection model could detect whether the semantic is coherent between the two paragraphs. The model structure figure is shown in Fig. 1.

Model Inputs
First, we pre-trained the dataset through Word2vec [12] model to get a vector representation of each word in the dataset. Then each word in paragraph can be represented as a word vector with d dimension. In Fig. 1, the first paragraph contains m words and it can be represented as a matrix $W_1 = \{w_{1,1}, w_{1,2}, \ldots, w_{1,t}, \ldots, w_{1,m}\}, w_{1,t} \in R^d$, each element in W_1 is a Word2vec vector of each word in paragraph. Similarly, the second paragraph can also be represented as a matrix $W_2 = \{w_{2,1}, w_{2,2}, \ldots, w_{2,t}, \ldots, w_{1,n}\}, w_{2,t} \in R^d$. We use the two word vectors matrixes as the inputs of the RNN cell.

RNN-based Detection Model
RNN [13, 14] is used to process the current outputs and the previous outputs related sequence data. The inputs of the current moment contain the hidden states of the previous moment, and the nodes between the hidden layers are connected. In other words, the recurrent neural networks can memorize the previous information and then apply to the calculation of the current moment. The detail calculation is as follows:

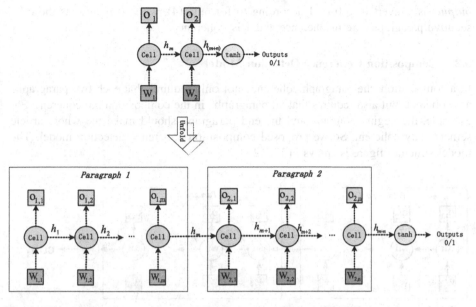

Fig. 1. The consecutive paragraphs coherence detection model. *W1* represents the first paragraph's input matrix and *W2* represents the second input matrix. The *outputs* is the final detect result, while *0* represents the consecutive paragraphs are incoherence and *1* represents coherence.

$$h_t = \sigma\left(U^1 \cdot W_t + U^2 \cdot h_{(t-1)} + b\right) \tag{1}$$

$$o_t = \sigma(V \cdot h_t + c) \tag{2}$$

$$outputs = tanh\left(Z \cdot h_{(m+n)} + d\right) \tag{3}$$

$$outputs(x) = \begin{cases} 0, & x < 0.5 \\ 1, & x \geq 0.5 \end{cases} \tag{4}$$

$$\sigma(x) = \frac{1}{1 + e^{-x}} \tag{5}$$

$$tanh(x) = \frac{e^x - e^{-x}}{e^x + e^{-x}} \tag{6}$$

where h_t is the hidden state of RNN cell in time step t, and o_t is the output value in time step t. The *outputs* is the final detection results. U^1, U^2, V, Z, b, c and d are the model parameters. σ and *tanh* represented the activate functions, and the function is defined in formula (5) and (6). Particularly, the final detect results is calculated as formula (3), while we use the hidden state of the RNN cell $h_{(m+n)}$ in final time step $m + n$, supposed that paragraph 1 has m words and paragraph 2 has n words. And the value of *outputs* is converted to 0 or 1 according to formula (4), while 0 represents the consecutive paragraphs are incoherence and 1 is coherence.

3.2 Composition Coherence Detection Model

In a composition, the paragraph coherence not only requires that each two paragraphs are coherent, but also requires that all paragraphs in the composition are coherent. For example, the begin paragraph and the end paragraph should make the whole article semantically coherent. So we proposed composition coherence detection model. The model structure figure is shows in Fig. 2.

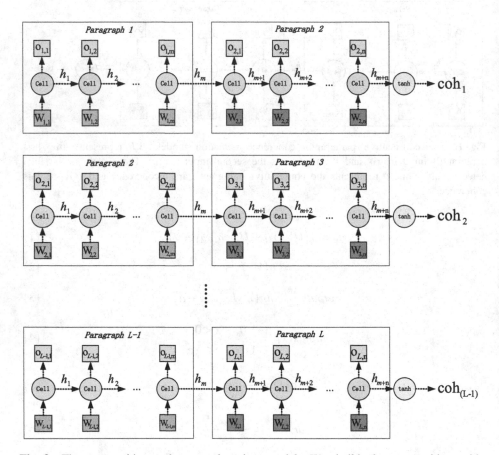

Fig. 2. The composition coherence detection model. We build the composition with *L* paragraphs into *L–1* parts, the model needs to perform *L–1* times of coherence detection and get *L_1* numbers of coherence values. Then we calculate the final coherence values based on the *L_1* numbers of coherence values.

Model Inputs

First, we build the model input sample data. When a composition has L paragraphs, we input $L-1$ parts into the model. For example, if a composition has 5 paragraphs, then the 4 parts of the composition are constructed as {*paragraph 1, paragraph 2*}, {*paragraph 2, paragraph 3*}, {*paragraph 3, paragraph 4*} and {*paragraph 4, paragraph 5*}. Then, we get a word vector representation based on Word2vec for the words in each paragraph. Finally, the word vector matrix for each paragraph is used as the input for the model, which is same with the consecutive paragraphs coherence detection model.

RNN-based Detection Model

The detailed calculation process of the coherence detection value is the same as in Sect. 3.1. So, when a composition has L paragraphs, we calculate $L-1$ coherence detection values $\{coh_1, coh_2, \ldots, coh_{L-1}\}$ for the following coherence detection of the whole composition.

Composition Coherence Detection

The coherence detection value of the whole composition coh_value is calculated as follows:

$$coh_i = \begin{cases} 0, & When\ part_i\ is\ incoherent \\ 1, & When\ part_i\ is\ coherent \end{cases} \tag{7}$$

$$coh\_weight_i = 1/(L-1) \tag{8}$$

$$coh\_value = \sum_{i=1}^{L-1} coh\_weight_i \cdot coh_i \tag{9}$$

where coh_i represents the coherence detection value of each part of the composition and the value is 1 when the part is coherent, the value is 0 when the part is incoherent. And we define the weights for each part of the composition, the coh_weight_i represents the weight of each part. What need special explanation are the weights of each part is the same here. Finally, the final composition coherence detection value is calculated by Eq. (9). We also divide the value of coh_value by 0.5 threshold as the coh value, and when the coh_value is 1 to indicate that the composition is coherent, coh_value is 0 to indicate that the composition is in coherent.

4   Experiments

4.1   Dataset

The dataset contains 4,545 compositions which are manually collected and come from primary and secondary school Chinese compositions. The manually collected dataset are considered to be coherent in the compositions, so we need to construct inconsistent negative sample data for the training of the model. For the consecutive paragraphs coherence detection model, we use the two paragraphs reserved order in the dataset as a positive sample, and the inverted two paragraphs as a negative sample. For the composition coherence detection model, we use the composition in the original paragraph order as a positive sample, and the compositions in the chaotic order of the paragraph as a negative sample. All the positive samples are labeled 1 and the negative samples are labeled 0. The ratio of the number of positive and negative samples is 1:1, and then we randomly divide the data set into a training set and a test set in a ratio of 8:2.

4.2 Training and Evaluation

For the training of the models, we use the 0–1 loss function to optimize the models. The loss function is defined as follows:

$$loss(y, f(x)) = \begin{cases} 0, & When \ y = f(x) \\ 1, & When \ y \neq f(x) \end{cases} \tag{10}$$

where y represents the standard result, and $f(x)$ represents the model predict result. Besides, we use the standard accuracy evaluation indicators to evaluate the model, which means the model predicts the ratio of the correct number of samples to the total number of samples.

4.3 Results of Consecutive Paragraphs Coherence Detection Model

In this section, we conducted three comparative experiments to emphasize the performance of the consecutive paragraphs coherence detection model. All the three experiments employed the consecutive paragraphs coherence detection model, the detailed steps are described in Sect. 3.2. The model results are shown in Fig. 3.

For the first experiment, we only removed the stop words from the paragraphs and then input them into the model, which we called the full words inputs experiment and the results are shown in (a) in Fig. 3. For the second experiment, we only kept the verbs in the paragraph as the inputs for the model, which we called the verbs inputs experiment and the results are shown in (b) in Fig. 3. For the third experiment, we kept the verbs and adjectives in the paragraph as the inputs for the model, which we called the verbs and adjectives inputs experiment and the results are shown in (c) in Fig. 3.

From the results figures, we observed that when the model inputs are verbs the model achieves 70% accuracy value, and when the model inputs are verbs and adjectives the model also achieves 70% accuracy value. But the full words inputs experiment only achieves 54% accuracy value. So we considered that input all the words into the model, which will reduce the accuracy of the model prediction due to the inclusion of more noise data. Therefore, these experiments not only emphasize that our model can achieve 70% accuracy, but also show that verbs and adjectives are representative in the paragraphs coherence detection.

4.4 Results of Composition Coherence Detection Model

Based on the results of the consecutive paragraphs coherence detection model, we considered that the verbs and adjectives in the composition can achieve excellent results for the coherence detection. So in this section, we also conducted two

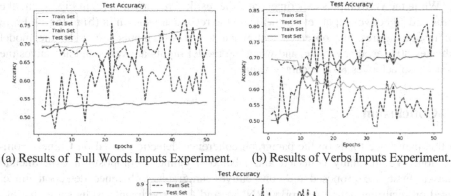

(a) Results of Full Words Inputs Experiment.   (b) Results of Verbs Inputs Experiment.

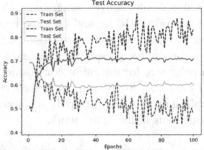

(c) Results of The Verbs and Adjectives Inputs Experiment.

Fig. 3. Results of the consecutive paragraphs coherence detection model. The results of three parts of experiments are shown in (a), (b) and (c). Where the red line is the test set accuracy, the yellow line is the test set loss function value; the black line is the training set accuracy, and the blue line is the training set loss function value. (Color figure online)

comparative experiments to emphasize the performance of the composition coherence detection model. The results of the experiments are shown as follows:

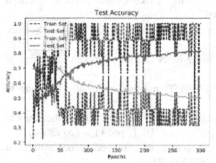

(a) Results of Verbs Inputs Experiment.

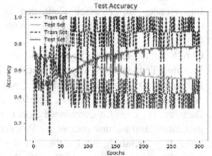

(b) Results of Verbs and Adjectives Inputs Experiment.

Fig. 4. Results of the composition coherence detection model. The results of two parts of experiments are shown in (a) and (b). Where the red line is the test set accuracy, the yellow line is the test set loss function value; the black line is the training set accuracy, and the blue line is the training set loss function value. (Color figure online)

While the verbs inputs experiment and the results are shown in (a) in Fig. 4, and the verbs and adjectives inputs experiment and the results are shown in (b) in Fig. 4. From the results figures, we observed that when the model inputs are verbs the model achieves 80% accuracy value, and when the model inputs are verbs and adjectives the model also achieves 80% accuracy value.

5 Conclusion

In this paper, we focus on the paragraph coherence detection based on Chinese composition. We manually collected and labeled a Chinese composition experimental dataset. First, we proposed the consecutive paragraphs coherence detection model based on recurrent neural networks (RNNs), and the experiment results show that our model achieves 70% accuracy value. After that, we proposed a composition coherence detection model based on consecutive paragraphs coherence detection model, which can detect the paragraph coherence for the entire composition. The results show that our model can achieve 80% accuracy for the composition coherence detection, which is satisfactory result for application. So we will apply our model approach to specific composition auto-evaluation tools in the future work.

Acknowledgement. This work is supported by Key Special Projects of National Key R&D Program of China (2018YFC0830100), National Natural Science Foundation of China (61672361), and Beijing Municipal Education Commission-Beijing Natural Fund Joint Funding Project (KZ201910028039).

References

1. Xiong, W., et al.: Achieving human parity in conversational speech recognition. IEEE/ACM Trans. Audio Speech Lang. Process. (2016)
2. Tang, J., Yang, Y., Carton, S., Zhang, M., Mei, Q.: Context-aware natural language generation with recurrent neural networks. In: 31th AAAI Conference on Artificial Intelligence, San Francisco, California, USA (2017)
3. Graves, A.: Generating Sequences With Recurrent Neural Networks. Computer Science (2013)
4. Cho, K., et al.: Learning Phrase Representations using RNN Encoder-Decoder for Statistical Machine Translation. Computer Science (2014)
5. Bahdanau, D., Cho, K., Bengio, Y.: Neural Machine Translation by Jointly Learning to Align and Translate. Computer Science (2014)
6. Barzilay, R., Lee, L.: Catching the drift: probabilistic content models, with applications to generation and summarization. In: Proceedings of NAACL-HLT, pp. 113–120 (2004)
7. Foltz, P.W., Kintsch, W., Landauer, T.K.: The measurement of textual coherence with latent semantic analysis. Discourse Process. 25(2&3), 285–307 (1998)
8. Guinaudeau, C., Strube, M.: Graph-based local coherence modeling. In: Proceedings of ACL, pp. 93–103 (2013)
9. Feng, V.W., Hirst, G.: Extending the entity-based coherence model with multiple ranks. In: Proceedings of EACL, pp. 315–324 (2012)

10. John, A.K., Di Caro, L., Boella, G.: Text segmentation with topic modeling and entity coherence. In: Abraham, A., Haqiq, A., Alimi, A.M., Mezzour, G., Rokbani, N., Muda, A.K. (eds.) HIS 2016. AISC, vol. 552, pp. 175–185. Springer, Cham (2017). https://doi.org/10. 1007/978-3-319-52941-7_18
11. Li, J., Hovy, E.: A model of coherence based on distributed sentence representation. In: Proceedings of the EMNLP, pp. 2039–2048 (2014)
12. Mikolov, T., Chen, K., Corrado, G., Dean, J.: Efficient Estimation of Word Representations in Vector Space. Computer Science (2013)
13. Martens, J., Sutskever, I.: Learning recurrent neural networks with hessian-free optimization. In: International Conference on International Conference on Machine Learning (2011)
14. Schuster, M., Paliwal, K.K.: Bidirectional recurrent neural networks. IEEE Trans. Sig. Process. **45**(11), 2673–2681 (1997)

Use of Artificial Neural Networks in Determining Domestic Violence Predictors

Jesús Silva[1]($\boxtimes$), Erick Guerra Aleman[2], Génesis Camargo Acuña[2],
Osman Redondo Bilbao[3], Hugo Hernandez-P[3], Bella León Castro[3],
Pedro Arrieta Meléndez[3], and Dionicio Neira[2]

[1] Universidad Peruana de Ciencias Aplicadas, Lima, Perú
`jesussilvaUPC@gmail.com`
[2] Universidad de la Costa, St. 58 #66, Barranquilla, Atlántico, Colombia
`{eguerra4,gcamargo2,dneiral}@cuc.edu.co`
[3] Corporación Universitaria Latinoamericana, Barranquilla, Colombia
`{oredondo,hhernandez,nleon,parrieta}@ul.edu.co`

Abstract. This paper aims to determine the predictors of violence against women by their partners, according to the National Survey of Demography and Health - ENDS - Colombia, 2017 using artificial neural networks. The results indicate that the best forecasting model found is the artificial neural network, perceptron model, multilayer associative memory with a hidden layer of 20 units, through functions of sigmoidal activation and sum of square of the error as error function. The ten main explanatory variables are: respect for human rights of the partner, respect for wishes, love expressed by the partner, a history of domestic violence, engaging in joint decision making, decision of contraceptive use, number of connections (partners) of the respondent, decision-making at the financial level, correction of children behavior, and decisions regarding women's health at home.

Keywords: Artificial neural network · Multilayer perceptron ·
Domestic violence

1 Introduction

At international level, Colombia signed the convention on the elimination of all forms of discrimination, CEDAW, by means of Law 51 in 1981, which regulated the commitment of States to reduce violence against women, which led the government to include new rights in the Carta Magna (constitution) [1]. This Convention is one of the first commitments that the State acquires with the United Nations to improve the women conditions. Similarly, in 1994, it signs the Inter-American Convention for Preventing, Punishing, and Eradicating Violence against Women, Convention of Belém Do Pará. Later, the Colombian government attends the Sixth Regional Conference on the Integration of Women into the Economic and Social Development in Latin America and the Caribbean, which enacts the guarantee of equalitarian inclusion of women to regional development and, finally, reiterates the commitment to advance the elimination of violence against women in the United Nations Conference for Women in Cairo. While these events occur at international context, a powerful activity

© Springer Nature Switzerland AG 2019
Y. Tan et al. (Eds.): ICSI 2019, LNCS 11656, pp. 132–141, 2019.
https://doi.org/10.1007/978-3-030-26354-6_13

of women for the advancement of these commitments from the state is developed in the country [2–4].

According to [5], "In Colombia, until the promulgation of the current Constitution (1991), gender inequality was backed by laws. In fact, until 1932, women were considered incapable, like mentally ill people and minors. For this reason, married women could not manage their assets, or even their wages, which was responsibility of the spouse" [6]. For this reason, the articles of the Constitution that favor women is one of the greater achievements of the social movement that supported the female constituents in the discussions that took place at the national constituent assembly. After these recognitions, there was a comprehensive policy for Colombian women that was defined as "a structural policy for women, which passes through all planning processes in the development of the State" [7].

During the time period 1995–2010 [8], three (3) government proposals were made, including the fulfilment of Human Rights, International Humanitarian Law, and the decentralization of state action as the basis of social, economic, and political development of the country. The National Office for Equality for Women was created during these governments (1995) now known as High Presidential Counselor for Women's Equity and laws aimed at gender equity were approved as the Law 823 of 2003. This law rules on equality of opportunity between men and women, the National Agreement on equity between men and women, and the Law 1009 of 2006, by which a permanent observatory of gender issues was created (OAG), as well as the law 1257 in 2008 which aims to guarantee and protect the dignity of women and to avoid any kind of discrimination or victimization toward them [9–11].

The Law 1257 in 2008 and its regulatory decrees allowed a legal progress to face gender-based violence against women that applies to domestic and sexual violence in Colombia as the scenario where different forms of physical, psychological, and sexual abuse are committed. However, violence has increased in Colombia in recent years, so it is important to use mechanisms to predict these facts [12, 13].

Given the above, the objective of this work is to use current technologies to determine the predictors of violence against women by their partners, according to the National Survey of Demography and Health - ENDS - Colombia, 2017, using artificial neural networks.

2 Theoretical Review

2.1 Risk Factors of Violence Against Women

The risk factors for domestic and sexual violence are of the individual, family, community and social type. Some of them are associated to the commission of violent acts, others to the kind of suffering, and others to both [14]. Among the risk factors for both, domestic and sexual violence, are the following: a low level of instruction (perpetrators of sexual violence and victims of sexual violence); a history of exposure to child abuse (perpetrators and victims), the experience of domestic violence (authors and victims); antisocial personality disorder (authors); the harmful use of alcohol (authors and victims); the fact of having many partners or inspire suspicions of infidelity in partners (authors); attitudes that tolerate violence (authors); the existence of social norms that favor men or attribute them to a higher status and give an inferior status to women; and reduced access of women to paid employment [15–17].

Among the factors specifically associated with domestic violence include: the history of violence; marital discord and dissatisfaction; difficulties of communication among the members of the couple; the male dominating behavior toward his partner. And among the factors specifically associated with sexual violence include: the belief in the family honor and sexual purity; the ideologies that enshrine sexual privileges of man; and the lightness of the legal sanctions against acts of sexual violence. The inequalities between men and women and acceptance of violence against women are the main cause of violence against them [10, 14, 18].

2.2   Elements of a Neural Network

The Artificial Neural Networks (ANN) are models that attempt to reproduce the behavior of the brain. Such models perform a simplification, finding out the relevant elements of the system, either because the amount of information that is available is excessive or because it is redundant. An appropriate choice of its features, plus a convenient structure, is the conventional procedure used to build networks capable of performing a task [19–22].

- It is known as a layer or level to a set of neurons whose entries come from the same source and whose outputs are directed to the same destination.
- Unit of process: Artificial Neuron. There are three types of units in any system: inputs, outputs, and hidden. The input units receive signals from the environment, output units send signals outside the network, and the hidden unit is that whose inputs and outputs are within the system.
- Activation State. The states of the system at a time t are represented by a vector A(t). The values of activation can be continuous or discrete, limited or unlimited. If they are discreet, they often take a discrete set of binary values, as well as an active state would be indicated by a 1 and a passive state represented by a zero. Other models consider a set of states of activation with value between [0,1], or in the interval [–1,1], as a sigmoidal function.
- Transference or Output Function. Associated with each unit, there is an output function which transforms the current state of activation into an output signal.

3   Materials and Methods

3.1   Database

Colombia has multiple sources of information for the formulation, monitoring, and evaluation of policies, action plans, and projects. These sources are, among other, administrative records of the State entities, the national accounts, and population-based surveys such as the National Survey of Demography and Health (ENDS). The ENDS has been a source for the definition of health policies of women and children and has allowed to follow the behavior and changes in the reproductive life of Colombian women, as well as the causes of gender-based violence. In the present research, the data from the survey carried out in 2017 were used [23]. The selection of variables was the result of the consultation to experts of the questionnaire ENDS 2017 [24, 25]. For that purpose, the independent variables that explain the violence against women by their partners are shown in Table 1:

Table 1. Study variables according to ENDS 2017.

Type	Code	Description
Independent	X_1	She was punished when she was a child
	X_2	Who corrects to children when they misbehave?
	X_3	As much as you know, did your father ever harm your mother?
	X_4	The partner gets (got) drunk frequently
	X_5	Respondent considers that physical harm is necessary in child's formation
	X_6	Could you tell me if your husband is (was) kindly with you?
	X_7	Could you tell me if your husband spends (or spent) spare time with you?
	X_8	Can you tell me if your husband asks (asked) for your opinion in different issues at home?
	X_9	Could you tell me if your husband respects (respected) your desires?
	X_{10}	Could you tell me if your husband respects (respected) your rights?
	X_{11}	In your opinion, do you agree that your husband (partner) harms his wife if she goes out home without permission?
Independent	X_{12}	In your opinion, do you agree that your husband/partner harms his wife if she neglects the children?
	X_{13}	In your opinion, do you agree that your husband/partner harms his wife if she discusses with him?
	X_{14}	In your opinion, do you agree that your husband/partner harms his wife if she refuses to have sexual relations with him?
	X_{15}	In your opinion, do you agree that your husband/partner harms his wife if she burns the food?
	X_{16}	The husband/partner lives at home
	X_{17}	Who mainly decides the use of contraceptives?
	X_{18}	Number of partners of the respondent
	X_{19}	Who mainly decides how to spend the money?
	X_{20}	In your home, who has the last word in your health care?
	X_{21}	In your home, who has the last word in big purchases for home?
	X_{22}	In your home, who has the last word in shopping for daily household needs?
	X_{23}	In your home, who has the last word in visiting relatives, friends or family?
	X_{24}	In your home, who has the last word about daily meals?
	X_{25}	In your home, who has the last word on how to spend the partner's money?
Dependent	Y_1	Psychological violence by the partner
	Y_2	Physical violence by the partner
	Y_3	Sexual violence by the partner

3.2   Methods

All selected variables were transformed to dichotomous variables with zero (no) and one (yes) [21], so that the variables X_2, X_{17}, X_{19}, X_{20}, X_{21}, X_{22}, X_{23}, X_{24} y X_{25} were unfolded in two variables each, where X_{21}, X_{171}, X_{191}, X_{201}, X_{211}, X_{221}, X_{231}, X_{241} y X_{251} correspond to the role of man in such activity, while X_{22}, X_{172}, X_{192}, X_{202}, X_{212}, X_{222}, X_{232}, X_{242} y X_{252} correspond to the role women in such activity, see Table 2.

Table 2. Dichotomous transformation by role

X_{i1}	X_{i2}	Gender role
0	1	Mostly role of woman
1	0	Mostly role of man
1	1	Role for both

Likewise, the dependent variables were recoded including variables resulting from combinations of Y_1, Y_2 y Y_3, it being added to the variables:

$Y_{12} \rightarrow$ Psychological and physical violence by the partner
$Y_{13} \rightarrow$ Psychological and sexual violence by the partner
$Y_{23} \rightarrow$ physical and sexual violence by the partner
$Y_{123} \rightarrow$ psychological, physical, and sexual violence by the partner

All the dependent variables were dichotomized, where the value zero (0) means the absence of the type of violence in the variable, while the value one (1) means the presence of the type of violence in the variable.

In this paper, a supervised network was used for the prediction, assessment, and generalization, and its learning is based on associating a set of input variables with their corresponding set of output variables [26]. The Perceptron Memory of Multilayer correlation is an artificial neural network of forward feed composed of a layer of input units (independent variables), a certain number of hidden layers and a layer of output units (dependent variables). The output units (dependent variables) are connected only with the units of the last hidden layer [27].

The hidden layer performs a nonlinear processing of the input layer units (independent variables), extracting the most important characteristics. Correlation Memory defines the total map between the input and output of the binary associative memory [21]:

$$\widehat{M} = \sum_{i=1}^{k} Y_i X_i^T = w_i \tag{1}$$

$$Y_i = g_1 \left(\sum_{j=1}^{M} w_{ij} s_j \right) = g_1 \left(\sum_{j=1}^{M} w_{ij} \left(g_2 \left(\sum_{r=1}^{L} t_{jr} X_r \right) \right) \right) \tag{2}$$

Where:

w_{ij}: are the synaptic weights
L: is the number of units of the hidden layer process
g_1: is the transfer function of the output units, sigmoidal function in this case:

$$g_1(*) = \frac{1}{1 + e^{-(*)}} \tag{3}$$

t_{jr}: is the synaptic weight that connects the processing unit j of the hidden layer with the input sensor r
g_2: is the transfer function of the hidden layer units, which in this case is also the sigmoidal function.

Learning Algorithm (retropropagation): Aims to adjust the synaptic weights and biases to minimize overall error or sum of the error [25].

This learning supervised method is continuously carried out, changing weights and biases in the contrary direction to the slope of the error, which is called the descendant gradient technique. The followed steps were [24, 28]:

Step 1: Weights and thresholds are initialized.
Step 2: For a training pattern, the signal is spread forward, obtaining an output.
Step 3: Evaluates the error committed by the network for the pattern.
Step 4: The generalized delta rule is applied (multiple layers and non-linear and distinguishable transfer functions).

To modify the weights and thresholds of the network [29, 30]:

i. Values are calculated for all neurons in the output layer.
ii. Values are calculated for the rest of the neurons in the network, beginning from the last hidden layer and retropropagating these values toward the input layer.
iii. Weights and thresholds are changed.

Step 5: Repeat steps 2, 3, and 4 for all training patterns, thus completing a learning cycle.
Step 6: Evaluates the total error reached by the network. It is the training error. (Can measure the average error or accumulated error for all patterns).
Step 7: Repeat steps 2, 3, 4, 5, and 6, till reaching a minimum training error, for which "m" learning cycles are made. Another stop criterion can be used (small variation of training error, increase of the error of the test set, etc....).

4 Results

The modeling of the artificial neural network, perceptron model, multilayer associative memory has the following features:

- Training sample: 70.0%
- Sample of test: 30.0%
- Activation function in the hidden layer: Sigmoid
- Activation function in the output layer: Sigmoid
- Error function in the output layer: Sum of Squares
- Units in the input layer: 68
- Units in the output layer: 14

The results of the prognosis of the type of violence against women by their partners are shown in Table 3 where the memory model of multilayer perceptron correlation was performed with a hidden layer and two hidden layers. These results show a slight advantage in the model of two hidden layers to predict the psychological violence and sexual violence, while the model of a layer has a slight advantage to predict the physical violence and psychological and physical violence exercised by the partner against women.

Table 3. Predictions of the memory model of multilayer perceptron correlation of the women assaulted by their partners in Colombia.

Type of violence	A hidden layer	Two hidden layers
Psychological violence by the partner	76.4	76.5
Physical violence by the partner	69.4	69.3
Sexual violence by the partner	93.2	93.3
Psychological and physical violence by the partner	82.1	82.2
Psychological and sexual violence by the partner	96.0	96.0
Physical and sexual violence by the partner	93.0	93.0
Psychological, physical, and sexual violence by the partner	99.0	99.0

In view of the results, the perceptron model, multilayer associative memory with a hidden layer was performed, since it is the easiest model regarding the parsimony criterion.

Table 4 shows the summary of the estimate of the perceptron model memory of multilayer correlation with a hidden layer, where an error of the sum of squares is present in the training of 1550.616 and an error of sum of squares in the tests of 662,763, with an average percentage of incorrect forecasts of 12.5% and 12.3% in both the training sample and the test sample. It may be inferred that the percentage of correct prognosis of the types of violence against women exercised by the partner is an average of 87.6%.

Table 4. Summary of the perceptron model memory of multilayer correlation with a hidden layer of women assaulted by their partner

	Description		Value
Training	Error of sum of squares		1523.514
	Average percentage of incorrect forecasts		11.4%
	Percentage of incorrect forecasts for categorical dependent	Psychological violence by the partner	21.4%
		Physical violence by the partner	28.5%
		Sexual violence by the partner	5.1%
		Psychological and physical violence by the partner	15.9%
		Psychological and sexual violence by the partner	4.3%
		Physical and sexual violence by the partner	4.9%
		Psychological, physical, and sexual violence by the partner	4.2%
	Stop Rule used		1 step(s) in a row(s)
	Training Time		without reducing the error 0:00:00.72
Test	Error of sum of squares		665.458
	Average percentage of incorrect forecasts		11.98%
	Description		Value
Test	Percentage of incorrect forecasts for categorical dependent	Psychological violence by the partner	21.2%
		Physical violence by the partner	29.8%
		Sexual violence by the partner	3.98%
		Psychological and physical violence by the partner	15.98%
		Psychological and sexual violence by the partner	3.5%
		Physical and sexual violence by the partner	4.4%
		Psychological, physical, and sexual violence by the partner	3.6%

5   Conclusions

After the use of the perceptron model, the ten main variables that explain the prognosis of violence in women by their partners are: 1. Could you tell me if your husband respects (respected) your rights? 2. Could you tell me if your husband respects (respected) your desires? 3. Could you tell me if your husband is (was) kindly with you? 4. As much as you know, did your father ever harm your mother? 5. Can you tell me if your husband asks (asked) for your opinion in different issues at home? 6. Who mainly decides the use of contraceptives (Woman) 7. Number of connections (partners) of the respondent 8. In your home, who has the last word in shopping for daily household needs (Male)? 9. Who corrects to children when they misbehave (Mother)? 10. In your home, who has the last word in your health care (Woman).

References

1. Abramovich, V.: De las violaciones masivas a los patrones estructurales: nuevos enfoques y clásicas tensiones en el Sistema Interamericano de Derechos Humanos. Derecho PUCP **1** (63), 95–138 (2009). http://revistas.pucp.edu.pe/index.php/derechopucp/article/
2. Arroyo Vargas, R.: Acceso a la justicia para las mujeres... El laberinto androcéntrico del derecho. Revista IIDH **53**, 35–62 (2011). http://www.corteidh.or.cr/tablas/r26673
3. Ferrer Araujo, N.: El acceso a la justicia como elemento indispensable del ejercicio de la ciudadanía femenina. Opinión Jurídica **9**(17), 113–124 (2010)
4. Acosta, M.: Comportamiento de la Violencia de Pareja: Colombia 2015. En Revista Forensis. Grupo Centro de Referencia Nacional sobre la Violencia. Instituto Nacional de Medicina Legal y Ciencias Forenses (INML). Bogotá (2015)
5. Amnistía Internacional. Las mujeres sufren discriminación, ya sea institucionalizada por ley o en la práctica, incluso en países con leyes que garantizan la igualdad (2017). https://www.es.amnesty.org/en-que-estamos/temas/mujeres/
6. Cardona, J., et al.: Sexismo y concepciones de la violencia de género contra las mujeres en cuatro universidades de la ciudad de Manizales (Colombia). Archivos de Medicina **15**(2), 200–219 (2015)
7. Fernández, J.: Análisis y evolución de las campañas publicitarias promovidas por el gobierno de España tras la aprobación del Plan Nacional de Sensibilización y Prevención de la Violencia de Género. Pensar la Publicidad **7**(2), 409–424 (2013)
8. Consejería Presidencial para la Equidad de la Mujer. Avances de la tolerancia social e institucional de las violencias contra las mujeres en Colombia. Boletín No. 19 (2015). http://www.equidadmujer.gov.co/oag/Documents/oag_boletin-19-marzo2015.pdf
9. Chávez, J.: Percepción de la igualdad de género en jóvenes universitarios. Trabajo Social UNAM **10**(4), 75–90 (2015)
10. Echeburúa, E., Amor, P., Sarasua, B., Zubizarreta, I., Holgado-Tello, F.: Inventario de pensamientos distorsionados sobre la mujer y el uso de la violenciarevisado (IPDMUV-R): propiedades psicométricas. Anales de Psicología **32**(3), 837–846 (2016)
11. Hoxmeier, J.C., Flay, B.R., Acock, A.C.: Control, norms, and attitudes: differences between students who do and do not intervene as bystanders to sexual assault. J. Interpers. Violence. **33**(15), 2379–2401 (2016). https://doi.org/10.1177/0886260515625503
12. Ingrassia, P.: La universidad como agente de igualdad de género. RevIISE **9**(9), 63–69 (2017). http://www.ojs.unsj.edu.ar/index.php/reviise/article/view/135/pdf

13. Mérida, R., Salazar, O., Agudo, M.: Protocolo para la prevención y protección frente al acoso sexual y por razón de sexo en la Universidad de Córdoba (2015). https://www.uco.es/igualdad/protocolo/documentos/protocolo-prevencion-v2.pdf
14. Ordorika, I.: Equidad de género en la Educación Superior. Revista de la Educación Superior **44**(2), 7–17 (2015)
15. Palaudi, M.: Campus Action Against Sexual Assault: Needs, Policies, Procedures and Training Programs. Abc-clio, California (2016)
16. Rozo, L.: Rompiendo el silencio. Análisis de encuesta sobre violencia sexual a estudiantes mujeres. Dirección de Bienestar Universidad Nacional de Colombia, Bogotá (2016)
17. Vásquez, V.: Ya somos una Red Interuniversitaria por la Igualdad de Género y contra las violencias. UNSAM en la Red (2015). http://www.unsam.edu.ar/pcvg/pdf/Revista2015.pdf
18. Vasquez, V., Palumbo, M., Fernández, C.: ¿Cómo prevenir, sancionar y erradicar la violencia de género en las universidades? Revista Ciencias Sociales **92**, 106–114 (2016)
19. Reardon, S.: Worldwide brain-mapping project sparks excitement—and concern. Nature **537**, 597 (2016)
20. Tait, A.N., et al.: Neuromorphic photonic networks using silicon photonic weight banks. Sci. Rep. **7**, 7430 (2017)
21. Bakeer, H., Abu-Naser, S.S.: Photo copier maintenance expert system vol 01 using SL5 object language. Int. J. Eng. Inf. Syst. (IJEAIS) **1**(4), 116–124 (2017)
22. AbuEl-Reesh, J.Y., Abu Naser, S.S.: A knowledge based system for diagnosing shortness of breath in infants and children. Int. J. Eng. Inf. Syst. (IJEAIS) **1**(4), 102–115 (2017)
23. Fernández Matos, D.C., González-Martínez, M.N.: La paz sin las mujeres ¡No va! El proceso de paz colombiano desde la perspectiva de género. Revista CIDOB d' Afers Internacionals. **121**, 113–134 (2019)
24. Viloria, A., et al.: Determination of dimensionality of the psychosocial risk assessment of internal, individual, double presence and external factors in work environments. In: Tan, Y., Shi, Y., Tang, Q. (eds.) Data Mining and Big Data. DMBD 2018. Lecture Notes in Computer Science, vol. 10943. Springer, Cham (2018). https://doi.org/10.1007/978-3-319-93803-5_29
25. Bucci, N., et al.: Factor analysis of the psychosocial risk assessment instrument. In: Tan, Y., Shi, Y., Tang, Q. (eds.) Data Mining and Big Data. DMBD 2018. Lecture Notes in Computer Science, vol. 10943. Springer, Cham (2018). https://doi.org/10.1007/978-3-319-93803-5_14
26. Khella, R., Abu-Naser, S.S.: Rule based system for chest pain in infants and children. Int. J. Eng. Inf. Syst. **1**(4), 138–148 (2017)
27. Abu Naser, S.S., Baraka, M.H., Baraka, A.R.: A proposed expert system for guiding freshman students in selecting a major in Al-Azhar University, Gaza. J. Theor. Appl. Inf. Technol. **4**(9), 889–893 (2008)
28. Varela Izquierdo, N., Cabrera, H.R., Lopez Carvajal, G., Viloria, A., Gaitán Angulo, M., Henry, M.A.: Methodology for the reduction and integration of data in the performance measurement of industries cement plants. In: Tan, Y., Shi, Y., Tang, Q. (eds.) Data Mining and Big Data. DMBD 2018. Lecture Notes in Computer Science, vol. 10943. Springer, Cham (2018). https://doi.org/10.1007/978-3-319-93803-5_4
29. Abu-Nasser, B.S.: Medical expert systems survey. Int. J. Eng. Inf. Syst. **1**(7), 218–224 (2017)
30. Kamatkar, S.J., Kamble, A., Viloria, A., Hernández-Fernandez, L., Cali, E.G.: Database performance tuning and query optimization. In: Tan, Y., Shi, Y., Tang, Q. (eds.) Data Mining and Big Data. DMBD 2018. Lecture Notes in Computer Science, vol. 10943. Springer, Cham (2018). https://doi.org/10.1007/978-3-319-93803-5_1

Acute Lymphoblastic Leukemia Cell Detection in Microscopic Digital Images Based on Shape and Texture Features

Eva Tuba, Ivana Strumberger, Nebojsa Bacanin, Dejan Zivkovic, and Milan Tuba[(✉)]

Singidunum University, Danijelova 32, 11000 Belgrade, Serbia
tuba@ieee.org

Abstract. Leukemia or blood cancer is a disease that affects a large population, especially children. Fast and early detection of four main types of leukemia is crucial for successful treatment and patient's recovery. Leukemia can be detected in microscope blood images by detecting blasts, i.e. not fully developed white blood cells. Computer-aided diagnostic systems can improve the quality and speed of abnormal lymphocytes detection. In this paper we proposed a method for automatic detection of one type of leukemia, acute lymphoblastic leukemia, by classifying white blood cells into normal cells and blasts. The proposed method uses shape and texture features as input vector for support vector machine optimized by bare bones fireworks algorithm. Based on the results obtained on the standard benchmark set, ALL-IDB, our proposed method shows a competitive accuracy of classification comparing to other state-of-the-art method.

Keywords: Acute lymphoblastic leukemia detection · Segmentation · Local binary pattern · Support vector machine · Optimization · Swarm intelligence · Bare bone fireworks algorithm

1 Introduction

Digital images have a great impact on the modern world and led to great advancement in numerous fields. Nowadays digital images can be obtained from various sources and they can be used in countless purposes. One of the main advantages of digital images over analog ones is much more powerful techniques for their processing.

One of the fields that made significant progress after introducing digital images is medicine. Precise and early disease detection and recognition is crucial for successful recovery of patients. Most of the diseases can be detected only by analyzing digital images obtained by different sources. Since the human eye

This research is supported by Ministry of Education, Science and Technological Development of Republic of Serbia, Grant No. III-44006.

is a rather imperfect organ, small details in the images can be overlooked and neglected. By using digital image processing techniques it is possible to detect anomalies even before they become visible to the human eye. By using different digital image processing techniques and methods various details can be detected and recognized which would be impossible by the naked eye. Besides this quality, usage of digital image processing algorithms can drastically reduce the time needed for analyzing them. Previously named advantages represent some of the main reasons for widespread usage of digital images in various areas, especially in medicine.

Since human body represents a complex set of different types of tissues, bones, liquids, etc. it is necessary to use various sources to capture all of them, e.g. X-ray is used for capturing bones, MRI for soft tissues, etc. Medical digital image processing represents an active research field that consists of a wide range of topics since each type of images and each disease has to be analyzed separately. In the literature numerous papers deal with medical image processing methods and they proposed various approaches for problems such as abnormality detection [1], segmentation [2], registration [3], compression [4], etc.

Medical digital images can be obtained by microscope and they are very important for detecting different infections [5], liver diseases [6], cancers [7,8], etc. Due to the fact that all named diseases and many others manifest rather differently, it is a common practice of researchers to focus on the detection and recognition of one of them or a smaller group of anomalies with similar characteristics. One of the diseases that can be detected by processing and analyzing microscope medical digital images is leukemia and it represents an active research topic [9–11].

Leukemia or blood cancer is manifesting by a high number of immature white blood cells that are also called blasts. There are four main types of leukemia: acute myeloid leukemia (AML), chronic myeloid leukemia (CML), acute lymphocytic leukemia (ALL) and chronic lymphocytic leukemia (CLL) [12]. The main difference between these types is the rate of progression and the place where it develops. In this paper, we focused on the detection of ALL in microscope images. ALL is a type of leukemia where blood marrow starts to produce abnormal, i.e. not completely formed, white cells that cannot fight infections which is their main purpose. The number of abnormal (leukemia) cells or blasts rapidly grows and they spread to other organs and tissues such as brain and liver. Early diagnosis of ALL is crucial for the patient's recovery and treatment determination.

In this paper we propose a method for classification of normal white blood cells and blasts. Shape and texture features are used for describing cells that were extracted by morphological operations in the preprocessing step. Selected features represent input vector for support vector machine that is used for classifying cells as a normal or blast.

2   Literature Review

Automatic detection of leukemia, especially ALL, is an active research topic and numerous methods were proposed in the recent years. Usual steps in these methods include preprocessing step where the white blood cells are extracted from the microscopy image followed by the feature extraction step. Features used for describing blood cells are color, shape and/or texture based. When appropriate set of features is chosen, the final step is classification of extracted cells based on that features. In this step different classifiers can be used and some of the most common are naive Bayesian, K-nearest neighbor, artificial neural networks, support vector machine, etc.

In [13] computer-aided diagnostic method for ALL detection. Automated detection and recognition of blasts was achieved by using morphological, color and texture features of binary, gray and color image. Some of the features that were used are: nucleus and cell size, shape, nucleus/cytoplasm ration, couture signature, gray level co-occurrence matrix, wavelet coefficients and many others. Extracted features were used for ensemble classifier that showed higher accuracy comparing to other classifiers such as naive Bayesian, K-nearest neighbor, radial basis functional network, etc.

Another automatic ALL detection method based on different color, shape and texture features were proposed in [14]. Rather complex set of features was extracted, i.e. 131 different descriptors: 30 shape, 21 color descriptors and 80 texture features, but only 50 of them were used as input vector for support vector machine. Comparing to Naive Bayes classifier and k-nearest neighbor algorithm, the proposed method achieved better results, i.e. higher classification accuracy.

On contrary to rather complex features that were used in [13] and [14], in [15] white blood cell classification method based only on three shape features was proposed. K-nearest neighbor algorithm was used to distinguish normal white blood cells and blasts based on area, perimeter and circularity. Even though it is rather simple method it achieved rather high classification accuracy.

The better results compared to [15] were obtained by the method proposed in [16] where support vector machine was used as classifier. Besides different classifier, larger feature set was used. Features that were used for describing previously extracted white blood cells included 11 features obtained from gray level co-occurrence matrix and 13 shape features.

In [17] k-means clustering algorithm was used for white blood cell segmentation. After the segmentation, color, shape, texture and statistical features were extracted and cells were classified by support vector machine.

Another method for leukemia detection based on k-means and morphological features was proposed in [18]. The proposed method consisted of three steps: contrast enhancement with a goal to emphasize the nuclei done by addition and subtraction operations, morphological segmentation that searched for the nuclei edges and removed normal blood cells and fuzzy k-means detection of leukemia. Features used by fuzzy k-means were texture, geometry, color and statistical features.

In [19], random forest was used for blood cell classification. In order to select features used by random forest marker-based segmentation and gray level co-occurrence matrix were used. Number of the extracted features was reduced by probabilistic principal component analysis.

Features used by many classifiers was proposed in [20]. The best results were achieved with kNN classifier. Preprocessing step included transformation into CMYK color model, image enhancement and background removal. Microscope images were enhanced by histogram equalization and segmentation was done by Zack thresholding technique. Color, texture and shape features were extracted from each cell and they were scaled and after normalized by z-score and min-max methods.

3   Problem Description

Automated ALL detection in microscope digital images represents rather complex problem and all mentioned steps (preprocessing, feature extraction and classification) should be carefully analyzed and chosen. Based on the state-of-the-art methods and also hematologists procedures it is clear that various factors need to be considered when analyzing blood cells in order to obtain a good classification of normal cells and blasts. Example of healthy and abnormal (blasts) white blood cells from the used standard benchmark dataset of microscope images, ALL-IDB2 [21], are shown in Fig. 1.

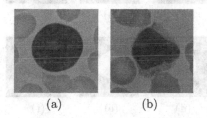

(a)   (b)

Fig. 1. Example of white blood cells from ALL-IDB2 database (a) normal and (b) blast

Normal white blood cells, i.e. fully formed cells, usually have nuclei eccentric in location, a small amount of cytoplasm and regular circle shape. On the other hand, blasts have an irregular shape, not centered nuclei, a larger amount of cytoplasm and a different texture than the normal cell. Because of these differences, it can be assumed that shape and texture descriptors can be the proper features for blast detection.

4   Our Proposed Method

The proposed computer-aided diagnostic systems for ALL detection contains three steps: segmentation where lymphocytes (white blood cells) are extracted from the microscope blood image, feature extraction where shape and texture descriptors of the extracted cells are chosen and the last step is classification.

The first step in ALL detection is lymphocyte extraction. Segmentation was performed in HSI color space because differences between white blood cells and the rest of the microscope blood image are more visible than in RGB color space. Intensity cannot distinguish different types of blood cells thus it will not be used. Normal lymphocyte can be detected with both, hue and saturation component, but in the case of blast, the best segmentation can be obtained by combining these two components.

For segmentation, i.e lymphocyte extraction, we empirically determined threshold values for both, hue and saturation components to be 0.3 (both components are in the range [0,1]). Thresholding on the hue component will result by extracting the complete cell while after applying a threshold on saturation nucleus will be extracted. For more precise nucleus and cell detection, after the segmentation, morphological operation opening with mask size 6×6 was performed. Once that nuclei and cells are determined, the cytoplasm can be obtained by removing the nucleus from the cell. Example of the segmentation is presented in Fig. 2.

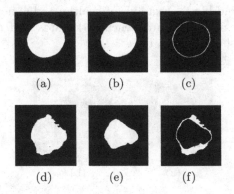

(a)   (b)   (c)

(d)   (e)   (f)

Fig. 2. (a), (d) cell, (b), (e) nuclei and (c), (f) cytoplasm

4.1 Feature Extraction

Hematologists differentiate normal white blood cells from blasts based on shape, color, and texture. Finding good descriptors for these three is crucial for making a good computer-aided diagnostic system. Color features are already used in the segmentation step where nucleus, cell, and cytoplasm were extracted based on the hue and saturation. It has been proven that shape features are most important for detecting blasts [14].

In this paper we included several shape features such as area, ratio of areas of cytoplasm to nucleus and ratio of areas of the nucleus to cell, perimeter, and circularity. The area represents number of pixels in the cell while the perimeter is the maximal distance between the adjoining pair of pixels on the border of the nucleus. Circularity measures the roundness of the nucleus and it is an important feature since blasts are not rounded as normal cells. Circularity is a function of the perimeter and the area. Ratios of the areas of cytoplasm to nucleus and nucleus to the cell are used since blasts are not fully formed white blood cells and that can be determined based on these two values.

Besides shape features we used uniform local binary pattern (LBP) as texture descriptor. LBP is a rather simple and computationally inexpensive yet powerful texture description. Simple LBP version is not rotation invariant which is desirable for the considered problem. In order to overcome this problem, various LBP modifications were presented in the past and one of them is uniform LBP which reduces the number of patterns that are considered as different. All patterns with 2 or more transitions from 0 to 1 or vice verse are considered as the same pattern. In the case of 8-neighborhood which is used in this paper, 256 different patterns are reduced to 59 different texture patterns. We created a histogram that represents the frequency of each pattern and extracted different features such as mean, standard deviation, skewness, kurtosis, energy and entropy. These six numerical values were used along with the previously described shape features as input vectors for the classifier.

4.2 Classification

In this paper we used a support vector machine (SVM) as a classifier. SVM searches for the optimal hyperplane that separates instances from two classes. It uses kernel function to map input data into a space with higher dimension and in that way makes them linearly separable. Kernel function used in this paper is radial biases function (RBF) as one of the most used kernel function. RBF has one free parameter that needs to be tuned for optimal classification, parameter γ. In order to achieve the best possible results, i.e. the highest classification accuracy, it is necessary to find the optimal value for this parameter for the considered classification problem.

Another parameter of the SVM is the soft margin parameter C that determines the tolerance for misclassified instances which is necessary for real life data classification due to the outliers and errors.

Instead of finding the optimal values for each parameter, C and γ separately, the pair of values should be considered. SVM parameters tuning is a hard optimization problem and exhaustive search is impossible. In order to choose the best configuration we used the bare bone fireworks algorithm (BBFWA) [22]. The BBFWA is a recent and simplified version of the fireworks algorithm [23] proposed in 2018 by Li and Tan. FWA is originally proposed in 2010 and since than it has been applied to numerous problems such as image compression [24], maximal coverage location problem [25, 26], data clustering [27], etc. One of FWA versions, enhanced FWA [28] was tested for SVM parameters tuning in [29].

In BBFWA only the best solution is saved through generations and exploration and exploitation is done by controlling the size of the search space around the best solution where the new solution will be randomly generated. SVM was trained to classify input data, i.e. vector with shape and texture features, into one of two classes: normal white blood cell or blast.

In order to analyze the classification accuracy, we used the basic metrics for machine learning algorithms such as sensitivity, specificity and accuracy that were also used in [30] so the fair comparison is provided. Confusion matrix should be created first so that these metrics can be calculated. Confusion matrix contains data about true positive (TP), true negative (TN), false positive (FP) and false negative (FN) classified data. If we consider class where blasts belong in positive class and normal white cells are considered as a negative class, then TP represents the number of correctly classified blasts while FN is the number of blasts classified as normal cells and similarly for TN and FN. After determining the confusion matrix, sensitivity and specificity are calculated. Sensitivity, which is also called the true positive rate, is used to express the proportion of the correctly identified abnormal white blood cells while the specificity measures the ratio of correctly detected normal blood cells to the total number of them.

5   Experimental Results

The method proposed for automatic ALL detection was tested on Intel® Core™ i7-3770K CPU at 4 GHz, 8 GB RAM, Windows 10 Professional OS computer and it was implemented in Matlab R2016b. For classification we used support vector machine from the LIBSVM 3.21 toolbox [31].

In order to test our proposed method and fairly compare it to other state-of-the-art methods, we organized experiments same as in [30]. We used the standard benchmark dataset ALL-IDB [21], and more specifically, we used ALL-IDB2 dataset where for training we used 50 blast images and 50 normal white blood cell images and the obtained SVM model was tested on the rest of the set that has 66 blast and 76 normal cell images.

Our proposed method was compared to the method proposed in [30]. A method based on shape features and DCT coefficients was proposed in [30]. The first step of that method was noise reduction by Weiner filter along with the contrast enhancement. The second step was segmentation process by watershed segmentation. DCT coefficients were calculated for each segmented cell and SVM was used for classification. The proposed method was compared to Naive Bayes classifier (NC), k-nearest neighbors (KNN) and back propagation neural network (BPNN) and we included these results in this paper.

Compared to the method proposed in [30], our method uses less features as input vector for the classifier. Another difference is that we did not include any image enhancement before extracting the blood cells. All these makes our proposed method simpler than the method proposed in [30].

Comparison between the results presented in [30] and the results obtained by our proposed method is shown in Table 1. The method proposed in [30] is named DCT. Better results are printed in bold.

As it can be seen, our proposed method achieved better accuracy compared to all four approaches presented in [30]. Considering the fact that we did not

Table 1. Comparison of the results obtained by method proposed in [30] and our proposed method

	NB	KNN	BPNN	DCT	SVM
Sensitivity	88.70	**98.38**	80.64	84.67	94.21
Specificity	75.38	69.23	37.67	**94.61**	89.37
Accuracy	81.66	83.46	58.70	89.76	**91.84**

include image enhancement in the preprocessing step and that the number of features is smaller, it can be assumed that the proposed method can be even more improved while staying less or equally complex then the method in [30].

Even though the accuracy of the proposed method is larger compared to the method proposed in [30] (91.84% compared to 89.76%), the sensitivity and specificity are not uniformly better comparing to other methods. The best sensitivity (correctly recognized blasts) was obtained with the features proposed in [30] and k-nearest neighbors as a classifier, 98.38% while with the our proposed algorithm it was 94.21%. The problem with KNN method is that numerous healthy blood cells very not recognized correctly. It can be concluded that the KNN method in most cases classifies cells as blasts which lead to the high sensitivity but rather low specificity.

In the case of specificity, the highest value was achieved with DCT, the method proposed in [30], 94.61% while our proposed algorithm had 89.34%. Since the sensitivity achieved by the method presented in [30] was low, the overall accuracy was worse than the accuracy obtained by our proposed method. The worst results were achieved when back propagation neural networks were used. The sensitivity was 80.64% while the specificity was only 37.67%. The overall accuracy was 58.70%. Neural networks has many parameters to be set and the quality of the classification highly depends on them. Usage of inappropriate parameters can lead to the poor results such the one presented in [30].

6 Conclusion

In this paper we proposed a method based on shape, color and texture features for detecting blasts in microscope blood images with aim to detect acute lymphoblastic leukemia. We used local binary pattern as texture descriptor while shape of each cell was presented by area, ration of area of cytoplasm to nucleus and ratio of area of nucleus to cell, perimeter and circularity. We used support vector machine, where parameters are determined by the bare bone fireworks algorithm, for classifying the extracted white blood cells. Based on the results of the comparative analysis, we can conclude that the proposed method is suitable for ALL detection in microscope images. In the future work we can adjust the proposed method for detecting different leukemia types, test with larger benchmark sets and compare the method to other state-of-the-art methods that provide detailed analysis of the results.

References

1. Stojak, A., Tuba, E., Tuba, M.: Framework for abnormality detection in magnetic resonance brain images. In: 24th Telecommunications Forum (TELFOR), pp. 1–4. IEEE (2016)
2. Tuba, E., Mrkela, L., Tuba, M.: Retinal blood vessel segmentation by support vector machine classification. In: 27th International Conference Radioelektronika (RADIOELEKTRONIKA), pp. 1–6. IEEE (2017)
3. Tuba, E., Tuba, M., Dolicanin, E.: Adjusted fireworks algorithm applied to retinal image registration. Stud. Inform. Control 26(1), 33–42 (2017)
4. Tuba, E., Jovanovic, R., Beko, M., Tallón-Ballesteros, A.J., Tuba, M.: Bare bones fireworks algorithm for medical image compression. In: Yin, H., Camacho, D., Novais, P., Tallón-Ballesteros, A.J. (eds.) IDEAL 2018, Part II. LNCS, vol. 11315, pp. 262–270. Springer, Cham (2018). https://doi.org/10.1007/978-3-030-03496-2_29
5. Pirnstill, C.W., Coté, G.L.: Malaria diagnosis using a mobile phone polarized microscope. Sci. Rep. 5, 13368 (2015)
6. Tao, Z., et al.: Early tumor detection afforded by in vivo imaging of near-infrared II fluorescence. Biomaterials 134, 202–215 (2017)
7. McCann, M.T., Ozolek, J.A., Castro, C.A., Parvin, B., Kovacevic, J.: Automated histology analysis: opportunities for signal processing. IEEE Signal Process. Mag. 32(1), 78–87 (2015)
8. Xing, F., Yang, L.: Robust nucleus/cell detection and segmentation in digital pathology and microscopy images: a comprehensive review. IEEE Rev. Biomed. Eng. 9, 234–263 (2016)
9. Bhattacharjee, R., Saini, L.M.: Detection of acute lymphoblastic leukemia using watershed transformation technique. In: International Conference on Signal Processing, Computing and Control, pp. 383–386. IEEE (2015)
10. Shankar, V., Deshpande, M.M., Chaitra, N., Aditi, S.: Automatic detection of acute lymphoblasitc leukemia using image processing. In: International Conference on Advances in Computer Applications, pp. 186–189. IEEE (2016)
11. Amin, M.M., Kermani, S., Talebi, A., Oghli, M.G.: Recognition of acute lymphoblastic leukemia cells in microscopic images using k-means clustering and support vector machine classifier. J. Med. Signals Sens. 5(1), 49 (2015)
12. Kumar, A., Shaik, F., Abdul Rahim, B., Sravan Kumar, D.: Image enhancement of leukemia microscopic images. In: Signal and Image Processing in Medical Applications. SAST, pp. 17–37. Springer, Singapore (2016). https://doi.org/10.1007/978-981-10-0690-6_4
13. Mohapatra, S., Patra, D., Satpathy, S.: An ensemble classifier system for early diagnosis of acute lymphoblastic leukemia in blood microscopic images. Neural Comput. Appl. 24(7–8), 1887–1904 (2014)
14. Putzu, L., Caocci, G., Di Ruberto, C.: Leucocyte classification for leukaemia detection using image processing techniques. Artif. Intell. Med. 62(3), 179–191 (2014)
15. Joshi, M.D., Karode, A.H., Suralkar, S.: White blood cells segmentation and classification to detect acute leukemia. Int. J. Emerg. Trends Technol. Comput. Sci. 2(3), 147–151 (2013)
16. Rawat, J., Singh, A., Bhadauria, H., Virmani, J.: Computer aided diagnostic system for detection of leukemia using microscopic images. Procedia Comput. Sci. 70, 748–756 (2015)

17. Patel, N., Mishra, A.: Automated leukaemia detection using microscopic images. Procedia Comput. Sci. **58**, 635–642 (2015)
18. Viswanathan, P.: Fuzzy C means detection of leukemia based on morphological contour segmentation. Procedia Comput. Sci. **58**, 84–90 (2015)
19. Mishra, S., Majhi, B., Sa, P.K., Sharma, L.: Gray level co-occurrence matrix and random forest based acute lymphoblastic leukemia detection. Biomed. Signal Process. Control **33**, 272–280 (2017)
20. Abdeldaim, A.M., Sahlol, A.T., Elhoseny, M., Hassanien, A.E.: Computer-aided acute lymphoblastic leukemia diagnosis system based on image analysis. In: Hassanien, A.E., Oliva, D.A. (eds.) Advances in Soft Computing and Machine Learning in Image Processing. SCI, vol. 730, pp. 131–147. Springer, Cham (2018). https://doi.org/10.1007/978-3-319-63754-9_7
21. Labati, R.D., Piuri, V., Scotti, F.: All-IDB: the acute lymphoblastic leukemia image database for image processing. In: 18th IEEE International Conference on Image Processing (ICIP), pp. 2045–2048. IEEE (2011)
22. Li, J., Tan, Y.: The bare bones fireworks algorithm: a minimalist global optimizer. Appl. Soft Comput. **62**, 454–462 (2018)
23. Tan, Y., Zhu, Y.: Fireworks algorithm for optimization. In: Tan, Y., Shi, Y., Tan, K.C. (eds.) ICSI 2010, Part I. LNCS, vol. 6145, pp. 355–364. Springer, Heidelberg (2010). https://doi.org/10.1007/978-3-642-13495-1_44
24. Tuba, E., Tuba, M., Simian, D., Jovanovic, R.: JPEG quantization table optimization by guided fireworks algorithm. In: Brimkov, V.E., Barneva, R.P. (eds.) IWCIA 2017. LNCS, vol. 10256, pp. 294–307. Springer, Cham (2017). https://doi.org/10.1007/978-3-319-59108-7_23
25. Tuba, E., Dolicanin, E., Tuba, M.: Guided fireworks algorithm applied to the maximal covering location problem. In: Tan, Y., Takagi, H., Shi, Y. (eds.) ICSI 2017, Part I. LNCS, vol. 10385, pp. 501–508. Springer, Cham (2017). https://doi.org/10.1007/978-3-319-61824-1_55
26. Tuba, E., Tuba, M., Simian, D.: Wireless sensor network coverage problem using modified fireworks algorithm. In: 2016 International Wireless Communications and Mobile Computing Conference (IWCMC), pp. 696–701. IEEE (2016)
27. Tuba, E., Jovanovic, R., Hrosik, R.C., Alihodzic, A., Tuba, M.: Web intelligence data clustering by bare bone fireworks algorithm combined with k-means. In: Proceedings of the 8th International Conference on Web Intelligence, Mining and Semantics, p. 7. ACM (2018)
28. Zheng, S., Janecek, A., Tan, Y.: Enhanced fireworks algorithm. In: IEEE Congress on Evolutionary Computation, pp. 2069–2077. IEEE, June 2013
29. Tuba, E., Ribic, I., Capor-Hrosik, R., Tuba, M.: Support vector machine optimized by elephant herding algorithm for erythemato-squamous diseases detection. Procedia Comput. Sci. **122**, 916–923 (2017)
30. Mishra, S., Sharma, L., Majhi, B., Sa, P.K.: Microscopic image classification using DCT for the detection of Acute Lymphoblastic Leukemia (ALL). In: Raman, B., Kumar, S., Roy, P.P., Sen, D. (eds.) Proceedings of International Conference on Computer Vision and Image Processing. AISC, vol. 459, pp. 171–180. Springer, Singapore (2017). https://doi.org/10.1007/978-981-10-2104-6_16
31. Chang, C.-C., Lin, C.-J.: LIBSVM: a library for support vector machines. ACM Trans. Intell. Syst. Technol. **2**, 27:1–27:27 (2011)

Novel Algorithm for Blind Classification of Space-Time Block Codes in Cognitive Radio

Wenjun Yan$^{(\boxtimes)}$, Qing Ling, and Limin Zhang

Naval Aviation University, Yantai 264001, China
wj_yan@foxmail.com

Abstract. The blind classification of space-time block codes (STBCs) is a key research issue related to cognitive radio. There have been numerous studies attempting to classify STBCs, but the blind classification of STBCs with transmission impairments merits further research. The novel blind classification algorithm proposed in this paper exploits the fourth-order cyclostationarity of STBCs to classify them with a single receiver antenna in the presence of transmission impairments. The proposed algorithm relies on the fourth-order cyclic moment as a discriminating feature and employs the distance between adjacent spectral lines to classify the transmitted STBCs. As opposed to other methods, this algorithm does not require a priori information regarding the modulation scheme, channel coefficients, or noise power; consequently, it is very well-suited to non-cooperative scenarios. According to rough estimation of symbol duration and carrier frequency offset, the distance between adjacent spectral lines remains almost the same with value dependent on the transmitted STBCs. Simulations indicate that the proposed method performs well even at low signal-to-noise ratios (SNRs).

Keywords: Cognitive radio · Blind classification ·
Transmission impairments · Fourth-order cyclic moment ·
Non-cooperative scenarios

1 Introduction

In cognitive radio, the blind classification of signal parameters is an intermediate step between signal detection and signal decoding/demodulation. Signal parameters include modulation information, channel coding information and code parameters. In recent years, blind classification of signal parameters, an important task of intelligent receivers, has been extended to both military applications and commercial applications, such as interference identification, signal confirmation, radio surveillance and spectrum monitoring.

Most previous work on blind signal classification has focused on single-input single-output (SISO) scenarios [1,2]. The advent and rapid development of multi-input multi-output (MIMO) techniques, however, has added an extra layer of

© Springer Nature Switzerland AG 2019
Y. Tan et al. (Eds.): ICSI 2019, LNCS 11656, pp. 152–163, 2019.
https://doi.org/10.1007/978-3-030-26354-6_15

complexity to this process. These multiple antenna systems introduce new and challenging signal classification problems such as estimating the quantity of transmit antennas and space-time block code (STBC).

STBC is a set of practical signal design techniques aimed at obtaining the theoretical capacity of MIMO channel information [3]. Integrating STBCs into MIMO communication systems is a promising approach to signal classification problems; MIMO-STBC communication systems have already been standardized in IEEE 802.16e and IEEE 802.11n, and are commonly considered an ideal technology for the next generation of wireless communication. The blind classification of STBCs have become a popular research issue in non-cooperative MIMO communication scenarios accordingly. The blind classification of STBC can be divided into four categories: Maximum likelihood [4,5], second-order statistics [6–11], cyclostationarity-based [12 15] and fourth-order statistics [16–18]. Maximum likelihood algorithms employ the maximum likelihood criterion to find optimum solutions, however, they require a priori information such as channel coefficients, modulation information, carrier frequency offset, and carrier phase. The computational complexity is too high for higher-order modulation, as well [4,5]. The space-time second-order correlation function is used as a discriminating feature to classify the received signals with multiple receiver antennas [6–9], while the cyclostationarity features of received signals are exploited to classify of STBCs in single or multiple receiver antenna scenarios [12–15]. The fourth-order statistics of received signals are used as discriminating signal features to classify the STBCs with a single antenna [16–18]. Most of the previous studies in this field [5–19] were conducted with relatively little information regarding carrier phase, frequency offset, Doppler shift, or data rate, apart from a study by Marey [13]. In addition, Shi found that the receiver requires optimum sampling time and knowledge of channel parameters [12]. Marey pointed out that the second-order time-varying correlation function can not provide a discriminating feature when a single receiver antenna is available [13]. In fact, the correlation function does not have any cycle frequency that can provide a discriminating feature for STBC signals; there are existing classifiers, however, one classifier was discussed in studies by Marey [8] and Shi [12], but applies only to multiple received antennas. Another classifier appears in [10], but for Alamouti (AL) code and spatial multiplexing (SM). These two classifiers are not applicable to a single receiver antenna with different STBC candidates, however, and since these constraints are unrealistic in practice, further research is needed to solve the problem of classifying STBCs with a single receiver affected by transmission impairments.

In this paper, we established and analyzed an STBC classification algorithm based on the fourth-order cyclic moment with a single receiver antenna in the presence of transmission impairments over frequency-flat channels. Our algorithm does not require a priori modulation scheme, channel coefficient, or noise power information, making it well-suited to non-cooperative scenarios. Moreover, the distance test proposed here can provide a lower computational complexity than the statistical test for the presence of fourth-order cyclostationarity [13].

The distance between adjacent spectral lines remains almost the same with value dependent on transmitted STBCs. Taken together, the results discussed below suggest that ours is a feasible and effective recognition algorithm.

The rest of this paper is organized as follows: Sect. 2 describes the signal model and assumptions, and the derivation of the fourth-order cyclic moment of STBCs is introduced in Sect. 3. Section 4 describes the proposed STBC classification algorithm. Simulation results are provided in Sect. 5, and conclusions are drawn in Sect. 6.

2   Signal Model and Assumptions

2.1   Linear STBC Model

The N transmitted symbols can be divided into blocks with length of N_s. Each block of N_s modulated symbols is encoded to generate N_t parallel signal sequences of length L. In most cases, STBCs can be interpreted as a single map, this changes a set of N_s complex symbols into a $N_t \times L$ matrix X. The mapping can be expressed as follows:

$$\{s_1, \dots s_{N_s}\} \longrightarrow X. \tag{1}$$

Theoretically, the form of the map is not restricted. STBCs can be divided into two categories: Linear STBCs and non-linear STBCs. (Most STBCs are linear.)

The matrix X can be expressed as follows:

$$X = \sum_{n=1}^{N_s} (\bar{s}_n A_n + i\tilde{s}_n B_n). \tag{2}$$

where $\bar{s}_n$ and $\tilde{s}_n$ denote the real and imaginary parts of the transmitted symbol s_n, respectively. A_n and B_n form an coding matrix set. For example, the coding matrix A_n and B_n for Alamouti coding is

$$A_1 = \begin{bmatrix} 1 & 0 \\ 0 & -1 \end{bmatrix}, A_2 = \begin{bmatrix} 0 & 1 \\ 1 & 0 \end{bmatrix}, B_1 = \begin{bmatrix} 1 & 0 \\ 0 & 1 \end{bmatrix}, B_2 = \begin{bmatrix} 0 & -1 \\ 1 & 0 \end{bmatrix}$$

For any communication system with linear STBCs, it is reasonable to assume that the symbols belonging to the same complex linear modulation are independent and identically distributed (i.i.d) random variables. The real and imaginary parts of the transmitted symbols in complex linear modulation are also i.i.d. The information-bearing symbols $\{x_z\}_{z=-\infty}^{\infty}$ are drawn from a finite alphabet Q; the symbols to be transmitted are sent in a block of N_s through N_t parallel transmit antennas in L time slots. The space-time block encoder generates an $N_t \times L$ block matrix. The bth transmit block can be denoted $X_b = [x_{b,0}, x_{b,1}, \dots, x_{b,N_s-1}]$. Here, we denote the bth code matrix by $C(X_b)$. The code matrices for SM, AL, OSTBC-3/4 coding (ST3), and OSTBC-1/2 coding (ST4) are available in the Appendix.

2.2   Signal Model with Transmission Impairments

Considering a wireless communication system with N_t transmit antennas and a single receiver antenna, the received signal can be expressed as

$$r(t) = y^\lambda(t)e^{j2\pi(\Delta f_e t + \theta_0 + \varphi(t))} + v(t). \tag{3}$$

where j refers to imaginary unit, Δf_e refers to the residual carrier frequency offset, the carrier phase noise is denoted by $\varphi(t)$, and θ_0 is the carrier phase offset. $v(t)$ refers to the zero-mean Gaussian white noise, $y^\lambda(t)$ is the signal without transmission impairments and noise, and $\lambda \in \{SM, AL, ST3, ST4\}$. $y^\lambda(t)$ can be expressed as follows:

$$y^\lambda(t) = \sum_{l=1}^{L}\sum_{i=1}^{N_t} h_i(t) \sum_{k=-\infty, k\in nL}^{\infty} C_{i,l}(X_b)g_{T,\varepsilon}^{k,l-1}(t). \tag{4}$$

where $h_i(t)$ refers to the channel coefficient between the i transmitted antenna and received antenna. $g_{T,\varepsilon}^{k,l-1}(t)$ can be expressed as $g(t - (k + l - 1)T + \varepsilon)$. $g(t)$ is the impulse response of the cascaded transmitted and received filters, T refers to the symbol period, and ε is the timing delay between the receiver and transmitter. $C_{i,l}(X_b)$ represents the code matrix element, which lies in array i^{th} and column l^{th} in code matrix $C(X_b)$, with $0 < i \leq N_t$ and $0 < l \leq L$, i and l take integer values.

2.3   Main Assumptions

In this study, the following conditions are assumed to hold.

AS1) T is known in advance.

AS2) ASK and BPSK signals are excluded.

AS3) Channel gains are unknown deterministic parameters.

AS4) The transmitted signal is uncorrelated with noise: $E\{y^\lambda(t)v(t+\tau)\} = 0$, $\forall\lambda \in \{SM, AL, ST3, ST4\}$, and $\tau \in R$ with R as the set of real numbers.

AS5) Data symbols are uncorrelated with each other: $E\{x_z x_z'\} = 0$, $E\{x_z x_{z'}^*\} = \sigma_s^2\delta_{zz'}$, $\forall x_z$, $x_z' \in Q$, where σ_s^2 is the transmitted signal power, $\delta_{zz'}$ is the Kronecker delta, and $E[.]$ and $*$ indicate statistical expression and complex conjugate, respectively.

3   Fourth-Order Cyclic Moment of STBCs

In this section, the expression of fourth-order cyclic moment is deduced in order to identify the characteristic parameters able to blindly classify STBCs with transmission impairments in a non-cooperative scenario.

3.1   Principles

A complex valued random process is said to have nth-order cyclostationarity if any of its nth-order time-varying moments/cumulants is a periodic function of time. In such a case, the nth-order time-varying moments/cumulants are expressed as a Fourier series, the coefficients of which are referred to as the nth-order cyclic moments/cumulant; its non-zero frequencies are called cycle frequencies. The time-varying kth order moment $m_{k,r}(t;\tau)$, $\tau \triangleq (\tau_1, \tau_2, \ldots, \tau_{k-1})$ of the process $r(t)$ can be defined accordingly as a Fourier expansion of the kth cyclic moment M_{kr} as follows [20]:

$$m_{k,r}(t;\tau) = E\{r(t)r(t+\tau_1)\ldots r(t+\tau_{k-1})\},$$

$$M_{k,r}(\eta,\tau) = \lim_{T\to\infty} \frac{1}{T} \sum_{t=0}^{T-1} m_{k,r}(t;\tau)e^{-j\eta t}. \tag{5}$$

where η denote a cycle frequency.

3.2   Derivations of Fourth-Order of Cyclic Moment for STBCs

(1) SM
Based on (3) and (4) and the information presented in Sect. 3.1, the fourth-order cyclic moment of SM is:

$$m^{SM}(t,\tau) = 0. \tag{6}$$

Therefore, SM does not have any cycle frequency.

(2) AL
Again, based on (3) and (4) and the discussion in Sect. 3.1, the fourth-order cyclic moment for Alamouti STBC can be expressed as follows:

$$m^{AL}(t;\tau) = E[r(t)r(t+\tau)r(t)r(t+\tau)]$$
$$= a(t,\tau)b(t,\tau). \tag{7}$$

where

$$a(t,\tau) = \frac{1}{2T}\sigma_s^4 e^{j\theta(t,\tau)}[h_1^2(t)h_2^2(t+\tau) + h_2^2(t)h_1^2(t+\tau)]. \tag{8}$$

$$b(t,\tau) = \sum_{k=-\infty, k\in nL}^{\infty} (g_{T,\epsilon}^{k,0}(t)g_{T,\epsilon}^{k,1}(t+\tau))^2. \tag{9}$$

$$\theta(t,\tau) = 8\pi\Delta f_e t + 4\pi\Delta f_e \tau + 8\phi_0 + 4\varphi(t) + 4\varphi(t+\tau). \tag{10}$$

where h_i represents the channel coefficient between the i transmitted antenna and received antenna and τ represents the delay value. (The other symbols in (8)–(10) were explained in Sect. 2.2). $b(t,\tau)$ is a periodic function in t with period $2T$. (7) can be rewritten with periodic function properties as follows:

$$m^{AL}(t,\tau) = a(t,\tau)[(g_{T,\epsilon}^{0,0}(t)g_{T,\epsilon}^{0,1}(t+\tau))^2] \otimes \sum_{k=-\infty, k\in nL}^{\infty} \delta(t-kT). \tag{11}$$

where $\otimes$ denotes convolution. The Fourier transform of (11) is:

$$M^{AL}(\eta,\tau) = A(\eta,\tau) \otimes [B(\eta,\tau) \sum_{k=-\infty}^{\infty} \delta(\eta - \frac{k}{LT})]. \tag{12}$$

$$B(\eta,\tau) = FFT[(g_{T,\epsilon}^{0,0}(t)g_{T,\epsilon}^{0,1}(t+\tau))^2]. \tag{13}$$

where $A(\eta,\tau)$ is the Fourier transform of $a(t,\tau)$. When the code is AL, L is equal to 2.

(3) ST3 and ST4
Since the derivation of ST3 and ST4 is same to AL, derivation process will not be listed here.

For ST3, the Fourier transform of the fourth-order cyclic moment is denoted as:

$$M^{ST3}(\eta.\tau) = \sum_{i=1}^{6} C_i(\eta,\tau) \otimes [F_i(\eta,\tau) \sum_{k=-\infty}^{\infty} \delta(\eta - \frac{k}{LT})]. \tag{14}$$

Where $F_i(\eta,\tau)$ represent FFT of received symbols like (9).

For ST4, the Fourier transform of the fourth-order cyclic moment is denoted as:

$$M^{ST4}(\eta,\tau) = Z_i(\eta,\tau) \otimes [M_{i,j}(\eta,\tau) \sum_{k=\infty}^{\infty} \delta(\eta - \frac{k}{LT})]. \tag{15}$$

When the code is ST4, L is equal to 8. $Z_i(\eta,\tau)$ and $M_{i,j}(\eta,\tau)$ are the Fourier transforms of $z_i(t,\tau)$ and $m_{i,j}(t,\tau)$, respectively.

4 Proposed STBC Classification Algorithm Based on Fourth-Order Cyclic Moment

The impact of the transmission impairments on $M(\eta,\tau)$ can be analyzed based on the expressions provided in Sect. 3.2. Based on (7)–(13), $M(\eta,\tau)$ is comprised of the convolution of $B(\eta,\tau)$ and $A(\eta,\tau)$. For $B(\eta,\tau)$, ϵ gives rise to a phase rotation of $M(\eta,\tau)$ but does not change the magnitude and location of the cyclical frequencies of $M(\eta,\tau)$. For $A(\eta,\tau)$, the effect of θ_0 is the same as that of ϵ. Δf_e not only causes a phase rotation but also a frequency shift $2\Delta f_e$. φ and $h(t)$ lead to two disruptive effects: (1) Destroying the magnitude and phase of the $M(\eta,\tau)$ and (2)introducing new frequency components between cycle frequencies.

In effect, due to the presence of Δf_e, ϵ, and θ_0 as well as the absence of phase noise and channel Doppler shift, $M^{AL}(\eta, \tau)$ has spectral lines only at $\{\frac{k}{2T} + 2\Delta f_e, k \in integer\}$ and the corresponding magnitudes are unaffected by these impairments.

4.1 Proposed Algorithm

Based on (6), (12), (14) and (15), $M^{SM}(\eta, \tau)$ does not exhibit peaks. $M^{AL}(\eta, \tau)$ does, however, at frequencies equal to integer multiples of $\frac{1}{2T}$ and delays $\pm T$; $M^{ST3}(\eta, \tau)$ does at frequencies equal to integer multiples of $\frac{1}{4T}$ and delays $\pm T$, $\pm 2T$, and $\pm 3T$, and $M^{ST4}(\eta, \tau)$ does at frequencies equal to integer multiples of $\frac{1}{8T}$ and delays $\pm T$, $\pm 2T$, ..., and $\pm 7T$.

The proposed algorithm can be summarized accordingly as follows.

Required signal pro-processing: Mean removal and T estimation.

Step 1: Calculate the $M(\eta, \tau)$ value of the received signals at delays $\pm T$, $\pm 2T$, $\pm 3T$, $\pm 4T$. If $M(\eta, \tau)$ exhibits peaks at frequencies equal to integer multiples of $\frac{1}{8T}$, the ST4 code is distinguished from the other STBCs.

Step 2: Calculate the $M(\eta, \tau)$ value of the received signals at delays $\pm T$, $\pm 2T$, $\pm 3T$. If $M(\eta, \tau)$ exhibits peaks at frequencies equal to integer multiples of $\frac{1}{4T}$, the ST3 code is distinguished from the other STBCs.

Step 3: Calculate the $M(\eta, \tau)$ value of the received signals at delays $\pm T$. If $M(\eta, \tau)$ exhibits peaks at frequencies equal to integer multiples of $\frac{1}{2T}$, the AL code is distinguished from SM.

4.2 Test for the Presence of Cyclostationarity

Most second-order cyclostationarity can be determined via binary hypothesis testing [21,22], but the computational complexity of testing for fourth-order cyclostationarity is impractically high. In this study, the presence of fourth-order cyclostationarity was determined according to the distance between $\eta = 0$ and a peak near $\eta = 0$. $M^{ST4}(\eta, \tau)$, as mentioned above, exhibits peaks at cycle frequencies equal to integer multiples of $\frac{1}{8T}$ and delays $\pm 4T$, but other STBCs do not exhibit peaks; to this effect, if the distance between $\eta = 0$ and peak near $\eta = 0$ is equal to $\frac{1}{4T}$, ST4 is chosen. Secondly, as $M^{ST3}(\eta, \tau)$ exhibits peaks at cycle frequencies equal to integer multiples of $\frac{1}{4T}$ and delays $\pm 3T$ (and again, other STBCs do not). If the distance between $\eta = 0$ and the peak near $\eta = 0$ is equal to $\frac{1}{2T}$, ST3 is chosen. Finally, because $M^{AL}(\eta, \tau)$ exhibits peaks at cycle frequencies equal to integer multiples of $\frac{1}{2T}$ and delays $\pm T$ (but not other STBCs). If the distance between $\eta = 0$ and the peak near $\eta = 0$ is equal to $\frac{1}{T}$, AL is chosen. For a 1000 Monte Carlo trial, the distance $\hat{d}$ was calculated while the degree of confidence α was set to 0.99, SNR $= 10$ dB and $N = 4096$.

Step 1: Calculate the mean of the distance $\hat{d}$.

Step 2: The left border c_1 is equal to the mean of the distance $\hat{d}$ minus α; the right border c_2 is equal to the mean of the distance $\hat{d}$ plus α.

Step 3: If the experimental value $c_1 < \hat{d} < c_2$, AL is chosen, otherwise SM is chosen.

5 Simulation Results

5.1 Simulation Setup

One thousand Monte Carlo trials were performed to evaluate the performance of the proposed algorithm. SM, AL, ST3, and ST4 were under consideration throughout the simulation. The conditions for each Monte Carlo trial included quadrature phase shift keying (QPSK) modulation, $N = 4096$, and $\alpha = 0.99$. The channel was assumed to be a frequency-flat fading channel and was modeled as a zero-mean independent complex Gaussian random variable. The channel coefficients were set as constants during each observation period, and the over-sampling factor ρ was 8. The SNRs were defined as the ratio of the signal and noise powers at the output of the receiver filter. A raiser cosine filter with 0.35 roll-off factor was employed for spectral shaping. A Butterworth low-pass filter was used at the receiver side with bandwidth equal to the signal bandwidth. The time offset ϵ and phase offset θ_0 were set to be random variables uniformly distributed over $[0, T]$ and $[0, 2\pi]$, respectively, and the frequency offset Δf_e was set to $0.04/T$. The phase noise φ was set to zero originally. (Scenarios including channel Doppler shift and phase noise were also considered, as discussed separately in Sect. 5.6) Two performance measures, the average probability of correct classification, P_c, and the probability of correct classification, $p(\lambda|\lambda)$, were applied to the simulation as well.

The average probability of correct classification, (P_c), can be expressed as follows:

$$P_c = \frac{1}{4} \sum_{\lambda \in \Omega} p(\lambda|\lambda). \tag{16}$$

where, $\Omega = (SM, AL, ST3, ST4)$ and λ represents the estimated STBCs.

5.2 Magnitude of the Estimated $\hat{M}(\eta, \tau)$

The magnitudes of $\hat{M}(\eta, \tau)$ for STBCs are shown in Fig. 1, respectively. Where unlike the SM code, AL exhibits peaks at frequencies equal to integer multiples of $\frac{1}{2T}$ and delays $\pm T$. These results are consistent with the theoretical derivation (Sect. 3.2).

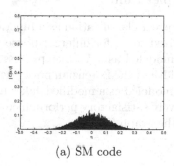
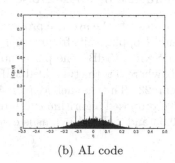

(a) SM code   (b) AL code

Fig. 1. Sample fourth-order cyclic moment as a function of η with delay vector $\tau = (0, T, 0, T)$

5.3   Influence of the Modulation Scheme

We have illustrated the behavior of the proposed algorithm for four complex modulation schemes: 16-quadrature amplitude modulation (QAM), 64-QAM, 16-phase shift keying (PSK) and QPSK as shown in Fig. 2. It follows that the performance of the proposed algorithm is not dependent on the modulation scheme used at the transmitter.

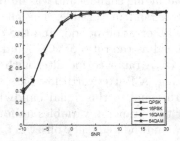   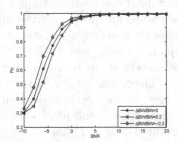

Fig. 2. Effect of the modulation on P_c.   **Fig. 3.** Effect of the bandwidth estimation on P_c

5.4   Influence of Bandwidth Estimation Error

Figure 3 presents the average probability of correct classification with respect to bandwidth estimation error, to which the proposed algorithm is relatively insensitive. As shown, the decreased noise resulting from a decrease in bandwidth only slightly affects the cyclostationarity of the received signals, as does increase in noise due to increase in bandwidth. At low SNRs, the average probability of correct classification slightly improved as $\Delta BW/BW = -0.2$ and slightly decreased with $\Delta BW/BW = 0.2$ as shown in Fig. 3. At high SNRs, however, the average probability of correct classification was independent of bandwidth estimation.

5.5   Influence of Phase Noise and Doppler Shift

Figure 4 presents the average probability of correct classification as a function of maximum Doppler shift frequency f_d normalized to $\frac{1}{T}$, for different phase noise rates at SNR = 15 dB. The phase noise was modeled as a Wiener process with rate βT, where β is the two-sided 3 dB bandwidth of the Lorenzian power density spectrum [23]. The channel doppler shift was modeled as a modified Jakes model [24]. The proposed algorithm exhibited relatively satisfactory performance when $\beta T \leq 0.03$ and $f_d T \leq 10^{-5}$, as is evident in the graph.

5.6 Performance Comparison

Figure 5 compares the average probability of correct classification, P_c, achieved by the proposed algorithm, fourth-order statistics algorithms [15,16], Kolmogrov-Smirnov (K-S) algorithm [9], and cyclostationarity-based algorithms [11,13]. FOLP-A, FOLP-B and FOLP-C algorithms are representative of a study by DeYoung [15]. Choqueuse [16] extended the work by DeYoung [15] to consider the classification of a larger pool of space-time block codes. Firstly, there is substantial improvement in the average probability of correct classification due to increase in N at intermediate or even low SNR values. At low received symbols, the average probability of correct classification had unacceptable correct classification performance even at high SNRs; this enhancement was facilitated by the more accurate estimation of the fourth-order cyclic moment $\hat{M}(\eta, \tau)$. Secondly, V. Choqueuse's algorithm [16] shows similar performance as FOLP-C; DeYoung's [15] and Choqueuse's [16] algorithms classify the received signal with a single receiver antenna, however, the correct classification probability $P(ST4|ST4)$ and $P(ST3|ST3)$ affect the average probability of correct classification in [16]. Therefore, the average probability of correct classification is worse than DeYoung's [15] algorithm. As expected, Eldemerdash's algorithm [9] outperformed than others as it relies on the binary decision tree with a non-parametric goodness-of-fit test applied at each node. Other previously proposed algorithms [11,13] showed the worst performance, as accurate estimation of fourth-order cyclic statistics requires a relatively large observation period. These algorithms are not applicable to the scenario described here, however. As can be seen, the proposed method shows satisfactory performance, and meets our needs in practical application.

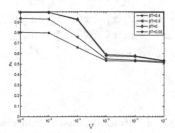

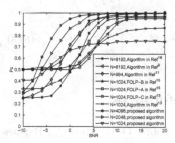

Fig. 4. Effect of the phase noise and Doppler shift on P_c

Fig. 5. Effect of the bandwidth estimation on P_c

5.7 Computational Complexity Analysis

The N-point FFT algorithm has complexity of $\rho N log_2(\rho N)$, the fourth-order algorithm has complexity of $O(NlogN)$, so the proposed algorithm has complexity of $O(\rho N log_2 \rho N)$, but both the K-S-based algorithm and FOLP-C algorithm have complexity of $O(NlogN)$. The proposed algorithm thus represents an increase in computational cost.

6   Conclusions

In this paper, we proposed a novel method for blind classification of STBCs based on the cyclostationarity of STBCs with a single receiver antenna in the presence of transmission impairments. The fourth-order cyclic moment exhibited peaks with corresponding cycle frequencies dependent on the transmitted STBCs. The proposed algorithm relies on the fourth-order cyclic moment as a discriminating feature and employs the distance between adjacent spectral lines to detect the transmitted STBCs. Unlike other, similar methods, this algorithm does not require a priori information regarding the modulation scheme, channel coefficients, or noise power; this makes it particularly well-suited to non-cooperative scenarios.

The proposed algorithm was evaluated in term of classification performance on four STBCs with different code lengths: Spatial multiplexing, Alamouti code and two orthogonal STBCs; it performed quite well even at low SNRs. Further, we found that its performance is enhanced as the number of received signals increases. Additional experiments showed that the algorithm is relatively insensitive to bandwidth estimation error, phase noise, and Doppler shift.

Appendix

The STBCs under consideration are SM, AL, ST3 and ST4. The corresponding transmission matrices are

$$C^{(SM)} = \begin{bmatrix} x_1 \\ x_2 \end{bmatrix}, \qquad C^{(ST3)} = \begin{bmatrix} x_1 & -x_2^* & x_3^* & 0 \\ x_2 & x_1^* & 0 & -x_3^* \\ x_3 & 0 & -x_1^* & x_2^* \end{bmatrix}$$

$$C^{(AL)} = \begin{bmatrix} x_1 & -x_2^* \\ x_2 & x_1^* \end{bmatrix}, \quad C^{(ST4)} = \begin{bmatrix} x_1 & -x_2 & -x_3 & -x_4 & x_1^* & -x_2^* & -x_3^* & -x_4^* \\ x_2 & x_1 & x_4 & -x_3 & x_2^* & x_1^* & x_4^* & -x_3^* \\ x_3 & -x_4 & x_1 & x_2 & x_3^* & -x_4^* & x_1^* & x_2^* \end{bmatrix}$$

References

1. Dobre, O.A., Abdi, A., Bar-ness, Y.: A survey of automatic modulation classification techniques: classical approaches and new developments. IEEE Trans. Commun. **1**(2), 137–156 (2007)
2. Swami, A., Sadler, B.: Hierarchical digtial modulation classification using cumulants. IEEE Trans. Commun. **48**(3), 416–429 (2000)
3. Larsson, E., Stoica, P.: Space-Time Block Coding for Wireless communications. Cambridge Press, Cambridge (2003)
4. Marey, M., Dobre, O.A., Liao, B.: Classification of STBC systems over frequency-selective channels. IEEE Trans. Veh. Technol. **64**(5), 2159–2164 (2014)
5. Choqueuse, V., Marazin, M.: Blind recognition of linear space-time block codes: a likelihood-based approach. IEEE Trans. Signal Process. **58**(3), 1290–1299 (2010)
6. Choqueuse, V., Yao, K.: Hierarchical space-time block code recognition using correlation matrices. IEEE Trans. Wirel. Commun. **7**(9), 3526–3534 (2008)

7. Choqueuse, V., Yao, K.: Blind recognition of linear space time block codes. In: 2008 IEEE International Conference on Acoustics, Speech and Signal Processing, Las Vegas, USA, pp. 2833–2836 (2008)
8. Marey, M., Dobre, O.A., Inkol, R.: Blind STBC identification for multiple-antenna OFDM systems. IEEE Trans. Commun. 62(5), 1554–1567 (2014)
9. Eldemerdash, Y.A., Dobre, O.A., Liao, B.J.: Blind identification of SM and Alamouti STBC-OFDM signal. IEEE Trans. Wirel. Commun. 14(2), 972–982 (2015)
10. Mohammadkarimi, M., Dobre, O.A.: Blind identification of spatial multiplexing and Alamouti space-time block code via Kolmogorov-Smirnov (K-S) test. IEEE Commun. Lett. 18(10), 1711–1714 (2014)
11. Mohamadkarmi, M., Dobre, O.A.: A novel non-parametric method for blind identification of STBC codes. In: 2015 IEEE 14th Canadian workshop on Information Theory (CWIT), St. John's, Canadian, pp. 97–100 (2015)
12. Shi, M., Bar-ness, Y.: STC and BLAST MIMO modulation recognition. In: IEEE GLOBECOM 2007-IEEE Global Telecommunications Conference, Washington, USA, pp. 3034–3039 (2007)
13. Marey, M., Dobre, O.A.: Classification of space-time block codes based on second-order cyclostationarity with transmission impairments. IEEE Trans. Wirel. Commun. 11(7), 2574–2584 (2012)
14. Karami, E., Dobre, O.A.: Identification of SM-OFDM and AL-OFDM signals based on their second-order cyclostationarity. IEEE Trans. Veh. Technol. 64(3), 942–953 (2015)
15. DeYoung, M., Heath, R., Evans, B.: Using higher order cyclo-stationarity to indentify space-time block codes. In: 2008 IEEE Global Telecommunications Conference GLOBECOM 2008, New Orleans, USA, pp. 1–5 (2008)
16. Choqueuse, V., Mansour, A., Burel, G.: Blind channel estimation for STBC system using higher-order statistics. IEEE Trans. Wirel. Commun. 10(2), 495–505 (2011)
17. Eldemerdash, Y.A., Marey, M., Dobre, O.A.: Fourth-order statistics for blind classification of spatial multiplexing and Alamouti space-time block code signals. IEEE Trans. Commun. 61(6), 1–12 (2013)
18. Eldemerdash, Y.A., Dobre, O.A., Marcy, M.: An efficient algorithm for space-time block code classification. In: 2013 IEEE Global Communication Conference, Atlanta, USA, pp. 3034–3039 (2013)
19. Eldemerdash, Y.A., Dobre, O.A., Oner, M.: Signal identification for multiple-antenna wireless systems: achievements and challenges. IEEE Commun. Surv. Tutor. PP(99), 1–28 (2016)
20. Gardner, W., Spooner, C.: The cumulant theory of cyclostationarity time series, Part I: foundation. IEEE Trans. Signal Process. 42(12), 3387–3408 (1994)
21. Dandawate, A.V., Giannakis, G.B.: Statistical test for the presence of cyclostationarity. IEEE Trans. Signal Process. 42(9), 2355–2359 (1994)
22. Lunden, J., Koivunen, V., Huttunen, A., Poor, H.V.: Spectrum sensing in cognitive radios based on multiple cyclic frequencies. In: 2007 2nd International Conference on Cognitive Radio Oriented Wireless Networks and Communication, Orlando, USA, pp. 37–43 (2007)
23. Demir, A., Mehrotra, A., Roychowdhury, A.: Phase noise in oscillator: a unifying theroy and numerical methods for characterization. IEEE Trans. Circ. Syst. 47(8), 655–674 (2000)
24. Zheng, Y., Xiao, C.: Simulation models with correct statistical properties for Rayleigh fading channels. IEEE Trans. Commun. 51(6), 920–928 (2003)

Spiking Neural Models and Their Application in DNA Microarrays Classification

Roberto A. Vazquez[1]([✉]) and Beatriz A. Garro[2]

[1] Intelligent Systems Group, Facultad de Ingeniería, Universidad La Salle México,
Benjamin Franklin 47, Condesa, 06140 Mexico, D.F., Mexico
ravem@lasallistas.org.mx
[2] IIMAS-UNAM, Ciudad Universitaria, Mexico, D.F., Mexico
beatriz.garro@iimas.unam.mx

Abstract. Gene expression in DNA microarrays has been widely used to determine which genes are related with a disease, identify tumors, determine a treatment for a disease, etc.; all of this based on the classification of DNA microarrays. Several pattern recognition and computational intelligence techniques such as Artificial Neural Networks (ANN) have been used to predict diseases in terms of the gene expression levels. However, to train an ANN using a reduced number of DNA microarray samples, it is necessary to apply more robust neural models due to the samples are composed of an enormous quantity of genes. In this paper, we described how a spiking neural model can be applied to solve a DNA microarrays classification task. The proposed methodology selects the most relevant genes that are related with a particular disease by means of the artificial bee colony algorithm. After that, the selected genes are used to train a spiking neural model (SNM) using a learning approach based on the particle swarm optimization algorithm. Finally, to asses the accuracy of the proposed methodology, a DNA microarrays dataset related to identify leukemia was used. The experimental results obtained with the proposed methodology are compared against those obtained with traditional distance classifier, feedforward neural networks and support vector machines. The results suggest that SNM provides acceptable results and comparable with those obtained with classical neural networks.

Keywords: Spiking neurons · Izhikevich model · Swarm intelligence · Artificial bee colony · DNA microarrays

1 Introduction

DNA microarrays are a new kind of technology capable to analyze the expression level of millions of genes. This technology has been widely used to diagnose diseases, select the best treatment to resist illness, and identify different types of tumors or cancer. Several techniques have been proposed to analyze the expression level of the genes and perform the DNA microarray classification to diagnose

© Springer Nature Switzerland AG 2019
Y. Tan et al. (Eds.): ICSI 2019, LNCS 11656, pp. 164–172, 2019.
https://doi.org/10.1007/978-3-030-26354-6_16

a disease, among the most popular, we could mention pattern recognition techniques such as Artificial Neural Networks (ANN). For example, the authors in [1] train an ANN using a singular value decomposition (SVD) technique for DNA microarray cancer classification. In [2], the authors use predictive genes to train an ANN for detecting recurrence of cancer. In [3] and [4], the authors also applied ANN to diagnose different kinds of cancer using ANN.

A DNA microarray contains several expressions of genes and usually, the number of DNA microarray samples related with a disease is reduced. Under this condition, it is more difficult for the ANN learn relevant information from the genes and perform the classification task with an acceptable accuracy, due to the reduce amount of training sample and the high number of features that compose the samples. One approach to avoid this problem is: before training the ANN, it is necessary to perform a gene selection step and, at the same time, select a number of genes less than the number of available DNA microarray samples. In [5], bioinspired techniques were used for selecting the most relevant genes associated with a disease.

Although the combination of gene selection with an ANN has provided acceptable results in a DNA microarrays classification task, in order to improve the accuracy of this approach, it is necessary to propose more robust ANN (easy to design and train) such as in [6].

Recently, the third generation of neural models [7] has gained the attention from the ANN scientific society [8]. The spiking neural models (SNM) are abstractions (differential equations) that try to reproduce the behavior of real neurons. These kind of neurons are excited with a stimulus during a period of time, and its output responds with a spike train, similar to real neurons. Originally, these neurons were used in the computational neuroscience field [9, 10] and nowadays, they have shown their robustness solving complex pattern recognition problems [11–14] with a better accuracy than classical ANN. For that reason, we consider that SNM could provide acceptable results in this task.

Following the described approaches, in this paper, it is presented how a SNM can be applied to perform a DNA microarrays classification task. First, we perform a dimensional reduction of the DNA microarray selecting the set of genes that best describes the disease using the artificial bee colony (ABC) algorithm. Finally, a SNM is trained using an evolutionary learning approach based of the particle swarm optimization (PSO) algorithm.

2   Spiking Neural Models

Spiking neural models (SNM) have the capability of modeling different neurodynamic properties of real neurons [7]. Several types of neurons have been proposed: the integrate-and-fire, Hodgkin-Huxley, Izhikevich models, among others [15–17]. Due to its simplicity and its low computational cost, in this paper, we use the well-known Izhikevich neuron model with a regular spiking pattern behavior described in Eq. (1):

$$C\dot{v} = k\left(v - v_r\right)\left(v - v_t\right) - u + I \quad \text{if} v \geq v_{peak} \text{ then}$$
$$\dot{u} = a\left\{b\left(v - v_r\right) - u\right\} \qquad v \leftarrow c, u \leftarrow u + d\,. \tag{1}$$

where v corresponds to membrane potential, u to the recovery current and C to the membrane capacitance. The resting membrane potential, the instantaneous threshold potential as well as the spike cutoff value are denoted with v_r, v_t, v_{peak}, respectively. The parameter a is the recovery time constant and b determines if the model behaves as an amplifying (when $b < 0$) or as a resonant (when $b > 0$). Finally, the voltage reset value is defined by c and the total amount of currents activated during the spike is denoted with d.

3 Particle Swarm Optimization (PSO) Algorithm

Particle Swarm Optimization (PSO) is a technique widely used for optimizing non-linear and non-differentiable continuous space functions with a great accuracy. This algorithm has been very popular as a learning strategy for training Artificial Neural Networks [18,19]. This technique defines a set of SN particles $\mathbf{s}_i$ that codify the solutions (positions) to an optimization problem. During the optimization process, each particle modifies its current position in terms of a social component (best solution of the population) and the cognitive component (best solution of the particle).

For more details of this algorithm, the reader could refer to [20]. The basic PSO algorithm is described in Algorithm 1.

Algorithm 1. PSO pseudo-code.

1: $t = 0$

2: Initialize the swarm population of solutions $\mathbf{s}_i(t) \forall i, i = 1, \ldots, SN$

3: Evaluate the population $f(\mathbf{s}_i(t)) \forall i, i = 1, \ldots, SN$

4: Initialize best local position $\mathbf{p}_i = f(\mathbf{s}_i(t)) \forall i, i = 1, \ldots, SN$

5: Initialize best global position $\mathbf{p}_g = min(f(\mathbf{s}_i(t)) \forall i, i = 1, \ldots, SN)$

6: **for** $t = 0$ to $MAXITER$ **do**

7:     **for** $i = 1$ to SN **do**

8:         Compute velocity $\mathbf{v}_i(t+1) = \omega \mathbf{v}_i(t) + c_1 r_1 (\mathbf{p}_i(t) - \mathbf{s}_i(t)) + c_2 r_2 (\mathbf{p}_g(t) - \mathbf{s}_i(t))$

9:         Compute new position $\mathbf{s}_i(t+1) = \mathbf{s}_i(t) + \mathbf{v}_i(t+1)$

10:         Evaluate the fitness of the particle $f(\mathbf{s}_i(t+1))$

11:         **if** $f(\mathbf{s}_i(t+1)) < \mathbf{p}_i =$ **then**

12:             Update best local position $\mathbf{p}_i = f(\mathbf{s}_i(t+1))$

13:         **end if**

14:     **end for**

15:     **if** $min(f(\mathbf{s}_i(t+1) \forall i, i = 1, \ldots, SN) < \mathbf{p}_g =$ **then**

16:         Update best global position $\mathbf{p}_g = min(f(\mathbf{s}_i(t+1)) \forall i, i = 1, \ldots, SN)$

17:     **end if**

18:     $t = t + 1$

19: **end for**

---

4   Methodology for DNA Classification

The proposed methodology is based on [5] and consider two main steps: the first stage is focused on selecting the most relevant genes, capable of discriminating and describing the DNA microarray, and other stage is focused on improving the accuracy during the classification task training a spiking neural model.

The first step applies a dimensional reduction over the DNA microarray, selecting those genes that best represent a specific disease using the artificial bee colony (ABC) algorithm. After that, this information is used in the second step for training an Izhikevich spiking neural model.

According to [5], the selection of the most relevant genes can be defined as an optimization problem. Given a set of p DNA microarrays $\mathbf{X} = \{\mathbf{x}_1, \ldots, \mathbf{x}_p\}$, $\mathbf{x}_i \in \mathbb{R}^n, i = 1 \ldots, p$ and its corresponding associated disease $\mathbf{d} = \{d_1, \ldots, d_p\}$. The aim is to find a subset of genes from the DNA microarray $G \in \{0, 1\}^n$ such that a fitness function defined by $\min (F(\mathbf{X}|_G, \mathbf{d}))$ is minimized.

The artificial bee colony (ABC) algorithm was originaly proposed by Karaboga [21]. This is based on the behavior of bees, particularly in the process of foraging. In this algorithm, the bees $\mathbf{x}_i \in \mathbb{R}^n, i = 1, \ldots, NB$ are possible solutions to the problem and represent the position of the food sources that are distributed in the search space (NB represents the size of the population). For more details, see [21].

To evaluate and determine which set of genes is the best optimal solution, the ABC algorithm requires of a fitness function that measures the aptitude of an individual. Particularly, the fitness function used in this methodology, measures the number of samples that have been wrongly classified in terms of an error function (Eq. 2).

$$F(\mathbf{X}|_G, \mathbf{d}) = \frac{\sum_{i=1}^{p} \left(\left| \underset{k=1}{\overset{K}{\arg\min}} \left(D\left(\mathbf{x}_i|_G, \mathbf{c}^k|_G\right)\right) - d_i \right| \right)}{p}. \tag{2}$$

where p is the total number of gene expressions to be classified, D is a Euclidean distance, K is the number of classes, $\mathbf{c}$ is the center of each category, $\arg\min$ provides the class to which the input pattern belongs in terms of the distance classifier and d_i is the expected class.

The solutions represent a subset of genes defined by an array $I \in \mathbb{R}^n$. Each individual $I_q, q = 1, \ldots, NB$ is binarized using Eq. (3) with a threshold level th. This threshold select the best set of genes defined as $G^k = T_{th}(I^k), k = 1, \ldots, n$; whose component is set to 1, indicates that this gene will be selected to make up the subset of genes.

$$T_{th}(x) = \left\{ \begin{array}{l} 0, x < th \\ 1, x \geq th \end{array} \right\}. \tag{3}$$

The next step is to train the spiking neural model (SNM) using the best set of genes selected by the ABC algorithm. Based on the work described in [11,12], in order to perform a pattern recognition task using SNM, the next behavior must be reached: "patterns from the same class produce similar firing rates in the output of the spiking neuron and patterns from other classes produce firing rates different enough to discriminate among the classes". In [11,12], the authors proposed a four stage methodology for pattern classification using spiking neural models, composed of the next steps: data acquisition, input current computation, firing rate computation, classification.

First of all, an input current is computed in terms of an input pattern that represents the presynaptic potential of different receptive fields $\mathbf{x}^i \in \mathbb{R}^n$ using Eq. (4)

$$I = \mathbf{x} \cdot \mathbf{w} . \tag{4}$$

where $\mathbf{w}^i \in \mathbb{R}^n$ represents the synaptic weights of the neuron model.

After that, a firing rate is computed from the output of the spiking neuron model. To do that, the neuron is stimulate during T ms using the input current to provoke the spike train at the output of the neuron. The firing rate is computed according to Eq. (5)

$$fr = \frac{N_{sp}}{T} . \tag{5}$$

where N_{sp} denotes the number of spikes generate at the output of the neuron within the time T. In addition, the average firing rate of each class $\mathbf{AFR} \in \mathbb{R}^K$ is computed considering the input patters that belongs to the same class.

Finally, to classify an unknown input pattern $\tilde{\mathbf{x}}$, the spiking neuron is stimulated with the current computed with $\tilde{\mathbf{x}}$, the firing rate fr is computed and compared against the average firing rate of each class by mean of Eq. (6)

$$cl = \arg \min_{k=1}^{K} \left(|AFR_k - fr| \right) . \tag{6}$$

The learning process is conducted by means of a particle swarm optimization (PSO) algorithm [18] where each particle from the swarm corresponds to a set of synaptic weights, and the size of particle is determined in terms of the number of selected genes used to stimulate the SNM. The value of the synaptic weights are adapted to maximize the performance of the SNM during the DNA microarray classification task using fitness function described in (7)

$$f(\mathbf{w}, \mathbf{X}, \mathbf{d}) = 1 - \frac{\sum_{i=1}^{p} c(\mathbf{w}, \mathbf{x}_i, d_i)}{p} . \tag{7}$$

where $\mathbf{w}$ represents the synaptic weights of the Izhikevich neuron model, $\mathbf{X}$ represents the set of input patterns, $\mathbf{d}$ represents the set of desired patterns associated to each pattern, p represents the number of patterns, and $c(\mathbf{w}, \mathbf{x}, d)$ represents a function that computes if the pattern was classified correctly and is defined as:

$$c(\mathbf{w}, \mathbf{x}, d) = \begin{cases} 1, & |d - y(\mathbf{w}, \mathbf{x})| = 0 \\ 0, & |d - y(\mathbf{w}, \mathbf{x})| \neq 0 \end{cases} . \tag{8}$$

where $\mathbf{x}$ is the input pattern, d is the desired class, y corresponds to the class detected with the SNM, and $\mathbf{w}$ are the synaptic weights of the SNM.

5   Experimental Results

In this section, we evaluate the accuracy of the proposed methodology using the *Leukemia benchmark ALL-AML* dataset contains measurements corresponding to acute lymphocytic leukemia (ALL) and acute myeloid leukemia (AML) samples from Bone Marrow and Peripheral Blood. It is composed of samples for training (27 ALL and 11 AML) and 34 samples for testing (20 ALL and 14 AML) where each sample contains information of 7129 gene expressions. In [22], the authors demonstrate that is possible to classification ALL and AML using DNA microarrays.

After evaluate different values for the parameters, we found that the best results are achieved with the next parameters to select the most relevant genes using the artificial bee colony (ABC) algorithm and an euclidean distance classifier: population size ($NB = 40$), maximum number of cycles $MNC = 2000$, limit $l = 100$ and food sources $NB/2$ [5]. After concluding all experiments as was described in [5], the ABC algorithm select three genes (SLC17A2 Solute carrier family 17 (L13258_at), MLC gene (M22919_rna2_at) and FBN2 Fibrillin 2 (U03272_at)), achieving an average accuracy of 74.6% and a maximum accuracy of 88.2% during the testing stage.

During the second stage, three selected genes were used to training the SNM by means the particle swarm optimization (PSO) algorithm. As equal as in the previous experiments, after evaluate different values for the parameters, we found the next parameters for the PSO algorithm $NP = 40$, $MAXGEN = 1000$, $VMAX = 4$, $VMIN = -4$, $c_1 = 2$, $c_2 = 2$, $XMAX = 10$, $XMIN = -10$ and ω was varied in the range $[0.95 - 0.4]$ through the generations. The parameters for the Izhikevich neuron were defined as $C = 100$, $v_r = -60$, $v_t = -40$, $v_{peak} = 35$, $k = 0.7$, $a = 0.03$, $b = -2$, $c = -50$, and $d = 100$. The Euler method was used to solve the differential equation of the model with $dt = 1$. The parameter to compute input current I from the input pattern was set to $\theta = 100$ with a duration of $T = 1000$. Finally, 30 experiments were performed to statistically validate the results obtained with the spiking neural model using two different partitions from the dataset: Original partition (O) where data is partitioned as in the original dataset and Random partition (R) where 80% of the samples were selected randomly from the original dataset to construct the training dataset and the remaining for the testing dataset.

In order to asses the advantage of using a SNM instead of a classical artificial neural network, the results achieved with the SNM were compared against the results obtained using a multilayer perceptron (MLP) with the next architecture: input layer with three linear neurons, hidden layer with five sigmoidal neurons and output layer with two sigmoidal neurons. A winner-takes-all strategy was used to determine the class to which the input pattern belongs. Finally, the proposed MLP was trained with a Levenberg-Marquardt algorithm using a learning rate of 0.1, 5000 epochs and a goal error of 0.

The results obtained with the MLP and the SNM are shown in Table 1. First of all, it was observed that both types of neuron models (MLP and SNM) improve the performance achieved with the euclidean distance classifier. Nonetheless, during the testing phase, the SNM obtain a better accuracy than the MLP, reaching an average performance of 88.2% with the original partition and a 94.1% with a random partition. The best accuracy was obtained with the MLP reaching a 94.1% of recognition using the original partition. On the other hand, both neural models achieved an accuracy 100% using the random partitions. Although in this case, both neural models achieved similar results, it is important to remark that only one SNM was enough to reach an accuracy of 100%. This is an advantage against MLP that required at least seven neurons.

Table 1. Best accuracy obtained with the SNM and MLP.

P	Type NN	Average accuracy		Best accuracy		Worst accuracy		# of genes
		Tr. cl.	Te. cl.	Tr. cl.	Te. cl.	Tr. cl.	Te. cl.	
O	MLP	0.819 ± 0.213	0.740 ± 0.170	1.000	0.941	0.289	0.412	3
R	MLP	0.844 ± 0.185	0.833 ± 0.182	0.983	1.000	0.328	0.357	3
O	SNM	1.000 ± 0.000	0.882 ± 0.019	1.000	0.912	1.000	0.853	3
R	SNM	0.970 ± 0.010	0.929 ± 0.094	1.000	1.000	0.948	0.571	3

Tr. cl. = Training classification rate, Te. cl. = Testing classification rate.

In Table 2, we present some results obtained using a support vector machine (SVM) in order to compare the accuracy of the proposed methodology. Based of these results, we can conclude that the proposed methodology provide better compared to those reported in the literature.

Table 2. Comparison against other techniques

Classification technique	Selection technique	# of genes	% of accuracy	References
SNM	ABC	3	1.0000	Proposed methodology
MLP	ABC	3	1.0000	[5]
SVM	PSO	10	1.0000	[23]
SVM	PLS-RFE	16	1.0000	[24]
SVM	GBC	3	0.9583	[25]

These results corroborate the robustness of the SNM and suggest that this model can be used as an alternative technique for performing the classification of DNA microarrays. On the other hand, the SNM has some advantage against the MLP and SVM, particularly, the SNM has less parameters to be adapted and most important, it is not necessary to deal with the architecture design because only one neuron was enough to classified the two types of leukemia.

6   Conclusions

The paper present a two steps methodology to apply a spiking neural model in a DNA microarrays classification task. First of all, a dimensional reduction technique based on the ABC algorithm was applied to select the most relevant genes of a DNA microarray. Once discover the most relevant genes for classifying the two types of leukemia contained in the dataset, we evaluated its accuracy using a simple distance classifier. Although we obtained a highly acceptable accuracy during the second stage, we tried to improve the results using a spiking neural model (SNM).

During the second stage, the SNM was trained using the genes discovered by the proposed methodology (SLC17A2 Solute carrier family 17 (L13258_at), MLC gene (M22919_rna2_at) and FBN2 Fibrillin 2 (U03272_at)). The accuracy achieved with the SNM trained with the PSO algorithm was compared against the performance of a multilayer perceptron (MLP). After analyzing the experimental results, we observed that the SNM as well as the MLP improve the results obtained with the distance classifier. Furthermore, the results confirm that the SNM provides a better performance than the MLP, concluding that the SNM trained with the proposed methodology is capable of detecting, predicting and classifying a disease with an acceptable accuracy using only one neuron instead of several neurons as MLP.

Acknowledgment. The authors would like to thank Universidad La Salle México for the economic support under grant number NEC-10/18.

References

1. Huynh, H.T., Kim, J.J., Won, Y.: Classification study on DNA micro array with feed forward neural network trained by singular value decomposition. Int. J. Bio-Sci. Bio- Technol. **1**(1), 17–24 (2009)
2. Peterson, L., et al.: Artificial neural network analysis of DNA microarray-based prostate cancer recurrence. In: Proceedings of the 2005 IEEE Symposium on Computational Intelligence in Bioinformatics and Computational Biology, 2005. CIBCB 2005, pp. 1–8, November 2005
3. Lancashire, L.J., Lemetre, C., Ball, G.R.: An introduction to artificial neural networks in bioinformatics-application to complex microarray and mass spectrometry datasets in cancer studies. Briefings Bioinform. **10**(3), 315–329 (2009)
4. Khan, J., et al.: Classification and diagnostic prediction of cancers using gene expression profiling and artificial neural networks. Nat. Med. **7**(6), 673–679 (2001)
5. Garro, B.A., Rodriguez, K., Vazquez, R.A.: Classification of DNA microarrays using artificial neural networks and ABC algorithm. Appl. Soft Comput. **38**, 548–560 (2016)
6. Garro, B.A., Sossa, H., Vázquez, R.A.: Evolving neural networks: a comparison between differential evolution and particle swarm optimization. In: Tan, Y., Shi, Y., Chai, Y., Wang, G. (eds.) ICSI 2011. LNCS, vol. 6728, pp. 447–454. Springer, Heidelberg (2011). https://doi.org/10.1007/978-3-642-21515-5_53
7. Maass, W., Graz, T.U.: Networks of spiking neurons: the third generation of neural network models. Neural Networks **10**, 1659–1671 (1997)

8. Schuman, C.D., et al.: A survey of neuromorphic computing and neural networks in hardware. CoRR abs/1705.06963 (2017)

9. Hasselmo, M.E., Bodelón, C., Wyble, B.P.: A proposed function for hippocampal theta rhythm: separate phases of encoding and retrieval enhance reversal of prior learning. Neural Comput. **14**, 793–817 (2002)

10. Thorpe, S.J., Guyonneau, R., Guilbaud, N., Allegraud, J.M., VanRullen, R.: Spikenet: real-time visual processing with one spike per neuron. Neurocomputing **58–60**, 857–864 (2004). Computational Neuroscience: Trends in Research 2004

11. Vazquez, R.A., Garro, B.A.: Training spiking neural models using artificial bee colony. Comput. Intell. Neurosci. **2015** (2015). Article ID 947098

12. Cachón, A., Vazquez, R.A.: Tuning the parameters of an integrate and fire neuron via a genetic algorithm for solving pattern recognition problems. Neurocomputing **148**, 187–197 (2015)

13. Wade, J., Mcdaid, L., Santos, J., Sayers, H.: Swat: a spiking neural network training algorithm for classification problems. IEEE Trans. Neural Networks **21**(11), 1817–1830 (2010)

14. Kasabov, N.: Evolving spiking neural networks for spatio-and spectro-temporal pattern recognition. In: 2012 6th IEEE International Conference Intelligent Systems (IS), pp. 27–32 (2012)

15. Hodgkin, A.L.: The local electric changes associated with repetitive action in a non-medullated axon. J. Physiol. **107**(2), 165–181 (1948)

16. Abbott, L.: Lapicque's introduction of the integrate-and-fire model neuron (1907). Brain Res. Bull. **50**(56), 303–304 (1999)

17. Izhikevich, E.M.: Dynamical Systems in Neuroscience: The Geometry of Excitability and Bursting. Computational Neuroscience. MIT Press, Cambridge (2007)

18. Vázquez, R.A., Garro, B.A.: Training spiking neurons by means of particle swarm optimization. In: Tan, Y., Shi, Y., Chai, Y., Wang, G. (eds.) ICSI 2011. LNCS, vol. 6728, pp. 242–249. Springer, Heidelberg (2011). https://doi.org/10.1007/978-3-642-21515-5_29

19. Garro, B.A., Vazquez, R.A.: Designing artificial neural networks using particle swarm optimization algorithms. Comput. Intell. Neurosci. **2015** (2015). Article ID 369298

20. Eberhart, R.C., Shi, Y., Kennedy, J.: Swarm Intelligence (The Morgan Kaufmann Series in Evolutionary Computation), 1st edn. Morgan Kaufmann, San Francisco (2001)

21. Karaboga, D.: An idea based on honey bee swarm for numerical optimization. Technical report, Computer Engineering Department, Engineering Faculty, Erciyes University (2005)

22. Golub, T.R., et al.: Molecular classification of cancer: class discovery and class prediction by gene expression monitoring. Science **286**(5439), 531–537 (1999)

23. Sahu, B., Mishra, D.: A novel feature selection algorithm using particle swarm optimization for cancer microarray data. Procedia Eng. **38**, 27–31 (2012). International Conference on Modelling Optimization and Computing

24. Wang, A., An, N., Chen, G., Li, L., Alterovitz, G.: Improving PLSRFE based gene selection for microarray data classification. Comput. Biol. Med. **62**, 14–24 (2015)

25. Alshamlan, H.M., Badr, G.H., Alohali, Y.A.: Genetic bee colony (GBC) algorithm: a new gene selection method for microarray cancer classification. Comput. Biol. Chem. **56**, 49–60 (2015)

An Unified View on the Feedforward Neural Network Architecture

Ping Guo and Bo Zhao[✉]

Image Processing and Pattern Recognition Laboratory, School of Systems Science,
Beijing Normal University, Beijing 100875, China
{pguo,zhaobo}@bnu.edu.cn

Abstract. In this paper, an unified view on feedforward neural networks
(FNNs) is provided from the free perception of the architecture design,
learning algorithm, cost function, regularization, activation functions,
etc. Furthermore, we consider the ensemble networks and swarm intelligence as the same sytems which consists of multiple learning algorithms
or collective behavior of decentralized, self-organized systems with similar unified view of FNNs based architecture. This work is a small step
on the road toward to the general theory of neural networks.

Keywords: Unified view · Feedforward Neural Networks ·
Ensemble learning · Swarm intelligence · Particle swarm optimization

1 Introduction

In the viewpoints of Physical scientists, they always attempt to unify different
theories of complex phenomenons to a set of concepts, and it is helpful to make
successful predictions by using the mathematical formulas which express these
concepts. For example, Smolin et al. [1] have ever described that "Physics's long-
cherished wish, like bad love stories, is for unity. When possible, it is the greatest
surprise and joy of science to combine two things that used to be considered
different of an entity".

The same opinion appears in machine learning. Manuel et al. [2] expressed an
opinion as "Do we need hundreds of classifiers to solve real world classification
problems?" The answer to this question is that it is surely not required to design
many classifiers. It implies that these classifiers should be unified. To achieve this
goal, this paper presents a brief unified view on architectures, cost functions,
learning methods, activation functions of different machine learning tools, such
as feedforward neural network, ensemble learning, swarm intelligence, etc. To
achieve the general theory of neural networks [3], this work is a small step toward
to this goal.

This work was supported in part by the National Natural Science Foundation of China
under Grants U1531242, 61603387 and 61773075, and in part by the Early Career
Development Award of SKLMCCS under Grant 20180201.

Y. Tan et al. (Eds.): ICSI 2019, LNCS 11656, pp. 173–180, 2019.
https://doi.org/10.1007/978-3-030-26354-6_17

2   Multi-layer Feedforward Neural Network

As a typical feedforward neural network, multi-layer perceptron (MLP) has been paid great attention of researchers from 1980's. With more than three hidden layers, MLP is called deep neural network (DNN), and training DNN is a deep learning procedure, which is successful in various supervised learning tasks. Both theoretical and empirical studies have shown that the MLP has powerful capabilities for pattern classification and universal approximation [4]. When there are few hidden layers, weight parameters of the network can be trained by the gradient descent learning algorithm, namely the well-known error back propagation (BP) algorithm [5,6]. As we know, the disadvantages of the BP algorithm lies in the poor convergence rate and trapping local minima [7]. The selection of hyper-parameters in the BP algorithm, i.e., the learning rate and the momentum constant, is critical for the success of the algorithm.

Architecture. The layers between the input layer and the output layer are called hidden layers. The neuron numbers in the input and output layers depend on users how to model the given task, while hidden layer neuron number is dependent on the user's design. In the following, a single hidden layer network (SHLN) is employed to illustrate our viewpoints. The schematic diagram of SHLN is shown in Fig. 1. There are $n+1$ neurons in the input layer, $l+1$ neurons in the hidden layer, and m neurons in the output layer. $\mathbf{x} = (x_1, x_2, ..., x_n)$ and $\mathbf{o} = (o_1, o_2, ..., o_m)$ represent the input vector with n dimensions and the output vector with m dimensions. b_1 and b_2 are bias neurons in the corresponding layers. $\mathbf{V}$ and $\mathbf{W}$ are the weight matrices which connect input-hidden layer and the hidden-output layer, respectively. The network mapping function is expressed as $o_k = f_k(\mathbf{x}, \mathbf{\Theta}) = \sigma(\sum_{j=1}^{l} W_{k,j} g_j + b_2)$, $g_j = \sigma(\sum_{i=1}^{n} V_{j,i} x_i + b_1)$, where $\mathbf{\Theta}$ stands for the network parameter group, including connecting weights $\mathbf{W}, \mathbf{V}$,

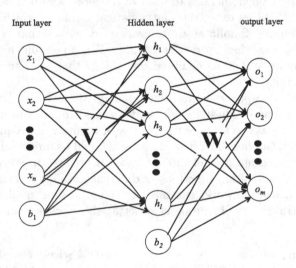

Fig. 1. A schematic diagram of single hidden layer neural networks.

and bias neurons b_1, b_2. Activation function $\sigma(\cdot)$ is always selected as sigmoid, hyperbolic, step, radial basis function, and so on. $\mathbf{g}(\mathbf{Vx} + \mathbf{b}_1)$ and $\mathbf{f}(\mathbf{Wg} + \mathbf{b}_2)$ are the outputs of the hidden layer and the last layer, respectively.

Let $\sum_{i=1}^{n} V_{j,i} x_i + b_1 = \sum_{i=0}^{n} V_{j,i} x_i$, with $V_{j,0} = b_1$, $x_0 = 1$ and $\sum_{j=1}^{l} W_{k,j} g_j + b_2 = \sum_{j=0}^{l} W_{k,j} g_j$, with $W_{k,0} = b_2$, $g_0 = 1$. It implies that the matrix $\mathbf{V}, \mathbf{W}$ is an augmented matrix. Bias neuron is used to prevent zero input vector to destroy weight updating in sequentially training, the value of the bias is set to be $+1$ or a variable. For simplicity, the hidden layer bias neuron b_2 is often omitted.

Hidden Layer Number. In the SHLN, the number of hidden neurons l is a hyperparameter of the neural network architecture. When a given problem is formulated, the number of neurons in the input layer is determined by the input data dimension, and the number of the output layer neurons depends on the specific problem. The number of hidden layer neurons is only one hyperparameter for SHLN and it perhaps the most difficult problem for most beginners. In the work of Guo et al. [8], l is set to be N for the purpose of exact learning.

Activation Function. In artificial neural networks, the activation function of a node defines the output of that node given an input or set of inputs. In the multilayer perceptrons, sigmoidal activation function is always selected as hyperbolic tangent, which is commonly expressed as $\phi(v_i) = \tanh(v_i)$, which varies in $[-1, 1]$, and $\phi(v_i) = (1 + \exp(-v_i))^{-1}$, which varies in $[0, 1]$. The latter model is often considered much closer to biologically realistic, but it runs into theoretical and experimental difficulties with certain computational problems.

Cost Function. Cost function, which is also called loss function, error function or objective function, is often used to be the metric to evaluate the similarity (dissimilarity) between two functions. As we all know, the hinge loss and Minkowski distance are the two main approaches.

Learning Algorithms. As a kind of gradient decent algorithm, BP algorithm received great success in neural network learning. However, it has slow convergence and local minima. To address these difficulties, non-gradient descent based algorithms have been considered from the late 1990s or early 2000. As a typical approach, the PIL algorithm received great success [8,9] for MLP (or multi-layer neural networks).

Given a data set $D = \{\mathbf{x}^i, \mathbf{t}^i\}$, the network is trained to find the weight parameters $\mathbf{V}, \mathbf{W}$ by minimizing cost function. The cost function, also known as the loss function or error function, is used to measure the difference between actual outputs and expected outputs of the network. When the error distribution is the Gaussian distribution, the cost function is the sum of the squared error as $E = \frac{1}{2N} \sum_{i=1}^{N} \sum_{j=1}^{m} \|f_j(\mathbf{x}^i, \boldsymbol{\Theta}) - t_j^i\|^2$. For simplicity, the system error function can be rewritten in the matrix form as $E = \frac{1}{2N} \|\mathbf{O} - \mathbf{T}\|_F^2$, where subscript F stands for Frobenius norm.

In order to overcome the aforementioned drawbacks of the BP algorithm, Guo et al. [8] proposed the PIL algorithm to train a SHLN in 1995. The activation function was taken as the hyperbolic function $Tanh(\cdot)$. The weight parameter matrix was obtained by minimizing the error function

$$\min \| \mathbf{YW} - \mathbf{B} \|^2 . \tag{1}$$

where $\mathbf{Y} = Tanh(\mathbf{XV})$ is the output matrix of the hidden layer, $\mathbf{X}$ is the input matrix which consists of N input vectors as its rows and $d = n + 1$ columns as input vector dimension, $\mathbf{B} = ArcTanh(\mathbf{T})$, and $\mathbf{T}$ is the target label matrix which consists of N label vectors as its rows and m columns as target vector dimension.

Equation (1) is formally a problem of least squares in linear algebra. However, only the $\mathbf{B}$ matrix is available at present. Weight matrices $\mathbf{V}$ and $\mathbf{W}$ are unknown, which are required to be obtained by the network learning. From Eq. (1), the formal solution is $\mathbf{W} = \mathbf{Y}^+\mathbf{B}$, where $\mathbf{Y}^+$ is the pseudoinverse of $\mathbf{Y}$. Substitute the formal solution into Eq. (1), we can also get

$$\mathbf{YW} - \mathbf{B} = \mathbf{YY}^+\mathbf{B} - \mathbf{B} = \mathbf{0} . \tag{2}$$

Thus, $\mathbf{YY}^+ = \mathbf{I}$ satisfies the requirement if Eq. (2) holds. Hence, $\mathbf{Y}$ should be a full rank matrix if $\mathbf{Y}^+$ is the final solution. With this new objective function, the input matrix $\mathbf{V}$ is set to guarantee the hidden layer output matrix $\mathbf{Y}$ to be full rank. To achieve this goal, $\mathbf{V}$ is set to be a random value matrix with nonlinear transformation, or the pseudoinverse of the input matrix $\mathbf{X}$.

Hence, a fast learning algorithm which calculates the weight matrix to instead of iterative approach is proposed. It implies that the perfect learning is obtained by one step only (See detailed Algorithm PIL in [9,10]).

When a weight decay regularization technique, (in statistics, weight decay is called as ridge regression), is adopted to improve the network's generalization performance, the pseudoinverse matrix can be computed with following equation:

$$\mathbf{W} = (\mathbf{Y}^T\mathbf{Y} + \lambda\mathbf{I})^{-1}\mathbf{Y}^T\mathbf{X} . \tag{3}$$

where $\lambda > 0$ is a user-specified regularization parameter. This hyper parameter also can be considered as smooth parameter in kernel density distribution, it can be estimated with the formula derived by Guo et al. in 2003 [11].

Since weight parameters in PIL algorithm are calculates with pseudoinverse solution, it does not need to be tuned further. In [8,12], the algorithm to randomly set input weight V is also investigated as Algorithm PIL0. A deep neural network also can be fast trained with PIL for autoencoder (PILAE) [13] under the strategy of greedy layer-wise training, which is also can be regarded as a quasi-automatic machine learning (AutoML) technique. More about PIL algorithm and its variants can be found on a recent survey work [14].

3   Unified View

Both the FNNs and support vector machines (SVMs) can be regarded as a single hidden layer neural network with different activation functions. The main difference lies in the loss function and regularization term between them, and SVMs have one neuron in output layer only. Recall the hidden layer output matrix in [8] as

$$
\mathbf{H} = \begin{pmatrix}
\tanh[\mathbf{v}_1^\mathsf{T}\mathbf{x}_1 + b_1] & \tanh[\mathbf{v}_1^\mathsf{T}\mathbf{x}_2 + b_1] & \cdots & \tanh[\mathbf{v}_1^\mathsf{T}\mathbf{x}_N + b_1] \\
\tanh[\mathbf{v}_2^\mathsf{T}\mathbf{x}_1 + b_1] & \tanh[\mathbf{v}_2^\mathsf{T}\mathbf{x}_2 + b_1] & \cdots & \tanh[\mathbf{v}_2^\mathsf{T}\mathbf{x}_N + b_1] \\
\vdots & \cdots & \ddots & \vdots \\
\tanh[\mathbf{v}_N^\mathsf{T}\mathbf{x}_1 + b_1] & \tanh[\mathbf{v}_N^\mathsf{T}\mathbf{x}_2 + b_1] & \cdots & \tanh[\mathbf{v}_N^\mathsf{T}\mathbf{x}_N + b_1]
\end{pmatrix}.
$$

where $\mathbf{v}_i$ is the ith row of the matrix $\mathbf{V}$. And the kernel matrix with MLP kernel function is $k(\mathbf{v}, \mathbf{x}) = \tanh(\mathbf{v}^\mathsf{T}\mathbf{x} + b_1)$. In our previous work [8,12], vector $\mathbf{v}$ is derived from the pseudoinverse matrix $\mathbf{X}^+$ in PIL algorithm, and $\mathbf{v}$ is a random vector in PIL0 algorithm.

Substituting the kernel into feedforward neural networks, we have $\Omega_{ij} = \phi(v_i)^\mathsf{T}\phi(x_j) = K(v_i, x_j)$. We can also use other kernel functions to replace x_i, i.e., $K(x, x_i) \Rightarrow K(x, v_i)$. Now we call these two kernel functions as random kernel and pseudoinverse kernel, respectively. Moreover, in our deep neural network learning work [9,10], the kernel transformation can be explained as nesting kernel, thus the last hidden layer (feature map) output is $k(\mathbf{v}_i^L, \mathbf{w}_j^L) = k(\phi(\phi(\ldots\phi(v_i))), \phi(\phi(\ldots\phi(x_j))))$. From this view point, we can regard Wong et al.'s work [15] as a simple variant of our PIL work. Specially, by assigning the proper scale parameter k and bias parameter b in tanh kernel, $\Omega_{ij} = \delta_{ij}$ if the data matrix $\mathbf{X}$ is a full rank square matrix (More strict condition is that $\mathbf{X}$ is a orthogonal matrix). It connects with orthogonal least square closely.

Now, we further consider the unified view on ensemble learning (EL) and swarm intelligence (SI) system.

Ensemble Learning. Ensemble learning (EL) is a multiple learning algorithm which integrates statistics and machine learning to obtain better predictive performance than any constituent learning algorithms alone. Different from the infinite statistical ensemble in statistical mechanics, a machine learning ensemble consists of only a concrete finite set of alternative models with much more flexible structure. Since an ensemble neural network is trained for predictions, it can be considered as integrated system, in which some modules (or sub-networks) are trained with supervised learning algorithm. Therefore, the trained ensemble network represents a single hypothesis, which is not necessarily contained within the hypothesis space of the models from which it is built. Thus, ensembles can be shown to have more flexibility to over-fitting the training data more than a single model. In practice, some ensemble techniques (especially bagging) tend to reduce over-fitting problems for the given training data.

Random algorithms (like random decision trees) produces a stronger ensemble than very deliberate algorithms (like entropy-reducing decision trees) [16]. Random forests or random decision forests are ensemble learning methods for classification, regression and other tasks by constructing a multitude of decision trees at training time and outputting the class that is the mode of the classes (classification) or mean prediction (regression) of the individual trees. Random decision forests [17] correct decision trees' habit of overfitting to the training set.

For the large data set, the "divide and conquer" strategy leads to ensemble learning for combining many sub-networks. When different kernel functions are taken for the given data set or sub-data set, this leads to multi-kernel learning research field. We can generate many random kernels, e.g. random vectors with or without zero mean vector from uniform distribution data set, Gaussian distribution data set, Poisson distribution data set, Boltzmann distribution data set, Gibbs distribution data set, Generalized gamma distribution data set, Generalized gamma distribution data set, Student's t-distribution data set, etc. Without the zero mean vector, we can regard these random kernels as the mean vector with small perturbation (Algorithm PIL1) [10,12].

4 Swarm Intelligence Systems

As a concept in artificial intelligence, swarm intelligence (SI) [18] is the collective behavior of decentralized, self-organized systems, natural or artificial. The nature inspired SI systems are composed of many simple agents or boids interacting locally with one another and with their environment. The agents follow very simple rules, and no centralized control structure dictating how individual agents should behave, local, and to a certain degree random. However, interactions between such agents lead to the emergence of "intelligent" global behavior, unknown to the individual agents. Nowadays, SI systems include such as ant colonies, bird flocking, animal herding, bacterial growth, fish schooling and microbial intelligence, etc. Taking particle swarm optimization (PSO) as an example of SI, by randomly generating a set of particles in searching space for obtaining optimal solution, the fitness value of each particle is determined by fitness function. Through comparing the fitness value of each particle with itself "*pbest*" and global optimum "*gbest*" or local optimum "*lbest*" iteratively, the velocity and position vectors are updated and recorded to derive the optimal solution in the solution space [19].

Figure 2 shows the unified view on an ensemble neural network with FNN architecture based base learners. In this figure, the first layer is used to distribute the data to multiple "agents", such as radial basis function (RBF) neural network, SVM, convolutional neural network (CNN), DNN, etc., which are considered as an particle in PSO or other SI schemes. After the operation of these agents, the meta data is synergetic synchronized in a meta learner, which can distribute the data to different agents iteratively according to the result of meta learner. Then, the output is derived. Hence, this FNN based ensemble network architecture can be regarded as a SI system under our unified viewpoint.

From above, we can consider the feedforward neural network based artificial intelligence systems, including EL based and SI based systems, will be able to realized under our unified view framework.

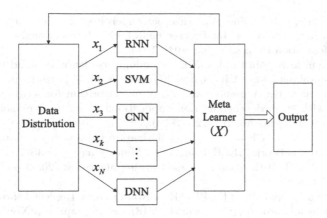

Fig. 2. The unified view on FNN

5 Conclusion

This paper provides an unified view on FNNs from view angles of its architecture, learning algorithm, cost function and activation function. In this framework, we can design an ensemble network to perform the tasks of classification, regression and prediction. The base learners and meta learner can be realized with pseudoinverse learner modules, which can be agile deployment with the PIL algorithm. We also proposed that a swarm intelligence system can be implemented with FNN based neural network agents. Under an unified view framework, it will become easy to learn various classifiers with various architectures. Thus, a small progress is made towards the general theory of neural networks.

References

1. Smolin, L., Harnad, J.: The trouble with physics: the rise of string theory, the fall of a science, and what comes next. Math. Intelligencer **30**(3), 66–69 (2008)
2. Fernćndez-Delgado, M., Cernadas, E., Barro, S., et al.: Do we need hundreds of classifiers to solve real world classification problems? J. Mach. Learn. Res. **15**(1), 3133–3181 (2014)
3. Hartnett, K.: Foundations Built for a General Theory of Neural Networks (2019). https://www.quantamagazine.org/foundations-built-for-a-general-theory-of-neural-networks-20190131/
4. Bishop, C.M.: Neural Networks for Pattern Recognition. Oxford University Press, Oxford (1995)
5. Rumelhart, D.E., Hinton, G.E., Williams, R.J.: Learning internal representations by error propagation. California Universuty San Diego La Jolla Institute for Cognitive Science (1985)
6. LeCun, Y., Bottou, L., Bengio, Y., et al.: Gradient-based learning applied to document recognition. Proc. IEEE **86**(11), 2278–2324 (1998)
7. Wessels, L.F.A., Barnard, E.: Avoiding false local minima by proper initialization of connections. IEEE Trans. Neural Networks **3**(6), 899–905 (1992)

8. Guo, P., Chen, C.L.P., Sun, Y.: An exact supervised learning for a three-layer supervised neural network. In: Proceedings of 1995 International Conference on Neural Information Processing, pp. 1041–1044 (1995)
9. Guo, P., Lyu, M.R., Mastorakis, N.E.: Pseudoinverse learning algorithm for feedforward neural networks. Adv. Neural Networks Appl. 321–326 (2001)
10. Guo, P., Lyu, M.R.: A pseudoinverse learning algorithm for feedforward neural networks with stacked generalization applications to software reliability growth data. Neurocomputing **56**, 101–121 (2004)
11. Guo, P., Lyu, M.R., Chen, C.L.P.: Regularization parameter estimation for feedforward neural networks. IEEE Trans. Syst. Man Cybern. (B) **33**(1), 35–44 (2003)
12. Guo, P.: A VEST of the pseudoinverse learning algorithm (2018). arXiv preprint arXiv:1805.07828
13. Guo P., Zhou X., and Wang K.: PILAE: A Non-gradient Descent Learning Scheme for Deep Feedforward Neural Networks (2018). arXiv preprint arXiv:1811.01545
14. Guo, P., Zhao, D., Han, M., Feng, S.: Pseudoinverse learners: new trend and applications to big data. In: Oneto, L., Navarin, N., Sperduti, A., Anguita, D. (eds.) INNSBDDL 2019. PINNS, vol. 1, pp. 158–168. Springer, Cham (2020). https://doi.org/10.1007/978-3-030-16841-4_17
15. Wong, C.M., Vong, C.M., Wong, P.K., et al.: Kernel-based multilayer extreme learning machines for representation learning. IEEE Trans. Neural Networks Learn. Syst. 2018 **29**(3), 757–762 (2018)
16. Breiman, L.: Random forests. Mach. Learn. **45**(1), 5–32 (2001)
17. Ho, T.K.: Random decision forests. In: Proceedings of 3rd International Conference on Document Analysis and Recognition, pp. 278–282. IEEE (1995)
18. Bonabeau, E., Marco, D.R.D.F., Dorigo, M., Theraulaz, G.: Swarm Intelligence: From Natural to Artificial Systems. Oxford University Press, Oxford (1999)
19. Guo, P.: Computational Intelligence for Software Reliability Engineering. Science Press, China (2012). (In Chinese)

Machine Learning

Efficient Android Phishing Detection Based on Improved Naïve Bayes Algorithm

Dawei Liu, Dong Liu, Yang Li, Mengqi Zhu, Erzhou Zhu, and Xuejian Li[✉]

School of Computer Science and Technology, Anhui University,
Hefei 230601, People's Republic of China
zjmsjtul6@gmail.com, dlahu@gmail.com, liycs@gmail.com,
mqzhu@gmail.com,
{ezzhu,lxj}@ahu.edu.cn

Abstract. With the rapid development of the mobile Internet, phishing attacks are becoming more common on mobile phones. In order to effectively detect phishing attacks on Android platforms, this paper proposes an improved framework based on the revised Naive Bayes algorithm. Under this framework, the K-means algorithm is used to supplement missing values of attributes to get the complete datasets. The probability is enlarged to resolve the problem of low biased estimation of the Bayesian algorithm. Weights of different attributes are evaluated to avoid neglecting the relationship among them to improve the accuracy of phishing website detection. The probability ratio of phishing websites to legitimate websites is adjusted to further improve the correct rate of detection. Experimental results have demonstrated that the proposed framework can effectively detect the phishing attacks with relatively small time cost.

Keywords: Android platform · Phishing · Naïve Bayes

1 Introduction

With the rapid development of mobile technology and the Internet, mobile network attacks and frauds happen constantly. Mobile phishing is an emerging threat targeting mobile users of online shoppers, financial institutions, and social networking companies. Phishing attacks aim to steal private information such as usernames, passwords, and credit card details by way of impersonating legitimate entities. At present, there are a number of defense and protection schemes for phishing attacks on the PC, but the threat is not well mitigated for that on mobile platforms [1]. Mobile platforms are now the new targets of phishing attacks.

Current phishing detection schemes can be roughly divided into three categories: backlist-based schemes, heuristics-based schemes and vision-based schemes [2]. Blacklist based schemes are based on existing phishing blacklists, which are mainly provided by well-known IT companies. These schemes could accurately detect phishing websites that are in the blacklist, but cannot detect zero-day phishing attacks. Heuristics-based schemes extract features from URLs and HTML source code at first. Then, other techniques such as machine learning are used to determine the validity of

© Springer Nature Switzerland AG 2019
Y. Tan et al. (Eds.): ICSI 2019, LNCS 11656, pp. 183–190, 2019.
https://doi.org/10.1007/978-3-030-26354-6_18

websites [3]. In these schemes, the method of choosing features from websites is crucial [4]. Vision-based schemes depend on visual differences between phishing websites and legitimate websites. If the difference exceeds the value of the given threshold, a phishing attack might be alerted. This technique requires complex image processing operations. So, it is not suitable for mobile platforms.

In this paper, we put forward an efficient phishing detection framework based on the improved Naïve Bayes algorithm. Actually, the Naïve Bayes algorithm has solid mathematical foundations and stable performance in classification. It has been widely used in many classification fields [5]. However, traditional Naïve Bayes algorithm also has some deficiencies. For the deficiencies of Naive Bayes algorithm, this paper has made some improvements as follows:

(1) In the process of collecting sample points, some attribute values of sample points are constantly missing. This is because that some information cannot be obtained, or one attribute of some points is unavailable. In this paper, we use the K-means algorithm to fill the missing attribute values.
(2) When the dimension of feature attributes is overmuch, there will be a large number of conditional probability multiplications for Naïve Bayes algorithm. However, these probabilities are always less than 1. So, when these conditional probabilities multiply, it is possible to get low biased estimation. In this paper, we enlarge these probabilities so as to resolve the problem of result underflow.
(3) The traditional Naïve Bayes algorithm neglects the relationship among attributes. It considers attributes to be independent of each other. However, in reality, there is inevitable relevance between attributes and categories. In this paper, we evaluate the weight of different attributes according to the importance of the attributes so as to enhance the classification performance and accuracy of Naïve Bayes algorithm.
(4) In the actual situation, the number of phishing websites is relatively small. In this paper, we adjust the probability ratio (*PR*) of phishing websites to legitimate websites to further improve the accuracy of phishing websites detection.

2   Improvements of Naïve Bayes Algorithm

For the deficiencies of the traditional Naïve Bayes algorithm in phishing websites detection, this section gives the corresponding improvements.

2.1   Filling Values of Missing Attributes

In the process of collecting sample data, some attribute values of sample points are frequently incomplete. Generally, there are two ways to deal with these missing values: deleting them or filling them. The method of deleting data is simple. However, it may result in problem of data deviation (which will lead to error conclusion of the Naïve Bayes algorithm). For this reason, we use the method of filling data to complete the missing attribute values.

As a classical partitional clustering algorithm, K-means is one of the most popular in reality because of its simplicity and effectiveness. For this reason, we use the K-means algorithm to fill the missing values of some attributes. During the procedure of using K-means algorithm to process datasets composed of phishing websites, it is needed to specify two measurements: the average value of an attribute and the similarity among different sample points. In this paper, datasets of phishing websites are the discrete ones. The average value (A) of an attribute is calculated as $A = B_i$. Where, B_i is the corresponding attribute value of the object with the highest usage frequency. Meanwhile, since there are only two states (0 specifies the legitimate website and 1 specifies the phishing one) of the value of an attribute, the similarity $(sim(x_i, x_j))$ between points x_i and x_j can be measured by the Jaccard similarity coefficient as: $sim(x_i, x_j) = |x_i \cap x_j|/|x_i \cup x_j|$. Where, $x_i = x_{i1}, x_{i2}, \ldots, x_{im}$; $x_j = x_{j1}, x_{j2}, \ldots, x_{jm}$; $i, j = 1, 2, \ldots, n$; n is the number of sample points of the target dataset. Based on measurements of average value of attributes and similarity between different points, we can give the main steps of utilizing the K-means algorithm to fill missing values of attributes as:

(1) *Divide the original dataset.* The original dataset is split into two parts, the complete dataset and the incomplete dataset. The complete dataset incorporates sample points with no missing attribute values. While, the incomplete dataset contains sample points with missing attribute values.
(2) *Cluster the complete dataset.* By utilizing the K-means algorithm, the complete dataset is divided into K clusters. Duo to only two states, legitimate website and phishing website, for each point in our dataset, the value of K in the K-means algorithm is set as 2.
(3) *Filling missing attribute values.* In this step, each sample point with missing attribute value is firstly put into its nearest cluster. Then, the missing value of an attribute is substituted by the most appeared value of this attribute.
(4) *Recalculate the mean value.* Repeatedly execute step (2) and step (3) until all the missing values of attributes are filled.

2.2 Eliminating Low Biased Estimation

Traditionally, the Naïve Bayes algorithm is based on the equation as:

$$P(B_i|X) = \sum_{1 < k < n} (P(X_k|B_i)P(B_i))/P(X) \tag{1}$$

In this equation, $P(X)$ specifies the occupancy probability of event X; $P(B_i)$ is the priori probability of B_i; $P(X_k|B_i)$ is the posteriori probability. Actually, $P(X_k|B_i)$ is equal to s_{ik}/s_i. Where, s_i is the number of sample points in category B_i. s_{ik} is the number of sample points in category B_i, meanwhile, the value of the k-th attribute of these sample points is equal to X_k. Under this circumstance, the value of $P(X_k|B_i)$ is estimated by s_{ik}/s_i. However, we will get a low Biased Estimation when the value of s_{ik} is very small. Meanwhile, the value of an arbitrary probability is always not more than 1, the multiple of many attributes values (they are probability values) will get a much smaller value than the original probability values. This result may result in the situation of underflow. However, the result underflow will result in inaccuracy of classification of Naïve Bayes algorithm.

In order to resolve this drawback, we enlarge the samples probability based on the m-estimate of probability [6]. Specifically, the new calculation method is shown as:

$$P(X_k|B_i) = (s_{ik} + mP)/(s_i + m) \tag{2}$$

In this equation, s_{ik} and s_i are defined as before; P is a priori estimate of the definite probability, and m is the size of virtual samples obtained by P distribution. If an attribute has K kinds of values, we set $P = 1/K$.

2.3   Weighting Attributes

The Naïve Bayes algorithm neglects the relationship among different attributes. In reality, there is inevitable relevance among different attributes and categories. If we do not consider their relationships, the classification performance of the Naïve Bayes algorithm will decrease significantly.

To this end, we quantify the relationships between categories and attributes and use the quantization value as the weighted coefficient [7] to weight attributes. In this case, different attributes will obtain different weights based on degrees of quantization values. Based on these observations, the weighted Naïve Bayes formula can be revised as:

$$P(B_i|X) = \left(P(B_i)\sum_{1 \leq k \leq n} (P(X_k|B_i) * w_i)\right)/P(X) \tag{3}$$

Where, w_i represents the weight of the i-th attribute. Obviously, the greater weight of an attribute is assigned, the more degree of influence on the classification performance. In order to get the weight of the i-th attribute (w_i), we firstly define $P(B_i \wedge X_k)$ as:

$$P(B_i \wedge X_k) = \text{count}(B_i \wedge X_k)/\text{count}(X_k) \tag{4}$$

Where, $count(X_k)$ is the number of sample points with the value of the k-th attribute is equal to X_k; $count(B_i \wedge X_k)$ specifies the number of sample points in the category B_i and meanwhile their k-th attribute value is equal to X_k. Then, according to the mathematical knowledge, w_i can be acquired by the following equation ($count(K)$ is the number of values of the k-th attribute):

$$w_i = (count(K) + P(B_i \wedge X_k))/count(K) \tag{5}$$

2.4   Adjusting Probability Ratio (*PR*)

According to the traditional method in Eq. (1), if $P(B_1|X) > P(B_2|X)$ (B_1 is the phishing category, B_2 is the trusted category), website X will be marked as a phishing one. Otherwise, X is a trusted website. However, in actual situations, the number of trusted websites is larger than that of phishing websites. For this reason, the unrevised Naïve Bayes algorithm will get low accuracy of phishing detection. In order to improve the accuracy of phishing detection, we adjust the probability ratio of phishing sites to trusted sites. Specifically, we set a threshold value PR. If $P(B_1|X)/P(B_2|X) > PR$ $(PR > 0)$, we will classify it as phishing sites, otherwise it will be classified into trusted sites.

Actually, the value of PR is obtained by a mass of experiments. In this paper, the value of PR is initialized to 0.1, then gradually increasing PR with step length of 0.1 to observe the correct rate of the framework. For example, Fig. 1 shows the relationship between PR and the accuracy rate our framework. In this experiment, the tested dataset is composed of 500 URLs with 300 trusted sites and 200 phishing sites. After a large number of experiments, we found that the correct rate of our framework reaches the highest value when $PR = 1.5$.

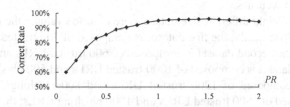

Fig. 1. Relationship between PR and the correct rate.

3 Framework Implementation

According to behaviors of phishing websites, this paper extracts eight features of them. These features are organized as a vector as $V = <F_1, F_2, F_3, F_4, F_5, F_6, F_7, F_8>$. Among these features, F_1 is used to specify whether the target URL contains the IP address; F_2 is used to specify whether the target URL contains special characters (such as '_' and '@'); F_3 is used to determine the corresponding URL has multi-level of domains; F_4 is used to determine the length of the target URL greater than 30 (in the common cases, the length legal URLs often less than 30 characters); F_5 is used to determine whether the target HTML source code contains 'Form' ('Form' is usually used to submit the verification information); F_6 is used to determine whether the target HTML source code contains 'username ' ('username' usually contains the identities of users); F_7 is used to specify whether the target HTML source code contains 'password'; F_8 is used to determine whether the target HTML source code contains 'hyperlink'.

Based on the revised Naïve Bayes algorithm and the collected feature vector of URLs, we can give the main steps of the proposed phishing websites detection framework as:

(1) According to the loaded URL, the proposed framework is initialized;
(2) Features of the target URL are extracted immediately after the web browser loading a web page;
(3) According to the source code of the HTML, features of web page are extracted;
(4) Based on the collected features of URL and the source code of HTML, the feature vector is constructed;
(5) The improved Naïve Bayes algorithm is used to determine whether the target URL is a phishing website or not.

4 Experimental Results

The tested datasets of this section are all composed of two parts, the phishing URLs (from "anquan.org") and the trusted URLs (from "alexa.cn"). Our framework is evaluated by three indexes: the correct rate $(R_C = (r_1 + r_4)/(r_1 + r_2 + r_3 + r_4))$, the precise rate $(R_P = r_1/(r_1 + r_2))$ and the recall rate $(R_R = (r_1)/(r_1 + r_3))$. In our experiments, r_1 is the number of phishing websites that are correctly marked as phishing websites by our framework; r_2 is the number of trusted websites that are wrongly marked as phishing websites; r_3 is the number of phishing websites that are wrongly marked as trusted websites; r_4 is the number of trusted websites that are correctly marked as trusted websites.

In this section, eight different size datasets are used to evaluate the performance of our framework. Specifically, the first dataset is composed of 300 trusted URLs and 200 phishing URLs; the second dataset is composed of 600 trusted URLs and 400 phishing URLs; the third dataset is composed of 1000 trusted URLs and 500 phishing URLs; the forth dataset is composed of 1200 trusted URLs and 800 phishing URLs; the fifth dataset is composed of 1500 trusted URLs and 1000 phishing URLs; the sixth dataset is composed of 2000 trusted URLs and 1000 phishing URLs; the seventh dataset is composed of 2500 trusted URLs and 1000 phishing URLs; the eighth dataset is composed of 2500 trusted URLs and 1500 phishing URLs;

Figure 2 gives the average experimental results on testing eight datasets. Specifically, Fig. 2(a), (b) and (c) give the R_C, R_P and R_R comparisons between the original Naïve Bayes algorithm (marked by "*Original*") and our new proposed framework (marked by "*improved*") respectively. From these experiments, we can see that indexes R_C, R_P and R_R of our proposed framework are increased by 10% than the original Naïve Bayes algorithm. Meanwhile, the R_C of our framework reaches 97.32% when the size of the tested dataset contains more than 3000 samples.

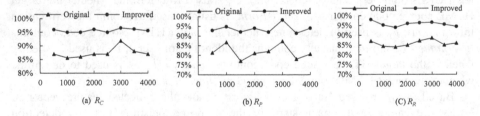

(a) R_C (b) R_P (C) R_R

Fig. 2. Correct rate (R_C), precise rate (R_P) and the recall rate (R_R) comparisons between the original Naïve Bayes algorithm and our new framework.

Table 1 lists the accuracy comparisons among different phishing detection schemes. In this table, "*SVM*" is the classifier that uses the SVM scheme to classify the attributes of URLs; "*Bayes and SVM*" is the classifier that uses Bayes algorithm to classify RULs and uses SVM to process web contents respectively; "Logistic Regression" is the logistic regression classifier that uses the regularization logic methods to detect the URL of a website. From this table, we can see that the accuracy of our proposed framework is slight higher than the traditional methods.

Table 1. Accuracy (R_C) comparisons among different schemes.

Schemes	SVM	Bayes and SVM	Logistic regression	Our framework
R_C	95.6%	94%	95.5%	96.7%

Meanwhile, since the Bayesian algorithm has the merit of time efficiency of classification, our framework incurs relatively lower time cost compared with other classifiers. Table 2 lists the time cost of our framework when it is used to process an input URL. As listed in this table, the process time of our framework can be divided into three stages: (1) the first stage extracts feature attributes from the target URL; (2) the second stage loads the HTML source code through the URL and extracts feature attributes from the content of the target website; (3) the third stage obtains the detection result according to sample data.

Table 2. Time consumption of our framework.

Stages	Time cost	Total time cost
First stage	0.0012 s	1.3739 s
Second stage	1.2897 s	
Third stage	0.0830 s	

5 Conclusion

Since the traditional Naïve Bayes algorithm cannot properly process datasets with URLs of phishing websites, in this paper, we revised this algorithm from four directions. Firstly, the K-means algorithm was used to supplement missing values of attributes to get the complete dataset. Secondly, the probability was enlarged to eliminate the problem of low biased estimation of Naïve Bayes algorithm. Thirdly, the weights of different attributes were evaluated to avoid neglecting the relationship between attributes. Lastly, the probability ratio of phishing sites to trusted sites was adjusted to resolve the problem of small probability of the occurrence of the phishing site in the actual situation. Based on these improvements, we designed a new phishing websites detection framework. Experimental results had demonstrated that the new framework can effectively detect the phishing attacks without incurring much time cost. However, duo to frequently update of phishing websites, we need continuously collect more features of phishing websites to make our framework keep pace with the times.

Acknowledgement. This work was supported by the Natural Science Foundation of Education Department of Anhui province (China) [Grant No. KJ2018A0022] and the National Natural Science Foundation of China [Grant No. 61300169].

References

1. Bicakci, K., Unal, D., Ascioglu, N., Adalier, O.: Mobile authentication secure against man-in-the-middle attacks. Procedia Comput. Sci. **34**, 323–329 (2014)
2. Zhu, J., Wenbo, H.: Recent advances in Bayesian machine learning. J. Comput. Res. Dev. **52** (1), 16–26 (2015)
3. Ramesh, G., Krishnamurthi, I., Kumar, K.S.S.: An efficacious method for detecting phishing webpages through target domain identification. Decis. Support Syst. **61**, 12–22 (2014)
4. Yang, H., Zhang, Y., Yupu, H., et al.: A malware behavior detection system of Android applications based on multi-class features. Chin. J. Comput. **37**(1), 15–27 (2014)
5. Zhang, W., Gao, F.: An improvement to Naive Bayes for text classification. Procedia Eng. **15**, 2160–2164 (2011)
6. Bianchi, A., Corbetta, J., Invernizzi, L., et al.: What the app is that? Deception and countermeasures in the Android user interface. In: Proceedings of the 2015 IEEE Symposium on Security and Privacy (SP 2015), San Jose, CA, USA, 17–21 May 2015, pp. 931–948 (2015)
7. Khonji, M., Iraqi, Y., Jones, A.: Phishing detection: a literature survey. IEEE Commun. Surv. Tutor. **15**(4), 2091–2121 (2013)

Parkinson Disease Analysis Using Supervised and Unsupervised Techniques

Paola Ariza-Colpas[1]([✉]), Roberto Morales-Ortega[1],
Marlon Piñeres-Melo[2], Emiro De la Hoz-Franco[1],
Isabel Echeverri-Ocampo[3], and Katherinne Salas-Navarro[1]

[1] Universidad de la Costa, CUC, Barranquilla, Colombia
{parizal,rmorales,edelahoz,ksalas2}@cuc.edu.co
[2] Universidad del Norte, Barranquilla, Colombia
pineresm@uninorte.edu.co
[3] Instituto Colombiano de Neuropedagogia, Barranquilla, Colombia
isabelceo@gmail.com

Abstract. Parkinson's disease is classified as a disease of neurological origin, which is degenerative and chronic. Currently, the number of people affected by this disease has increased, one in 100 people over 60 years old, although it has been shown that the onset of this disease is approximately 60 years of age. Cases have also been identified of this disorder in patients as young as 18 years old suffer from this disease. Many tests have been developed throughout the literary review in order to identify patients tending to suffer from this disease that currently massifies its prevalence in the world. This article shows the implementation of different machine learning techniques such as LWL, ThresholdSelector, Kstar, VotedPercepton, CVParameterSelection, based on a test performed on experimental individuals and controls in order to identify the presence of the disease.

Keywords: Parkinson's disease · Neurodegenerative analysis ·
Spiral drawings · Machine learning approach

1 Introduction

Parkinson's disease is a chronic, progressive and neurondegenerative illness that affect many people around the world. James Parkinson described this illness in 1817 [1] as "shaking palsy" and fifty years later, Jean-Martin Charcot considered the name of Parkinson's disease. Parkinson's disease is characterized by motor affections as rest tremors, bradykinesia, rigidity, and instabilities in gait and posture and nonmotor symptoms as hyposmia, constipation, or rapid eye movement (REM) sleep behavioral disorder. The spectrum of clinical features varies greatly, some patients have a benign disorder with minimal nondopaminergic symptoms and others presents malignant symptoms with an early predominance of a nondopaminergic motor and nonmotor features.

This paper using the digitized graphics tablet data set for Parkinson disease spiral drawings that consist of 62 people with Parkinson and 15 people healthy who

© Springer Nature Switzerland AG 2019
Y. Tan et al. (Eds.): ICSI 2019, LNCS 11656, pp. 191–199, 2019.
https://doi.org/10.1007/978-3-030-26354-6_19

participated of study of Department of Neurology of the Faculty of Medicine of Cerrahpasa, University of Istanbul. People were taken three handwriting recordings as Static Spiral Test (SST), Dynamic Spiral Test (DST) and Stability Test on Certain Point (STCP). This data set was made using Wacom Cintiq 12WX table that consist of a graphics tablet and LCD monitor rolled into one with special software for recording handwriting drawings and testing the coordination of the PD patients using the recordings [2]. In this experiment, different techniques are used for the identification of Parkinson's disease taking as input data the dataset mentioned above, the techniques were tested, LWL, ThresholdSelector, Kstar, VotedPercepton, CVParameterSelection which showed different performances in the detection of the disease as it is shown in the development of the article.

The article is organized in the next section. First, the brief of literature about the use of different techniques defined in the literatura for detection of Parkinson disease are shown. Second, we explain the dataset that was taken to perform the implementation process and a description of the different techniques selected to perform the analysis is shown. Third, the experimentation is detailed, showing the different results associated with the quality measures of the techniques. Fourth, the result are shown and we explain the reason for select the classifier that was implemented. Fifth, the conclusions of the experimentation are shown and future works.

2 Brief Review of Literature

In the development of the systematic review of the literature, it was possible to show that different authors have made different experiments for the purpose of being able to make accurate diagnoses of Parkinson's disease. Specifically, Mostafa [3] allows to improve the diagnosis of this pathology through the analysis of the existing changes in the patient's voice, by means of a new Multiple Characteristic Evaluation Approach (MFEA) of a multiagent system, which uses different Forms of classification such as: the Decision Tree, Naïve Bayes, The neural network, the randomized forests and the support vector machine in the diagnosis of Parkinson's before and after applying the MFEA, the methodological framework defines the use of cross-validation and an improvement in the implementation of this model is observed in comparison with other existing ones. The average rate of improvement in the diagnostic accuracy of the classifiers is Decision tree 10.51%, Naïve Bayes 15.22%, Neural network 9.19%, Forests random 12.75% and Machine support vectors 9.13%.

Sharma [4], achieved a modification of the modified gray wolf optimization algorithm (MGWO), which achieves the identification in early stages of the disease, due to the different treatments that can be offered by the medical personnel for the purpose of providing care integral that improves the quality of life of the patient. The algorithm proposed by the author performs a previous process of selection of characteristics, it is a metaheuristic type algorithm. The presented algorithm helps in the prediction of Parkinson's disease with an estimated accuracy of 94.83%, a detection rate of 98.28%, a false alarm rate of 16.03% and further helps individuals to receive functional treatment in a early stage.

Glaab [5], raises the use of the molecular image to facilitate the process of diagnosing Parkinson's disease. This type of analysis was contracted through the application of blood plasma tests to patients, 60 with the disease and 15 controls who had the same age and gender. The data groups were analyzed by means of automatic learning techniques, applying machines of linear support vectors or random forests within a cross-validation scheme without interruptions and curves of operating characteristics of the computer receiver (ROC), obtaining as a result that the integration of blood metabolomics data combined with PET data significantly improves the power of diagnostic discrimination. Ferraris [6], does so of the motor analysis to perform the diagnosis of Parkinson's disease. By means of the analysis of the RGB bands of the images of the gestures of the patients, it is possible to carry out the process of the characterization of those who have this affectation. The analysis of the kinetic factors of the different limbs and the postures are considered as an important input for the identification of the pathology. During an experimental campaign, neurologists simultaneously rated and analyzed the performance of patients affected by Parkinson's disease. The results on the ease of use of the system and the accuracy of the evaluation, in comparison with the clinical evaluations, indicate that the system is feasible for an objective and automated evaluation of Parkinson's disease in the home, based on the treatments in home through telemedicine.

Nilashi [7] analyzes the prediction of the presence of Parkinson's disease through the study of speech qualities, as a valid sound signal for the process of implementation of the Singular Value Decomposition (SVD) algorithms and the sets of the Adaptive System of Neuro-Diffuse Inference (ANFIS). The results showed that the proposed method is effective in predicting the progression of PD by improving the accuracy and timing of the diagnosis of the disease. The method can be implemented as a medical decision support system for the diagnosis of PD in real time when large patient data are available in the medical data sets.

3 Materials and Methods

3.1 Description and Preparation of Dataset

The Parkinson Disease Spiral Drawings were made by hand by 62 people with Parkinson's and 15 healthy, for which a Wacom Cintiq 12WX digital graphic tablet was used. The tests were carried out in the Department of Neurology of the Faculty of Medicine of Cerrahpasa, University of Istanbul. For this test three types of recordings were taken: Static Spiral Test - SST, Dynamic Spiral Test - DST and a stability test - STCP. The TSM test was carried out with the objective of determining the motor performance, the tremor measurement and the diagnosis of PE. The second test was DST where the Archimedean spiral simply appeared and disappeared at certain time intervals. In the third test (STCP), people were asked to hold the digital pen in a red dot located in the center of the screen without touching it. The class criterion indicates whether the person has parking (one) or does not (zero). The data set has 77 instances and 79 characteristics, including class criteria.

From the consolidated data set each instance contains: temporal and spatial characteristics, based on arithmetic statistics. The temporal characteristics refer to the time in seconds that it took the individual to perform each of the three tests. The spatial characteristics are: X, Y, Z coordinates, pressure and the GripAngle, for each test. From these characteristics, the range, the standard deviation, the average, the arithmetic mean and the asymmetry, kurtosis, range and skewness were calculated. The mean μ is the average value of the data, i.e., the sum of all occurrence vector fields divided by the total number of data:

$$\mu = \frac{1}{S}\sum_{i=1}^{S}\sigma_i$$

The median is the middle value in a sorted list of data:

$$median = \begin{cases} O_{\frac{S+1}{2}}, & \text{if } S \text{ is odd} \\ \frac{1}{2}\left(O_{\frac{S}{2}} + O_{\frac{S}{2}+1}\right) \end{cases}$$

The range is the difference between the largest value and the smallest value of a dataset

$$O_{range} = O_{max} - O_{min}$$

The standard deviation is the square root of the variance. The variance is the sum of all squared differences from each occurrence value to the mean divided by the number of data S minus 1:

$$\sigma = \sqrt{\frac{1}{S-1}\sum_{i=1}^{S}(O_i - \mu)^2}$$

The kurtosis κ is defined as the quotient of the fourth central moment of a dataset $m4$, and the standard deviation σ power 4:

$$k = \frac{m_4}{\sigma^4} = \frac{\frac{1}{S}\sum_{i=1}^{S}(O_i - \mu)^4}{\left(\sqrt{\frac{1}{S}\sum_{i=1}^{S}(O_i - \mu)^2}\right)^4}$$

The skewness γ is defined as the quotient of the third central moment $m3$ of a dataset, and the cubed standard deviation.

$$\gamma = \frac{m_3}{\sigma^3} = \frac{\frac{1}{S}\sum_{i=1}^{S}(O_i - \mu)^3}{\left(\sqrt{\frac{1}{S}\sum_{i=1}^{S}(O_i - \mu)^2}\right)^3}$$

3.2   Materials and Methods

3.2.1   LWL

LWL or rather known as locally weighted learning, consists of a specific class of techniques that allow the approximation of function [8], the prediction in this model is done through approach points near the current point of interest. This method is not considered to be parametric, therefore, predictions are made through the use of subsets of data. The main objective of the LWL is the creation of models of local type associated to certain points of interest adjacent to a central point of consultation, instead of having a general model. The definition of these points is achieved through the weighting of these points in relation to the influence of the data for the prediction process. All the datums are close to the current point, but those that are farther away take greater weight. This algorithm is also called as the lazy algorithm because of the displacement that must be made to each point to perform the respective query. Normally this algorithm has a very high precision because it adds new points to the training [9].

3.2.2   ThresholdSelector

The methods of the threshold value are a group of algorithms whose purpose is to segment rasterized graphics [10], that is, to separate the objects of an image that interest us from the rest. With the help of threshold value methods in the simplest situations you can decide which pixels make up the objects you are looking for and which pixels are just the environment of these objects. This method is especially useful to separate the text of a document from the background of the image (yellowish paper, with spots and wrinkles for example) and thus be able to carry out the optical recognition of text (OCR) with more guarantees of obtaining the correct text. This is especially useful if we want to digitize old books, in which the contrast between the text (which has already lost some of its pigments) and the paper (darkened and thumbed) is not too high [11].

3.2.3   KStar

The methods of clustering of hierarchical type have as objective the optimization of a specific function [12]. That is, objects in the same cluster should be similar to each other, while those in different groups should be as different as posible. The different algorithms framed within this method vary mainly in the measure of similarity and the criterion to evaluate the overall quality of the grouping carried out K-Star is known as a method framed in the hierarchical typology, in which different groups of clusters are generated where different similar characteristics can be identified [13].

3.2.4   VotedPercepton

The Voted-Perceptron algorithm is an algorithm that is based on the original Rosenblatt and Frank algorithm [14]. The algorithm has good performance due to the use of data that has high separability takes advantage of data that are linearly separable with large data margins. This method is simpler to implement and much more efficient in terms of calculation time compared to Vapnik's SVM. The algorithm can also be used in very high dimensional spaces using core functions [15].

4 Experimentation

For this experimentarrion we used the The Parkinson Disease Spiral Drawings Using Digitized Graphics Tablet Data Set provided by UCI Machine Learning, consists of 62 PWP (People with Parkinson) and 15 healthy individuals at the Department of Neurology in Cerrahpasa Faculty of Medicine, Istanbul University. Three types of recordings (Static Spiral Test - SST, Dynamic Spiral Test - DST and Stability Test on Certain Point STCP) are taken. Handwriting dataset was constructed using Wacom Cintiq 12WX graphics table [16, 17].

Para el analisis de la calidad de los resultados de la expermentación fueron utilizadas las siguientes metricas de calidad, las cuales son descritas a continuación: accuracy, preccission, recall, F-measure.

$$Accuracy = \frac{(true\ positive + true\ negative)}{total} \tag{1}$$

$$\Pr ecision = \frac{true positive}{(true\ positive + false\ positive)} \tag{2}$$

$$Recall = \frac{true\ positive}{true\ positive + false\ negative} \tag{3}$$

$$F - measure = \frac{2 * precision * recall}{precision + recall} \tag{4}$$

5 Results

In the present experimentation, the data preparation process was taken as a starting point, afterwards the selection of the most adequate technique to be applied to the constructed dataset. The result of the algorithms coverage are shows (Figs. 1, 2, 3 and 4and Table 1):

Table 1. Algorithm result

	Accuracy	Precision	Recall	F-measure
LWL	91.67%	94.12%	88.89%	91.43%
ThresholdSelector	86.90%	82.98%	92.86%	87.64%
Kstar	79.76%	100%	59.52%	74.63%
VotedPercepton	64.29%	65.79%	59.52%	62.50%
CVParameterSelection	47.62%	48.48%	76.19%	59.26%

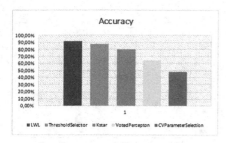

Fig. 1. Accuracy results

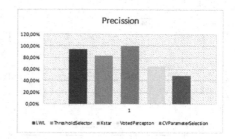

Fig. 2. Precission results

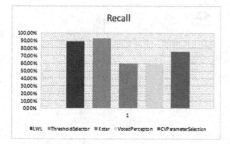

Fig. 3. Recall results

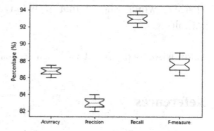

Fig. 4. F-measure results

Product of the cross validation application with each of the selected classification algorithms, the mean and the variation in each of the four metrics in the algorithm with the best LWL and the others algorithms results performance are shown next (Figs. 5, 6, 7, 8 and 9).

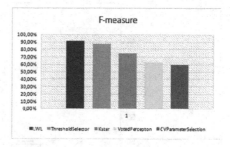

Fig. 5. LWL variation

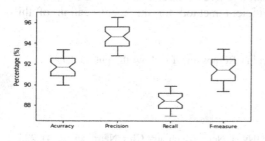

Fig. 6. ThresholdSelector variation

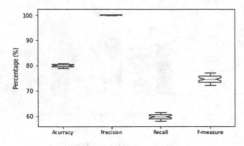

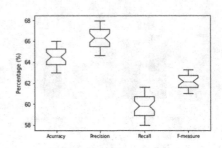

Fig. 7. Kstar variation   **Fig. 8.** VotedPercepton variation

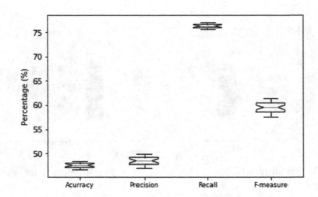

Fig. 9. CVParameterSelection variation

6   Conclusions

The LWL technique provide a good result for identify the Parkinson disease with this metric result: Accuracy 91.67%, Precision 94.12%, Recall 88.89% and F-measure 91.43%, which shows that it is an efficient method for the identification of this pathology.

Acknowledgment. The UCI Machine Learning Respository for show the public dataset.

References

1. Parkinson, J.: An essay on the shaking palsy. J. Neuropsychiatry Clin. Neurosci. **20**(4), 223–236 (1817)
2. Braak, H., Bohl, J.R., Müller, C.M., Rüb, U., de Vos, R.A., Del Tredici, K.: Stanley Fahn Lecture 2005: the staging procedure for the inclusion body pathology associated with sporadic Parkinson's disease reconsidered. Mov. Disord.: Off. J. Mov. Disord. Soc. **21**(12), 2042–2051 (2006)

3. Mostafa, S.A., et al.: Examining multiple feature evaluation and classification methods for improving the diagnosis of Parkinson's disease. Cogn. Syst. Res. **54**, 90–99 (2019)
4. Sharma, P., Sundaram, S., Sharma, M., Sharma, A., Gupta, D.: Diagnosis of Parkinson's disease using modified grey wolf optimization. Cogn. Syst. Res. **54**, 100–115 (2019)
5. Glaab, E., et al.: Integrative analysis of blood metabolomics and PET brain neuroimaging data for Parkinson's disease. Neurobiol. Dis. **124**, 555–562 (2019)
6. Ferraris, C., et al.: Feasibility of home-based automated assessment of postural instability and lower limb impairments in Parkinson's disease. Sensors **19**(5), 1129 (2019)
7. Echeverry, I., Urina-Triana, M., Ariza-Colpas, P., Mantilla, M.: El trabajo colaborativo entre ingenieros y personal de la salud para el desarrollo de proyectos en salud digital: una visión al futuro para lograr tener éxito. Revista Latinoamericana de Hipertensión **13**(4) (2018)
8. De-La-Hoz-Franco, E., Ariza-Colpas, P., Quero, J.M., Espinilla, M.: Sensor-based datasets for human activity recognition–a systematic review of literature. IEEE Access **6**, 59192–59210 (2018)
9. Yin, S., Xie, X., Sun, W.: A nonlinear process monitoring approach with locally weighted learning of available data. IEEE Trans. Ind. Electron. **64**(2), 1507–1516 (2017)
10. Calabria-Sarmiento, J.C., et al.: Software Applications to Health Sector: A Systematic Review of Literature (2018)
11. Lehnert, C., Wyeth, G.: Locally weighted learning model predictive control for nonlinear and time varying dynamics. In: 2013 IEEE International Conference on Robotics and Automation, pp. 2619–2625. IEEE, May 2013
12. Jimeno Gonzalez, K., Ariza Colpas, P., Piñeres Melo, M.: Gobierno de TI en Pymes Colombianas.¿ Mito o Realidad (2017)
13. Xie, X., Lam, J., Yin, S., Cheung, K.C: A novel nonlinear process monitoring approach: locally weighted learning based total PLS. In: IECON 2016-42nd Annual Conference of the IEEE Industrial Electronics Society, pp. 7137-7142. IEEE, October 2016
14. Palechor, F.M., De la Hoz Manotas, A., Colpas, P.A., Ojeda, J.S., Ortega, R.M., Melo, M.P.: Cardiovascular disease analysis using supervised and unsupervised data mining techniques. JSW **12**(2), 81–90 (2017)
15. Vijayakumar, S., Schaal, S.: Local dimensionality reduction for locally weighted learning. In: Proceedings 1997 IEEE International Symposium on Computational Intelligence in Robotics and Automation CIRA 1997. Towards New Computational Principles for Robotics and Automation, pp. 220–225. IEEE, July 1997
16. Mendoza-Palechor, F.E., Ariza-Colpas, P.P., Sepulveda-Ojeda, J.A., De-la-Hoz-Manotas, A., Piñeres Melo, M.: Fertility analysis method based on supervised and unsupervised data mining techniques (2016)
17. Palechor, F.M., De la hoz Manotas, A., De la hoz Franco, E, Ariza-Colpas, P.: Feature selection, learning metrics and dimension reduction in training and classification processes in intrusion detection systems. J. Theor. Appl. Inf. Technol. **82**(2) (2015)

Implementation of the Eclipse Process Framework Composer Tool for the Documentation of Quality Management Systems: A Case Applied in Healthcare Services

Juan-David De-la-Hoz-Hernández[1] ,
Alexander Troncoso-Palacio[2(✉)] , and Emiro De-la-Hoz-Franco[2]

[1] Corporación Universitaria Latinoamericana, Barranquilla, Colombia
jdelahozh@ul.edu.co
[2] Universidad de la Costa, Barranquilla, Colombia
{atroncos1, edelahoz}@cuc.edu.co

Abstract. This document presents the implementation of the Eclipse Process Framework Composer EPFC tool, in a company in the health sector, which where it were using physical documentation to register the processes QMS Quality Management Systems, in this one it is explained the process of adapting the tool, to migrate the documentary structure of the company, through the application of a model that correlates the attributes of the tool with the documentary structure. The proposed model allows the construction of document structures for the QMS that guide the user in their processes and procedures within the organization. Therefore, it is proposed that by promoting knowledge management and reducing the execution time of the processes, it will be possible for companies to be more productive, improve customer service, failure rates in the development of activities be minimized and, and reduces the lead time in the processes. Finally, it was obtained a documentary platform developed under a process approach that implements interactive diagrams that aim to facilitate the understanding of each of the elements that make up the QMS.

Keywords: Quality Management System - QMS ·
Eclipse Process Framework Composer - EPFC ·
Document Management System - DMS · Delays in documentation

1 Introduction

Starting from the premise that the latest scientific and technological advances in the world increase every day, is necessary the companies will be more competitive, staying reducing the waiting time and delays in the consulting their processes. According to [1–3], the companies must have increasingly efficient systems, where it can track their processes in an agile way, organized and in a timely manner with which certification will be achieved in international standards such as ISO 9001. Most of the world's organizations, have aligned their strategy and operation to the standards established for

© Springer Nature Switzerland AG 2019
Y. Tan et al. (Eds.): ICSI 2019, LNCS 11656, pp. 200–210, 2019.
https://doi.org/10.1007/978-3-030-26354-6_20

the Integrated Management System - IMS, allowing the merger of the Quality, Environment, Health and Safety Management Systems - QMEHSS. For this, the companies from all productive sectors use technology to increase productivity. This document was implemented for the construction of the documentary structure for the QMS of a health company, through a model that allows the development of documentary platforms for QMS. Where a set of interrelated and highly interactive flow diagrams facilitate the understanding of the macro processes, processes and procedures of the organization. Many organizations currently use documentation mechanisms through text formats. This project will be used to solve problems related to the way in which processes are documented and access to QMS information. With the implementation on the platform EPFC, The processes were developed, identifying the antecedents and the interactions between them, allowing to achieve the following objectives: The Efficient development of processes, and the reduction of execution times. Consequently, whit based on the methodology implemented by [4–7], where was established that in the processes is fundamental to take into account the interactions, the resource utilization, the productivity rate and proportion of tardy jobs. Due to the above, the search parameters used in the literary review was determined according to the set of combinations shown in the Fig. 1.

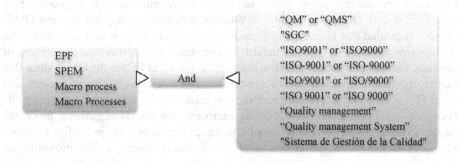

Fig. 1. Search combinations. The databases used: IEEE Xplorer, ProQuest, Science Direct, Ebsco, Scopus and ACM

2   Literary Review

According with [8], the information is the most important resource for an organization, so it is essential that it is easy to understand for the people involved in companies, whether internal or external. In the research by [9], it is manifest that when the information is poorly documented, it can be misunderstood by the parties involved, and can also create barriers in the communication. The previous problem extremely affects the execution of the processes and knowledge management in the QMS. In order to solve this situation, a series of documentary platforms have emerged, such as: [10–17], among others. Most of the current applications these platforms are based on the use of overpriced software packages, as explained by [18], where is wanted to safeguard all the information related to the quality of the company and facilitate access to it.

However, although these tools are adequately structured, many of them document the processes and the procedures under simple text formats, that is, they use vast texts for the description of the processes and the procedures of the organization. In the same way, those QMS software that apply flowcharts tend to have very high costs for SMEs. Situation that notably affects the way in which the QMS is applied in these companies. In [19], it is affirmed that the cluster of employees responsible of the processes inside the companies declare dissatisfaction with the technique in which information concerning the processes and the procedures is documented, which generates a lack of interest by the users, and additionally preventing that the information being sought in the documentation systems tools for QMS. Therefore, it is fundamental the way information is recorded in the documentary platforms. According to [20], this influences the active participation of employees, in the implementation, the maintenance and the improvement of the organization. Further in [19], the role of information in the QMS is presented, in order to provide a specific execution route for the implementation of complementary processes and [21], is indicated that the information must be considered in relation to the person who receives it. In general, EPFC, has been implemented for the documentation and structure of software processes, but not for the documentation of a QMS. In [22], The EPFC, tool has been used to create a manual for the teacher induction process, which demonstrates the use of this software as a mechanism for documentation in the management systems. In [23] is provided an overall framework of the implementation process, which can be applied to every QMS. It is recommended that all companies make improvements in operations, to adjust the requirements of the ISO 9001 standard to corporate audit processes. In review of literature, founding no background has been of the use of EPFC for the QMS, since this is currently used as a tool to document software processes. In [24] it can be seen that the EPFC, aims to be a technological support structure for software engineering the processes, this being a tool for modeling elements that allows organizing processes without making great efforts in terms of coding. In the same way, in [25], it is shows the use of EPFC for the development of an electronic process guide, providing an effective and erasable process addressing. Complementarily, in [26], it is stated that EPFC is an industrial software engineering tool that supports the modularization and composition of the process elements, using them to generate customized processes.

Based on the above, this paper seeks to generate a correlation model that allows the use of the EPFC tool for QMS, creating interactive documentary platforms that use flowcharts that allow the staff of the organization to understand agile and simple way everything related to existing the processes and the procedures. It is possible to consider the unification of these documentary requirements to generate a structure that not only fully complies with the requirements of the different standards, but also allows the creation of a QMS that uses a management effective documents. In the Table 1, is possible appreciate the documentary requirements. For greater accuracy, each element of the table, was defined based on the Quality standards.

Quality policies: In accordance with [27], the policies define the orientation of an organization towards quality, to the [28], there must be documented statements of these.

Table 1. Component and relations

Items	9000:2004	9000:2015	9001:2008	9001:2015	10013:2002
Quality policies	x	x	x	x	x
Quality objectives	x	x	x	x	x
Quality manual	x	x	x		x
QMS scope				x	
Quality plans	x	x			x
Guidelines	x				
Documented procedures	x	x	x		x
Records		x	x	x	x
Works instructions and drawings	x				x
External documents			x	x	x
Forms					x

Quality objectives: According [29] objectives are defined as something ambitious related to quality and like quality policies [28], indicates that it is necessary to handle documented statements of quality.

Quality manual: In the Technical Standards [27, 29] define it as that document that discloses the specifications of the Quality Management System of an organization. The [28] indicates that this should be established and maintained within the organization taking into account the elements that comprise it, which are described in detail in ISO 10013:2002. It should be noted that although the [30] does not mention the existence of this document, it does indicate that those elements that make it up must be documented.

Scope of the QMS: According to the technical norms [27–29] and [30], the scope of the QMS contains information regarding the limitations, applicability and exclusions of the system, which is why it must be available and remain as documented information.

Quality plans: It is that document that contains the specifications of the procedures, resources and those responsible [27, 29]. This commonly referenced different parts of the quality manual and according to [31], belongs to the documentation of the Quality Management System.

Guidelines: The [29], defines guidelines as documents that is part of the person in charge of providing suggestions or recommendations.

Documented procedures: The [27, 29], define it as that specific form in which an activity or a process is carried out, its documentation is optional, notwithstanding the [28], indicates that the quality manual should establish the documented procedures of the Quality Management System and a documented procedure that defines the necessary controls in relation to the documentation of the QMS.

Work instructions: the [27], indicates that they are documents that provide information on how the activities and processes are carried out in a coherent manner and their documentary structure is specified in numbers 4.6 and 3.1 of ISO 10013: 2002.

Specifications: These are the documents that establish the requirements, whether of an activity, procedure or product [27, 29, 31].

Registration: The records defined according to [27, 29], as those documents that provide evidence of the activities carried out, according to [28], these must be controlled, For this reason, a documented procedure must be established for its control, in addition to keeping said records legible, identifiable and recoverable. The [27], lists the records that are mandatory according to the standard (Annex B).

Forms: According [31] these documents are developed and maintained in order to give accuracy of compliance with the requirements of the QMS.

External documents: According to the [31], organization must consider the external documents and their controls, the [30], indicates that information of external activities must be kept, because it is necessary information for the planning and operation of the QMS [28].

3   Data Collection and Methodology

The processes architecture alludes to a methodology of business engineering that according to [32], seeks to instantiate the relevant macro processes of an organization and determine their relationships through a generic structure, all this to reach a strategic positioning. In [33], it is argued that one of the main implications for the organization is that these architectures allow aligning the products and processes generating better demand opportunities in the different environments of the organization. Consequently, it is considered that this methodology focused on the macro process approach seeks to through time generate improvements in the organization through the strategic structure of the processes.

A descriptive analytical methodology was used, that carried out a systematic literature´s review, which allowed analyze the rules that establish the documentary requirements for the QMS, in order to identify, which are the required documents that must be handled. With that, it was proceeded to identify the structure and configure EPFC, metadata´s parameters, achieving apply the documentary requirements of the QMS. In the Fig. 2, is showed the diagram that structures the methodology used in this study, to organize the documents collected during the systematic literature review.

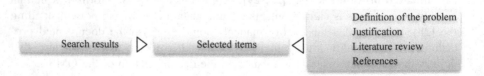

Fig. 2. Methodology for the systematic review of the literature.

4   Case Study: Documentation a Quality Management System in Healthcare Services

Due to the fact that there are smalls and medium companies that wish to carry out the documentation of their processes in a better approach, without implying a considerable increase in their software acquisition or development costs. For this reason, is proposed the application of a model in the Table 2, where can recognize how each of the documents established by quality standards should be created to design an adequate documentary platform.

Table 2. Correlation model

QMS elements	EPFC settings	EPF view
Politics	Guidance/Checklist	Company information
Objectives-Scope-Exclusions Mission-Vision	Guidance/Supporting materials	Company information
Procedures	Task or processes	Sub processes and activities
Responsible	Role	Responsible
Products	Work product (Artifact, derivable or Outcome)	Products
Processes	Processes	Processes maps
Records – Controls Support documents	Guidance supporting materials	Support documents
Definitions	Concepts	Definitions

This model indicates in the first column the types of documents necessary to build a Document Management System (DMS) according with the provisions in the standards NTC-ISO 9000: 2005, NTC-ISO 9000: 2015, NTC-ISO 9001: 2008, NTC-ISO 9001: 2015 and GTC-ISO 10013: 2002, besides, the past versions of the standard were taken into account due to the fact that many companies are currently doing the updating process. In the second column are the configuration elements by which the documentary components of the QMS are created. Finally, column three indicates the section within which each document is lodged according to its typology.

4.1   Structures Developed in HTML

With the correlation model presented in the Table 2, is possible to build a documentary software that contains the entire outline of the processes of a company. To do so, is necessary to know the information corresponding to each of the documents indicated in column one of the correlation model, and must be transcribed, either by simple text or by HTML code, to enter basic information of one of the strategic processes of the company that was taken in the present case study as shown in the Fig. 3.

Fig. 3. Structure HTML

Subsequently, is ordered each of the activities and the procedures, taking into account the structure of the processes used by the company, in the Fig. 4 present the PDCA cycle and the set of activities that are part of this.

4.2 Development of UML Diagrams Used for the Construction of Flowcharts

The processes and activities ordered with the UML structure, it is based on the hierarchy managed by the company, as shown in the Fig. 4.

Presentation Name	Index	Predecessors	Model Info	Type	Planned
◢ ⬢ Ciclo PHVA	0			Capability P...	☑
⬡ Liderazgo	1			Task Descri...	☐
⬡ Apoyo	2			Task Descri...	☐
⬡ Contexto de la organización	3			Task Descri...	☐
⬡ Operación	4	1,6		Task Descri...	☐
⬡ Evaluación de desempeño	5	4,1		Task Descri...	☐
⬡ Planificación	6	1,3		Task Descri...	☐
⬡ Mejoramiento	7	1,5		Task Descri...	☐

Fig. 4. Insertion of activities and procedures.

Afterwards, the flowcharts of each of the procedures, the processes and the macro processes that are part of the company are generated. It´s important realize that the processes maps must be distributed according to their typology: Strategic, Missionary or Support process.

4.3 Building of Documentary Platforms for Quality Management Systems (QMS) Through the Correlation Model

The previous steps and the purposed model, show that EPFC, despite being designed for the documentation in software processes, can be applied in the creation of a documentary structure that allows management knowledge and the understanding of the quality processes in an agile approach, by means of the implementation of flowcharts and a focus of the processes as established in international quality standards. Allowing that EPFC, as a tool could be useful for companies that wish to move from physical documentation to an inexpensive electronic document system. It should be noted that one of the benefits obtained using this tool is that its approach through the use of flow charts seeks to facilitate the understanding of the processes, in order to reduce the indices of failures in the development of activities through an appropriate transmission of knowledge, in such a way that each operator identifies his role within this. The above statements are supported through the case applied to a company in the health sector of the city of Barranquilla. All physical documentation was migrated to a documentary structure for its QMS, based on the proposed model of the Fig. 5. It was possible to visualize the whole scheme of the company through a platform on the intranet, based in international quality standards and that seeks to allow small and medium companies to begin to familiarize themselves with this type of digital tools, which aim to facilitate the handling of information in a company.

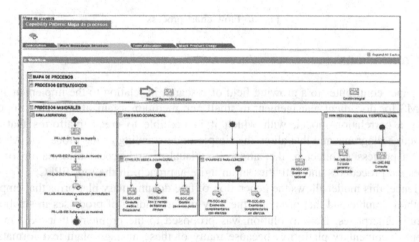

Fig. 5. Map of the process of a company in the healthcare

Finally, it is been obtained a documentary platform developed under a process approach that implements interactive diagrams that aim to facilitate the understanding of each of the elements that make up the QMS. Figure 6 shows the flowchart developed.

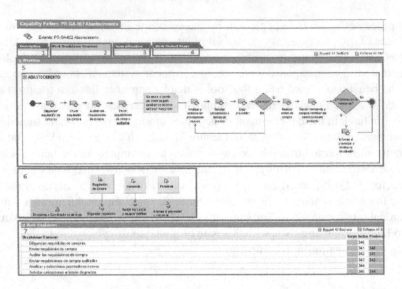

Fig. 6. Flow chart process

5 Conclusions

This paper contributes to a growing field of research in relation to the implementation of QMS for document management in small and medium organizations. The proposal shows a correlation model, with which it is possible to create platforms that use interactive diagrams and that allow the simple understanding of the processes. All this using a process architecture that allows to visualize and access information of the processes, procedures and activities in an agile approach, in the tool EPFC.

Hence, this model allows the generation of free documentary platforms that employ a method graphic and that promotes the easy understanding of processes in small and medium enterprises. Here a solution was proposed to the problems that exist in the current documentary platforms, because many of these manage plain text formats to document their processes and procedures.

This model is completely replicable, and in the future it can be complemented with any other Management System in companies of all sectors, to develop the documentation in an agile way.

Acknowledgments. This paper is derived from the degree project: "Model for the documentary support of Quality Management Systems in the Eclipse Process Framework Composer Software Platform". Which, Juan David De-la-Hoz-Hernandez, is the author. Therefore, the authors would like to thank the tutors Andres-Sanchez-Comas, Aurora Piñeres-Castillo and also to company where this study was implemented.

References

1. Pho, H.T., Tambo, T.: Integrated management systems and workflow-based electronic document management: an empirical study. J. Ind. Eng. Manag. **7**(1), 194–217 (2014)
2. Pino, F.J., García, F., Piattini, M.: Software process improvement in small and medium software enterprises: a systematic review. Softw. Qual. J. **16**(2), 237–261 (2008)
3. Alič, M.: www.intechopen.com. http://dx.doi.org/10.5772/intechopen.71372. Accessed 20 Dec 2017
4. Troncoso-Palacio, A., Neira-Rodado, D., Ortíz-Barrios, M., Jiménez-Delgado, G., Hernández-Palma, H.: Using discrete-event-simulation for improving operational efficiency in laboratories: a case study in pharmaceutical industry. In: Tan, Y., Shi, Y., Tang, Q. (eds.) ICSI 2018. LNCS, vol. 10942, pp. 440–451. Springer, Cham (2018). https://doi.org/10.1007/978-3-319-93818-9_42
5. Caicedo García, M.A., Pérez Vargas, M.d.J.: Marco para la aplicación de mejoras radicales en los procesos durante la implementación y certificación de sistemas de gestión de la calidad, Barranquilla (2017)
6. Acosta-Coll, M., Ballester-Merelo, F., Martinez-Peiró, M., De la Hoz-Franco, E.: Real-time early warning system design for pluvial flash floods-a review. Sensors **18**(7), 2255 (2018)
7. De-La-Hoz-Franco, E., Ariza-Colpas, P., Quero, J.M., Espinilla, M.: Sensor-based datasets for human activity recognition - a systematic review of literature. IEEE Access **6**, 59192–59210 (2018)
8. Salaün, Y., Flores, K.: Information quality: meeting the needs of the consumer. Int. J. Inf. Manag. **21**(1), 21–37 (2001)
9. Burgin, M., Semenovich, M.: Theory of Information: Fundamentality, Diversity and Unification. World Scientific (2010)
10. Daruma Software. darumasoftware.com. http://darumasoftware.com/. Accessed 24 Nov 2018
11. ISODOC. https://isodoc.co. Accessed 24 Nov 2018
12. Solución® Calidad. Guías soluciones TIC. https://www.guiadesolucionestic.com/sistemas-de-informacion/gestion-de-procesos-de-negocios-bpm-herramientas-de-productividad/gestion-de-calidad-mejoramiento-continuo-iso-9001-ntcgp1000-meci/1891-isolucion-calidad. Accessed 26 Nov 2018
13. kawak. kawak.net. https://kawak.net/. Accessed 26 Nov 2018
14. Mejoramiso. mejoramiso.com. https://www.mejoramiso.com/. Accessed 26 Nov 2018
15. Open km. openkm.com. https://www.openkm.com/es/. Accessed 26 Nov 2018
16. Open Doc Man. opendocman.com. http://www.opendocman.com/free-download/. Accessed 30 Nov 2018
17. Alfresco. alfresco.com. https://www.alfresco.com/es/. Accessed 30 Nov 2018
18. Calvo, I., López, F., Zulueta, E., González-Nalda, P.: Towards a methodology to build virtual reality manufacturing systems based on free open software technologies. Int. J. Interact. Des. Manuf. **11**(3), 569–580 (2016)
19. Grudzień, Ł., Hamrol, A.: Information quality in design process documentation of quality management systems. Int. J. Inf. Manag.: J. Inf. Prof. **36**(4), 599–606 (2016)
20. Lazär, L.-V., Gheorghe, M.: Modeling of documents and flowcharts from service quality management system. UPB Sci. Bull. Ser. D: Mech. Eng. **77**(3), 163–172 (2015)
21. Stefanowicz, B.: Informacyjne systemy zarządzania: przewodnik, Szkoła Główna Handlowa - Oficyna Wydawnicza, Varsovia, Warszawa (2007)
22. Abad Londoño, J.H.: Repositorio Institucional Universidad EAFIT. http://hdl.handle.net/10784/691. Accessed 08 Nov 2012

23. Seppälä, R.: Implementing a Quality Management System for an Engineering and Services Company (2015)
24. Baumgarten, G., Rosinger, M., Todino, A., de Juan Marín, R.: SPEM 2.0 as process baseline meta-model for the development and optimization of complex embedded systems. In: 2015 IEEE International Symposium on Systems Engineering (ISSE), Roma (2015)
25. Koolmanojwong, S., Phongpaibul, M., Laoteppitak, N., Boehm, B.: Comparative experiences with software process modeling tools for the incremental commitment model. Center for Software Engineering, California (2008)
26. Aleixo, F.A., Freire, M., Alencar, D., Campos, E.: A comparative study of compositional and annotative modelling approaches for software process lines. In: 26th Brazilian Symposium on Software Engineering, Natal, Brazil (2012)
27. ISO: NTC-ISO 9000 Sistemas de Gestión de la Calidad - Fundamentos y vocabulario (2015). https://www.iso.org/obp/ui/#iso:std:iso:9000:ed-4:v1:es
28. ISO: Fundación Centro Colombiano de estudios profesionales. https://www.cecep.edu.co/documentos/calidad/ISO-9001-2008.pdf. Accessed 14 Nov 2008
29. ISO: NTC-ISO 9001 Sistemas de Gestión de la Calidad. Requisitos. https://www.cecep.edu.co/documentos/calidad/ISO-9001-2008.pdf. Accessed 14 Nov 2008
30. ISO: International Organization for Standardization (2015). https://www.iso.org/obp/ui/#iso:std:iso:9001:ed-5:v1:en
31. ISO: Organización Internacional de Normalización (2002). https://www.iso.org/obp/ui#iso:std:iso:tr:10013:ed-1:v1:es
32. Barrios Fernández, N., Ricard Delgado, M., Fernández Elías, R.: La definición de funciones en la gestión de la calidad de los procesos universitarios. Cofin Habana 10(2), 95–114 (2016)
33. Colón Sáenz, S.J., Siple De La Espriella, A.F.: Arquitectura Empresarial Para Alinear Las Tic Con Los Procesos De Negocio De Las Pyme Del Sector Hoteles Y Restaurantes De Cartagena (2016)

Enkephalon - Technological Platform to Support the Diagnosis of Alzheimer's Disease Through the Analysis of Resonance Images Using Data Mining Techniques

Paola Ariza-Colpas[1]([⊠]), Marlon Piñeres-Melo[2],
Ernesto Barceló-Martinez[3], Emiro De la Hoz-Franco[1],
Juan Benitez-Agudelo[3], Melissa Gelves-Ospina[1],
Isabel Echeverri-Ocampo[3], Harold Combita-Nino[1],
and Alexandra Leon-Jacobus[4]

[1] Universidad de la Costa, CUC, Barranquilla, Colombia
{parizal,edelahoz,mgelves1,hcombital}@cuc.edu.co
[2] Universidad del Norte, Barranquilla, Colombia
pineresm@uninorte.edu.co
[3] Instituto Colombiano de Neuropedagogia, Barranquilla, Colombia
ebarcelo@yahoo.es, investigacion2@icnweb.org,
isabelceo@gmail.com
[4] Universidad Metropolitana de Barranquilla, Barranquilla, Colombia
aleonj@unimetro.edu.co

Abstract. Dementia can be considered as a decrease in the cognitive function of the person. The main diseases that appear are Alzheimer and vascular dementia. Today, 47 million people live with dementia around the world. The estimated total cost of dementia worldwide is US $ 818 billion, and it will become a trilliondollar disease by 2019 The vast majority of people with dementia not received a diagnosis, so they are unable to access care and treatment. In Colombia, two out of every five people presented a mental disorder at some point in their lives and 90% of these have not accessed a health service. Here it´s proposed a technological platform so early detection of Alzheimer. This tool complements and validates the diagnosis made by the health professional, based on the application of Machine Learning techniques for the analysis of a dataset, constructed from magnetic resonance imaging, neuropsychological test and the result of a radiological test. A comparative analysis of quality metrics was made, evaluating the performance of different classifier methods: Random subspace, Decorate, BFTree, LMT, Ordinal class classifier, ADTree and Random forest. This allowed us to identify the technique with the highest prediction rate, that was implemented in ENKEPHALON platform.

Keywords: Resonance images · Image processing · Image mining · Alzheimer's disease

© Springer Nature Switzerland AG 2019
Y. Tan et al. (Eds.): ICSI 2019, LNCS 11656, pp. 211–220, 2019.
https://doi.org/10.1007/978-3-030-26354-6_21

1 Introduction

Alzheimer's disease is a significant public health problem, which causes serious problems of thinking, memory and activities of daily living, in older adult between the ages of 80 and 90 years. People with mild dementia generally exhibit impairments of memory, reasoning and thought. Requiring in some cases, support or supervision of a family member or caregiver to complete the activities, which they carry out daily. This solution is not always practical, because it leads to a decrease in the level of autonomy of the individual with Alzheimer's and because the costs of hiring a caregiver are always accessible to people suffering from this disease. Around one-third of people with dementia currently live alone without this caring presence [1].

Furthermore, the cost of providing such care is unsustainable and represents an average annual cost of £32,250 per person. In the UK alone, the overall financial impact of dementia is £26.3billion which is disaggregated in: £3.4 billion of healthcare costs, £10.3 of social care (£4.5 billion spent on publically-funded social care and £5.8 billion spent on privately-funded social care), £11.6 billion of unpaid care and £111 million on other dementia costs. Moreover, the total of £26.3 billion is 24% higher in comparison with the cost reported in 2007 (£21.2 billion) and continues to rise with a projected future cost of £34.8 billion, which is considered as a huge drain on the public purse and it is of particular concern to policy makers. Additionally, 66.6% of the cost of dementia is paid by people with dementia and their families, either in unpaid care (£11.6 billion) or in paying for private social care (£5.8 billion). Nevertheless, the cost derived from the attention to people with dementia might be meaningfully reduced through improvements in care and support for these people and their carers, avoiding future admissions and better clinical management. That are where assistive technologies may provide an opportunity to alleviate the burden faced the people Alzheimer's disease. In this paper, we explain the use of ENKEPHALON platform, that analyzing the resonance magnetic images for identify Alzheimer's disease. This is the result of the project "Technological platform to support the diagnosis of Alzheimer's disease through the analysis of resonance images using DataMining techniques", that was funds by Colciencias in Colombia.

The paper is organized in five sections. The section second, the brief of literature about the use of neuroimaging for identify the Alzheimer disease are shown. In the section third, we explain the construction and the details of the attributed of the dataset, that we used during the experimentation, also we describe the techniques used to identified the best classifier, which will be implemented in the platform. In the fourth section, the experimentation is detailed, and we specify the methods and the platform interface. In the fifth section, the results are shown and we explain the reason for select the classifier that was implemented. The work ends showing, the conclusions, the acknowledgments and the references.

2 Brief Review of Literature

During the analysis of the review of literature, was possible to find different applications that can to help to identify Alzheimer using magnetic resonance imaging - MRIs, these applications are explain next. In 2011, researchers of the Polytechnic University of Valencia and INSCANNER [2], have jointly developed two software tools (BRAIM and MergeBRAIM) to help the early diagnosis of neurodegenerative diseases, such as Parkinson, Multiple Sclerosis or Alzheimer as for the monitoring and treatment of brain tumors. On the other hand, the National University of Colombia, campus Manizales [3], based on the structure of the brain reflected in magnetic resonances, developing a tool identifies morphological characteristics that help diagnose people with cognitive deficiency, with the Alzheimer's disease or healthy. This tool has an effectiveness of 70% identifying people with Alzheimer's, using fuzzy logic in the analysis of MRIs. The Bilbomática technological company, in collaboration with Vicomtech-ik4, the Castilla La Mancha University and Virgen del Rocío Hospital [4] developed a computer application to early diagnosis of alzheimer's disease performing the data analysis with a semantic ontology.

Varatharajan [5], apply the foot movement continuously monitoring technique using Internet of Things – IoT, for the early detection of Alzheimer. Was implemented the algorithm Dynamic Time Warping - DTW to compare the different position of the patient's feet, in experimental scenarios, with cross-validation techniques. Beheshti [6], developed a computer-aided diagnostic - CAD system that classifies the data that come from MRIs by techniques based on genetic algorithms in order to identify pathologies associated with Mild Cognitive Impairment – MCI and Alzheimer. Zheng [7], uses the LUPI algorithm for the learning of characteristics, from the data extracted of MRIs as a prevalent technique for the detection of Alzheimer. The experimental results demonstrate the good functioning of the algorithm with superior performance of this compared to other predictive models.

Palafox [8], also uses MRIs to identify typical changes in Alzheimer's disease and MCI. To do this, they proposed an image segmentation using the Mean Shift algorithm, applying probabilistic maps and Support Vector with Linear Base and Radial Core for hippocampal segmentation in MRIs, which obtained comparable results with the manual segmentation performed by a radiologist. Dolui [9], also uses the method of processing ASL signals obtained from a 3T scanner for the diagnosis of Alzheimer's disease, the longitudinal data of the control participants that were processed three months apart served to evaluate the coefficient of variation within the subject – wsCV.

Gomez-Sancho [10], studied the different characteristics of each one of the cerebral regions making use of techniques such as: support vector machines and regularized logistic regression), achieving a wide and significant difference when making the detection of the disease. Lahmiri [11], performed experiments with Support Vector Machine (SVM) trained with cortical thickness, allowing in this way the extraction of the best features that can guide the early detection of Alzheimer's disease.

3 Materials and Methods

3.1 Data Preparation and Analysis

First, the sample space of patients was defined who would participate in the development of the project. At the same time, the set of neuropsychological tests that 4 would be implemented on patients were defined. Subsequently, neuropsychological tests were applied to a population defined as a sample space to achieve a final selection of the individuals that would be part of the study. For this study, the dataset was generate from data extracted of neuropsychological tests and MRIs to 101 patients and 103 attributes. The patients signed an informed consent form for participation in the Project. The data set was used for training and testing a predictive model based on machine learning techniques. Specifically, the quality metrics of the following techniques were evaluated: random subspace, Decorate, BFTree, LMT, ADTree and RandomForest. Each of these is described below.

3.2 RandomSubSpace

Tin Kan Ho [12] defined a RandomSubSpace algorithms like a classifier to consists of multiple trees constructed systematically by pseudorandomly selecting subsets of components of the feature vector, that is, trees constructed in randomly chosen subspaces. The subspace method is compared to single-tree classifiers and other forest construction methods by experiments on publicly available datasets, where the method's superiority is demonstrated.

3.3 Decorate

This methods was introduced by Melville and Mooney [13, 14], they used a dataset ensemble generated iteratively, learning a classifier at each iteration and adding it to the current ensemble. They initialize the ensemble to contain the classifier trained on the given training data. The classifiers in each successive iteration are trained on the original training data and also on some artificial data.

3.4 BFTree

This methods was introduced by Athanassoulis and Ailamaki [16, 17], the authors defined that the data is necessary organized, based on the indexing key. A BF-tree defined two different types of nodes. consists of nodes of two different types. The root and the internal nodes has the similarity morphology to a normal B++ Tree.

3.5 LMT

LMT is define like a combination of two concepts previous logistic regression and induction tree [18, 19]. This algorithm makes good use of the reduction of computational costs and complexity. The best results of this algorithm are given for sets of attributes of numerical type. Within several experiments, the best results of this algorithm have been demonstrated in comparison with others such as J48, RandomTree.

3.6   ADTree

The ADTree was introduced by Yoav Freund and Llew Mason in 1999 [20]. An ADTree consists mainly of an alternation of different decision nodes, from which a condition can be identified which is considered determinant and which normally contain a number that defines the prediction. An alternative decision tree is made up of two types of nodes: decision and prediction. In the decision nodes the condition of the predicate is usually specified and in the prediction nodes a single number is stored.

3.7   RandomForest

Random forest, is a combination of different predictive trees in such a way that each of the trees depends in turn on a random vector that is previously tested and that has the same distribution of each of the trees [21]. This algorithm modifies the Bagging algorithm. This algorithm was developed by Leo Breuman and the selection of attributes in random form that was introduced by Tin Kam.

4   Experimentation

To make the experimentation it was necessary to build an integrated dataset with 103 attributes, that could contemplate all the analyzed aspects of each one of the patients, among them the results of the neuropsychological test, the result of the radiological test and also the amount of black pixels found in the Temporal Temporary Lobe Atrophy (MTA). Frisoni, [22] define the medial temporal lobe atrophy score: 0 = absent, 1 = minimal, 2 = mild, 3 = moderate, and 4 = severe. The MTA-score should be rated on coronal T1-weighted images at a consistent slice position. Select a slice through the corpus of the hippocampus, at the level of the previous pons (Fig. 1).

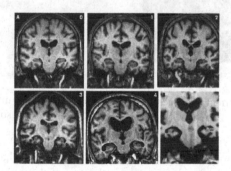

Fig. 1. Level of MTA define by Fisoni [1].

During the process of preparation of data was necessary to applied SMOTE to balanced the number of the instance that the patients that have or not have the disease. After the classifications techniques RandomSubSpace, Decorate, BFTree, LMT, OrdinalClassClassifier, ADTree and RandomForest was applied for analysing the better result that can obtain during the experimentation. The Accuracy [23], Precision [24], Recall and F-measure [25] metric was used for the interpretation of the better results. This equations are shown next.

$$Accuracy = \frac{(true\,positive + true\,negative)}{total} \tag{1}$$

$$Precision = \frac{true\,positive}{(true\,positive + false\,positive)} \tag{2}$$

$$Recall = \frac{true\,positive}{true\,positive + false\,negative} \tag{3}$$

$$F - measure = \frac{2 * precision * recall}{precision + recall} \tag{4}$$

The process of testing and training process of the date was made using crossed validation and after was compared the result using the metric mentioned before. This evaluations is done automatically, using ENKEPHALON software. In this applications the user can select the resonance image for folder scan where we will locate the content of the cd of the resonance and we will select the file (Figs. 2 and 3).

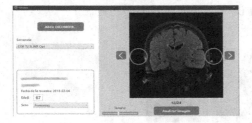 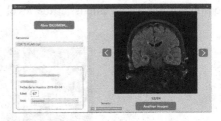

Fig. 2. Selecting the current sequence of the images.

Fig. 3. Define the analysis zone in ENKEPHALON software.

In this new window we can see the name of the patient, the identification of the patient, the date in which sample was taken, the age of the patient and the sex of the patient. On the left side we can see a drop-down list, here we can change the sequence current that we are visualizing in the right part; By default, the sequence "COR T2 FLAIR Opt" which is the sequence that was used for the detection of Alzheimer's. With the selected sample we drag each circle of blue color over the area where choroid fissure, temporal horn, and hippocampal formation. If we need to adjust the size of the circles we can change it with the scroll bar located at the bottom that says "Size". Clicking on the "Analyze Image" button invokes the use of the selected RandomSubSpace algorithm to identify the presence or absence of the disease.

5 Results

In the present experimentation, the data preparation process was taken as a starting point, afterwards the selection of the most adequate technique to be applied to the constructed dataset. In the following graphs, the results of each classifier studied are presented (Fig. 4 and Table 1).

Table 1. Algorithm result

	Accuracy	Precision	Recall	F-measure
RandomSubSpace	91.67%	94.12%	88.89%	91.43%
Decorate	90.74%	92.31%	88.89%	90.57%
BFTree	89.81%	92.16%	87.04%	89.52%
LMT	88.89%	95.65%	81.48%	88.00%
OrdinalClassClassifier	88.24%	86.54%	90.00%	88.24%
ADTree	87.96%	91.84%	83.33%	87.38%
RandomForest	87.04%	88.46%	85.19%	86.79%

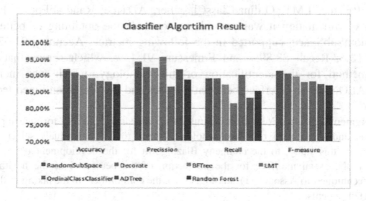

Fig. 4. Define the analysis zone in ENKEPHALON software.

Product of the cross validation application with each of the selected classification algorithms, the mean and the variation in each of the four metrics in the algorithm with the best RandomSub Space performance are shown in Fig. 5.

Taking into account the evaluation of the above-mentioned algorithms, it can be specified that the best performance is RandomSubSpace, given that it allows establishing more accurately the existence or not of the disease taking into account the results of the quality metrics and this models was used for developing the ENKEPHALON software.

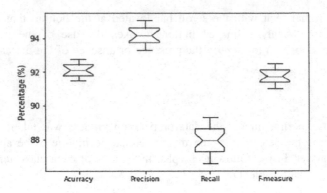

Fig. 5. Variation in classifier performance

6   Conclusions

This research proposed a classification method to support the early identification of Alzheimer's disease through the analysis of magnetic resonance imaging. A dataset was used from the development of each of the stages developed in the project "Technological platform to support the early diagnosis of Alzheimer's disease through the analysis of resonance images using data mining techniques" funded by Colciencias.

First the SMOTE method was used for the balancing process of the respective data instances and then different classification techniques are applied: RandomSubSpace, Decorate, BFTree, LMT, OrdinalClassClassifier, ADTree, RandomForest. From the previous experimentation it was possible to conclude the obtaining of better results with RandomSubSpace, supported in the following metrics: Accuracy 91.67%, Precision 94.12%, Recall 88.89% and F-measure 91.43%, which shows that it is an efficient method for the identification of this pathology, which was included in ENKEPHALON, as an interface between the user and the aforementioned technique.

Acknowledgments. To the Colombian institute of neuropedagogy (ICN), for the support in the identification and application of neurosychological tests to the individuals selected for the development of this study, to the company BlazingSoft for the development of the software ENKEPHALON, as an interface for the interaction of the personnel of the health and the developed techniques, to Associated Radiologists, for the commitment in the taking of the images to the selected patients.

References

1. Kane, M., Cook, L.: Dementia 2013: The hidden voice of loneliness. Alzheimer's Society, London (2013)
2. Universidad Politécnica de Valencia: Un software español facilita el diagnóstico precoz de alzhéimer o párkinson. Disponible (2011). http://www.abc.es/salud/noticias/20150515/abci-cerebro-braim-valencia-201505131203.html

3. Universidad Nacional de Colombia, Sede Manizales: Software identifica cerebros con Alzheimer. Disponible. http://www.unperiodico.unal.edu.co/dper/article/emsoftwareem-identifica-cerebros-con-alzheimer.html
4. Universidad de Castilla la Mancha y Hospital Vírgen del Rocío: Diagnóstico precoz del Alzheimer. Disponible. http://www.elmundo.es/elmundo/2011/07/10/paisvasco/131032-2549.html
5. Varatharajan, R., et al.: Wearable sensor devices for early detection of Alzheimer disease using dynamic time warping algorithm. Clust. Comput. **21**, 1–10 (2017)
6. Beheshti, I., et al.: Classification of Alzheimer's disease and prediction of mild cognitive impairment-to-Alzheimer's conversion from structural magnetic resource imaging using feature ranking and a genetic algorithm. Comput. Biol. Med. **83**, 109–119 (2017)
7. Zheng, X., et al.: Improving MRI-based diagnosis of Alzheimer's disease via an ensemble privileged information learning algorithm. In: 2017 IEEE 14th International Symposium on Biomedical Imaging (ISBI 2017). IEEE (2017)
8. Palafox, G.D.L., et al.: Hippocampal segmentation using mean shift algorithm. In: 12th International Symposium on Medical Information Processing and Analysis. International Society for Optics and Photonics (2017)
9. Dolui, S., et al.: Structural Correlation-based Outlier Rejection (SCORE) algorithm for arterial spin labeling time series. J. Magn. Reson. Imaging **45**(6), 1786–1797 (2017)
10. Gomez-Sancho, M., Tohka, J., Gomez-Verdejo, V., Alzheimer's Disease Neuroimaging Initiative: Comparison of feature representations in MRI-based MCI-to-AD conversion prediction. Magn. Reson. Imaging **50**, 84–95 (2018)
11. Lahmiri, S., Shmuel, A.: Performance of machine learning methods applied to structural MRI and ADAS cognitive scores in diagnosing Alzheimer's disease. Biomed. Signal Process. Control **52**, 414–419 (2018)
12. Ho, T.K.: The random subspace method for constructing decision forests. IEEE Trans. Pattern Anal. Mach. Intell. **20**(8), 832–844 (1998)
13. Echeverry, I., Urina-Triana, M., Ariza-Colpas, P., Mantilla, M.: El trabajo colaborativo entre ingenieros y personal de la salud para el desarrollo de proyectos en salud digital: una visión al futuro para lograr tener éxito. Revista Latinoamericana de Hipertensión **13**(4) (2018)
14. Melville, P., Mooney, R.J.: Constructing diverse classifier ensembles using artificial training examples. In: IJCAI, vol. 3, pp. 505–510, August 2003
15. Han, M., Zhu, X., Yao, W.: Remote sensing image classification based on neural network ensemble algorithm. Neurocomputing **78**(1), 133–138 (2012)
16. De-La-Hoz-Franco, E., Ariza-Colpas, P., Quero, J.M., Espinilla, M.: Sensor-based datasets for human activity recognition–a systematic review of literature. IEEE Access **6**, 59192–59210 (2018)
17. Athanassoulis, M., Ailamaki, A.: BF-tree: approximate tree indexing. Proc. VLDB Endow. **7**(14), 1881–1892 (2014)
18. Calabria-Sarmiento, J.C., et al.: Software applications to health sector: a systematic review of literature (2018)
19. Sumner, M., Frank, E., Hall, M.: Speeding up logistic model tree induction. In: Jorge, A.M., Torgo, L., Brazdil, P., Camacho, R., Gama, J. (eds.) PKDD 2005. LNCS, vol. 3721, pp. 675–683. Springer, Heidelberg (2005)
20. Ooi, M.P.L., Sok, H.K., Kuang, Y.C., Demidenko, S.: Alternating decision trees, chapter 19. In: Handbook of Neural Computation, pp. 345–371. Academic Press (2017). ISBN 9780128113189
21. Sok, H.K., Ooi, M.P.L., Kuang, Y.C., Demidenko, S.: Multivariate alternating decision trees. Pattern Recogn. **50**, 195–209 (2016)

22. Frisoni, G.B., et al.: Neuroimaging tools to rate regional atrophy, subcortical cerebrovascular disease, and regional cerebral blood flow and metabolism: consensus paper of the EADC. J. Neurol. Neurosurg. Psychiatry **74**(10), 1371–1381 (2003)
23. Palechor, F.M., De la Hoz Manotas, A., Colpas, P.A., Ojeda, J.S., Ortega, R.M., Melo, M.P.: Cardiovascular disease analysis using supervised and unsupervised data mining techniques. JSW **12**(2), 81–90 (2017)
24. Mendoza-Palechor, F.E., Ariza-Colpas, P.P., Sepulveda-Ojeda, J.A., De-la-Hoz-Manotas, A., Piñeres Melo, M.: Fertility analysis method based on supervised and unsupervised data mining techniques (2016)
25. Palechor, F.M., De la hoz Manotas, A., De la hoz Franco, E, Ariza-Colpas, P: Feature selection, learning metrics and dimension reduction in training and classification processes in intrusion detection systems. J. Theor. Appl. Inf. Technol. **82**(2) (2015)

Experience on Learning Through an AR-Based Course

Waraporn Jirapanthong[✉]

Dhurakij Pundit University, Bangkok 10210, Thailand
Waraporn.jir@dpu.ac.th

Abstract. Augmented Reality (AR) technology is one of rapidly growing areas in the digital field. There are numerous applications in the market. Our research focus on applying AR technology to support learning for students. In particular, the course materials are provided and prepared by applying AR technology. The AR contents are created and the learning style is purposed. The case study is performed by having a group of participants experienced with AR-based course. The pre- and post- test learning scores are used to assess the students' satisfaction and attitudes.

Keywords: Augmented Reality · AR technology · Hybrid learning

1 Introduction

Recently, a lot of studies focus on game-based learning since it has become more appealing than conventional instructional methods and can increase learners' dedication to their study. The pattern of study not only relies on cognitive abilities, but also affective, functional, and social skills. According to [1], computer games are appealing to students because they can experience with adventures, challenges, and novelty.

Presently, Augmented Reality (AR) is a type of interactive, reality-based display environment that takes the capabilities of computer generated display, sound, text and effects to enhance the user's real-world experience. Augmented reality combines real and computer-based scenes and images to deliver a unified but enhanced view of the world. Advanced AR technologies e.g. adding computer vision and object recognition are developed. They allow users to have the information about the surrounding real world of the user becomes interactive and digitally manipulable. Information about the environment and its objects is overlaid on the real world. This information can be virtual or real, e.g. seeing other real sensed or measured information such as electromagnetic radio waves overlaid in exact alignment with where they actually are in space [2–4]. Augmented reality also has a lot of potential in the gathering and sharing of tacit knowledge. Augmentation techniques are typically performed in real time and in semantic context with environmental elements. Immersive perceptual information is sometimes combined with supplemental information like scores over a live video feed of a sporting event. This combines the benefits of both augmented reality technology and heads up display technology (HUD).

© Springer Nature Switzerland AG 2019
Y. Tan et al. (Eds.): ICSI 2019, LNCS 11656, pp. 221–227, 2019.
https://doi.org/10.1007/978-3-030-26354-6_22

Our research focus on the use of AR technology for the development of educational content. In particular, the AR technology is designed inclusively for teaching. It is essential to understand how instructors can benefit or have the potential of adopting the technology. The resources for creating an innovative classroom with AR technology. (i) software for AR content creation, it is applied with a traditional computer desktop that allows a student to explore a virtual environment using a computer, keyboard, mouse, and other devices; (ii) mobile application which is required to be installed in a smart phone. Moreover, our work we create a case study of AR-based course. The course is based on AR content. We planned to evaluate the result of learning through the AR contents by a case study. In particular, the case study is being developed in order to find out how the AR-based materials can support the teaching process. The design of this course has been divided into two parts: (i) learning through AR content such as video clips, and (ii) evaluating the learning through AR cards. We conducted the teaching course as a game. As believed, AR games become the absolutely most immersive learning technology that gives learners a powerful sense of presence in the augmented reality environment. The case study of using AR technology for learning was created and used to observe training both hard and soft skills. also, our research conducted the review based on Kitchenham [5]. Particularly, it was adapted for the purposed of the systematic review. We planned to select journals, defined criteria for studies and categories of analysis, and then selected the study. Finally, we have performed an observation and used a questionnaire to collect data and feedback on the use of the AR-based materials. The questionnaire consisted of open and closed questions. Those questions are based on the perspective of the use of the contents.

2   Literature Review

According to [6], the authors performed a comparative study based on students' learning performance and satisfaction. They studied mobile-learning by using an AR application during fieldwork. Particularly, the AR and Mobile Pedestrain Navigation application was used with iPads. Software used was Apple Maps and Junaio for developing AR resources using geo-location. Qualitative and quantitative data collection with pre- and post- tests including satisfaction questionnaire and interviews. The authors found that AR application combined with fieldwork increases the effectiveness of teaching-learning processes, promotes the interaction of students with contents for learning, and improves students' performance in the educational process.

Additionally, Chiang and others [7] developed the study by using questionnaire. They also studied mobile-learning using an AR application during fieldwork. Particularly, the AR-based mobile learning system used iPad mini devices which had inbuilt GPS and were Wi-Fi enabled. The area of learning involved natural science topics relating to aquatic animals and plants. A pre-test questionnaire was used to ensure that the two groups of students had equivalent prior knowledge before the learning activity. A post-test questionnaire was used to assess the students' learning achievements after the learning activity. The work was shown to improve learning achievements. Students who learned with the AR-based mobile learning approach showed significantly higher motivations relating to attention, confidence, and relevance than those who learned with the conventional inquiry-based mobile learning approach.

Moreover, the authors [8] proposed the instructor interview survey and quasi-experimental study. They developed an interactive learning in an outdoor/indoor location using a mobile AR astronomy simulation software. Particularly, the mobile digital armillary sphere (MDAS) using AR combined a digital compass with a G-sensor on a mobile device and connected the target content with the users' physical movements to provide the experience of human-computer field interaction. The study took place both indoors and outdoors. The software was used during outdoor observation activities effectively enhanced both the students' learning of astronomical observation content and their performance of astronomical observations and learning, which had a substantial effect on retention. They found that students more significantly more active and engaged in interactions with the teacher compared to those students using traditional tools.

Also, the authors [9] proposed the a mobile game including multiple interaction forms and combined AR with non-AR mini games. They performed a comparative study based on quantitative and qualitative data collection with pre- and posts- tests. Particularly, they proposed two students at a time played the mobile game using AR and VR technology by using smartphone and tablet PC with external casing. It was found that students showed significant learning gains after intervention.

3 AR-Based Course

3.1 Learning Through AR Contents

We provided teaching materials by using AR technology. To create AR, a camera is used to capture video images of an external environment. The video clips are created by using phone camera and converted to be mp4 files. The images and information for teaching materials are prepared. Subsequently, the images are analyzed to determine whether predefined objects of interest are present in the video. After the objects are detected, virtual objects are superimposed over the detected objects for viewing on a display. Subsequently, the position and alignment of a virtual object can be adjusted according to the viewer's relative position to create a sense of reality.

We applied Vidinoti [10] in which is developed as a multi-lingual application and allows users to scan the markers, and interact with the contents. At this point, students can follow the course corresponding to AR contents appear on the screen. In particular, the students can scan the markers, see all the contents corresponding to the learning cards and select one of them to get more details (Fig. 1).

3.2 Interactive AR Cards

AR cards are used to be interactive materials for learning. We applied AR technology to create AR cards in which markers on the card are used to identify different contents. In particular, we evaluate the learning through a quiz game. The game is composed of questions regarding the learning contents. The questions and answers are presented by

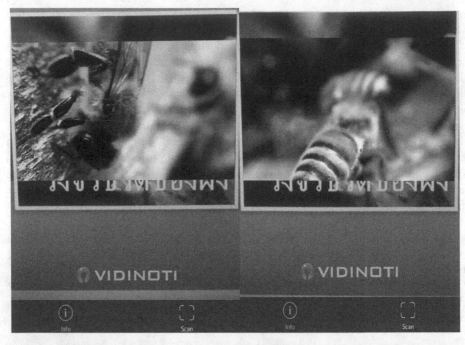

Fig. 1. Example of AR contents for learning materials.

AR application. The application was installed on smartphones. A student used the phone's camera to capture a card. A marker in the card is identified and then the question with alternatives are presented. The application determined whether the correct or incorrect answer cards were presented by the student and then provided feedback accordingly (Fig. 2).

Fig. 2. Example of AR contents for learning materials.

4 Experiences and Results

To evaluate our work, we created a case study of learning class. The participants were fifth-grade (n = 16) students. Each student was required to complete a pretest of learning before AR-based learning class. The learning class took 50 min to complete the learning materials. Before the class started, the authors spend 10 min to explain the class objectives and rules. The participants spent 50 min through AR-based learning materials. They then answered the questions via AR cards. Finally, they were required to complete a posttest of learning.

The results of answering the questions showed that the participants have correctly answered as 87% of all questions. The pre- and post- test learning scores were compared as shown in Table 1. The result shows that most items received a score higher than 4, indicating that the students felt positive about the learning. Therefore, they

Table 1. An example of questionnaires questions

No	Questionnaire questions	Average score
1	I stayed focused when learning through the AR-based class	4.18
2	I can enjoy the AR-based class without technical difficulty	4.21
3	When learning through AR-based class, I am not worried about answering the questions incorrectly and I want to continue the class	4.29
4	I want to learn through AR-based class again in the future	4.52
5	I look forward to the next level of learning through AR-based class	4.48

regarded the AR-based learning materials as an aid for teachers to test their learning outcomes and were overly careful when answering the questions in the class. The learning attitudes yield positive learning outcomes. Therefore, learning materials should be concerned on the mix of class contents and motivation in order to pursue the students' attitudes.

Furthermore, these students could not hold both the tablet device and the cards for a long time, and therefore required the help from teaching assistants, which interrupted their learning pace and focus. This problem can be solved by using a mount to secure the tablet device so that students are required to handle only the cards.

5 Conclusion and Future Work

Learning assessment are primarily aimed at identifying a student's progress in affective learning. Focusing on elementary school students, the scale adopted in the present study involved affective subscales for measuring students' attention, learning motivation, and anxiety. We adopted this scale to investigate whether the proposed interactive card game positively influenced the students' performance in the affective domain. The pretest and posttest learning motivation scores were compared using an ANOVA. The results revealed a significant improvement between the pretest and posttest scores, indicating that the students' learning motivation increased considerably after learning through AR technology.

In summary, we proposed AR technology as a driven tool to support for hybrid learning. Students are allowed to participate and have interact activities with the class through AR contents and materials. According to the case study, the following strengths are found: (a) the AR contents can be prepared using an ordinary tools e.g. printers and white paper, and the AR application can be installed on any smartphones. The AR-based course is possibly held in elementary schools because it does not require any special hardware or teaching aid, (b) the AR-based materials encourage the students participate and answer questions, and (c) the three-dimensional models can allow the students to have virtual real-experience of the lessons.

We plan to further develop the game to complete many courses i.e. mathematics and science. Also, the levels of questions are created to make different learning classes for different levels of learners.

References

1. Carroll, J.M.: The adventure of getting to know a computer. IEEE Comput. **15**(11), 49–58 (1982)
2. Mann, S.: Phenomenal augmented reality. IEEE Consum. Electron. **4**(4), 92–97 (2015)
3. Mann, S.: Wavelets and "Chirplets": time-frequency perspectives, with applications. In: Advances in Machine Vision, Strategies and Applications. World Scientific Series in Computer Science, volume 32. C Archibald and Emil Petriu, pp. 99–128 (1992)
4. Mann, S., et al.: Wearable computing, 3D Aug* reality, photographic/videographic gesture sensing, and veillance. In: Proceedings of the Ninth International Conference on Tangible, Embedded, and Embodied Interaction - TEI 2014, pp. 497–500. ACM, 15 January 2015. https://doi.org/10.1145/2677199.2683590. ISBN 9781450333054
5. Kitchenham, B.A.: Guidelines for performing systematic literature reviews in software engineering Version 2.3. EBSE Technical report, Keele University and University of Durham (2007)
6. Joo-Nagata, J., Abad, M., Giner, G., Garcia-Penalvo, F.: Augmented reality and pedestrian navigation through its implementation in m-learning and e-learning: evaluation of an educational program in Chile. Comput. Educ. **11**(1), 1–17 (2017)
7. Chiang, T.-H.-C., Yang, S.-J.-H., Hwang, G.-J.: An augmented reality-based mobile learning system to improve students' learning achievements and motivations in natural science inquiry activities. Educ. Technol. Soc. **17**(4), 352–365 (2014)
8. Zhang, J., Sung, Y.-T., Hou, H.-T., Chang, K.-E.: The development and evaluation of an augmented reality-based armillary sphere for astronomical observation instruction. Comput. Educ. **73**, 178–188 (2014)
9. Furió, D., González-Gancedo, S., Juan, M.-C., Seguí, I., Rando, N.: Evaluation of learning outcomes using an educational iPhone game vs. traditional game. Comput. Educ. **64**, 1–23 (2013)
10. V-director. https://www.vidinoti.com

Identification and Recognition

Seismograph Design for Landslide Monitoring in the Andean Region Using Automatic Control Techniques and Mathematical Modeling

Sebastian Soto[1]([✉]) [iD], Yeyson Becerra[1] [iD], Carlos Suarez[2] [iD],
and Elmer Gamboa[3] [iD]

[1] Corporacion Unificada Nacional de Educacion Superior, Bogota, Colombia
{sebastian_soto,yeyson_becerra}@cun.edu.co
[2] Fundacion Universitaria Agraria de Colombia, Bogota, Colombia
suarez.carlosre@uniagraria.edu.co
[3] Universidade de Sao Paulo, Sao Paulo, Brazil
elmeralexis@gmail.com

Abstract. The countries of the Andean area, in particular Colombia, suffer great problems related to landslides of large amounts of soil. These landslides occur due to high mountain deforestation caused by inadequate agricultural practices and the large volume of rainfall in this region. Therefore, it is important to detect information about telluric movements and small vibrations to avoid ecological disasters and dangers for humanity, as well as to determine if the surface can be used to cultivate without erosive problems, thus minimizing economic risks for producers. Seismographs based on accelerometers and geophones are suitable for detecting small vibrations in the earth produced by erosion and movements of groundwater that can prevent soil instability. In this paper, a seismograph prototype is presented, which is based on the use of a high sensitivity accelerometer and a mathematically designed geophone. The proposed seismograph produces as output a spectrum of frequencies of the different types of movements that are damped by automatic control techniques, which serves as a base of information for the generation of reports on soil management and disaster prevention. In addition, the architecture of hardware and software used in the construction of the seismograph allows the connection to the network of several devices that can be distributed in different critical places.

Keywords: Seismograph · Accelerometers and geophone ·
Embedded Systems · Landslide · Automatic control

1 Introduction

Landslides cause ecological and humanitarian disasters. Also, they have a large economic impact for agricultural producers [1, 2]. A landslide can be caused action of gravitational forces. Also, climatic changes and intervention in the landscape by human must considered [3]. In countries with a high percentage of mountains, such as the countries covered by the Andean mountain range [11], the economic impact caused by landslides is high and is a topic that has been discussed in different economic and

© Springer Nature Switzerland AG 2019
Y. Tan et al. (Eds.): ICSI 2019, LNCS 11656, pp. 231–242, 2019.
https://doi.org/10.1007/978-3-030-26354-6_23

disaster prevention forums [4, 5]. Landslide problems can be mitigated or prevented by having key information about magnitudes and frequency that the vibrations of the earth present [6]. The vibration records contain information about the origin and means of propagation of the waves, from this information it is possible to determine the physical properties of the medium [7–9].

This paper presents the development of a model of seismograph capable of detecting very small vibrations of different nature. The prototype works with accelerometers anchored to a plate so that each x, y, z axis has an accelerometer in position. The system features a mathematically designed geophone that serves to detect multiple vibrations. Unlike the existing models the prototype very economic and robust, because it integrates a geophone and accelerometers in the same encapsulation.

Based the concepts of inertia and oscillating systems, the mathematical modeling of a mechanical suspension system is carried out, which responds to vibrations from different sources, whether of natural or artificial origin. Using control techniques and mathematical analysis, the signal is cushioned to avoid erroneous readings when the system is detecting vibrations.

The next sections of the paper are organized as follows. In Sect. 2 the basic concepts and the theoretical background about the physical processes of the generation of earthquakes and seismic waves are introduced. Section 3 explains the methodology used in the construction of the seismograph, the mathematical modeling process of the inertial suspension system, the control techniques used to cushion the signal, the analysis of physical variables involved in the system. In Sect. 4 the discussion and analysis of results are exposed. Finally, in Sect. 5 the conclusions and future works of the work are placed.

2 Theoretical Framework

2.1 Seismological Instrumentation

The instruments used to observe earthquakes must be able to detect transient vibration, to operate continuously with very sensitive sensing capability and moreover need to have absolute time in such a way that the movement can be registered as function as time. The instrument must also offer a known linear response to the ground movement (calibrated instrument) that allows the seismic records to be related to the frequency content and the amplitudes of soil movement [10]. However, since not all instruments can record all the possible movements with a linear response, it has been necessary to develop instruments that observe in the wide dynamic range of amplitudes and the wide bandwidth in frequencies, of all the possible signals of interest, avoiding the interference of environmental noise [13].

Most instruments that are used to measure and record the passage of seismic waves (seismometers) are designed according to inertia postulate: all bodies have a resistance to change their state of uniform motion or rest. The movement of soil can be measured with respect to position of mass suspended by an element that allows it to remain at rest for some instants before soil movement. Thus, now the mass leaves its resting state, the mass tends to oscillate; this oscillation does not reflect the true movement of soil, it is necessary to provide the instrument with a damping system. The weights of the masses used in this type of instruments can vary in a range from a few grams to hundreds of kilograms. Since the movement of the earth, in the presence of an earthquake, occurs in three dimensions of the space, the installation of instruments that monitor movement vertically and horizontally the movement are required to observe the phenomenon completely; additionally, a conditioning system is required to amplify the signals in order to obtain records that can be analyzed directly with a simple visual inspection, as well as also is required a digital system with the capacity to store the data to be analyzed later more detailed [12]. Each instrument, given its natural frequency of oscillation and its magnification system, detects each one of the many frequencies that compose a seismic wave in different way. For this reason, it is necessary to know specifically the magnification curves of the instruments to be able to estimate the real movement of the soil [14].

3 Methodology

According to the problem posed and the variables of interaction, the focus of the present investigation is quantitative and experimental. It is an idea delimited in a series of objectives and research questions based on a literary review that is constructed within the framework of which a theoretical perspective of the proposed problem is offered. The variables are determined according to the development context and a design of experiments to test them. The statistics are analyzed by mathematical methods that allow synthesizing a series of results and taking into account the descriptive and correlational aspects.

The investigation used empirical methods since observation, experimentation and measurement works were carried out with the purpose of achieving the correct functioning of the system in case of an earthquake.

3.1 Inertial Seismometer Design

An inertial seismometer consists of a mass M joined to a point on the Earth through a parallel arrangement of a spring and a buffer. Assuming that all motion is restricted to the z-direction, we denote the motion of the Earth in the inertial reference frame as u (r) and the motion of the mass M in relation to the Earth, the spring will exert a force proportional to its elongation, e.g. from -10 from its tension length to 10, and the buffer will exert a force proportional to the relative velocity (between the mass and the Earth).

Elasticity constant of a spring (k) equation and Natural frequency of the system mass spring equation (Wn) Eq. (1).

$$W_n = \sqrt{\frac{k}{m}} = \sqrt{\frac{3.6186}{0.03}} = \sqrt{120.62} = 10.9827 \, \text{Hz}. \tag{1}$$

Mechanical damping factor ꝣm Eq. (2).

$$x(t) = Ae^{-\frac{ꝣ}{2m}t}.$$
$$\left(\frac{-2 * 0,03}{34}\right) * \ln\left(\frac{0,103}{0,113}\right) = ꝣ.$$

(2)

Natural frequency of the system affected by mechanical damping Eq. (3).

$$W_n = \sqrt{\frac{k}{m} - \frac{ꝣ}{4m}} = \sqrt{\frac{3,6186}{0,03} - \frac{0,00016368}{4 * 0,03}} = \sqrt{120.62 - 0.1364}$$
$$= 19.9765 Hz.$$

(3)

Then by means of a free body diagram represents the proposed scheme for the design of the geophone with the variables involved (Fig. 1).

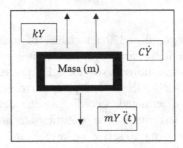

Fig. 1. Design of the geophone

According to the diagram and applying Newton's second law the sum of forces (f = m * a), $C\dot{Y}$ represents the opposite damping force proportional to the relative velocity of the mass with respect to the frame, $m\ddot{Y}$ is the force suffered by the mass when there is a disturbance, KY is the force exerted by the spring, now we divide in terms of m resulting in Eq. (4).

$$\ddot{Y} + \frac{C}{m}\dot{Y} + \frac{k}{m}Y = -\ddot{U}.$$

(4)

Knowing that Eq. (5).

$$ꝣ = \frac{C}{Cr}.$$

(5)

Where ꝣ is the damping reaction and Cr is the critical damping of the system, which is given by Eq. (6).

$$Cr = 2 * m * w_n.$$

(6)

The damping of the system will be given in a mechanical and an electrical one and for the general system Eq. (7) will be used.

$$\frac{c}{m} = 2 * \zeta * \omega. \tag{7}$$

Replacing Eqs. (7) and (2) in Eq. (4) results in Eq. (8)

$$\ddot{Y} + 2\zeta\omega_n\dot{Y} + \omega_nY = -\ddot{U}. \tag{8}$$

As mentioned above, the damping will be given in two parts, the mechanical damping and the electrical damping. Mechanical damping is a value inherent to the system and varies according to the physical and technical characteristics of the instrument. This could be found by calculating a logarithmic decrease. The mechanical damping coefficient is shown in Eq. (9).

$$\zeta_m = \frac{c}{2m}. \tag{9}$$

The electrical damping force shall be known as Eq. (10).

$$Fd = G * i. \tag{10}$$

Where G is the generation constant and $\dot{Y}$ represents the current. The voltage is known by the following Eq. (11).

$$E = G * \dot{Y}. \tag{11}$$

And the current is given by Eq. (12) due to ohm law.

$$i = \frac{E}{Rt} = \frac{G}{Rg + Re} * \dot{Y} = \frac{G}{33 + 20.000} * \dot{Y}. \tag{12}$$

Where E represents the output voltage in the system and Rt the total resistance which is known as Rt = Rg + Re, where Rg is the coil resistance and Rt is the External resistance.

Knowing that the damping coefficient is ζ, it is assumed that the electric damping coefficient is ζs. If $\zeta = 1$ is critically damped. If $\zeta > 1$, it is overshocked. And if $\zeta < 1$ is sub-damped. The following transfer function is given from the displacement frequency for a mechanical seismometer according to Eq. (13).

$$Td(\omega_d) = \frac{Y(\omega_d)}{U(\omega_d)} = \frac{\omega_d{}^2}{\omega_n{}^2 - \omega_d - i2\omega_d\omega_n\zeta}. \tag{13}$$

The phase answer in the equation is given by Eq. (14).

$$\phi(\omega_d) = \tan^{-1}\left(\frac{2\zeta\omega_d\omega_n}{\omega_n{}^2 - \omega_d{}^2}\right). \tag{14}$$

The output signal must be proportional to the speed of the mass and the frame of the coil; therefore, the output signal is a function of the frequency in response to the sensor and is given by $Y'(\omega d) = i\omega d\, Y(\omega d)$ also take into account that as it is a speed transducer intervenes the constant of generation G solving the equation is obtained Eq. (15).

$$Td(\omega_a) = \frac{Y(\omega_a)}{U(\omega_a)} = \frac{i\omega_d * \omega_d{}^2 * G}{\omega_n{}^2 - \omega_d - i2\omega_d\omega_n z} = \frac{\omega_d{}^3 * G}{\omega_n{}^2 - \omega_d - i2\omega_d\omega_n z}. \tag{15}$$

In Eq. (16) the function is presented in response to the travel of the seismometer.

$$Y(t) = \frac{Y_0}{\cos\phi} e^{-z\omega nt} \cos(\omega_1 t - \phi). \tag{16}$$

ϕ corresponds to the phase, $\phi = \cos^{-1}(z)$, and the frequency that this system has is given by $\omega 1 = \sqrt{\omega_n{}^2(1 - z^2)}$.

For the speed transducer it is assumed that the voltage is given by the following Eq. (17).

$$V(t) = Ge\dot{Y}(t). \tag{17}$$

Considering that Ge is the generator constant, effective or loaded, Eq. (18).

$$Ge = G * \frac{Re}{Re + Rg}. \tag{18}$$

Using mathematical tools and trigonometric identities such as, Eq. (19).

$$\cos(\omega 1 t - \phi) = \cos(\omega 1 t) * \cos(\phi) + sen(\omega 1 t) * sen(\phi).$$
$$\cos(\cos^{-1}(z)) = \sqrt{1 - z^2}. \tag{19}$$
$$sen(\cos^{-1}(z)) = z.$$

It is replaced in Eq. (17) to obtain Eq. (20).

$$Y(t) = \frac{Y_0}{\sqrt{1 - z^2}} e^{-z\omega nt} \left[\cos\left(\sqrt{\omega_n{}^2(1 - z^2)}\right) t \left(\sqrt{1 - z^2}\right) \right.$$
$$\left. + sen\left(\sqrt{\omega_n{}^2(1 - z^2)}\right) t * z \right]. \tag{20}$$

Equation (20) is replaced in Eq. (17) it is finally derived to obtain Eq. (21).

$$V(t) = \left(G\frac{Re}{Re + Rg}\right) \frac{Y_0}{\left(\sqrt{\omega_n{}^2(1 - z^2)}\right) * m} e^{-z\omega nt} \left(\left(\sqrt{\omega_n{}^2(1 - z^2)}\right) t\right). \tag{21}$$

This will be the equation of output voltage response of the system in relation to the relative velocity of the mass with respect to the frame. Transfer function of the mechanical part of the system, Eq. (22).

$$G(s) = \frac{s^2}{s^2 + 2\omega_n Z_m s + \omega_n{}^2}. \tag{22}$$

When graphing the transfer function of the previous section, the following graph is obtained (Fig. 2):

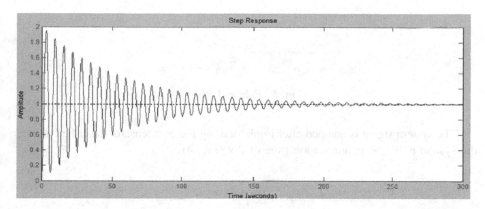

Fig. 2. System damping

In the graph can see that the system is oscillating, however, the damping time is 300 s, therefore, it is necessary to assign a gain and design a compensator to damp the system. Using Matlab 2016's sisotool graphical tool, the analysis of the obtained linear system was performed. With this tool the geometric location of the roots is obtained in a simpler way. From this it is possible to design controllers, compensators and filters, since it allows the visualization of the frequency of the system.

The design of the compensator to cushion the system is made a gain of 2.0485 is obtained and the resulting function that is implemented in the code is:

$$c = 2.0485 * \frac{(1 * s)}{(1 + 0.14\,s)}. \tag{23}$$

With the above equation it is possible to damp the geophone when the system stops oscillating avoiding erroneous readings in the absence of vibrations. The poles and zeros are identified next to the roots of the function, in order to obtain information on the response of the system in stable state (Fig. 3).

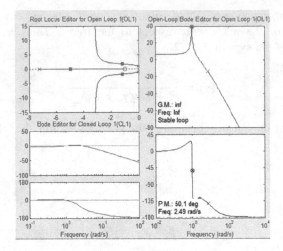

Fig. 3. Pole and zero

The system signal is damped after implementing the compensator described above, the system now has an attenuation time of 2 s (Fig. 4).

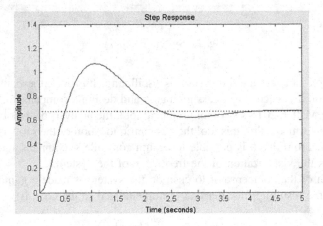

Fig. 4. Damped signal

Is possible to implement a RC circuit to improve the filtering of the signal. The filter added to the damping of the system allows that in the resulting seismogram the obtained signals do not present false wave vibration peaks which would not correspond to a real earthquake.

4   Results and Discussion

For the design of the prototype, the SCAMPER technique is used taking into account the parameters of substitution, combination, adaptation, modification, purpose, reduction, reorganization. Previously, in the design, each of the aspects is analyzed in detail. With the parameters of the geophone and accelerometers identified through mathematical design and automatic control, the prototype is modeled in CAD software, through a 3D printer, the pieces were materialized for the construction of the prototype (Fig 5).

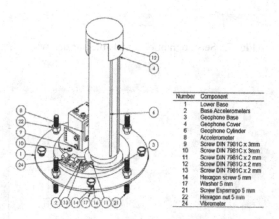

Number	Component
1	Lower Base
2	Base Accelerometers
3	Geophone Base
4	Geophone Cover
6	Geophone Cylinder
8	Accelerometer
9	Screw DIN 7981C x 3mm
10	Screw DIN 7981C x 3mm
11	Screw DIN 7981C x 2 mm
12	Screw DIN 7981C x 2 mm
13	Screw DIN 7981C x 2 mm
14	Hexagon screw 5 mm
17	Washer 5 mm
21	Screw Esparrago 5 mm
22	Hexagon nut 5 mm
24	Vibrometer

Fig. 5. Internal seismograph design.

The system integrates a geophone and an accelerometer in the same encapsulation, to register the waves in case they exceed the dynamic range. The data obtained is recorded in a table in real time, along with the date and time in parallel, they are sent to a folder in the form of an.xlsx file.

The following are seismograms of different types of waves detected by the developed seismograph (Figs. 6, 7, 8).

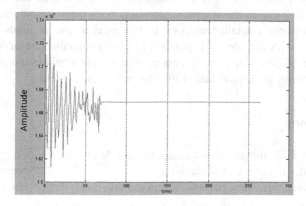

Fig. 6. Seismogram of constant disturbance.

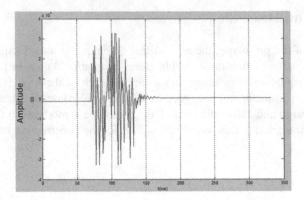

Fig. 7. Seismogram of a possible surface wave

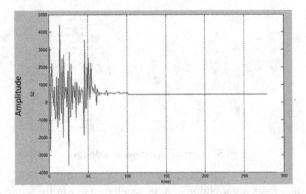

Fig. 8. Seismogram of the arrival of type p and s waves at different times.

The images show that the signals are buffered by the automatic control application. Each time a vibration stops producing from a natural or artificial source, the system finishes graphing the seismograms in response to the damping of the system.

The developed seismograph, it is possible to link a low-cost and high reliability monitoring network due to the system's damping. With the seismograms generated, it is possible to perform a detailed analysis of the areas at risk of landslides and help prevent disasters with the constant monitoring of a mountain system in the Andean region. In future investigations, it is necessary to carry out a calibration phase by going to the corresponding geological institutions to certify the system.

5 Conclusions

As recommended by the norm indicated by the National Seismology Network of Colombia (RSNC) in the factor of damping of the seismometers it must be close to the value of 7.07, since this value guarantees that the vibrations that do not correspond to a real earthquake will be, they can delete. For the prototype, the damping factor is lower than this value, therefore, it was necessary to develop a control system to achieve a damping of the system after the absence of a vibration.

The resulting design of the prototype allows the implementation of sensors with better performance without affecting the structure of the model. The modularity of the system allows the implementation of multiple hardware platforms according to the user's communication needs.

This prototype of a seismograph that uses an accelerometer to detect different types of seismic vibrations, including landslides, with the analysis of the resulting spectrograms, makes it possible to make decisions and design plans to prevent economic and social losses, mitigating financial and social disasters. The system has a very low cost and high reliability and, therefore, improves the development and rapid establishment of an integrated system of monitoring networks in certain regions of the Andes.

The system continues to be studied and constantly improved, applying the SCAMPER model to improve its qualities, and then achieving the calibration and certification of the National Seismology Network of Colombia (RSNC), as well as joining a network in the Andean region in cooperation with different countries. Universities and institutions.

References

1. Food and Agriculture Organization of the United Nations: status of the worlds soil resources, FAO, Rome, Italy (2015). http://www.fao.org/3/ai5199e.pdf. Accessed 11 Dec 2018
2. Food and Agriculture Organization of the United Nations: state of the worlds forest, FAO, Rome, Italy (2016). http://www.fao.org/3/a-i5588e.pdf. Accessed 11 Dec 2018
3. Montero, C.: Riesgos de origen geológico y geomorfológico: deslizamientos de tierras, identificación, análisis y prevención de sus consecuencias. Áreas. Revista Internacional de Ciencias Sociales 23, 34–39 (2003)
4. Federal Emergency Management Agency: Integrating Hazard Mitigation Into Local Planning, FEMA (2013). https://www.fema.gov/medialibrary-data/20130726-1908-250450016/integrating_hazmit.pdf. Accessed 11 Dec 2018
5. Advisory Committee On The International Decade For Natural Hazard Reduction, Confronting Natural Disasters: An International Decade for Natural Hazard Reduction. National Academy Press, Washington D.C. (1987). https://www.nap.edu/catalog/18896/confronting-natural-disasters-an-international-decade-for-natural-hazard-reductionAccessed 11 Dec 2018
6. Aki, K., Richards, P.: Quantitative Seismology, 2nd edn, pp. 7–35. University Science Books, Sausalito (2005)
7. Stein, S., Wysession, M.: An Introduction to Seismology, Earthquakes, and Earth Struc-ture, pp. 11–61. Blackwell, Malden (2005)
8. Nakatugawa, J.: Aceleration Sensor. Japan Patent 5962787, 5 October 1999
9. Yamashita, M.: Acceleration Sensor. Kyoto Patent US 6588276 B2, 8 July 2003
10. Young, H., Freedman, R.: Ondas Mecanicas, in Fisica Universitaria, pp. 487–516. Mexico, Pearson Educacion (2009)
11. Comisión Nacional del Agua: Manual de Mecánica de Suelos, 1st edn, pp. 15–50. Coyoacán, México, D.F., Secretaría de Medio Ambiente y Recursos Naturales (2012)

12. Departamento de Geología y Geoquímica. Facultad de Ciencias. UAM, Localización de un sismo, OPEN COURSEWARE, Madrid. https://formacion.uam.es/pluginfile.php/167/mod_resource/content/2/localizacion_de_un_sismo.pdf. Accessed 15 Dec 2018
13. Havskov, J., Alguacil, G.: Instrumentation in Earthquake Seismology, 2nd edn. Springer, Cham (2016). https://doi.org/10.1007/978-3-319-21314-9
14. OSSO: OSSO. http://www.osso.org.co/. Accessed 11 Dec 2018
15. Red sismológica Nacional de Colombia: Servicio Geologico Colombiano. http://200.119.88.135/RSNC/index.php/joomla-overview/red-sismologica-nacional-de-colombia. Accessed 02 Dec 2018
16. Gutenberg, B., Richter, F.: Frequency of earthquakes in California. Bull. Seismol. Soc. Am. **34**(4), 185–188 (1944). Appendix: Springer-Author Discount

Improving Chinese Named Entity Recognition with Semantic Information of Character Multi-position Representation

Yanru Zhong[ID], Leixian Zhao, Chaohao Jiang[✉], and Xiaonan Luo

Guilin University of Electronic Technology, Guilin, China
chaohaojiang@outlook.com

Abstract. Named entity recognition is an important basic task for information extraction and construction of knowledge graph, but the recognition rate needs to be further improved, especially in Chinese. There are two main implementations based on the sequence tagging method. Among them, the character-based method lacks the support of word information, and the word-based method is affected by the word segmentation efficiency. In order to comprehensively utilize the information of characters and words and to reflect the semantic information that changes due to different combinations of characters and words in a sentence. We designed a tagging scheme based on word segmentation and dictionaries. Then, neural networks are used for learning multi-position feature vectors and character-based tagging task. Experiments with MSRA datasets show that this method outperforms word-based and character-based baselines and achieves a higher recall rate compared to other methods.

Keywords: Chinese named entity recognition · Deep learning · Bi-LSTM-CRF · Word Tagging Scheme · Multi-position feature · Semantic information

1 Introduction

Named entity recognition (NER) has been extensively studied and focused as a fundamental task for information extraction. Converting recognition tasks to sequence tagging tasks is the primary processing method. And the method based on the LSTM-CRF model has obtained state-of-the-art results for NER [10, 21]. Chinese NER is different from other languages and has a closer relation with word segmentation. The boundaries of the Chinese words are blurred. And there are no clear features between words, such as spaces, capital letters, prefixes,

Supported by the Guangxi Science and Technology Plan Project (AD18216004, AA18118039-2).

etc. Building a neural network based on the results of the word segmentor is a relatively straightforward method. However, the error of word segmentation affects the recognition rate of entities [2, 15].

Compared with the word-based method, the character-based method avoids the influence of word segmentation and achieves superior results [5, 8]. However, The words and order contained in the sentence can be useful information. And research shows that words can further help character-based methods to improve recognition rate [19, 21].

In this paper, we proposed a novel method to use the word information contained in the sentence. We employ Bi-LSTM-CRF [6] to model the Chinese NER task as a character level sequence tagging problem. To integrate words, we design a scheme to construct position feature vectors for each character based on word segmentation and dictionaries. Our method effectively uses the information of the words in the sentence and avoids the erroneous effects of using a single word segmentation result.

2   Related Work

As a basic task of natural language processing, NER has been extensively studied, and a large number of solutions have been proposed in the literature. Generally, there are mainly the following methods: traditional approaches (rule-based and dictionary-based) [16, 24], statistical machine learning approaches [11, 17], and recently, deep learning and its hybrid approach have become more popular research directions in the NER field.

Following statistical methods, deep learning is widely concerned due to its advantages in feature learning. Collobert et al. [3] introduced the CNN-CRF structure to the NER task. Ma et al. [1]. [10] combined Bi-LSTM, CNN and CRF to build an end-to-end model in which CNN is used to learn character-level features in English. Simultaneously, joint training and construction of tagging schemes were used for NER and achieved superior results [23].

Because of the large differences in language backgrounds, one must explore different ways to deal with these differences in the NER field of different languages. Enriching network input is one of the effective methods. Dong et al. [4] used radical-level features. Wang et al. [19] used the words in the medical dictionary to provide boundaries for Chinese clinical entities. Joint training and multiple network structures have been validated. Peng and Dredze [12, 13] used joint training Embedding and word segmentation for Chinese social media. Zhao et al. [22] used a combined model of CNN, LSTM and CRF, where multi dimension convolution is used to get n-gram. Qiu et al. [14] used residual dilated convolutions for clinical named entities. Wang et al. [18] proposed a segment-level recognition method. Zhang and Yang [21] designed an additional control gate based on LSTM-CRF to utilize pre-trained words.

Based on the above research, words can be further integrated into character-based methods, especially considering the case where a character belongs to multiple related words. It is also necessary to consider the semantic changes due to the combination of different characters and words. Therefore, this paper constructs these features to improve recognition efficiency.

3   Model

We follow the best NER model using the character-based LSTM-CRF as the primary network structure. Formally, denote a sentence as $S = c_1, c_2, ..., c_m$, where c_i is the ith character. A sequence of sentences can also use words as a basic unit. So denote a sentence as $S = w_1, w_2, ..., w_m$, where w_i is the ith word. Similarly, a sentence contains multiple related words consisting of the same character. We denote a sentence as $S = rw_1, rw_2, ..., rw_m$, where rw_i is the ith related word. For example, a long word "南京市长江大桥 (Nanjing Yangtze River Bridge)", we can get "南京市 (Nanjing City)", "长江大桥 (Yangtze River Bridge)", "市长 (mayor)" and other related words. The model is shown in Fig. 1. For this model, Bi-LSTM and CRF act as the upper structure of the neural network, and the input determines the type of learning of the network. In this paper, we use IOB tagging scheme to label the sequence of entities.

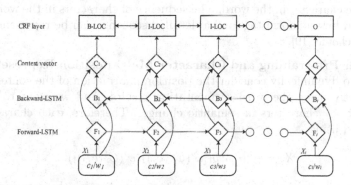

Fig. 1. Main architecture of character-based BLSTM-CRF

3.1   Input Embedding

Character Pre-training and Internal Features. Character-based models use characters and related features as input. For a sequence $c_1, c_2, ..., c_m$, each character c_i is represented using

$$X_j = [e^c(c_j); V_c] \tag{1}$$

e^c denotes a character embedding lookup table. V_c represents an additional feature vector of the character and is an optional item. Strokes and radicals have been used for pre-training and additional features, respectively [1,4].

Word Pre-training and Character Features. Word-based models use words as input units. And the sequence of words uses the result of word segmentation. For sequence $w_1, w_2, ..., w_m$, each word w_i is represented using

$$X_j = [e^w(c_j); V_w] \tag{2}$$

e^w denotes a word embedding lookup table. V_w represents an additional feature vector of the word. Similarly, characters can also be used as features of words and are additional optional features. CNN and LSTM have been used for the learning of character features [10].

Character Pre-training and Position Tags. It has been verified that using the positional information of character in the word can improve the recognition rate [12,19]. The result of word segmentation is represented by the position label of the character. The boundary information of the word acts as a soft feature on the model. Each character c_i is represented using

$$X_j = [e^c(c_j); e^p(s(c_j))] \tag{3}$$

e^p denotes a position label embedding lookup table. $s(c_j)$ denotes the position label of the character in the word. The sequence of characters in the word can be represented by a uniform tag, and a detailed sequence can be represented using a BMES scheme [19].

Character Pre-training and Character Multi-position Representation. We want to dynamically consider the position information of the context rather than directly using the word segmentation results. And we want to consider the role of key characters in semantic changes. Therefore, each character c_i is represented using

$$X_j = [e^c(c_j); g([e^p(C^c(c_j)); e^p(C^t(c_j))])] \tag{4}$$

$g()$ denotes a multi-position feature after neural network mapping. $C^c(c_j)$ denotes the tag of c_j under the semantics of the connection point. $C^t(c_j)$ denotes the tag of c_j under the semantics of the ambiguity point. For the ambiguity point, given the character c_i, the related word rw_i, and the related word rw_j, if $rw_i = \{c_m, c_{m+1}, ..., c_i\}$, $rw_j = \{c_i, c_{i+1}, ..., c_n\}$, and $c_m, ..., c_i, ..., c_n \in S$, then c_i is the ambiguity point.

For the connection point, given the related word $rw_j = c_m, c_{m+1}, ..., c_n$, the local sequence $LS = \{c_i, c_{i+1}, ..., c_k\} \in S$, and $rw_j = LS$, if $s(c_x) \neq s(c_y)$, and $c_x = c_y, c_x \in rw_j c_y \in LS$, then c_x is a connection point that extends semantic information through the combination of contexts. An example of constructing the feature vector is shown in Fig. 2. Two kinds of semantic information are represented due to various combinations of words. As shown in the figure, we have obtained all related words in the " 南京市长江大桥 (Nanjing Yangtze River Bridge)." The "长江 (Yangtze River)" and the "大桥 (Bridge)" acquired a longer entity "长江大桥 (Yangtze River Bridge)" through splicing. The bridge was further defined by the location and no semantic changes occurred. We use C

to tag connection points. Simultaneously, for the "市长 (mayor)", it belongs to "南京市 (Nanjing City)", "长江 (Yangtze River)" and itself. Therefore, it may have another colloquial expression "Mayor of Nanjing Daoqiao Jiang". We use T to tag ambiguity points.

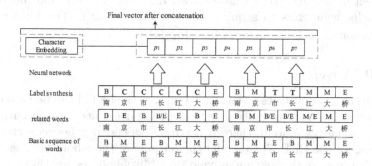

Fig. 2. Example of feature vector construction

In order to generate the feature, we first construct the related word set and the base word sequence, and label the corresponding sequence tags. The related word set contains all possible words in sentence S, which are obtained by dictionary matching. Considering the flexibility of Chinese words, the connection point may occupy most of the position tag, which may bring noise rather than flexible boundary information. Therefore, we use the result of word segmentation as the base sequence to be extended, which may be the optimal result. And the ambiguity points are individually tagged to provide some segmentation information. The two sequences contain connection points, ambiguity points, and partial boundary information. Finally, the two semantic features are fed into the neural networks after splicing and embedding. Similar to the feature learning described above, CNN, LSTM, and attention mechanisms can be used for feature learning.

3.2 LSTM

LSTM is a special model of RNN designed for sequential data. LSTM combines a memory cell to combat the issue that RNN tends to record their most recent inputs in the sequence, The memory cell mainly consists of input gate, output gate and forget gate to control the retained information. The implementation is:

$$i_t = \sigma(W_{xi}x_t + W_{hi}h_{t-1} + b_i) \tag{5}$$

$$f_t = \sigma(W_{xf}x_t + W_{hf}h_{t-1} + b_f) \tag{6}$$

$$c_t = f_t \odot c_{t-1} + i_t \odot \tan h(W_{xc}x_t + W_{hc}h_{t-1} + b_c) \tag{7}$$

$$o_t = \sigma(W_{xo}x_t + W_{ho}h_{t-1} + b_o) \tag{8}$$

$$h_t = o_t \odot \tan h(c_t) \tag{9}$$

where σ is the element-wise sigmoid function, $\odot$ is the element-wise product, W's are weight matrices, and b's are biases. A Bi-LSTM is used for each character in the sentence to learn the hidden vectors $\overrightarrow{h}$ and $\overleftarrow{h}$ in the left-to-right and right-to-left directions. Studies have shown that learning past and future information helps characters to acquire sentence-level features. The hidden vector representation of each character is $h_t = [\overrightarrow{h_t}; \overleftarrow{h_t}]$.

3.3 CRF Layer

As the output layer of the tag, the result vector of the LSTM can be used directly as a feature of Softmax to make independent tag decisions for each output [23]. However, in the tag system, there is a strong dependency between the output tags. Thus, we use CRF [7] to model the outputs of the whole sentence jointly. For training, we use the maximum conditional likelihood estimation.

A standard CRF layer is used on top of the Bi-LSTM. The CRF acquires the current node i and the front node i, and constructs local features and node features. After integrating features and weights, detailed formulas are as follows:

$$P(y|x) = \frac{1}{z(x)} \exp \sum_{k=1}^{k} w_k f_k(y, x) \tag{10}$$

$$Z(x) = \sum_{y} \exp \sum_{k=1}^{k} w_k f_k(y, x) \tag{11}$$

$$f_k(y, x) = \sum_{i=1}^{n} f_k(y_{i-1}, y_i, x, i) \tag{12}$$

Where $P(y|x)$ represented the probabilistic model for sequence CRF, $f_k(y, x)$ represented the feature function.

4 Experiments

We conducted experiments to study the effectiveness of the design method. And the method was compared to baseline and other methods. Standard accuracy (P), recall (R) and F1 score (F) were used as evaluation indicators. There are some basic indicators to evaluate the performance of model.

4.1 Experimental Settings

Data and Hyper-parameter Settings. We tested our model on the MSRA dataset. This dataset contains three types of named entities: location, people, and organization. The neural network is set accordingly. The sizes of the character embedding and position features are 100 and 40, respectively. The hidden size of

Bi-LSTM and full connected networks are both 300. The learning rate is 0.001, and the dropout of LSTM is 0.5.

Word Segmentation and Embedding. This paper uses Jieba segmentor's exact pattern to get the base word sequence. The Jieba segmentor's all pattern is used to get all related words. The word segmentation results may be erroneous and incomplete, so we use an external dictionary as the input of the segmentor to improve the quality of the related word set.

In theory, we built three dictionaries for experiments. The dictionary Dic1 is built directly using the segmentor's all pattern. We downloaded some dictionaries from the Internet as external input of the segmentor to build the dictionaries Dic2 and Dic3. For the Dic2, we focus on the words related to the entity, especially the proper nouns. Because proper nouns are complex in construction and long in length, they are difficult to be recognized by the network, especially the organization name. When building the dictionary Dic3, we randomly extracted words from the downloaded dictionary and added them to Dic2.

4.2 Results and Discussion

Baseline and Analysis. This paper uses character-based method, word-based method, and character and position tags method as baselines. Table 1 compares the results of our method with the baseline. The results of the Char and position baseline are superior to character-based and word-based methods, and got the highest F in the name of the person. Our best F is 1.28 higher than the best baseline. Our method has improved all indicators relative to baseline.

Table 1. Comparison of our method and baseline

Models	PER-F	LOC-F	ORG-F	P	R	F
Char baseline	92.57	91.12	85.07	89.72	89.83	89.78
Word baseline [21]	-	-	-	90.57	83.06	86.65
Char and position baseline	**94.15**	92.26	85.78	91.42	90.36	90.88
Character and Multi-position + Dic1	93.80	92.24	87.19	91.87	90.57	91.21
Character and Multi-position + Dic2	92.32	**92.84**	90.48	92.17	91.29	91.73
Character and Multi-position + Dic3	93.39	92.48	**90.58**	**92.98**	**91.36**	**92.16**

In the case of the dictionary Dic1, the F of the organization is increased by 1.41. However, there was no significant improvement in the total F and there was a decline in person and location entities. The organization name usually consists of a mixture of multiple words and characters. Therefore, the method improves the ability to determine the relation between multiple consecutive characters.

However, the shorter words tend to become long words due to the influence of character expansion. Dic2 enriches the organization name and location name. It provides connection information for medium and long entities and provides boundary information for some entities. Long words contain more connection semantics, which reduces the effect of ambiguity points and word segmentation. Therefore, the name of the person has further declined. Dic3 enriches common words, including person names, idioms, countries, etc. There are more ambiguity points, which make the words shorter or longer. Therefore, in the case of overall improvement, the location entity appears to decline. In general, our approach improves the overall recognition rate. This method improves the recognition efficiency of long entities. For short entities, the balance of the dictionary needs to be considered because it can have a negative effect.

Other Methods and Analysis. Table 2 shows the results of our method and other methods, including the statistical model [20, 24], character embedding Features [9] and segment-level recognition [18]. Our method provides competitive results without an external dictionary. Our best F has improved by 0.98 to 4.22 compared to other methods. In general, our method indirectly implements the dynamic selection of words and avoids the influence of word segmentation. Thanks to the multi-position representation of the characters, the method achieves a positive effect and the recognition effect can be further improved by utilizing external knowledge.

Table 2. Comparison of our method and other methods

Models	P	R	F
Zhang et al. [20]	**92.20**	90.18	**91.18**
Zhou et al. [24]	91.86	88.75	90.28
Lu et al. [9]	-	-	87.94
Dong et al. [4]	91.28	**90.62**	90.95
Wang et al. [18]	92.09	88.85	90.44
Our method + Dic1	91.87	90.57	91.21
Our method + Dic3	**92.98**	**91.36**	**92.16**

Entity and Dictionary. It can be seen from the experiment that the external dictionary plays a catalytic role in the recognition process. We counted the number of entities in the external dictionary of Dic2, which accounted for 16.8% of all entities including the train and test and accounted for 41.7% of the external dictionary. Simultaneously, we further add the same words as entities, especially long entities. The entity accounts for 25.2% of all entities in the corpus and 51.8% of the external dictionary. The result is an increase in person, location, and organization, and the total F increase of 1.15 compared to Dic3. The entity provides more semantic information about connections and ambiguities. It is mostly a composite structure of words and characters. And it may also provide boundary information when the entity is in the dictionary, especially long entities. Words can also cause noise, such as the organizational entity of Dic2 affecting the recognition rate of person. The quality of the dictionary affects the final recognition effect to a certain extent.

Entities in the dictionary play a facilitating role, but not all. There is no clear knowledge in the dictionary which words are entities. And because of our tagging method, entities may be extended or broken. The ultimate recognition and disambiguation capabilities still lie in the multi-position feature representation and supervised learning.

5   Conclusion

In this paper, we try to use the semantic connections and transitions in sentences, because we want to use word information flexibly. Therefore, the multi-positional information of the character is constructed as the feature vector through the designed labeling method. The sequence tag task was modeled by the character-based LSTM-CRF, and the experiment proved the effectiveness of the method. This method avoids word segmentation errors and references existing knowledge to supplement the need for word information based on character methods. In the future work, we hope to learn the word information by trying different neural networks, and add pre-trained embedding of words to the features.

References

1. Cao, S., Lu, W., Zhou, J., Li, X.: cw2vec: learning Chinese word embeddings with stroke n-gram information (2018)
2. Chen, X., Shi, Z., Qiu, X., Huang, X.: Adversarial multi-criteria learning for Chinese word segmentation. arXiv preprint arXiv:1704.07556 (2017)
3. Collobert, R., Weston, J., Bottou, L., Karlen, M., Kavukcuoglu, K., Kuksa, P.: Natural language processing (almost) from scratch. J. Mach. Learn. Res. **12**, 2493–2537 (2011)
4. Dong, C., Zhang, J., Zong, C., Hattori, M., Di, H.: Character-based LSTM-CRF with radical-level features for Chinese named entity recognition. In: Lin, C.-Y., Xue, N., Zhao, D., Huang, X., Feng, Y. (eds.) ICCPOL/NLPCC -2016. LNCS (LNAI), vol. 10102, pp. 239–250. Springer, Cham (2016). https://doi.org/10.1007/978-3-319-50496-4_20
5. He, J., Wang, H.: Chinese named entity recognition and word segmentation based on character. In: Proceedings of the Sixth SIGHAN Workshop on Chinese Language Processing (2008)
6. Huang, Z., Xu, W., Yu, K.: Bidirectional LSTM-CRF models for sequence tagging. arXiv preprint arXiv:1508.01991 (2015)
7. Lafferty, J., McCallum, A., Pereira, F.C.: Conditional random fields: probabilistic models for segmenting and labeling sequence data (2001)

8. Liu, Z., Zhu, C., Zhao, T.: Chinese named entity recognition with a sequence labeling approach: based on characters, or based on words? In: Huang, D.-S., Zhang, X., Reyes García, C.A., Zhang, L. (eds.) ICIC 2010. LNCS (LNAI), vol. 6216, pp. 634–640. Springer, Heidelberg (2010). https://doi.org/10.1007/978-3-642-14932-0_78

9. Lu, Y., Zhang, Y., Ji, D.H.: Multi-prototype Chinese character embedding. In: LREC (2016)

10. Ma, X., Hovy, E.: End-to-end sequence labeling via bi-directional LSTM-CNNS-CRF. arXiv preprint arXiv:1603.01354 (2016)

11. Mao, X., Dong, Y., He, S., Bao, S., Wang, H.: Chinese word segmentation and named entity recognition based on conditional random fields. In: Proceedings of the Sixth SIGHAN Workshop on Chinese Language Processing (2008)

12. Peng, N., Dredze, M.: Named entity recognition for Chinese social media with jointly trained embeddings. In: Proceedings of the 2015 Conference on Empirical Methods in Natural Language Processing, pp. 548–554 (2015)

13. Peng, N., Dredze, M.: Improving named entity recognition for Chinese social media with word segmentation representation learning. arXiv preprint arXiv:1603.00786 (2016)

14. Qiu, J., Wang, Q., Zhou, Y., Ruan, T., Gao, J.: Fast and accurate recognition of Chinese clinical named entities with residual dilated convolutions. arXiv preprint arXiv:1808.08669 (2018)

15. Qiu, L., Zhang, Y.: Word segmentation for Chinese novels. In: AAAI, pp. 2440–2446 (2015)

16. Song, M., Yu, H., Han, W.S.: Developing a hybrid dictionary-based bio-entity recognition technique. BMC Med. Inform. Decis. Making 15(1), S9 (2015)

17. Sun, W.: Chinese named entity recognition using modified conditional random field on postal address. In: 2017 10th International Congress on Image and Signal Processing, BioMedical Engineering and Informatics (CISP-BMEI), pp. 1–6. IEEE (2017)

18. Wang, L., Xie, Y., Zhou, J., Yanhui, G.U., Weiguang, Q.U.: Segment-level chinese named entity recognition based on neural network. J. Chin. Inf. Process. (2018)

19. Wang, Q., Xia, Y., Zhou, Y., Ruan, T., Gao, D., He, P.: Incorporating dictionaries into deep neural networks for the Chinese clinical named entity recognition. arXiv preprint arXiv:1804.05017 (2018)

20. Zhang, S., Qin, Y., Wen, J., Wang, X.: Word segmentation and named entity recognition for SIGHAN Bakeoff3. In: Proceedings of the Fifth SIGHAN Workshop on Chinese Language Processing, pp. 158–161 (2006)

21. Zhang, Y., Yang, J.: Chinese NER using lattice LSTM. arXiv preprint arXiv:1805.02023 (2018)

22. Zhao, J., Fang, W.: Chinese named entity recognition with inception architecture and weight loss. In: 2018 International Conference on Advanced Control, Automation and Artificial Intelligence (ACAAI 2018). Atlantis Press (2018)

23. Zheng, S., Wang, F., Bao, H., Hao, Y., Zhou, P., Xu, B.: Joint extraction of entities and relations based on a novel tagging scheme. arXiv preprint arXiv:1706.05075 (2017)

24. Zhou, J., Qu, W., Zhang, F.: Chinese named entity recognition via joint identification and categorization. Chin. J. Electron. 22(2), 225–230 (2013)

The Discourse Structure Recognition Model Based on Text Classification

Lan Li[1], Jie Liu[2（✉）], Xu Han[1], and Xiaohui Tan[1]

[1] Capital Normal University, Beijing 100048, China
{hanxu,tanxh}@cnu.edu.cn
[2] Information Engineering College, Research Center For Language Intelligence
of China, Capital Normal University, Beijing 100048, China
liujie@cnu.edu.cn

Abstract. Discourse structure recognition is an important aspect of the discourse structure rationality research. However, the assessment of discourse structure recognition usually suffer from the problems such as poor theory and lack of professional Chinese discourse structure corpus. We propose a discourse structure recognition model that consisted by the feature extraction method of "part-of-speech ratio & variance & Doc2vec" and three text classification methods that are Conditional Random Field (CRF), Support Vector Machine (SVM) and Naive Bayes for identifying discourse structure composition. We did two experiments to test the precision of the model and the highest precision reached 70.01%. What's more, we did an experiment to study the effects of five types of paragraph labels on the model and the highest precision reached 82.13%. All experiments uses our own composition corpus of primary and secondary school students. Experimental results on datasets demonstrate that our model can be feasible and effective on research on discourse structure composition.

Keywords: Discourse structure composition ·
Rationality of discourse structure · Text classification ·
Feature extraction

1 Introduction

The research on rationality of discourse structure is an important aspect of automatic composition evaluation technology. It aims to study whether the discourse structure is complete and logical. Specifically, it not only assist teachers to evaluate Chinese compositions more objectively, but also helps students to write a complete and logical composition. Recently, several research enjoyed success in

Supported by Key Special Projects of National Key R&D Program of China (2018YFC0830100), National Natural Science Foundation of China (61672361), and Beijing Municipal Education Commission-Beijing Natural Fund Joint Funding Project (KZ201910028039).

© Springer Nature Switzerland AG 2019
Y. Tan et al. (Eds.): ICSI 2019, LNCS 11656, pp. 253–262, 2019.
https://doi.org/10.1007/978-3-030-26354-6_25

many aspects of this task. The model based on Chinese frame nets can recognize the discourse relation and analyze it via frame semantics [5]. A coherence description scheme for Chinese discourse establishes the relationship between the frames and discourse units [6].

These research enjoyed great success in many aspects of discourse structure analysis, however, they are also encountered many problems. For instance, due to the differences between Chinese and English, the method of discourse structure analysis applicable to English cannot be applied in the study of Chinese discourse structure analysis directly. Another obstacle to the research on Chinese discourse structure is the lack of Chinese corpus, which makes the current research on Chinese discourse structure mainly focuses on specific fields.

To address the problem above, we propose a discourse structure recognition model consisted by unique feature extraction methods and three classify methods. Considering the different feature extraction methods can influence the results, we choose the combination of "part-of-speech ratio & variance & Doc2vec" instead of using single normal feature extraction method. We regard the recognition of discourse structure as a classification problem and CRF, SVM and Naive Bayes have shown their superiority in classification problems in past experiments. Thus, the three classification models were implemented to ensure that the results would not be biased by a single classification method and would be relatively objective. We aim to identify whether the structure of the composition of primary and secondary school students is complete. Thus, we established a corpus dataset that include 4545 compositions for primary and secondary school students. It must be clear what structure of a complete composition should contains. So we invited some professional teachers to divide the structure of a complete composition into five parts: article opening, character description, event description, conclusion and others. There are a total of 20,322 paragraph labels. There are three comparative experiments with the highest precision of 82.13%. The experiment result on the datasets of characters composition in primary and secondary schools show that our model is effective.

2 Related Work

The theories of discourse structure analysis mainly includes Rhetorical Structure Theory (RST) [12] and Penn Discourse Tree Bank (PDTB) [16]. Because English has natural spaces and Chinese requires word segmentation, the labeling of English corpus is different from that of Chinese and the research theories are different. Sun et al. use a Chinese Discourse Treebank based on RST to recognize implicit relations in 2014 [7]. Zhang et al. analyses Chinese discourse relation taxonomy based on PDTB and conducts annotation experiments on Chinese internet news texts [15].

With the development of machine learning, more machine learning methods have been applied to the research of discourse structure analysis. In the early studies, a series of models were proposed only for the concept of discourse, mainly focusing on the linguistic level of rhetorical structure theory, discourse centrality theory and discourse representation theory. In 2012, Louis and Nenkova put forward the idea of text consistency modeling based on hidden markov model [11]. In 2014, Li and Hovy proposed a discourse consistency model based on recurrent and recursive neural networks, which further improved the modeling performance [10].

In comparison, there are few studies on the automatic evaluation of Chinese composition, and they are only study some aspects of it. Xu et al. used composition in which Chinese is a second language, to study the establishment of shallow text feature index system and other specific issues, in 2015 [2]. Xu et al. proposed a connection-driven unsupervised discourse model, in 2014 [4]. Yang et al. studied the automatic scoring of 202 essays written by high school students, in 2012 [3].

In the aspect of text vectorization, deep learning method has achieved good results. In 2013, Mikolov et al. proposed word2vec, a word embedding method [14]. In 2014, he proposed doc2vec, also called paragraph2vec or sentence embedding, an unsupervised algorithm that can obtain sentences or paragraphs or vector expression of the Documents [13]. Doc2vec and classification model are often used for sentiment analysis of texts. Yang et al. used doc2vec and SVM to facilitate the sentiment inclination of the Sina Microblog texts in 2016 [18].

3   Model Description

3.1   Text Feature Extraction Methods

Text feature extraction is the foundation of text classification. Common text feature extraction methods include Mutual Information, Square Statistics, Information Gain, etc. However, According to the characteristics of primary and middle school students' compositions, we find that different paragraphs play different roles in the discourse structure, which is related to the proportion of parts of speech in the paragraphs. For instance, verbs and adverbs account for a higher proportion in the paragraph describing events, while adjectives and nouns account for a higher proportion than other parts of speech in the semantic block of the paragraph describing characters. Therefore, we use the part-of-speech ratio as an index to extract discourse structure feature. It is not enough to dig out the potential relationship by word level and sentence level alone. Doc2vec, as an effective text depth representation model, can better reflect the feature representation between sentences than word2vec [9]. According to the comprehensive analysis of the characteristics of discourse structure, we selects the proportion of part of speech, variance, Doc2vec and its combination as the feature extraction method.

Part-of-Speech Ratio. Part-of-speech is the nature of words. We use the Part-of-speech category provided by the Chinese word segmentation system NLPIR [1] (see Table 1), also called the ICTCLAS (Institute of Computing Technology, Chinese Lexical Analysis System) [17]. The part-of-speech ratio refers to the ratio of a certain class of words to all the words in a discourse structure. The different content described in the paragraph plays the role of linking and closing in the structure, and the part-of-speech ratio is also different.

In this paper, the part-of-speech ratio mentioned refers to the proportion of each Part-of-speech to all parts of speech in the corresponding paragraph by randomly selecting 100 texts from all preprocessed texts. The proportion of specific parts of speech refers to the situation in which the part-of-speech ratio is relatively high in a functional paragraph. Because in the character type composition, with "the event description, the character description" the label paragraph many. Therefore, the proportion of "noun, verb, adjective and adverb" which are representative parts of speech should be considered in Chinese character composition.

Table 1. Part-of-speech category table.

Part-of-speech	Abbreviations	Part-of-speech	Abbreviations
a	adjective	ni	organization name
b	other noun-modifier	nl	location noun
c	other conjunction	ns	geographical name noun
d	other adverb	nt	temporal noun
e	other nexclamation	nz	other proper noun
g	other morpheme	o	onomatopoeia
h	other prefix	p	preposition
i	idiom	q	quantity
j	abbreviation	r	pronoun
k	suffix	u	auxiliary
m	number	v	verb
n	general noun	wp	punctuation
nd	direction noun	ws	foreign words
nh	person name	x	non-lexeme

Doc2vec. Compared with the traditional vectorization representation model, word2Vec and doc2vec can distribute text more effectively [8]. Doc2vec can better express the relationship between sentences, which is useful for studying discourse structure. Doc2vec is to add a paragraph vector on the basis of word2vec, carry out semantic space mapping for paragraph text, and quantize paragraphs. In this paper, Doc2vec is also used as feature extraction technology to compress paragraph text into 400-dimensional feature vectors for research.

Variance. The variance methods filters out the trivial words, retains the high frequency features related to the overall performance of classification, and filters out the rare words within the class which are meaningless to classification. In this paper, the results of variance were sorted from large to small, and the first 5,000 words were selected as the characteristic words to be used.

3.2   Text Classification Models

Common text methods are CRF, SVM, Naive Bayes, and maximum entropy (ME), etc. Compared with the active deep learning algorithm in recent years, it is often supported by a large number of manual labelling corpus. The traditional classification algorithm has lower requirements for the quantity and quality of labelling corpus and better experimental results. Therefore, we adopts CRF, SVM and Naive Bayes as text classification models.

CRF is a typical discriminant model proposed by Lafferty in 2001. At present, CRF is widely used in natural language processing fields such as sequence segmentation, part-of-speech tagging, shallow syntactic analysis and Chinese word segmentation. Support vector machine was first proposed by V. Vapnik and A.J. Lerner in the 1960s, and was completely proposed by V. Vapnik in 1995. Achievements have been made in text classification. Naive bayes classification, a classification algorithm based on bayes' theorem, has been widely used in the field of statistics classification, such as text classification, mail filtering, emotion analysis, credit evaluation and other fields.

3.3   Evaluation Metrics

Common evaluation metrics used in machine model include precision, recall and F1 measure. In this paper, we use the precision.

$$P = \frac{TP}{TP + FP}. \tag{1}$$

TP indicates the number of classes that the classifier correctly classifies the input text into a category. FP indicates the number with which the classifier incorrectly excludes input text from a category.

4   Experiments

The following experiments are carried out for the textual structure recognition model studied. 1. For the feature extraction method of "proportion of Part-of-speech", a comparative experiment was conducted between "total proportion of Part-of-speech" and "specific proportion of Part-of-speech" in CRF, SVM and Naive Bayes 2. The text was extracted with different features. CRF, SVM and Naive Bayes were adopted to compare each feature extraction method. 3. On the basis of the previous research, the optimal method of "part-of-speech ratio & variance & Doc2vec" and CRF are adopted to study the influence of five types of tag texts on the "recognition model of Chinese composition structure and composition of characters".

4.1 Datasets

We have established our own corpus datasets for the lack of composition resources from primary and middle school students. We collected 4,545 character compositions written by grade 1 to grade 9 students as the original corpus samples on the websites. The most described types of characters were selected, including father, mother, teacher, brother, sister, friend, classmate and myself. Corpus was established according to the types of characters.

We processed the original corpus as follows: 1. We manually marked five categories of labels on the original corpus, and finally we get 20,322 labels, including 4,212 labels of "article opening, 5,142 labels of "character description", 5,364 labels of "event description", 4,031 labels of "conclusion" and 1573 labels of "others". The annotated text is called corpus block text. 2. We use the NLPIR system to conduct word segmentation for all corpus block texts. 3. Since stop word hardly reflect the characteristics of the text and take up storage space, we removed the stop words from the corpus block text. The stop word list comes from the website. The processed corpus has no stop words, and each processed corpus has five labels and the number of each label is greater than or equal to 1.

4.2 The Comparison Between the All Part-of-Speech Ratio and Specific Part-of-Speech Ratio

Part-of-speech account for "all Part-of-speech" and "specific Part-of-speech". According to table2, we processed the corpus block text. On the one hand, all parts of speech in corpus block texts are extracted for feature extraction, which is represented as "proportion of all parts of speech"; on the other hand, only verbs, adverbs, nouns, and adjectives in corpus block texts are extracted for feature extraction, which is represented as "proportion of specific parts of speech". CRF, SVM and Naive Bayes were adopted to train the model on the same training set and test set. Finally, we compared the precision of different feature extraction methods (see Table 2).

Table 2. Comparison of two kinds of ratio.

Part-of-speech kinds	Classification models		
	SVM (%)	Naive Bayes (%)	CRF (%)
All part-of-speech ratio	64.41	65.05	68.33
Specific part-of-speech ratio	**65.03**	**67.04**	**70.01**

We can see that the result of "specific Part-of-speech" are higher than that of "all Part-of-speech" in the three classification methods. This shows that "verb, adverb, noun and adjective" are representative in Chinese character composition, and can provide theoretical reference for relevant researches on Chinese character composition Thus, due to the better results of the proportion of specific part-of-speech ratio, the default of "proportion of Part-of-speech" in the following experiments was "proportion of specific part-of-speech ratio".

4.3 Precision of Different Text Feature Extraction Methods

We get seven feature extraction methods, including the single part-of-speech ratio, variance, Doc2vec and their combination as follows: part-of-speech ratio & variance; variance & Doc2vec; part-of-speech ratio & Doc2vec; and part-of-speech ratio & variance & Doc2vec. One third of the corpus was randomly selected as the test set, and the remaining two thirds as the training set. CRF, SVM and Naive Bayes were adopted to train the model on the same training set and test set. Finally, we compared the precision of different feature extraction methods (see Table 3 and Fig. 1).

Table 3. Precision of different text feature extraction methods.

Methods	Classification models		
	SVM (%)	Naive Bayes (%)	CRF (%)
part-of-speech ratio	63.23	65.12	66.26
variance	64.38	63.40	64.02
Doc2vec	64.06	65.76	67.20
part-of-speech ratio & variance	62.89	64.34	68.10
variance & Doc2vec	64.36	64.01	68.01
part-of-speech ratio & Doc2vec	63.21	66.89	69.96
part-of-speech ratio & variance & Doc2vec	**65.03**	**67.04**	**70.01**

From the results we can see that "Part-of-speech ratio & variance & Doc2vec" outperforms all other methods in classification models. The accuracy achieved by our model indicate that the combined feature extraction methods is significantly more accurate than the single feature extraction methods in the three classification methods. Comparing the two methods of "Part-of-speech ratio & Doc2vec" and "Part-of-speech ratio & variance & Doc2vec", the precision is similar in the case of CRF and Naive Bayes, but the latter gets the highest score. Furthermore, there is a big difference in the accuracy in case of the SVM method. Thus, the feature extraction methods of "Part-of-speech ratio & variance & Doc2vec" is more stable in general.

It can be seen that, the precision of CRF is the highest, reaching 70.01%, when use the same feature extraction method among the three classification models. On the other hand, under the same classification model, in different feature extraction methods, the precision of combined feature extraction methods is generally higher than that of single feature extraction methods. In combined feature extraction methods, "part-of-speech ratio & variance & Doc2vec" has the best and stable effect.

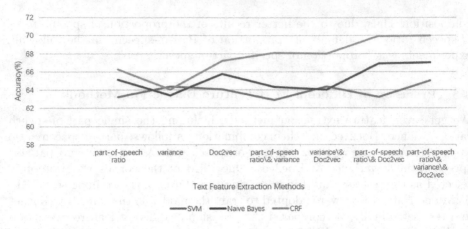

Fig. 1. Graph of the precision of CRF, SVM and Naive Bayes in seven feature extraction methods.

4.4 The Effects of Five Paragraph Labels on the Model

In our experiments, we used the word-of-speech & variance & Doc2vec feature extraction technique, combined with the best performing CRF algorithm for classification experiments (see Table 4). We divided 4545 corpus into separate data sets according to five kinds of labels, including 4212 "opening articles", 5142 "characters description", 5364 "event descriptions", 4031 "summary endings", and 1573 "others". We randomly selected 1/3 as test sets, and the other 2/3 is the training set.

Table 4. Precision of five paragraph labels on the model.

Labels	Opening articles	Characters description	Event descriptions	Summary endings	Others
Number	4212	5142	5364	4031	1573
Accuracy (%)	78.12	81.95	**82.13**	79.56	64.42

The precision of different label texts is between 64.42% and 82.13%, with a wide range of changes, but the regularity is strong. The number of characters in "character description and event description" is the highest, and the highest precision rate is 80% or more. In the Chinese composition of the character class, it is marked as "other" text, the writing style is complex, and the language standardization is poor. Therefore, in the implementation of the "text structure composition recognition model", selecting enough corpus can improve the precision of our recognize model.

5   Conclusion

We presented a discourse structure recognition model recognition via consisted by the feature extraction method of "part-of-speech ratio & variance & Doc2vec" and three text classification methods that are CRF, SVM and Naive Bayes. We demonstrate that the proposed model can help recognize the composition of students' character compositions.

In future work, we will attempt to study the influence of "other" paragraph label. In our study, due to the small number of "other" labels, we attributed "transition", "transition" and "connecting the preceding and the following" to "other" labels and did not conduct separate studies. However, the internal split of "other" label will inevitably result in the feature selection project failing to select the features that represent this category, resulting in poor recognition effect, and these functions are also an important part of achieving coherence. In addition, we will use F1 measure and recall to evaluate our model to make the evaluation more accurate. Furthermore, a more comprehensive quantitative comparison will be performed.

References

1. Ltp Cloud Homepage. http://www.ltp-cloud.com/. Accessed 8 Jan 2019
2. Changhuo, X., Dong, C.: A preliminary study on the automatic scoring of Chinese as a second language composition. International Chinese Teaching and Research (2015). (in Chinese)
3. Chen, Y.: The status quo and prospect of automatic scoring of composition. Language Teaching in Middle School (2012). (in Chinese)
4. Xu, F., Zhu, Q., Zhou, G., Wang, M.: Cohesion-driven discourse coherence modeling. J. Chin. Inf. Process. **28**, 11–21 (2014). (in Chinese)
5. Li, G., Zhang, Y., Li, R.: Discourse relation recognition based on Chinese framenet. J. Chin. Inf. Process. (2017). (in Chinese)
6. Lv, G., Su, N.: A study on Chinese discourse coherence based on CFN. J. Chin. Inf. Process. **31**, 40–49 (2017). (in Chinese)
7. Sun, J., Li, Y.: Research of Chinese implicit discourse relation recognition. ACTA Scientiaurm Naturalium Universitatis Pekinensis **50**, 111–117 (2014). (in Chinese)
8. Lau, J.H., Baldwin, T.: An empirical evaluation of doc2vec with practical insights into document embedding generation. Journal (2016)
9. Le, Q., Mikolov, T.: Distributed representations of sentences and documents. Journal (2014)
10. Li, J., Hovy, E.: A model of coherence based on distributed sentence representation. In: Proceedings of the EMNLP (2014)
11. Louis, A., Nenkova, A.: A coherence model based on syntactic patterns. In: Joint Conference on Empirical Methods in Natural Language Processing and Computational Natural Language Learning (2012)
12. Mann, W.C., Thompson, S.: A relational propositions in discourse. Journal (1986)
13. Mikolov, T., Sutskever, I., Chen, K., et al.: Distributed representations of words and phrases and their compositionality. In: Advances in Neural Information Processing Systems (2013)

14. Mikolov, T., Chen, K., Corrado, G., et al.: Efficient estimation of word representations in vector space. Computer Science (2013)
15. Zhang, M., Qin, B., Liu, T.: Chinese discourse relation semantic taxonomy and annotation. J. Chin. Inf. Process. **28**, 28–36 (2014). (in Chinese)
16. Prasad, R., Dinesh, D.: The Penn discourse TreeBank 2.0. Journal (2008)
17. Guo, X.: Research and implementation of ICTCLAS API with Delphi. Comput. Program. Skills Maintenance (2011). (in Chinese)
18. Yuting, Y., Mingyang, W.: Sina microblog sentiment classification based on distributed representation of documents. J. Intell. (2016). (in Chinese)

Ballistic Wind Speed Identification Method
Based on Hierarchical Optimization Algorithm

Wang Yafei[1], Liu Jianwei[1,2]([envelope]), and Liu Pengfei[1]

[1] Jiangsu Automation Research Institute, Lianyungang 222006, China
Wangyafei666@sohu.com, arctgljw@163.com,
liupengfeiheu@126.com
[2] School of Instrument Science and Engineering,
Southeast University, Nanjing 210096, China

Abstract. Wind has an important influence on the uncontrolled flight path of
the aircraft. If the wind speed variation law within the flight altitude range
cannot be obtained, it is difficult to accurately estimate the falling points of the
conventional projectile and the modified projectile. In order to improve the
accuracy of ballistic prediction, a method of using horizontal control algorithm
to measure horizontal wind speed using uncontrolled ballistic measurement data
and ammunition aerodynamic parameters is proposed. The theoretical trajectory
is calculated according to the six-degree-of-freedom equations of motion of
uncontrolled ammunition under windy conditions and compared with the
measured ballistics data. The optimal objective function is established. The
sequence quadratic programming method is used to estimate wind speed of the
vertical and horizontal heights. The simulation results show that the proposed
method can quickly and effectively estimate the horizontal wind speed at different heights and directions.

Keywords: Uncontrolled Trajectory · Wind speed ·
Stratification Optimization · Sequential Quadratic Programming(SQP)

1 Introduction

As a meteorological environment factor, wind has an important influence on the flight
path of the aircraft. Especially for the uncontrolled flight segments of conventional
uncontrolled projectiles and ballistic correction missiles, the change of wind speed
vector is one of the important factors that cause ballistic dispersion. Therefore, the
conventional projectile needs to compensate the angle of the ground according to the
surface wind speed before launching to improve the accuracy of the drop point. Ballistic wind speed plays a very important role in the process of predicting the drop point
for the guided munitions using the predicted drop point guidance [1, 2]. In the 1990s,
Mark F. Costello conducted a detailed study of the ballistic simulation model of the
guided projectile under windy conditions, which improved the accuracy of the drop
point prediction under the condition of known wind speed [3]. Zhao et al. studied the
ballistic model of the terminal guided projectile under windy conditions, and also
improved the accuracy of the predicted landing point [4]. Jing Yaxing et al. studied the

© Springer Nature Switzerland AG 2019
Y. Tan et al. (Eds.): ICSI 2019, LNCS 11656, pp. 263–271, 2019.
https://doi.org/10.1007/978-3-030-26354-6_26

`ballistic identification problem of forced bombs under non-standard meteorological conditions, and used the actual wind speed values to interpolate, effectively eliminating the adverse effects of wind on the accuracy of ballistic identification [5]. All of the above methods require wind speed measurement before shooting, and re-generate the shot table for pre-shot data binding. It can be seen that the measurement of wind speed plays an important role in improving the accuracy of the uncontrolled bomb and the correction projectile.

The wind speed varies not only with the geographical location, but even at the same location, the wind speed and direction change with time and space height. Wind speed can be divided into two types: constant wind speed and random wind speed. Relative to the constant wind speed, the random wind speed has little effect on the flight trajectory and can be ignored. In addition, considering that the constant wind speed has a small component in the vertical direction, the main factors affecting the ballistics are the horizontal constant wind speed and the wind direction, which is also the focus of wind speed measurement. Usually, the measurement of the ground wind field is easier, while the measurement of the air field is mainly done by the air balloon. The use of high air balls to measure wind speed has many limitations in practical applications, such as long measurement preparation time and poor timeliness of measurement results. Therefore, research on other wind speed measurement methods is of great value.

For the problem of wind speed measurement, Zhang Yanru et al. proposed a method for online identification of longitudinal wind speed based on the measured value of the sensor and the theoretical value of the drag coefficient [6], which improves the accuracy of range prediction. However, since the lateral wind speed cannot be estimated, this method can only predict the drop error in the range direction. Sun You et al. proposed a method to realize wind speed identification with overload control [7]. This method uses the function of the control loop to control the angle of attack to zero, and then performs online identification of wind speed according to the law of missile motion. Guided munitions with strong overload control capabilities. The problem is that the use restrictions are large and cannot be applied to uncontrolled projectiles. In literature [10], based on the uncontrolled ballistic measurement information and the approximate ballistic model under windy conditions, the optimization method is used to study the horizontal wind speed identification methods at different heights, but the method uses an approximate ballistic model and needs to measure uncontrolled ammunition. Acceleration curves at different heights therefore require higher ballistic accuracy and greater wind speed identification errors.

In this regard, in this paper, under the condition that the wind speed is unknown, the wind speed is identified by launching the uncontrolled projectile with known aerodynamic characteristics and then using the ballistic data measured by the ground ballistic measurement equipment or the missile-borne equipment. The method is easy to implement, has a short preparation time, and can be measured multiple times at any time. Firstly, the mathematical model of wind speed identification is established. Then, according to the position, velocity and acceleration measurement data of the projectiles in a period of time, the sequence quadratic programming(SQP) method is adopted for different heights. The wind speed is identified to obtain horizontal and lateral horizontal wind speeds. Finally, the effectiveness of the method is verified by mathematical simulation.

2 Model Establishment

2.1 Kinematic Model

In order to use the ballistic measurement data to identify the horizontal wind speed, it is first necessary to establish a mathematical model of the influence of wind speed on the ballistic characteristics. In windy conditions, the aerodynamic forces and aerodynamic moments of the projectile are related to the relative wind speed. The wind speed estimation model established in the paper involves multiple coordinate systems. The definitions of the ground coordinate system, the ballistic coordinate system and the quasi-elastic coordinate system have been introduced in detail in [8] and will not be described in detail in this paper. The definition of the velocity coordinate system $Ox_w y_w z_w$ and the relative ballistic coordinate system.

If the velocity vector of the missile relative to the ground coordinate system is V and the vector of the wind speed relative to the ground coordinate system is W, the relative velocity V_W of the projectile is

$$V_W = V - W. \tag{1}$$

Since the constant value of the wind on the surface of the earth is small in the vertical direction, it is negligible, so only the influence of the horizontal wind is considered. Set the x-axis direction of the ground coordinate system to the projection of the projectile's emission direction in the horizontal plane. The component of the wind speed in the ground coordinate system is $[W_x \ \ 0 \ \ W_z]^T$. Since the lateral movement speed of the projectile is much smaller than the longitudinal movement speed, W_x, W_z can be approximated as the longitudinal horizontal wind speed and the lateral horizontal wind speed at the position of the projectile. The relative wind speed of the projectile is in the form of a component in the ground coordinate system.

$$\begin{bmatrix} V_{Wx} \\ V_{Wy} \\ V_{Wz} \end{bmatrix} = \begin{bmatrix} V_x - W_x \\ V_y \\ V_z - W_z \end{bmatrix}. \tag{2}$$

Substituting equation (4) into the ballistic differential equations and calculating the angle of attack and side slip angle of relative wind speed for the calculation of aerodynamic force and aerodynamic moment, the six-degree-of-freedom rigid body ballistic model under windy conditions can be obtained. The specific mathematical model is deduced in detail in the literature [4] and will not be repeated here.

In order to facilitate the establishment of an optimization objective function between wind speed and ballistic measurement data, wind speed and ballistic measurement data can be converted to a transmission coordinate system. At this time, the origin O of the ground coordinate system is the emission point and the OX axis direction is the projection of the emission direction in the horizontal plane. In this coordinate system, the wind speed can be decomposed into a longitudinal wind speed W_c along the plane of incidence and a lateral wind speed W_n perpendicular to the plane of incidence.

If the stratified data of wind speed is known, the theoretical trajectory can be calculated from the ballistic simulation model. At the same time, the radar can be used to track the uncontrolled projectiles and the ballistic measurement data $[x, \; y, \; z, \; V_x, \; V_y, \; V_z, \; \theta, \; \psi_V]$ in the emission coordinate system can also be measured, where x, y, z, Vx, Vy, Vz are the emission coordinates. The three-axis position component and velocity component, θ is the ballistic inclination and ψ_V is the ballistic declination. By comparing the difference between the theoretical trajectory and the measured trajectory and modifying the wind speed data according to the optimization algorithm, the theoretical trajectory is matched with the measured trajectory as much as possible and the wind speed stratification data close to the actual meteorological conditions can be obtained.

2.2 Hierarchical Optimization Method

Large-range ammunition usually has a maximum ballistic height of more than 10 km. In order to use a computer to solve uncontrolled ballistic landings, stratified meteorological data at different altitudes is required. In order to obtain sufficiently accurate uncontrolled ballistic solution accuracy, it is generally required that the layered interval of meteorological data does not exceed 500 m. It can be seen that in order to meet the uncontrolled ballistic solution requirements of the ballistic computer, at least the wind speed of the 20-layer height needs to be identified. Even if the influence of the vertical wind speed is neglected, the wind speed needs at least two physical quantities in the horizontal direction to be expressed. Therefore, more than 40 parameters need to be optimized for identification. For high-dimensional systems, if the optimization algorithm is used directly for solving, there will be many problems such as large amount of calculation, slow convergence, and reduced optimization efficiency. To this end, this paper proposes a layered optimization algorithm.

Considering that the wind speed at different altitudes only affects the ballistic changes in the current altitude range, the wind speeds in the range can be optimized and calculated according to different height intervals, finally, the wind speeds in the whole ballistic height range are combined. If the stratification height of the wind speed is $\Delta h = 500 \, \text{m}$ and the ballistic height ranges from 0 to 12 km, the maximum weather stratification number is $n_{\max} = 25$. The wind speed of each layer is expressed in component form $[W_{ci}, \; W_{ni}]$ $(i \in N, i < n_{\max})$. For the wind speed in the range of h_j–h_{j+n} in the height range, the wind speed in the height range can be optimized based on the theoretical ballistics and the measured ballistics in the height range. By cyclically performing the process, the wind speed optimization calculation results in the full ballistic range can be obtained. Sequential Quadratic Programming (SQP) is a widely used nonlinear optimization method that can quickly solve unconstrained nonlinear optimization problems. Therefore, this paper chooses the sequence quadratic programming algorithm as the solution method to solve the horizontal wind speed optimization problem.

2.3   Optimization of the Choice of Objective Function

The choice of optimization function is very important for solving the optimization problem. Choosing a reasonable optimization function cannot only improve the convergence speed, but also reduce the sensitivity of the optimal solution to the system parameters. In the case of certain errors in the system parameters, a more accurate optimal solution can still be obtained.

For wind speed optimization problems, the choice of optimization function needs to consider the following factors:

(1)   The objective function needs to be easy to find;
Wind speed optimization relies on ballistic measurement data. The usual ballistic measurement methods mainly rely on ground radar, which can only obtain more accurate ammunition position and speed information, and it is more difficult to obtain acceleration and attitude parameters. Therefore, position, velocity or related angle information should be used as the source of information for the objective function calculation.

(2)   The correlation between the objective function and the optimization variable;
The objective function must be related to the optimization variable in order to reflect the pros and cons of the feasible solution through the change of the objective function value. Generally, the stronger the correlation between the objective function and the optimization variable, that is, the greater the influence of the optimization objective function on the wind speed, the more favorable it is to improve the convergence speed of the optimization solution and the calculation accuracy of the optimal solution.

(3)   The sensitivity of the objective function to system parameters;
The lower the sensitivity of the objective function to the system parameters, the smaller the influence of the optimal solution is affected by the system parameters, which can reduce the adverse effects of system parameter errors such as drag coefficient error and ballistic parameter measurement error on the accuracy of wind speed solution. By selecting the objective function with lower sensitivity, it is possible to obtain a more accurate wind speed in the case of a certain error in the drag coefficient and ballistic measurement.

According to the above analysis, according to the radar ballistic measurement data, the velocity error, position error, ballistic inclination and ballistic yaw error of the ballistics can be measured. By comparing and analyzing the sensitivity of each of the above functions and its correlation with the optimized variables, it can provide a basis for the selection of the objective function.

Let $\Delta x = x_m - x_s$, where, x_m is the actual x position of the radar, x_s is the theoretical x position of the simulation, Δx is the x position error of the actual ballistic and theoretical ballistics. Similarly, you can define Δy for y-direction position error, Δz for z-direction position error, Δv_x for x-direction velocity error, Δv_y for y-direction velocity error, Δv_z for z-direction velocity error and $\Delta \theta$ for ballistic inclination error, $\Delta \psi_V$ represents the ballistic yaw error. Set $g(x) = \sum \Delta x^2$, then $g(x)$ can be used as an objective function to represent Δx. And so on for each of the eight variables.

Figures 1 and 2 respectively show the influence of the longitudinal and lateral wind speed changes of 1 m/s on the values of the objective functions at different heights.

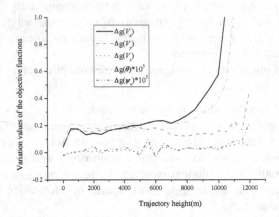

Fig. 1. Effect of longitudinal wind speed change 1 m/s on each function value

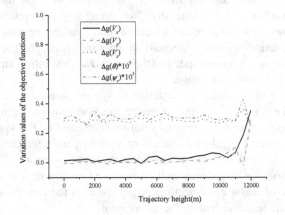

Fig. 2. Effect of lateral wind speed change 1 m/s on each function value

It can be seen from Figs. 2 and 3 that the change of longitudinal wind speed mainly affects the values of $\sum \Delta v_x^2$, $\sum \Delta v_y^2$ and $\sum \Delta \theta^2$, while the lateral wind speed mainly affects the values of $\sum \Delta v_z^2$ and $\sum \Delta \psi_V^2$. Therefore, in order to identify the longitudinal wind speed and the lateral wind speed at the same time, it is necessary to perform weighted summation on a plurality of objective functions.

In order to analyze the sensitivity of the optimal solution to various disturbance factors when different objective functions are used, the variation of the optimal solution is simulated under the error of drag coefficient. The results are as follows Fig. 3 shows.

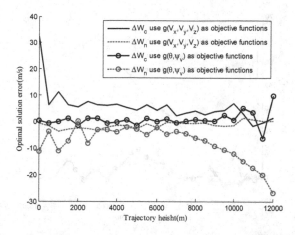

Fig. 3. 1% change in drag coefficient, change in optimal solution

It can be seen from the above results that the selection of the objective function has a great influence on the sensitivity of the optimal solution and must be considered. By comprehensive comparison, the weighted sum of squares of $\sum \Delta \theta^2$ and $\sum \Delta \psi_V^2$ can be selected as the objective function of the optimization.

$$\text{s.t.} \quad g = k_1 \sum \Delta \theta^2 + k_2 \sum \Delta \psi_V^2. \tag{3}$$

where k_1, k_2, k_3 are weight coefficients. In order to ensure that the order of magnitude of each objective function is consistent, $k_1 = k_2 = 1$ can be selected.

3 Simulation

In order to verify the effectiveness of the proposed horizontal wind speed identification method, a traditional rolling stable projectile is taken as an example for simulation. The initial velocity of the projectile is 930 m/s, the angle of incidence is 50° and the maximum ballistic height is about 12 km. The selected wind speed and wind direction are obtained based on the measured stratified wind speed.

If there is no error in the drag coefficient, initial velocity, initial ballistic inclination, and ballistic declination, use the wind speed identification method proposed above to simulate, and perform a round of stratified meteorological optimization for every 4 meteorological stratification heights, i.e., 2000 m intervals, and cycle 6 times, the wind speed optimization result in the range of 0–12000 m can be obtained. The wind speed optimization result and the wind speed optimization error curve are shown in Figs. 4 and 5.

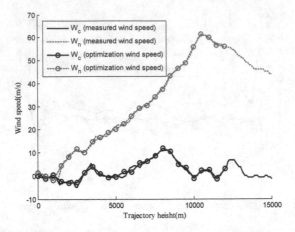

Fig. 4. Actual wind speed and identification wind speed comparison curve

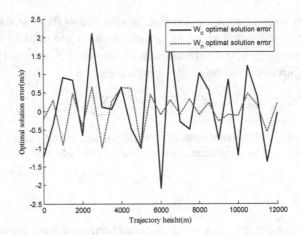

Fig. 5. Vertical and lateral wind speed identification error curve

It can be seen from the simulation results that under ideal conditions, the longitudinal and lateral wind speed identification errors are almost less than 2 m/s. Especially, the identification accuracy of lateral wind speed can reach the level of 1 m/s. As a comparison, the identification accuracy of the wind speed identification method proposed in literature [10] is about 4–6 m/s. It can be seen that the wind speed identification method proposed in this paper has a better effect. The wind speed identification method proposed in this paper can better estimate the horizontal wind speed values at different heights and meet the accuracy requirements of uncontrolled ballistic solution.

4   Conclusion

In this paper, a method for identifying horizontal wind speeds at different altitudes using ballistic measurement data is proposed. Using the difference between theoretical trajectory and radar measured trajectory under different wind speed conditions, the SQP method is used to solve the horizontal velocity at different altitudes. A better wind speed identification result. The simulation results show that the method can effectively identify the wind speed at different heights and it still has higher identification accuracy when the wind speed is large, which can meet the requirements of uncontrolled ejection angle correction and correction of the falling point prediction.

References

1. Burke, P.: XM1156 precision guidance kit (PGK) overview. In: NDIA-53rd Annual Fuze Conference (2009)
2. Habash, Y.: Roll control guided mortar (RCGM). In: America: NDIA Joint Armaments Conference (2012)
3. Costello, M.F.: Range extension and accuracy improvement of an advanced projectile using canard control. In: AIAA Atmospheric Flight Mechanics Conference in Baltimore, Maryland, pp. 324–331 (1995)
4. Zhao, Q., Song, W., Lu, F., et al.: Research on ballistic model of terminal guided projectile under windy conditions. J. Eng. Des. 5(15), 373–376 (2008)
5. Yaxing, J., Jing, L., Min, G.: A modified algorithm for the influence of wind on the trajectory identification accuracy. J. Detect. Control 3, 6–10 (2014)
6. Yanru, Z., Liangang, X., Jisheng, Z., et al.: Design of ballistic wind speed estimation algorithm based on aerodynamic parameter identification. Space Control 32(2), 29–34 (2014)
7. You, S., Guanghui, Y.: Online identification method of aircraft wind speed in the atmosphere. Space Control 30(6), 3–6 (2012)
8. Qian, X., Lin, R., Zhao, Y.: Missile Flight Mechanics [M]. Beijing Institute of Technology Press, Beijing (2000)
9. Han, Z.: External Ballistics of Missiles and Arrows [M]. Beijing Institute of Technology Press, Beijing (2014)
10. Qing, G., Yafei, W., Haichuan, W.: Horizontal wind speed identification method based on uncontrolled trajectory information. Command Simul. 39(4), 134–138 (2017)

BackgroundNet: Small Dataset-Based Object Detection in Stationary Scenes

Jian Cheng[1]([✉]), Shaoying Chen[1], Kun Liu[2], Lingkai Yang[3],
and Dongwei Wang[4]

[1] China University of Mining and Technology, Xuzhou 221116, Jiangsu, China
chengjian@cumt.edu.cn
[2] Information Center, Yankuang Group, Zoucheng 273500, Shandong, China
[3] Ulster University, Newtownabbey, County Antrim BT37 0QB, Northern Ireland
[4] HUAMI Co., Ltd., Hefei 230088, Anhui, China

Abstract. Deep learning algorithms have made remarkable progress on the object detection based on huge amount of images. However, it is really difficult to train a model with well generalization for the small-scale images with the limited computation resources. To address the problem, BackgroundNet is proposed to guide the learning process of deep learning-based object detection by the extracted information from the background images. The corresponding network learns not only the features of objects, but also the difference between the object and the non-object area, with the purpose of improve the classification performances for small-scale datasets. Based on YOLO, the background images are employed as the extra input data, and then the input layer of BackgroundNet is not traditionally three RGB but six channels. The experimental results done for coal mine dataset and six public datasets show that the proposed method has better performance when dealing with the object detection with small-scale images and their AP-values are averagely larger than YOLO about 27.8% for six public datasets.

Keywords: BackgroundNet · Small-scale · Background

1 Introduction

Object detection is an popular issue attracted the attention of many researchers. In practice, most of the detected objects are in stationary scenes and occupy the smaller portion of the image. The traditional object detection methods [1], including optical flow, inter-frame difference and background subtraction methods, are easily influenced by light condition or the environmental changes. However, deep learning-based object detection methods, such as Faster-R-CNN, You Only Look Once (YOLO) and Single Shot MultiBox Detector (SSD) [2,3], had high accuracy and generalization. They can be divided into two categories: object proposal-based and regression-based methods [4]. Proposal-based object detection methods generated a set of bounding-boxes containing the interesting

© Springer Nature Switzerland AG 2019
Y. Tan et al. (Eds.): ICSI 2019, LNCS 11656, pp. 272–281, 2019.
https://doi.org/10.1007/978-3-030-26354-6_27

objects with a high possibility. These bounding-boxes, subsequently, are introduced to the CNN classifiers, with the purpose of judging whether the surrounding images are the expected objects. Region-CNN (R-CNN) [5], spatial pyramid pooling network (SPPnet) and fast-R-CNN [6,7] are successively proposed to boost the training process or improve the detecting accuracy. Regression-based object detection methods, such as YOLO and SSD, transformed the problems to a regression task with the bounding-boxes and their probabilities to the associated classes, which have the faster detecting speed and more suitable for the real-time applications [3]. The above-mentioned algorithms focus on the general object detection problems with the huge amount of images, such as ImageNet and PASCAL [4]. Detecting objects in stationary scenes based on the small-scale dataset is still an open issue due to the enough training images are difficult to be collected and small-scale images make the generalization of deep learning-based object detection algorithms worse, causing over-fitting and low accuracy.

Transfer learning or knowledge transfer between different classification models becomes an active topic recently [8,9]. Especially, knowledge transfer in deep learning is to apply the trained deep network to a new situation, and then fine-tune the parameters of the existed deep network in terms of the images in the new situation, with the purpose of speeding up the learning process or improving the classification performance [10]. Following that, the pre-trained model for detecting objects in original scene is regarded as the pre-knowledge to guide the training process in new scene. Being different from the traditional knowledge transfer, the pre-knowledge employed in the paper is the background images in stationary scene rather than the information extracted from other models. Based on this, a novel deep learning-based object detection method called BackgroundNet is proposed, with the purpose of finding the interest objects from the small-scale dataset in stationary scenes. GoogLeNet InceptionV1 [11] is employed to extract the feature, and the object detection method is similar to YOLO. To be specific, the background images as six input channels containing both the object and background images are employed as the part of the input data. Corresponding classification model learns not only the features of objects, but also the difference between object and non-object, with the purpose of improve the generalization.

2 The Algorithm Description of BackgroundNet

Being different from YOLO, BackgroundNet fully utilizes the background information and the novel generating strategy of bounding boxes based on the gird cells. To be specific, L2 loss is replaced by the absolute-error loss. Without loss of generalization, the main issues of BackgroundNet include the input layer, the structure of the network, the loss function and non-maximum suppression. The input of BackgroundNet contains six channels, three BGR channels for the object images and the other channels for the background images, with the purpose of learning the features of objects and the differences between the object and the non-object area. The training images are randomly cropped, so as to overcome over-fitting. All images for training and testing are reshaped to 224 * 224.

GoogLeNet InceptionV1 is employed to extract the feature, but the number of feature maps in each layer is reduced to 1/4, with the purpose of avoiding over-fitting. The object detection of BackgroundNet is similar to YOLO and the input images are divided into 7 * 7 grids. However, the grids employed to draw the bounding boxes are different. In YOLO, only the grid occupied by the centre of the object takes the responsibility of detection. By contrast, all of the grids covering the target are participated in the detection of BackgroundNet and more than one bounding boxes may be produced for the same object. Non-maximum suppression [2] technique is employed to remove the redundant bounding boxes. The reason for multi-grid rather than the central grid in YOLO is that the objects are usually not rigid, and the complicated deformation may lead to the change of the actual bounding box for the objects. However, the small-scale dataset provides less central point. Based on this, multi-grid are employed to detect the objects, with the purpose of speeding up the learning process. Also, the detection accuracy is good enough as long as most of the bounding boxes cover the true bounding box of the objects.

In non-maximum suppression technique, the grid with larger confidence scores than the threshold T is defined as the basic box. Its position and confidence are denoted by $BBox_1$ and $Conf_1$. Other grids with larger confidence scores and IOU are regarded as the same $BBox_1$. The position of the final bounding box is calculated by all of the bounding boxes with confidence score higher than $0.9\ Conf_1$.

$$x = \frac{\sum Conf_i x_i}{\sum Conf_i}, y = \frac{\sum Conf_i y_i}{\sum Conf_i}, w = \frac{\sum Conf_i w_i}{\sum Conf_i}, h = \frac{\sum Conf_i h_i}{\sum Conf_i} \quad (1)$$

In BackgroundNet, the loss function is divided into two parts, including the classification loss and the regression loss. Cross entropy is employed as the classification loss.

$$L_{cls} = -\sum_{j=1}^{N^2}\sum_{i=1}^{2}\lambda_j^{cls}(s_{ji}^t log s_{ji} + (1 - s_{ji}^t)log(1 - s_{ji})) \quad (2)$$

λ_j^{cls} is the weight to balance the importance of object and non-object area. $\lambda_j^{cls} = 3$, if the grid contains object. Otherwise, $\lambda_j^{cls} = 1$. s_{ji} and s_{ji}^t are the classification output and the true label of the jth grid for the object. The regression loss calculated by the absolute-error loss shown as follows instead of L2 loss adopted in YOLO. Dropout [12] and local response normalization are also employed to avoid over-fitting. The size of the output for each grid is set to 6 and 2, with the purpose of judging whether there is the object in the grid, or 4, so as to positioning the bounding box.

$$L_{reg} = \frac{1}{\lambda_{reg}\sum_{j=1}^{N^2}1_j}\sum_{j=1}^{N^2}1_j(L(x_j, x_j^t) + L(y_j, y_j^t) + L(w_j, w_j^t) + L(h_j, h_j^t)) \quad (3)$$

x_j, y_j, w_j, h_j are the predicted position of the bounding box. $x_j^t, y_j^t, w_j^t, h_j^t$ are the true bounding box. $1_j = 1$, if there is an object in the grid. Otherwise,

Fig. 1. Examples of YOLO in coal mine

$1_j = 0$. λ_{reg} is employed to tradeoff the classification and regression loss. In the paper, $\lambda_{reg} = 1000$. L_{loss} is the totally error of BackgroundNet.

$$L_{loss} = L_{cls} + L_{reg} \tag{4}$$

3   Comparison and Discuss the Experimental Results

Scene Background Initialization (SBI) is a dataset used to evaluate and compare the algorithms for background initialization. Six datasets in SBI are employed to train the model and test its generalization in different situations [13,14]. In CAVIAR1, persons slowly walk along a corridor with mild shadows. A man stands and moves before the grassland in CaVignal. For Candela_m1.10 and Board, a man goes in and out a room, and two men moves in front of a dashboard, respectively. In HumanBody2 and IBMtest2, persons quickly walk indoor with mild shadows and corridors, respectively. Among them, CAVIAR1 is employed as the training dataset. CaVignal, Candela_m1.10, Board, HumanBody2 and IBMtest2 are adopted to test the performance of BackgroundNet in different situations. Moreover, a coal mine dataset shown in Fig. 1 is also employed to examine the algorithm performances.

Without loss of generalization, assuming that the background is known because the background images are easily obtained in stationary situations. In BackgroundNet, both the object and the true background images are considered as the input data. The output of the model includes the classification result judging whether there are motion objects and the regression result positing the objects. Xavier is employed to initialize the parameters. The size of a batch is set to 16. The momentum and learning rate are 0.9 and 0.0002, respectively. The detailed structure of the proposed method is shown in Table 1.

From the loss curves shown in Figs. 2 and 3, we see that YOLO and BackgroundNet both have the similar classification precision for training and testing in the same scene. However, the totally different testing performances for the different scenes, except for IBMtest2. Especially, BackgroundNet performs obviously better with the lower classification and regression loss for CaVignal, Candela_m1.10 and HumanBody2. To sum up, fully utilizing the background information improves the generalization of deep learning-based model in stationary scenes. Precision recall curves of BackgroundNet and YOLO are shown

Table 1. Structure of neural network

Layers	Output size	Input: 224 × 224 × 6			
Convolution 1	112 × 112 × 16	Conv7 × 7S2			
Pooling 1	56 × 56 × 16	Max 3 × 3S2			
LocalRespNorm					
Convolution 2	56 × 56 × 16	Conv1 × 1S1			
Convolution 3	56 × 56 × 48	Conv3 × 3S1			
LocalRespNorm					
Pooling 2	28 × 28 × 48	Max 3 × 3S2			
Inception 1_1	28 × 28 × 64	Conv1 × 1S1	Conv1 × 1S1	Conv1 × 1S1	Max 3 × 3S1
			Conv3 × 3S1	Conv5 × 5S1	Conv1 × 1S1
Inception 1_2	28 × 28 × 120	Conv1 × 1S1	Conv1 × 1S1	Conv1 × 1S1	Max 3 × 3S1
			Conv3 × 3S1	Conv5 × 5S1	Conv1 × 1S1
Pooling 3	14 × 14 × 120	Max 3 × 3S2			
Inception 2_1	14 × 14 × 128	Conv1 × 1S1	Conv1 × 1S1	Conv1 × 1S1	Max 3 × 3S1
			Conv3 × 3S1	Conv5 × 5S1	Conv1 × 1S1
Inception 2_2	14 × 14 × 128	Conv1 × 1S1	Conv1 × 1S1	Conv1 × 1S1	Max 3 × 3S1
			Conv3 × 3S1	Conv5 × 5S1	Conv1 × 1S1
Inception 2_3	14 × 14 × 128	Conv1 × 1S1	Conv1 × 1S1	Conv1 × 1S1	Max 3 × 3S1
			Conv3 × 3S1	Conv5 × 5S1	Conv1 × 1S1
Inception 2_4	14 × 14 × 132	Conv1 × 1S1	Conv1 × 1S1	Conv1 × 1S1	Max 3 × 3S1
			Conv3 × 3S1	Conv5 × 5S1	Conv1 × 1S1
Inception 2_5	14 × 14 × 208	Conv1 × 1S1	Conv1 × 1S1	Conv1 × 1S1	Max 3 × 3S1
			Conv3 × 3S1	Conv5 × 5S1	Conv1 × 1S1
Pooling 4	7 × 7 × 208	Max 3 × 3S2			
Inception 3_1	7 × 7 × 208	Conv1 × 1S1	Conv1 × 1S1	Conv1 × 1S1	Max 3 × 3S1
			Conv3 × 3S1	Conv5 × 5S1	Conv1 × 1S1
Inception 3_2	7 × 7 × 256	Conv1 × 1S1	Conv1 × 1S1	Conv1 × 1S1	Max 3 × 3S1
			Conv3 × 3S1	Conv5 × 5S1	Conv1 × 1S1
Pooling 5	7 × 7 × 256	Average 7 × 7S1			
Convolution 4	7 × 7 × (2+4)	Conv1 × 1S1		Conv1 × 1S1	
		Softmax			

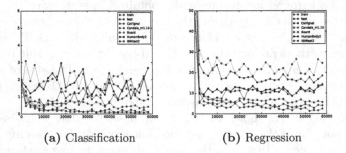

(a) Classification   (b) Regression

Fig. 2. The classification and regression loss of BackgroundNet

in Fig. 4. For BackgroundNet, the AP-values in the same scene are better than YOLO, except for Board.

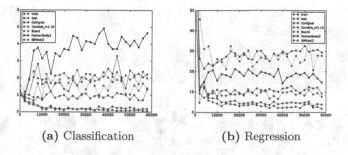

(a) Classification   (b) Regression

Fig. 3. The classification and regression loss of YOLO

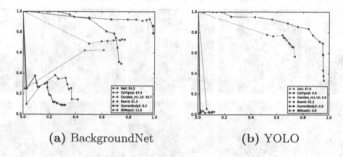

(a) BackgroundNet   (b) YOLO

Fig. 4. Precision recall curve

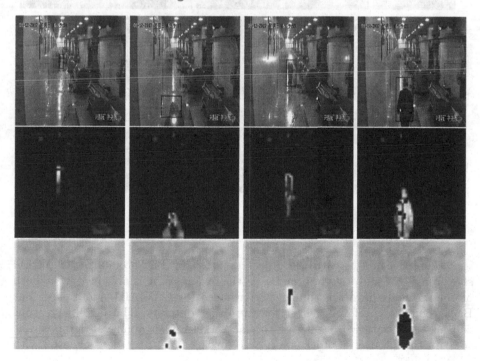

Fig. 5. Examples of BackgroundNet in coal mine

278   J. Cheng et al.

Fig. 6. Examples of BackgroundNet

Taking the images with the object detected by BackgroundNet or YOLO shown in Fig. 1 and Figs. 5, 6 and 7 as the examples, it is obviously that both of the methods have the similar performance for CAVIAR1 and Board, but BackgroundNet performs better for the other datasets. The possible reasons causing the unsatisfied results are the lack of data for training. It is impossible to learn the features of objects very well for the small-scale dataset, even with

Fig. 7. Examples of YOLO

data augmentation technique. Moreover, the learned model cannot catch all of the characteristics of objects. For example, all of the persons in the training set wear black clothes, which makes the learned model confused after changing the color of clothes.

4 Conclusion

A novel deep learning-based object detection method is proposed for small-scale datasets with stationary scenes, with the purpose of avoiding over-fitting and improve the generalization. Over-fitting can be overcame by many techniques, such as random cropping, dropout, and decreasing the complexity of the model. However, it is difficult to improve the generalization because the features in the training set are different from the datasets with another scenes. To address the problem, BackgroundNet utilizing the information extracted from the background images to guide the learning process of deep learning-based algorithms is proposed. It learns not only the features of objects, but also the difference between the object and the non-object area, with the purpose of improve the classification performances for small-scale datasets. The experimental results done for coal mine dataset and six public datasets show that the proposed method has better performance when dealing with the object detection with small-scale images and their AP-values are averagely larger than YOLO about 27.8% for six public datasets. More efficient strategies extracting the background information are the future works.

Acknowledgments. This work was supported in part by National key research and development program (2016YFC0801808) and National key research and development program (2016YFC0801406).

References

1. Cheng, Y.H., Wang, J.: A motion image detection method based on the inter-frame difference method. Appl. Mech. Mater. **490–491**, 1283–1286 (2014)
2. Ren, S., Girshick, R., Girshick, R., et al.: Faster R-CNN: towards real-time object detection with region proposal networks. IEEE Trans. Pattern Anal. Mach. Intell. **39**(6), 1137–1149 (2015)
3. Redmon, J., Farhadi, A.: YOLO9000: better, faster, stronger. In: Proceedings of the IEEE Conference on Computer Vision and Pattern Recognition, pp. 7263–7271 (2017)
4. Everingham, M., Gool, L.V., Williams, C.K.I., et al.: The Pascal, Visual Object Classes (VOC) challenge. Int. J. Comput. Vision **88**(2), 303–338 (2010)
5. Han, J., Zhang, D., Cheng, G., et al.: Advanced deep-learning techniques for salient and category-specific object detection: a survey. IEEE Signal Process. Mag. **35**(1), 84–100 (2018)
6. He, K., Zhang, X., Ren, S., et al.: Spatial pyramid pooling in deep convolutional networks for visual recognition. IEEE Trans. Pattern Anal. Mach. Intell. **37**(9), 1904–1916 (2015)
7. Girshick, R.: Fast R-CNN. In: Proceedings of the IEEE International Conference on Computer Vision, pp. 1440–1448 (2015)
8. Tzeng, E., Hoffman, J., Darrell, T., et al.: Simultaneous deep transfer across domains and tasks. In: Proceedings of the IEEE International Conference on Computer Vision, pp. 4068–4076 (2015)

9. Guo, Y.N., Cheng, J., Luo, S., Gong, D.W., Xue, Y.: Robust dynamic multi-objective vehicle routing optimization method. IEEE/ACM Trans. Comput. Biol. Bioinf. **15**(6), 1891–1903 (2018)
10. Wang, L., Guo, S., Huang, W., et al.: Knowledge guided disambiguation for large-scale scene classification with multi-resolution CNNs. IEEE Trans. Image Process. **26**(4), 2055–2068 (2017)
11. Szegedy, C., Liu, W., Jia, Y., et al.: Going deeper with convolutions. In: Proceedings of the IEEE Conference on Computer Vision and Pattern Recognition, pp. 1–9 (2015)
12. Srivastava, N., Hinton, G., Krizhevsky, A., et al.: Dropout: a simple way to prevent neural networks from overfitting. J. Mach. Learn. Res. **15**(1), 1929–1958 (2014)
13. Maddalena, L., Petrosino, A.: Towards benchmarking scene background initialization. In: Murino, V., Puppo, E., Sona, D., Cristani, M., Sansone, C. (eds.) ICIAP 2015. LNCS, vol. 9281, pp. 469–476. Springer, Cham (2015). https://doi.org/10.1007/978-3-319-23222-5_57
14. Guo, Y.N., Yang, H., Chen, M.R., Cheng, J., Gong, D.W.: Ensemble prediction-based dynamic robust multi-objective optimization methods. Swarm Evol. Comput. **48**, 156–171 (2019)

A New Method for Identification of Essential Proteins by Information Entropy of Protein Complex and Subcellular Localization

Jie Zhao[1], Xiujuan Lei[1(✉)], Xiaoqin Yang[1], and Ling Guo[2]

[1] School of Computer Science, Shaanxi Normal University,
Xi'an 710062, China
xjlei@snnu.edu.cn
[2] School of Life Science, Shaanxi Normal University, Xi'an 710062, China

Abstract. Essential proteins are critical components of living organisms. The identification of essential proteins from protein-protein interaction (PPI) networks is beneficial for the understanding of biology mechanism. This work presents a novel information entropy of protein complex and subcellular localization based method (IECS) for essential protein identification from PPI networks. First, extract the sample by stratified sampling to calculate the information gain of the protein complex and subcellular localization. Information gain can effectively determine the importance of biological characteristics. Then calculate the biological attribute score based on the information entropy of protein complex and subcellular localization. Finally combined with the network characteristics of the node. The proposed IECS method is implemented on two Saccharomyces cerevisiae datasets (DIP and Krogan), and the experimental results show that IECS overmatches most of the traditional methods for identifying essential proteins.

Keywords: Essential proteins · Information entropy · Information gain · Protein-protein interaction network

1 Introduction

Essential proteins are the fundamental components of many biological processes in a cell [1]. With the development of proteomics and computer technology, various computational methods for essential protein detection have been proposed and become effective complements to the experimental methods since most of them are usually laborious and time-consuming [2]. In general, these computational methods can be classified into two types: network topology based methods and multi-information integration based methods.

Many studies have shown that essentiality of a protein is closely related to its topological location in the protein-protein interaction (PPI) network [3], and the more important the position a protein lies in, the more likely it expresses essentiality. Based on the characteristics, a great number of topological centrality methods have been used for identifying essential proteins. Such as Degree Centrality (DC) [4], Betweenness Centrality (BC) [5], Closeness Centrality (CC) [6], Subgraph Centrality (SC) [7], Eigenvector Centrality (EC) [8], and Information Centrality (IC) [9] are the most representative

© Springer Nature Switzerland AG 2019
Y. Tan et al. (Eds.): ICSI 2019, LNCS 11656, pp. 282–291, 2019.
https://doi.org/10.1007/978-3-030-26354-6_28

topology based methods. Some other impactful methods taking advantage of topological properties have been developed for protein essentiality determination, for instance, Local Average Connectivity (LAC), which measures protein essentiality by evaluating the relationship between a protein and its neighbors [10]; Neighborhood Centrality (NC) which is based on edge clustering coefficient [11]; and Local Interaction Density (LID), which takes the essentiality of a protein from interaction densities among its neighbors [12]. These topology-based methods identify essential proteins in the light of the principle of scoring-sorting, more specifically, all proteins in a PPI network are scored according to a certain centrality method, and then are sorted on their decreasing scores, finally, those top ranked proteins are taken as identified essential proteins.

Furthermore, in order to enhance the identification accuracy, many attempts have been made to integrate topological as well as biological characteristics, and a series of information integration based methods are proposed. Li et al. proposed PeC [13] and Tang et al. developed WDC [14], both of which integrate the PPI network and gene expression data. Peng et al. proposed UDoNC [15], which is based on the integration of protein domain information and PPI networks. Lei et al. developed a new method RSG [16], which is based on the information combination of RNA-Seq, subcellular localization and GO annotation. Experimental results demonstrate that the methods integrating some biological information can produce better prediction results compared those methods based merely on network topology.

Although there have been all sorts of approaches designed for essential proteins identification, the accuracy level still needs further improvement. In this study, we propose a new method by utilizing information entropy of protein complex and subcellular localization to identify essential proteins named IECS. IECS measures protein essentiality by considering the network characteristics and biological characteristics of proteins. We apply our IECS method on two PPI networks of Saccharomyces cerevisiae and compare it with several competing methods including DC, BC, CC, SC, EC, IC, LAC, NC, PeC and WDC. The experimental results show that IECS outperforms other methods in predicting essential proteins from PPI networks.

2 Methods

2.1 Basic Concept

A PPI network is usually described as an undirected graph $G(V, E)$. The nodes V represents the proteins and the edges $E = \{e(v_i, v_j)\}$ represent the interaction of two proteins v_i and v_j. The pearson correlation coefficient (PCC) was calculated to evaluate how strong two interacting proteins are co-expressed [17]. Compared with traditional gene expression data, RNA-Seq data has better accuracy when analyzing gene expression profiles [18]. The *PCC* value of a pair of gene $x = \{x_1, x_2, \ldots, x_n\}$ and $y = \{y_1, y_2, \ldots, y_n\}$ is defined as:

$$PCC(x, y) = \frac{\sum_{k=1}^{n} (x_k - \mu(x))(y_k - \mu(y))}{\sqrt{\sum_{k=1}^{n} (x_k - \mu(x))^2}\sqrt{\sum_{k=1}^{n} (y_k - \mu(y))^2}} \tag{1}$$

where $\mu(x)$, $\mu(y)$ is the mean gene expression value. In this paper, PCC is used to weight the edges in the PPI network, and using RNA-Seq data for calculations. After the weighted network is constructed, the weighted edge aggregation coefficients (WECC) [16] is calculated which is a local variable that characterizes the closeness of two proteins v_i and v_j:

$$WECC_{ij} = \frac{\sum\limits_{e \in Z_{ij}} We}{\min(|Ni| - 1, |Nj| - 1)} \qquad (2)$$

where Z_{ij} are the triangles built on edge (v_i, v_j), We is the weight of edge in Z_{ij}. $|Ni|$ and $|Nj|$ are the degrees of protein v_i and v_j, respectively.

2.2 Information Entropy and Information Gain

Information entropy indicates the degree of chaos in a system. The higher the uncertainty of the system, the greater the information entropy. The measure of information entropy associated with each possible data value is the negative logarithm of the probability mass function for the value [19]:

$$E = -\sum_{i=1}^{n} p_i \log_2 p_i \qquad (3)$$

The information gain is used to select the characteristic index in the decision tree algorithm. The larger the information gain, the better the selectivity of this feature. The probability is defined as the entropy of the set Y to be classified minus the conditional entropy of the selected feature X [20].

$$IG(Y|X) = E(Y) - E(Y|X) \qquad (4)$$

Protein has many biological properties that have an impact on essential. Information gain can effectively determine the importance of biological properties.

2.3 Predicting Essential Proteins Based on IECS

Based on the information entropy of the protein complex and subcellular localization, a new method IECS is proposed to predict essential proteins. In Fig. 1, an example is shown to explain the IECS method. For each protein v, IECS determines its essentiality according to network attribute score $nscore$ and biological attribute score $bscore$.

$$nscore(v) = \sum_{u \in Nv} WECC(v, u) \qquad (5)$$

where Nv denotes the set of all neighbors of node v.

To analyze the biological properties of proteins, first, extract ns proteins from known essential proteins and non-essential proteins using stratified sampling and

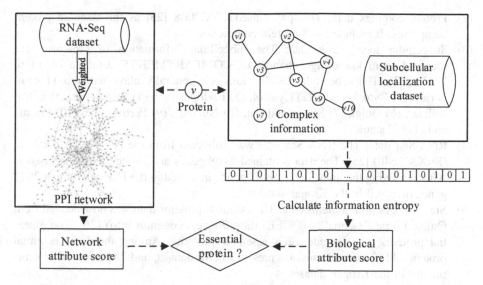

Fig. 1. An illustration of IECS method.

calculate the information gain of protein complex properties igc and subcellular localization properties igs to measure the importance of the two biological properties. we set ns equal to 100. Then construct vector eigenvectors using protein complexes and subcellular localization data, calculate the information entropy of the protein complex iec and subcellular localization ies data, respectively. The biological attribute score of the protein v is defined as follows;

$$bscore(v) = \frac{igc}{(igc+igs) \times iec_v} + \frac{igs}{(igc+igs) \times ies_v} \tag{6}$$

The final score of the protein v is calculated as follows:

$$score(v) = nscore(v) + bscore(v) \tag{7}$$

3   Experiments and Results

3.1   Experimental Data Description and Analysis

All algorithms are implemented in Matlab R2018a and executed on a quad-core processor 3.30 GHz PC with 8G RAM. All the data used were *Saccharomyces cerevisiae*.

(1) Protein-protein interaction data: In this study, two commonly used protein interaction databases DIP [21] (version of 20160114) and Krogan [22] were employed. After preprocessing, the DIP database contains 5028 proteins and 22302 interactions, the Krogan database contains 2674 proteins and 7075 interactions.

(2) Protein complex data: This paper used CYC2008 [23] as the standard protein complexes. It included 408 protein complexes.

(3) Subcellular localization data: The subcellular information of proteins were retrieved from knowledge channel of COMPARTMENTS database (April 6, 2017) [24]. The subcellular localizations are generally classified into 11 categories: (1) Cytoskeleton, (2) Cytosol, (3) Endoplasmic, (4) Endosome, (5) Extracellular, (6) Golgi, (7) Mitochondrion, (8) Nucleus, (9) Peroxisome, (10) Plasma and (11) Vacuole.

(4) RNA-Seq data: The RNA-Seq data was collected from the NCBI SPA database (SRX362640) [25]. The data contained 7108 genes at 12 time points in 3 tissues. After removing the unavailable, 4957 genes involved in the DIP dataset and 2673 genes involved in the Krogan dataset.

(5) Standard essential proteins data: The essential proteins data was downloaded from Online GEne Essentiality (OGEE) (http://ogee.medgenius.info) [26]. The essential proteins data include 1285 essential proteins. Among the 1285 essential proteins, 1150 essential proteins present in DIP dataset, and 784 essential proteins present in the Krogan dataset.

3.2   Comparison with Ten Existing Methods

The performance of IECS is compared with ten other previously proposed methods: DC, BC, CC, SC, EC, IC, LAC, NC, PeC, WDC. It is well known that DC, BC, CC, SC, EC and IC are six classics centrality measures. The results of these six methods are generated by a cytoscape plugin CytoNCA [27]. The comparison results in DIP and Krogan database are shown in Figs. 2 and 3 respectively. Proteins are sorted in descending order according to algorithm scoring. Then the top 100, 200, 300, 400, 500, 600 proteins were selected as candidate essential proteins to compare with standard essential proteins. As can be seen in Figs. 2 and 3, IECS performs better than all the ten other centrality methods for identifying essential proteins from the two databases.

3.3   Validated by Jackknife Methodology

To further evaluate the performance of our proposed method IECS, we cite the jackknife methodology developed by Holman et al. [28]. The experimental results validated by Jackknife method on DIP and Krogan are described in Fig. 4(a) and (b), respectively. The horizontal axis represents the top ranked proteins according to their ranked scores computed by corresponding methods. The vertical axis represents the cumulative count of essential proteins for each method.

The horizontal axis of Fig. 4(a) ranges from 0 to 1150 and the horizontal axis of Fig. 4(b) ranges from 0 to 784. The 1150 and 784 are the number of known essential proteins under current technical conditions in the DIP and Krogan databases. It demonstrates that our proposed method IECS performs better than other methods.

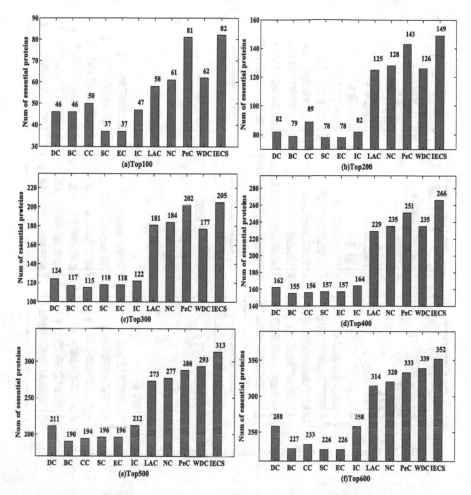

Fig. 2. Comparison of IECS and other ten methods from DIP database.

3.4   Validated by ROC Curves

The Area Under Curve (AUC) is used to measure the performance of corresponding methods, the bigger the area is, the better prediction performance the method has. As shown in Fig. 5, the areas under the curve for IECS is larger than other curves both in DIP database and Krogan database, it demonstrates that our proposed method IECS performs better than other ten methods.

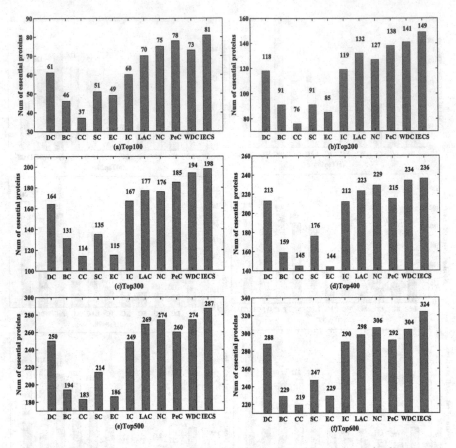

Fig. 3. Comparison of IECS and other ten methods from Krogan database.

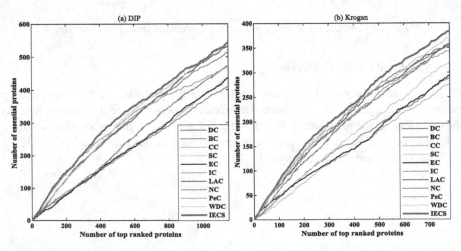

Fig. 4. Jackknife curves of IECS and other ten methods in (a) DIP database and (b) Krogan database.

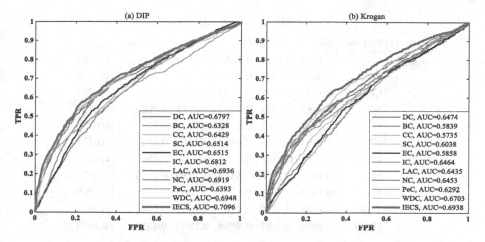

Fig. 5. ROC curves of IECS and other ten methods in (a) DIP database (b) Krogan database.

3.5 Validated by Statistical Measures

For evaluating the performance of IECS, the following six statistical sensitivity (*SN*), specificity (*SP*), positive predictive value (*PPV*), negative predictive value (*NPV*), F-measure and accuracy (*ACC*) used to evaluate the methods [16].

As shown in Table 2, it is obvious that the sensitivity, specificity, positive predictive value, negative predictive value, F-measure, and accuracy of IECS are higher than that of any other ten methods on two different databases, which shows that IECS can identify essential proteins more accurately.

Table 2. Comparison of IECS and other ten methods.

Dataset	Methods	*SN*	*SP*	*PPV*	*NPV*	*F-measure*	*ACC*
DIP	DC	0.4104	0.8250	0.4104	0.8250	0.4104	0.7301
	BC	0.3557	0.8087	0.3557	0.8087	0.3557	0.7050
	CC	0.3800	0.8160	0.3800	0.8160	0.3800	0.7162
	SC	0.3791	0.8157	0.3791	0.8157	0.3791	0.7158
	EC	0.3800	0.8160	0.3800	0.8160	0.3800	0.7162
	IC	0.4113	0.8252	0.4113	0.8252	0.4113	0.7305
	LAC	0.4618	0.8404	0.4626	0.8400	0.4622	0.7536
	NC	0.4488	0.8365	0.4496	0.8361	0.4492	0.7476
	PeC	0.4108	0.8250	0.4104	0.8252	0.4106	0.7303
	WDC	0.4661	0.8417	0.4670	0.8412	0.4666	0.7556
	IECS	**0.4726**	**0.8435**	**0.4730**	**0.8433**	**0.4728**	**0.7586**

(continued)

Table 2. (*continued*)

Dataset	Methods	SN	SP	PPV	NPV	F-measure	ACC
Krogan	DC	0.4554	0.7740	0.4554	0.7740	0.4554	0.6805
	BC	0.3673	0.7374	0.3673	0.7374	0.3673	0.6289
	CC	0.3533	0.7316	0.3533	0.7316	0.3533	0.6207
	SC	0.4082	0.7544	0.4082	0.7544	0.4082	0.6528
	EC	0.3737	0.7401	0.3737	0.7401	0.3737	0.6326
	IC	0.4503	0.7718	0.4503	0.7718	0.4503	0.6775
	LAC	0.4566	0.7745	0.4566	0.7745	0.4566	0.6813
	NC	0.4579	0.7750	0.4579	0.7750	0.4579	0.6820
	PeC	0.4375	0.7665	0.4375	0.7665	0.4375	0.6700
	WDC	0.4745	0.7819	0.4745	0.7819	0.4745	0.6917
	IECS	**0.4898**	**0.7882**	**0.4898**	**0.7882**	**0.4898**	**0.7007**

4   Conclusion

Essential proteins play a very important role in disease prediction and drug design. More and more computation-based methods have been proposed to fuse large amounts of biological information, but do not make full use of the relationship between biological information. In this paper, a new essential proteins discovery method IECS is presented based on information entropy and information gain, and tested on DIP, Krogan databases. The experimental results show that IECS achieves better performance than ten other methods.

Acknowledgement. This paper is supported by the National Natural Science Foundation of China (61672334, 61502290, 61401263) and the Fundamental Research Funds for the Central Universities, Shaanxi Normal University (GK201804006, GK201901010).

References

1. Winzeler, E.A., et al.: Functional characterization of the S. cerevisiae genome by gene deletion and parallel analysis. Science **285**, 901–906 (1999)
2. Acencio, M.L., Lemke, N.: Towards the prediction of essential genes by integration of network topology, cellular localization and biological process information. BMC Bioinform. **10**, 290 (2009)
3. Jeong, H., Mason, S.P., Barabasi, A.L., Oltvai, Z.N.: Lethality and centrality in protein networks. Nature **411**, 41 (2001)
4. Hahn, M.W., Kern, A.D.: Comparative genomics of centrality and essentiality in three eukaryotic protein-interaction networks. Mol. Biol. Evol. **22**, 803–806 (2005)
5. Joy, M.P., Brock, A., Ingber, D.E., Huang, S.: High-betweenness proteins in the yeast protein interaction network. Biomed. Res. Int. **2005**, 96–103 (2005)
6. Wuchty, S., Stadler, P.F.: Centers of complex networks. J. Theor. Biol. **223**, 45–53 (2003)
7. Estrada, E., Rodriguez-Velazquez, J.A.: Subgraph centrality in complex networks. Phys. Rev. E **71**, 056103 (2005)

8. Bonacich, P.: Power and centrality: a family of measures. Am. J. Sociol. **92**, 1170–1182 (1987)
9. Peng, X., Wang, J., Wang, J., Wu, F.-X., Pan, Y.: Rechecking the centrality-lethality rule in the scope of protein subcellular localization interaction networks. PLoS ONE **10**, e0130743 (2015)
10. Li, M., Wang, J., Chen, X., Wang, H., Pan, Y.: A local average connectivity-based method for identifying essential proteins from the network level. Comput. Biol. Chem. **35**, 143–150 (2011)
11. Wang, J.X., Li, M., Wang, H., Pan, Y.: Identification of essential proteins based on edge clustering coefficient. IEEE/ACM Trans. Comput. Biol. Bioinform. **9**, 1070–1080 (2012)
12. Luo, J., Qi, Y.: Identification of essential proteins based on a new combination of local interaction density and protein complexes. PLoS ONE **10**, e0131418 (2015)
13. Li, M., Zhang, H., Wang, J., Pan, Y.: A new essential protein discovery method based on the integration of protein-protein interaction and gene expression data. BMC Syst. Biol. **6**, 15 (2012)
14. Tang, X., Wang, J., Zhong, J., Pan, Y.: Predicting essential proteins based on weighted degree centrality. IEEE/ACM Trans. Comput. Biol. Bioinform. (TCBB) **11**, 407–418 (2014)
15. Peng, W., Wang, J., Cheng, Y., Lu, Y., Wu, F., Pan, Y.: UDoNC: an algorithm for identifying essential proteins based on protein domains and protein-protein interaction networks. IEEE/ACM Trans. Comput. Biol. Bioinform. (TCBB) **12**, 276–288 (2015)
16. Lei, X., Jie, Z., Fujita, H., Zhang, A.: Predicting essential proteins based on RNA-Seq, subcellular localization and GO annotation datasets. Knowl.-Based Syst. **151**, S095070511830159X (2018)
17. Shang, X., Wang, Y., Chen, B.: Identifying essential proteins based on dynamic protein-protein interaction networks and RNA-Seq datasets. Sci. China Inf. Sci. **59**, 1–11 (2016)
18. Oh, S., Song, S., Grabowski, G., Zhao, H., Noonan, J.P.: Time series expression analyses using RNA-seq: a statistical approach. BioMed Res. Int. **2013**(5), 203681 (2013)
19. Wang, G.Y.Y.H.: Decision table reduction based on conditional information entropy. Chin. J. Comput. **25**, 759–766 (2002)
20. Lee, C., Lee, G.G.: Information gain and divergence-based feature selection for machine learning-based text categorization. Inf. Process. Manag. **42**, 155–165 (2006)
21. Xenarios, I., Salwinski, L., Duan, X.Q.J., Higney, P., Kim, S.M., Eisenberg, D.: DIP, the database of interacting proteins: a research tool for studying cellular networks of protein interactions. Nucleic Acids Res. **30**, 303–305 (2002)
22. Krogan, N.J., et al.: Global landscape of protein complexes in the yeast Saccharomyces cerevisiae. Nature **440**, 637–643 (2006)
23. Pu, S., Wong, J., Turner, B., Cho, E., Wodak, S.J.: Up-to-date catalogues of yeast protein complexes. Nucleic Acids Res. **37**, 825–831 (2009)
24. Binder, J.X., et al.: COMPARTMENTS: unification and visualization of protein subcellular localization evidence. Database **2014**, bau012 (2014)
25. Frazee, A.C., Jaffe, A.E., Langmead, B., Leek, J.T.: Polyester: simulating RNA-seq datasets with differential transcript expression. Bioinformatics **31**, 2778–2784 (2015)
26. Cherry, J.M.: SGD: saccharomyces genome database. Nucleic Acids Res. **26**, 73–79 (1998)
27. Tang, Y., Li, M., Wang, J., Pan, Y., Wu, F.-X.: CytoNCA: a cytoscape plugin for centrality analysis and evaluation of protein interaction networks. Biosystems **127**, 67–72 (2015)
28. Holman, A., Davis, P., Foster, J., Carlow, C., Kumar, S.: Computational prediction of essential genes in an unculturable endosymbiotic bacterium, Wolbachia of Brugia malayi. BMC Microbiol. **9**, 243 (2009)

Research on Fault Diagnosis Method Based on RSAPSO-DBN

Jianjian Yang[1(✉)], Xiaolin Wang[1], Qiang Zhang[1], Chao Wang[1],
Zhihua Zhang[1], Yang Liu[1], Dunwei Gong[2], and Miao Wu[1]

[1] China University of Mining and Technology, Beijing 100083, China
yangjiannedved@163.com
[2] China University of Mining and Technology, Xuzhou 221116, China

Abstract. In view of the fact that the existing traditional methods of mechanical equipment have a large dependence on the data signal processing method, this paper uses the Deep Belief Network (DBN) based fault diagnosis method. The DBN is made up of a number of restricted Restricted Boltzmann Machines (RBM). The last layer uses a back propagation network (BP network) to fine tune the network. DBN directly uses the original data as input to reduce the influence of human factors in feature extraction, but the excessive interference factors in the original data make the diagnosis result difficult to reach the ideal result. Therefore, in order to further improve the diagnostic accuracy of DBN, this paper proposes a random self-adapting particle swarm optimization algorithm (RSAPSO) to optimize the BP classifier of the last layer of DBN. Through simulation experiments, it is found that the use of particle swarm optimization DBN effectively improves the accuracy of fault diagnosis than the standard DBN.

Keywords: Raw data · Fault identification · Particle Swarm Optimization · Deep Belief Network

1 Introduction

With the development of science and technology, industrial equipment is becoming more and more sophisticated, which makes the system gradually develop toward automation, which greatly improves production efficiency while reducing production costs. However, in the event of a malfunction in the equipment, it will lead to serious consequences, which will lead to a decrease in the production efficiency of the equipment, and serious consequences for personal safety. Therefore, it is very important for the condition monitoring and fault diagnosis of the equipment.

In the continuous development of machine learning, the shallow network [1–6] represented by BP network and SVM model has matured, but there is still a large dependence on big data and signal processing. In the current situation of big data processing, new troubleshooting methods are urgently needed to fill the gaps. As an emerging method of machine learning in recent years, deep learning has been widely used in the fields of image, voice, and vibration signal recognition. As one of the deep learning algorithms, Deep Belief Network (DBN) has achieved good results in pattern

© Springer Nature Switzerland AG 2019
Y. Tan et al. (Eds.): ICSI 2019, LNCS 11656, pp. 292–300, 2019.
https://doi.org/10.1007/978-3-030-26354-6_29

recognition. Compared with shallow network, DBN can directly input the original signal and reduce artificial extraction. Uncertainty caused by features, and has obvious advantages in dealing with big data, preventing the occurrence of dimensional disasters.

Since Geoffrey Hinton et al. proposed DBN in 2006, more and more scholars have begun to study the application of DBN in pattern recognition. For example, the literature [7, 8] has achieved good recognition in the field of imagery. [9–11] has obtained a good recognition effect in terms of speech. The literature [12–16] studied the state detection of DBN under vibration signal and proved that DBN also has a good recognition effect in this respect. Through the study of the above literature, it is found that although DBN has been applied in the field of fault diagnosis, it still has problems. Direct input of raw data as input vector leads to low diagnostic accuracy, and there are human factors in the extracted features.

At present, the population optimization algorithm is widely used in various fields, such as optimizing shallow neural networks, reducing the probability that the network falls into local optimum, optimizing the learning ability of the model, and adjusting parameters. The population-optimized model is applied to various fields such as fault diagnosis [17], path planning [18, 19], software learning [20, 21], and equipment control [22].

In order to make DBN widely applicable to the field of big data fault diagnosis, this paper proposes a fault diagnosis method based on Optimized Particle Swarm Optimization (PSO) to optimize DBN, and directly input the original vibration signal to train DBN network. The characteristics of the training classifier, reduce the impact of manual processing signals, complete the training of the entire DBN, and finally use the trained network to achieve fault diagnosis of the device.

2 DBN Model Based on RSAPSO Optimization

2.1 RSAPSO Algorithm

In order to improve the search accuracy of the standard particle swarm optimization algorithm and reduce its probability of falling into local optimum, this paper uses a random self-adapting particle swarm optimization algorithm (RSAPSO) to optimize the last layer of DBN. BP network [11].

The algorithm introduces a random adaptive mechanism based on PSO. The standard PSO update rules are detailed in the literature [1], which allows the particles to randomly reset the position with a certain probability, so that they jump out of the original position and search again, reducing the algorithm to fall into local optimum. probability:

$$x_{id} = \begin{cases} x_{\max} \times rands(1, D) & rand() \leq p \\ x_{id} & rand() < p \end{cases} \tag{1}$$

Where p is the probability of variation, xmax is the maximum allowed for the position, and rands(1, D) is the number of random numbers between 0 and 1.

In order to improve the search accuracy of PSO, the algorithm modifies the weight update formula of the standard PSO:

$$w = w_{\max} - \frac{(w_{\max} - w_{\min}) \times (f_{\max} - fitness(i))}{f_{\max} - f_{\min}}. \tag{2}$$

Where wmax and wmin represent the maximum and minimum values of the inertia weight, fmax represents the maximum fitness value of each generation of particles, fmin represents the minimum fitness value of each generation of particles, and fitness(i) represents the adaptation of the i-th particle of each generation. Degree value.

Literature [11] and so on prove that the proposed algorithm has better stability and higher convergence accuracy than the standard PSO, APSO, CFPSO and other particle swarm optimization algorithms.

2.2 Deep Belief Network

As one of the classical algorithms for deep learning, deep belief network can automatically extract low-level to high-level, concrete-to-abstract features from raw data through a series of nonlinear transformations.

The deep belief network is composed of multiple restricted Boltzmann machines (RBMs) and a layer of BP network. The lower layer represents the original data details, the upper layer represents the data attribute categories or features, and the layers are abstracted from the lower layer to the upper layer. The nature of the data.

The DBN network model is shown in Fig. 1, and its foundation is RBM. The core idea of the greedy layer-by-layer algorithm is to learn some simple models in an orderly manner and combine these models to achieve the effect of learning a complex model, namely, individual training. The first RBM, after full training, will be trained in the next RBM. Finally, fine-tuning through the BP network to adjust the weight of the entire network. See the literature [8] for DBN network update rules.

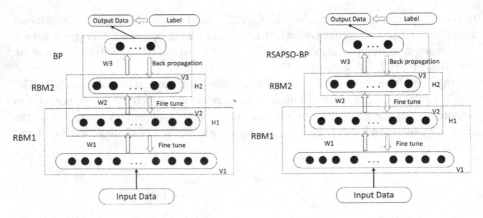

Fig. 1. DBN model   **Fig. 2.** RSAPSO-DBN

2.3 RSAPSO-DBN Model

The RSAPSO-DBN model network flow chart proposed in this paper, as shown in Fig. 2, firstly extracts the feature value by using the deep mining feature of DBN, and then uses the extracted feature value as the input of RSAPSO-BP to train the BP network. The main steps of the method include the following steps: (1) collecting sample data, collecting original vibration acceleration signals on the equipment to be monitored by different sensors; (2) constructing sample data according to the sampling principle; (3) collecting the collected data The original signal is directly input to the visible layer; (4) the feature is extracted by DBN, and the output value of the multi-layer RBM is input to the input vector of RSAPSO-BP; (5) the test is performed with the trained BP network.

It can be seen from the above steps that DBN combines feature extraction and classifier to directly input raw data without complicated signal processing, and does not cause the degradation of recognition accuracy due to human factors. DBN has certain Universality; DBN is a multi-layer network with a higher diagnostic ability than a shallow model.

3 Data Experiment Analysis

3.1 Simulation Signal Construction

To verify the performance of the proposed RSAPSO-DBN model, three different analog signals were used. The three signals are composed of different frequency modulation, amplitude modulation and frequency modulation and amplitude modulation signals. In order to make the simulation signal closer to the actual situation, a random noise signal is added to each signal. The simulation signal is as follows:

The simulation signal x(t) is a frequency modulation signal:

$$\begin{cases} x_1(t) = 5\sin(5\pi t) \\ x_2(t) = 10\sin(15\pi t) + 20\sin(20\pi t) \, . \\ w = rands(1, n) \end{cases} \tag{3}$$

$$x(t) = x_1(t) + x_2(t) + w. \tag{4}$$

The simulation signal y(t) is an amplitude modulation signal:

$$\begin{cases} y_1(t) = 5[1 + \sin(5\pi t)]\sin(20\pi t) \\ y_2(t) = 10[1 + \sin(5\pi t)]\sin(30\pi t) \\ y_3(t) = 20[1 + \sin(5\pi t)]\sin(40\pi t) \\ w = rands(1, n) \end{cases} \tag{5}$$

$$y(t) = y_1(t) + y_2(t) + y_3(t) + w. \tag{6}$$

The simulation signal z(t) is a frequency modulation-amplitude signal:

$$\begin{cases} z_1(t) = [15 + 10\sin(5\pi t)]\sin(40\pi t) \\ z_2(t) = 30\sin(30\pi t) + 20\sin(50\pi t) \\ z_3(t) = 20\sin(10\pi t)\sin(40\pi t) + 15\sin(20\pi t) \\ w = rands(1, n) \end{cases} \tag{7}$$

$$z(t) = z_1(t) + z_2(t) + z_3(t) + w. \tag{8}$$

The three simulated signals are discretized and then sampled at a sampling frequency of 12 kHz with a sampling time of 20 s. The sampled data was divided into 480 groups, 500 data points per group, and 3 signals totaled 1440 sets of data. 900 of them were selected as training data, and the remaining 540 groups were used as test data.

3.2   Simulation Results

The simulation signal experiment results are shown in the following table:

Table 1. Accuracy comparison

Method	Frequency				
	1	2	3	4	5
DBN	68%	75%	73%	72.5%	69.5%
RSAPSO-DBN	78%	80%	82.5%	78.5%	83.5%

The highest accuracy is selected for 5 times to draw a fit map, as shown in Figs. 3 and 4.

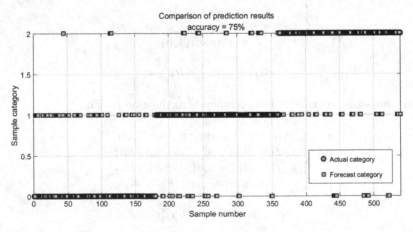

Fig. 3. Fit map of DBN

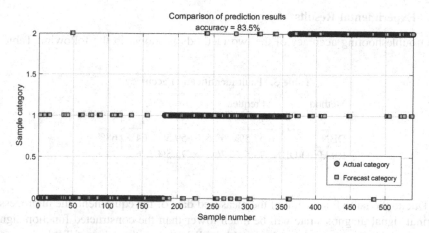

Fig. 4. Fit map of RSAPSO-DBN

From the above table, it can be found that the diagnostic accuracy of the DBN model after RSAPSO optimization is higher than that of the original DBN. It can be proved that the RSAPSO optimization model has certain improvement performance.

3.3 Selection of Actual Data Sets

The actual data validation selected data set is the Case Western Reserve University bearing fault data set. This data set is the data collected after the fault diagnosis of the motor bearing is fabricated by EDM. The sampling frequency includes two frequencies of 12 kHz and 48 kHz. The data at the sampling frequency of 12 kHz is used in this paper. The bearing experiment was collected under four loads of 0–3 hp, simulating normal, inner ring failure, outer ring failure and rolling element failure. The fault diameters ranged from 0.007 in. to 0.040 in.

In this paper, four types of data under 0 hp load are used, and normal data and inner ring, outer ring and rolling element fault data are taken, which are represented by Normal, OF, IF and RF respectively. The three fault data are selected to have a fault diameter of 0.021 in.

The number of single-sample data points is determined according to the sampling theorem. The bearing speed at 0 hp is 1797 r/min, and the number of sampling points $N = \frac{60}{1797} \times 12000 \approx 400$ is selected. The number of sampling points greater than two cycles is selected for analysis, so 1000 sampling points are used for analysis. The detailed data set is as shown in Table 2:

Table 2. Fault data set

Status category	Fault depth/inch	Data set training sample number	Data set test sample number	Single sample data points
Normal	0	200	80	1000
OF3	0.021	200	80	1000
IF3	0.021	200	80	1000
RF3	0.021	200	80	1000

3.4   Experimental Results

The troubleshooting accuracy of the two methods is shown in the following Table 3:

Table 3. Fault identification accuracy

Method	Frequency				
	1	2	3	4	5
DBN	57.5%	62.5%	59.5%	64%	68%
RSAPSO-DBN	78.5%	76%	75.5%	76%	74%

Due to the large fluctuation of the measured data of the equipment, the unprocessed original signal diagnosis rate will be much lower than the constructed function signal. Therefore, the accuracy of the above table will be lower than that of Table 1.

The fit of the actual data with the highest accuracy is shown in Figs. 5 and 6.

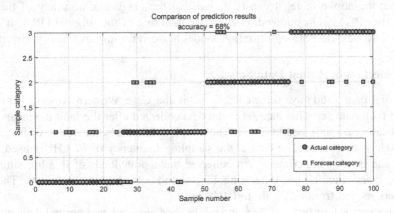

Fig. 5. Fit map of DBN

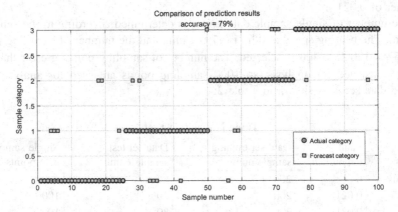

Fig. 6. Fit map of RSAPSO-DBN

As can be seen from the above table and fig, the accuracy of the unoptimized DBN in the case of the original data as input is between 50% and 70%, the accuracy is low, and it is difficult to correctly diagnose the type of fault; the highest accuracy of DBN diagnosis after optimization using RSAPSO It is more than 10% higher than the unoptimized DBN.

4 Conclusion

In this paper, the problem of low accuracy of deep neural network recognition for raw data without any processing is proposed. The RSAPSO algorithm is proposed to optimize the DBN network model to further improve the update accuracy of network weights and thresholds, thus improving the fault data of the entire network model. Recognition rate. The simulation results show that the RSAPSO-DBN model used in this paper can effectively improve the diagnostic accuracy of deep neural networks, and provides a new idea and new method for the model diagnosis method of raw data as direct input vector.

Fund. Shanxi Province Science and Technology Major Project (20181102027).
National Natural Science Foundation of China under Grant 51874308.

References

1. Yang, J., Tang, Z., Wang, Z., et al.: Fault diagnosis on cutting unit of mine roadheader based on PSO-BP neural network. Coal Sci. Technol. **45**(10), 129–134 (2017)
2. Wulandhari, L.A., Wibowo, A., Desa, M.I.: Condition diagnosis of multiple bearings using adaptive operator probabilities in genetic algorithms and back propagation neural networks. Neural Comput. Appl. **26**(1), 57–65 (2015)
3. Zhang, L.-P., et al.: Fault diagnosis technology of rolling bearing based on LMD and BP neural network. In: Proceedings of the 2016 12th World Congress on Intelligent Control and Automation, pp. 1327–1331 (2016)
4. Gangsar, P., Tiwari, R.: Comparative investigation of vibration and current monitoring for prediction of mechanical and electrical faults in induction motor based on multiclass-support vector machine algorithms. Mech. Syst. Signal Process. **94**, 464–481 (2017)
5. Yang, J.J., et al.: Improved fault Petri nets of unmanned seafloor drilling based on traces transition. J. Coast. Res. **83**, 479–485 (2018)
6. Islam, M.M.M., Kim, J.-M.: Reliable multiple combined fault diagnosis of bearings using heterogeneous feature models and multiclass support vector machines. Reliab. Eng. Syst. Saf. **184**, 55–66 (2019)
7. Wu, M.Y., Chen, L., IEEE: Image recognition based on deep learning. In: Chinese Automation Congress, pp. 542–546. IEEE, New York (2015)
8. Zhi-Qiang, G., Yi-Kang, Z.: An improved deep belief network inspired by Glia chains. Acta Automatica Sinica **42**(6), 943–952 (2016)
9. Zhang, X.L., Wu, J.: Deep belief networks based voice activity detection. IEEE Trans. Audio Speech Lang. Process. **21**(4), 697–710 (2013)

10. Mohamed, A.R., et al.: Deep belief networks using discriminative features for phone recognition. In: IEEE International Conference on Acoustics, Speech, and Signal Processing, pp. 5060–5063. IEEE, New York (2011)
11. Tao, J., Liu, Y., Yang, D., et al.: Rolling bearing fault diagnosis based on bacterial foraging algorithm and deep belief network. J. Vib. Shock **36**(23), 68–74 (2017)
12. Zhao, G., Ge, Q., Liu, X., et al.: Fault feature extraction and diagnosis method based on deep belief network. Chin. J. Sci. Instrum. **37**(09), 1946–1953 (2016)
13. Wen, H.: A Fault Diagnosis Method Based on Deep Belief Networks. Beijing Jiaotong University (2018)
14. Yang, J., et al.: Application of SVDD single categorical data description in motor fault identification based on health redundant data. In: Tan, Y., Shi, Y., Tang, Q. (eds.) ICSI 2018. LNCS, vol. 10942, pp. 399–410. Springer, Cham (2018). https://doi.org/10.1007/978-3-319-93818-9_38
15. Liang, J.J.Y., et al.: A novel multi-segment feature fusion based fault classification approach for rotating machinery. Mech. Syst. Signal Process. **122**, 19–41 (2019)
16. Hoang, D.T., Kang, H.J.: A survey on deep learning based bearing fault diagnosis. Neurocomputing **335**, 327–335 (2019)
17. Thelaidjia, T., Chenikher, S., IEEE: A new approach of preprocessing with SVM optimization based on PSO for bearing fault diagnosis. In: 13th International Conference on Hybrid Intelligent Systems, pp. 319–324. IEEE, New York (2013)
18. Guo, Y.-N., Cheng, J., Luo, S., Gong, D.-W., Xue, Y.: Robust dynamic multi-objective vehicle routing optimization method. IEEE/ACM Trans. Comput. Biol. Bioinf. **15**(6), 1891–1903 (2018)
19. Yang, J.J., et al.: Stochastic C-GNet environment modeling and path planning optimization in a narrow and long space. Math. Prob. Eng. (2018)
20. Guo, Y., et al.: Firework-based software project scheduling method considering the learning and forgetting effect. Soft Comput. (2018). https://doi.org/10.1007/s00500-018-3165-2
21. Guo, Y.-N., Zhang, P., Cheng, J., Wang, C., Gong, D.: interval multi-objective quantum-inspired cultural algorithms. Neural Comput. Appl. **30**(3), 709–722 (2018)
22. Guo, Y., Cheng, W., Gong, D., Zhang, Z., Zhang, Y., Xue, G.: Adaptively robust rotary speed control of an anchor-hole driller under varied surrounding rock environments. Control Eng. Pract. **86**, 24–36 (2019)

Standard Modeling Practice Research for a Safety Technical Disclosure of Wind Turbine Maintenance Systems

Min Liu[1], Guiping Liu[2(✉)], and Kunjie Liu[3]

[1] Erdos Ecological Environment of Career Academy,
Erdos Inner Mongolia, China
[2] The Department of Mathematics and Computer Science, Hetao College,
Bayannur Inner Mongolia, China
csguiping_liu@163.com
[3] Ningxia Huadian New Energy Power Generation Co. Ltd., Yinchuan, China

Abstract. A safety disclosure and a technical disclosures are important links of wind turbine generators in repair work and they directly affect the safety of maintenance work and the reliability of maintenance quality. Nevertheless, being implemented of safety disclosure and technical disclosure, it has some deficiencies in process property, the comprehensiveness, and the pertinence. To effectively improve the efficiency of wind turbine safety technology disclosure work, the paper recommends the wind turbine maintenance safety disclosure and technology disclosure based on a fault tree of PDCA modular. Practical work proves it greatly improved that the process property, the comprehensiveness and the pertinence of wind turbine maintenance for safety technology disclosure. The circular mechanism of PDCA makes disclosure more applicable and timely. The modular structure makes the disclosure more convenient and flexible.

Keywords: Wind turbine maintenance · PDCA ·
The Safety Technical disclosure · The cycle mechanism

1 Introduction

In recent years, with the rapid development of clean energy industry in China, wind power has been widely applied all over the world due to the maturity of the technology and the increasing growth of the installed capacity of wind power. According to the statistic from the China Wind Energy Association, the cumulative installed capacity in our country reached 188 million KW · h in 2017 [1]. With the increase of installed capacity of wind power units in China, the third-party market for operation and maintenance of wind power units is growing fast, but the technical level of companies are uneven in the market, bringing greater risk to the operation and maintenance of these wind turbines [2]. Therefore it how to improve the maintenance efficiency, reduce the maintenance and repair risk and effectively avoid the regulatory risk has become an urgent problem to be solved.

Y. Tan et al. (Eds.): ICSI 2019, LNCS 11656, pp. 301–308, 2019.
https://doi.org/10.1007/978-3-030-26354-6_30

2   Current Status of Safety Technology Disclosure for Maintenance of Wind Turbines

This paper divides the technical safety disclosure into two levels: safety disclosure and technical disclosure. The safety disclosure is to point to the safety of the personnel involved in the maintenance, which is to enable the maintenance personnel to have a detailed understanding of the danger points and safety measures in the maintenance process and make them operate as required to disperse security risks. Technical disclosure is a technical explanation of the personnel involved in the construction, which is to enable the construction personnel to have a more detailed understanding of the engineering features, technical quality requirements, maintenance methods and measures, in order to scientifically organize maintenance and ensure the stable quality of maintenance work.

The current operation and maintenance of wind turbines may be divided into three classes: operation and maintenance of the third party, operation and maintenance of equipment manufacturers, and owner's independent operation and maintenance [3]. The relevant requirements of the National Energy Board and the Production Safety Law can be effectively implemented and the Safety Technical disclosure has a sound under-structure, because the owner of Wind Power Equipment is generally central and local state-owned enterprises in China. Due to the technical barriers set by equipment manufacturers, the owners are prone to incomplete or insufficient depth of technology in the process of equipment technology. The manufacturer of wind power equipment has enough knowledge of their own equipment technology while they lack sufficient depth of the interpretation of electrical safety regulations and the National Energy Board's security documents, leading to inadequate infrastructure and uncomprehensive content of safety technical disclosure and its general focus on technical disclosure. The third-party operation and maintenance of manufacturers, as the service construction, fulfill its equipment operating and maintenance duties and is restricted to equipment manufacturers and owners. Compared with the owner's operation and maintenance and telecom-equipment makers and maintenance, the third-party operation and maintenance safety technology disclosure are relatively weak.

Based on the above deficiencies and the flexibility, complexity and high frequency of wind turbine maintenance tasks, this paper proposes modular wind turbines overhaul safety technology of event tree PDCA to make up for the lack of safety technology at work and improve the efficiency of the safety technology disclosure.

3   The Unified Modeling for Safety Technology Disclosure

Fault Tree Analysis is an important analytical method for safety system engineering. It is originally used for the design and maintenance in the field of aerospace, which is mainly used in some large equipment or large computer systems. With the continuous development of the concept of fault tree analysis, it is involved in more and more fields [4, 5], including the field of wind turbine maintenance [6]. FTA (Fault Tree Analysis) is also called event tree analysis. It starts with a possible accident (top event), top-down, layer-by-layer refinement decomposition and finally reaches the basic operational element (bottom event). Fault Tree Analysis is used to large and complex system reliability, security analysis and risk assessment, to provide a reference for decision-making management. This paper introduces the FTA framework, taking the specific maintenance task as the starting point (top event), from top to bottom, decomposing the task layer and finally forming a detailed safety technology disclosure (bottom event). Under the FTA framework maintenance tasks are streamlined and standardized decomposition, which is to ensure maintaining a safe workplace technical tests of integrity and thoroughness. Standardization modeling of security technology disclosure on FTA framework in Fig. 1, where in the arrow shows the direction of maintenance tasks decomposition. The non-decomposable task is indicated by no arrow, which is called the bottom task. Finally, the task can be operated, such as the maintenance subtask 1.n, 1.2.2. The task number indicates that the current task is in the level of the maintenance and the execution order, such as the maintenance subtask 1.1, indicating that the subtask is on the first floor and is executed in the first one. In the current system, the order of tasks is defined by the general rules of planned maintenance, which is an important computable indicator in the future construction of predictive maintenance systems for wind turbines [7].

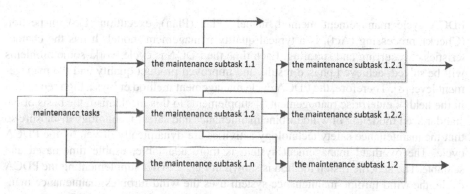

Fig. 1. Standardized modeling diagram of security technology disclosure based on FTA framework

Given the flexibility, complexity and high frequency of wind turbine maintenance and operation. According to the safety technology standardization modeling method and the recommended industry standards, we refine the wind turbine maintenance tasks and package the operation steps and safety technology into each task. As the task continues to decompose, security technology is also followed up. 1.2.2 maintenance subtask below to an example to describe the encapsulation of security procedures and technical tests, as shown in Table 1, Table 1 hypothesis, the maintenance subtask 1.2.2 includes a total of 3 operational steps; the task level describes the difficulty of the task and the level is changed from easy to difficult on 1–5. When the task is assigned, different security technologies disclosure can be displayed according to the level of maintained content. The operation steps and security technology are similar to the package of the class. The main advantages include: first, the safety technology is concrete to each operation step and has a strong pertinence; second, it is beneficial to the reuse of various components in the system, simplifying construction tasks and reducing construction costs; third, the task classification level helps to assign tasks and improve the quality of work order contents.

Table 1. Package table of operational procedures and safety technology disclosure

Task name	Maintenance subtasks
Task number	1.2.2
Contains the number of steps	3
Task level	1
Step 1	Operation step 1, Security disclosure 1, Technology disclosure 1
Step 2	Operation step 2, Security disclosure 2, Technology disclosure 2
Step 3	Operation step 2, Security disclosure 2, Technology disclosure 2

4 PDCA Cycle

PDCA cycle management method, namely Plan (Plan), execution (Do), inspection (Check), processing (Act), is a typical quality management model. It has the characteristics of recurring and spiraling. Each time the PDCA is cycle work, some problems will be solved, achieved phased results and improved product quality and the management level [8]. Therefore, the PDCA cycle management method enjoys a high reputation in the field of enterprise management. It supplements to this mechanism the basis of the standardized modeling of wind turbine maintenance and safety technology disclosure so that the maintenance safety technology activities are dynamically driven by the PDCA cycle. The overhaul management system is more adaptable, usable time-based and scalable. The specific fusion method is shown in Fig. 2. After supplementing the PDCA cycle, the wind turbine maintenance system uses the wind turbines maintenance management database as the medium to input the same kind of equipment failures, events, accidents and events of similar working nature and accidents into the top-level maintenance tasks, so as to drive the task decomposition and update and the bottom-level tasks package updates (operational steps and security technology disclosure).

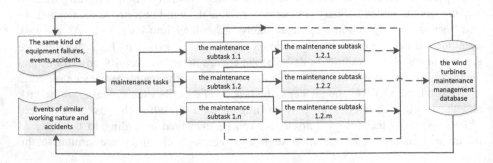

Fig. 2. PDCA cycle management model

5 Standardized Modeling Practice of Safety Technology Disclosure for Maintenance of Wind Turbines

The maintenance of a single wind turbine is generally a combination of maintenance of a multi-task and this combination is relatively flexible. In the process of Maintenance Mission Distribution, the dispatch personnel assigns the tasks according to the actual situation of the wind farm, the wind turbine and the staff.

According to the recommended standard for Electric Power Industry, the task of perambulation inspection contains multiple subtasks for wind turbine generators level. Such as: a hydraulic system inspection, a generator inspection, appearance and clean and inspect, lightning protection, a grounding system inspection, a wheel inspection, a gearbox inspection, a coupling inspection, brake inspection, a spindle inspection, blade and change paddle system inspection, a yaw system inspection, an electrical cabinet inspection, a wind turbine basic inspection. And each subtask can be broken down into multiple smaller subtasks, such as the yaw system tour check contains subtasks: (1) Visual Inspection; (2) Fastener Bolt Inspection; (3) Yaw Reducer Inspection; (4) Yaw Drive Motor Inspection; (5) Pinion and Rotary Ring Gear Appearance and Meshing Condition Inspection; (6) Yaw Brake Check, Brake Lining Clearance or Brake Damper Check; (7) Yaw Counting Device (Limit Switch, Proximity Switch) Check; (8) Yaw System Lubrication Device Check; (9) Yaw Whether there is abnormal sound; (10) Yaw System to check the wind and cable function. Sub-tasks after the generator patrol check is broken down include: (1) Elastic shock absorber inspection; (2) Generator and base bolt inspection; (3) Generator winding insulation, DC resistance inspection; (4) Generator bearing sound and grease inspection; (5) Cable and its fastening (6) Carbon brush, slipping ring, encoder and other accessories inspection; (7) Ventilation and Cooling System Inspection; (8) Motor Operation Sound Inspection and other work.

5.1 Top Task Construction

It is based on instrument maintenance and record in the logbook of the unit and the operating data of SL1500, #119 unit on April 13, 2018. Combined with the forecast of wind power and human resources and materials, the routine inspection of the generators was carried out at 08:30 on the same day. The task of the work is to check for equipment of #119 unit generator.

5.2 Subtask Selection

According to the tasks of schedule and safety regulations, operating procedures, maintenance procedures and other relevant regulations, the work content is refined. It prevents the lack of coverage of work contents. Resulting in the implementation of work is blocked. According to the needs of the work, the sub-tasks selected by the dispatcher including: (1) Generator Carbon Brush inspection and replacement; (2) Generator Grease Lubrication inspection and the oil-adding; (3) Generator Direct Resistance inspection; (4) Generator Winding insulation inspection.

5.3   Technical Safety Disclosure

We will take the sub-task "Generator Carbon Brush inspection and replacement" as an example to introduce detailedly the formation process and content of technical safety disclosure in this section. The formation of technical safety disclosure is divided into three steps: The first step is task selection. As shown in Fig. 3, the bold font part is the content of the task selection (the task selection of the #119 unit generator inspection work). The second step is to generate the Technical Safety Disclosure sheet. According to Fig. 3, the subtask of the generator grease lubrication inspection and the oil-adding, generator direct resistance inspection, generator winding insulation inspection, which generates the corresponding safety technology disclosure sheet. The third step is to synthesize all safety technology disclosure sheet and submit the sheet in order and grade. The task number of carbon brush inspection and replacement as shown in Table 2 will be revised to 1.1.2. If the skill level of the maintenance personnel is greater than or to level 2 and the specific safety technology Disclosure will not appear in the delivery order. Display the necessary headers and operating procedures to achieve the targeting and adaptability of safety technology.

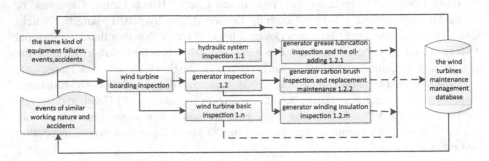

Fig. 3. Task selection for generator inspection work (#119)

The details of Sdi and Tdi are as follows:

Sd$_1$: Risk of inhaling dust, Wear a dust mask.

Sd$_2$: Risk of mechanical injury, Mechanical braking and standard use of tools.

Sd$_3$: Risk of electric shock, The generator power is disconnected and the power is checked.

Sd$_4$: Risk of mechanical injury, Wear cotton gloves to prevent mechanical scratches.

Sd$_5$: Risk of mechanical injury, Mechanical braking and standard use of tools.

Td$_1$: Perform torque relaxation according to manual and tool requirements to prevent damage to bolts and threaded holes.

Td$_2$: Carbon brush End Finger pressure should meet the maintenance specifications.

Td$_3$: The length of the carbon brush should be greater than 1/3 of its original length, Otherwise, it will be replaced.

Table 2. Safety technology disclosure list for carbon brush inspection and replacement

Task name	Generator carbon brush inspection and replacement maintenance		
Task number	1.2.2		
Contains the number of steps	6		
Task level	2		
Step	Operation step	Safety disclosure	Technology disclosure
1	Generator slip ring chamber cover removal	Sd_1 Sd_2 Sd_3	Td_1
2	Generator carbon brush End Finger removal	Sd_1 Sd_4	Td_1 Td_2
3	Carbon brush length measurement and carbon brush replacement	Sd_1 Sd_4	Td_3 Td_4 Td_5 Td_6 Td_7
4	Clean up carbon	Sd_1 Sd_4	–
5	Generator carbon brush End Finger recovery	Sd_1 Sd_4	Td_1 Td_8
6	Generator slip ring chamber cover recovery	Sd_1 Sd_5	Td_1 Td_9

Td_4: Carbon brushes should be replaced with the same model and should not be mixed.

Td_5: After the replacement of the new carbon brush, it should be ensured that the carbon brush and the collector ring are more than 80% area fit.

Td_6: The carbon brush tail and the collector ring bolt should be tightened, the reliable torque is correct, and the contact is sufficient.

Td_7: The carbon brush installation position should be one-to-one correspondence and must not be misplaced.

Td_8: Carbon brush End Finger pressure meets maintenance specifications.

Td_9: Inventory tools, clean up work site hygiene, prevent tools and debris left behind.

Based on the standardized modeling practice of safety technical disclosure for wind turbine maintenance, safety disclosure and technical disclosure are effectively integrated through subtask division. It has good process and guidance, which makes up for the lack of separation between safety disclosure and technical disclosure in the current wind turbine maintenance and improves the maintenance quality and safety of the wind turbine.

6 Conclusion

The FTA framework is introduced, maintenance tasks carry out as the starting point and the task layer decomposed to form detailed safety technical disclosure from top to bottom, which ensures the integrity and thoroughness of the maintenance work safety technology disclosure. The PDCA cycle mechanism is supplemented under the FTA framework, so that the maintenance safety technology disclosure activities can be dynamical and scalability drove by the PDCA cycle. Practice shows that the wind turbine maintenance and repair technology standardization modeling have good prospects for application and put forward new research ideas for the safety production and management of wind turbine maintenance.

Acknowledgements. This work was funded by Research Program of Science and Technology at Universities of Inner Mongolia Autonomous Region (Grant No. NJZY16339, NJZY17560).

References

1. Operational analysis of Wind Power Integration in 2017. Energy of China. vol. 40, no. 02, p. 5 (2018)
2. Notice on issuing the working train of thought and key task for 2018 electricity safety production of National Energy Administration. Electric Power Equipment Management. vol. 02, pp. 12–13 (2018)
3. Guiping, L., Kunjie, L., Na, L.: Maintenance management model of the closed-loop demand wind farm. Power Syst. Clean Energy **32**(06), 143–146+152 (2016)
4. Firuzabad, M., Billinton, R., Munian, T.: A novel approach to determine minimal tie-set of complex network. IEEE Trans. Reliab. **53**(1), 61–70 (2004)
5. Ruijters, E., Stoelinga, M.: Fault tree analysis: a survey of the state-of-the-art in modeling, analysis and tools. Comput. Sci. Rev. **15–16**(03), 29–62 (2015)
6. Dinwoodie, I., Mcmillan, D.: Operation and maintenance of offshore wind farms. Eng. Technol. Ref. **1**(1) (2014)
7. Ping, M., Jiejuan, T., Shuren, X.: Basic event ordering in fault tree analyses using binary decision diagram. J. Tsinghua Univ. (Sci. Technol.) **12**, 1646–1649 (2005)
8. Zhang, Z.: Application effects exploration of PDCA cycle management method in the management of equipment department. J. Imaging Res. Med. Appl. **2**(05), 23–25 (2018)

Social Computing and Knowledge Graph

The Critical Factor Prompting the Usage of a Social Computing

Su-Tzu Hsieh[(✉)]

Department of e-commerce, Economic and Management College, ZhaoQing University, Zhaoqing Avenue, Zhaoqing 526061, Guangdong Province, China
Helen_st_hsieh@yahoo.com

Abstract. The way of promoting new technology of social computing, swarm, data mining is to increase the user acceptance and usage of the technology. Technology Acceptance Model, TAM argued users' satisfaction can prompt their intention to use a new technology. Not only intention to use the new technology is important but also users' adhesion too. In marketing research, users' intention to use can be predicted by attitude. This study integrates users' attitude from marketing into TAM and argues that continuous intentional use of a new technology can be preciously predicted and facilitated by attitude. Research result showed attitude can preciously predict continuous intention, meanwhile, enhancing explanatory power of continuous intention. Research result also showed attitude mediating between satisfaction and continuous intention. Research result, the mediation of attitude, suggests top managers pay attention and allocate resources to build up users' attitude of favor to the new technology rather than rescue multifarious trivial dissatisfaction deviations. Research result showed dissatisfaction deviations will be diminished into attitude of favor; that is, deviation of dissatisfaction can be cover by user's attitude of favor.

Keywords: Attitude · Technology Acceptance Model TAM ·
Mediating effect · Continuous intention to use new technology

1 Introduction

New technology of social computing, swarm, data mining system needs support of usage from users. Continuous usage has been wildly used to measure the success of a new technology of information system, (Abdullah et al. 2019). Poor continuous usage of a new technology of a company information system could bring company disaster. One of the famous examples was the case of Fox Meyer Drug; a $5 billion pharmaceutical company that had file for bankruptcy as a result of poor continuance intention usage of enterprise information system. Some of failures of noted cases such as Dell Computer, Boeing, Dow Chemical, Mobil Europe, Applied Material, Hershey and Kellogg's. It was reported that 40% of enterprise information system, EIS implementations only achieve partial and 20% of EIS adoptions are reported as failure (Negahaban 2008 and Thomas 2004).

Attitude is an affective feeling to respond favor or unfavor to an object such as social computing technology (Azjen 1988). The loyal attitude of customers can predict their repurchase behaviours (Oliver 1999). Oliver (1999) claimed attitude was a result

Y. Tan et al. (Eds.): ICSI 2019, LNCS 11656, pp. 311–317, 2019.
https://doi.org/10.1007/978-3-030-26354-6_31

from satisfaction to predict repurchase behaviours because customers with affective attitude believe that firms will continuous offer their best products. Attitude was recognized as one of most immediate predictors of intention behaviour (Oliver 1999). Hence, it can be analogized that attitude can precisely predict continuous usage which result in a successfully new technology of information system such as social computing, swarm, data mining system...etc.

Attitude could fully mediate between satisfactions and continuous intention of usage. In new technology acceptance model, TAM, satisfaction is the key antecedents to continuous intention of usage (Mohammed-issa and Naseem 2010). However, Oliver revealed (1999) user's satisfaction was a short unstable emotion which soon diminished into a long term enduring affective attitude. Ajzen (1988) revealed affective attitude is an accumulating feeling which resulted from satisfaction and lead to continuous intention of usage. Support by previous scholars, this study argues attitude fully mediating between satisfactions and continue intention which could illustrate how to achieve success of a new technology usage.

Research result shows attitude fully mediate between satisfaction and continuous intention of usage. It implies in management meaning new information technologies of social computing, swarm and data mining systems can be promoted by increasing user affective attitude. Affective attitude toward the system resulted from user satisfaction and then works as a driver to stimulate system maximum usage by aroused continuous intention.

Bhattacherjee (2001) encouraged future researchers to find out more additional factors which influent continuous intention of usage. This study suggests extend TAM model with attitude as a more enhanced TAM model to enhance explanatory power of continuous intention of usage. Enhanced TAM model with attitude of this study are verified by empirical data collected from 295 enterprise information system end users scattered in 17 companies. Statistical explanatory power of continuous intention in enhanced TAM model is significantly higher than the original TAM model.

2 Literature Review

Previous researchers measured satisfaction in great various approaches with same consequential result of continuous intention. This research is not intending to critic which satisfaction measurement is the better one but to propose all these various of satisfactions can be deposited into an stable affective attitude as a driver to stimulate continuous intention. Here first review the diversely measured aspects of satisfaction of previous researches.

2.1 Attitude

Attitude research is depreciated in IT study field; only little research can be found. As our best knowledge, affective attitude research is even few. Bhattacherjee (2001) merged attitude into satisfaction with the reasons of satisfaction and attitude are similar with emotion elements. So did follower scholars viewed attitude as synonymous with satisfaction (Hsu et al. 2004 and Lin 2005) which result in attitude fled from IT study field. With inattention of attitude, even fewer researches focused on attitude.

Attitude can precisely predict IT system success through continuous usage. Oliver (1999) claimed attitude is recognized as one of most immediate predictors of behavioral intention. Attitude is a stable cognitive which is different from satisfaction. (Oliver 1999 and Suh and Yi 2006) Satisfaction is a finite users' complex emotional response soon decays into users' affective attitude (Oliver 1981). Attitude of summation every post-use satisfaction then ends up with customer loyalty (Suh and Yi 2006). So, it can be concluded that attitude is the key stable cognitive deposition container to take in user's satisfaction surplus and works as a preciously predictor to foresee customer loyal intention behaviour of usage. This research adopts this logic to argue attitude should be added back in TAM model to predict user's maximized continuous intention usage for the success of new technology of information system.

2.2 Technology Acceptance Model, TAM

Among previous studies of satisfaction and continuous Intension, Technology Acceptance Model, TAM is one of the most popular theories (Bhattacherjee 2001 and Liao et al. 2007). TAM stating user satisfaction leads to continuous intention when her/his initial expectation of products or services is confirmed (Oliver 1999 and Spreng 1996). As this research focus on success IT model through attitude to extends TAM model.

Bhattacherjee proposed TAM model as following Fig. 1 (Bhattacherjee 2001).

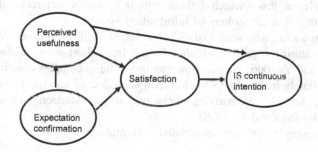

Fig. 1. Technology acceptance model, TAM, by Bhattacherjee (2001b)

3 Research Model and Hypotheses

Base on above literature review, this study proposes an extended TAM model to Information System's (IS) continuous intention model and hypothesis as below Fig. 2:

According to Bhattacherjee research, the original of hypothesis are list and re-test by this study as below:

H1: expectation confirmation is positively associated with Perceived Usefulness.
H2: Expectation confirmation is positively related with Satisfaction
H3: Perceived usefulness is positively associated with Satisfaction
H4: Perceived usefulness is positively associated with Continue Intention.
H7: Satisfaction is no directly associated with Information System's (IS) Continuous Intention.

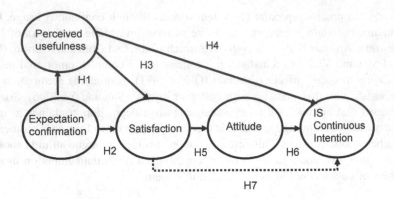

Fig. 2. Research model: extended the TAM model

3.1 Attitude

MacKenzie, Lutz and Belch define Attitude was an affective which composed by cognitive and affect strength (MacKenzie et al. 1986). Human attitude was composed by cognitive responses and affects response which elicited from actual experience of use then impact further continuous intention behaviour of the use (Bitner 1992 and Bloch 1995). Hence, this research defines attitude as user's preference affect strength assessment with a new technology of information system.

Satisfaction and attitude were two different stages of affect. (Oliver 1999). Attitude was a stable enduring cognitive which different from short term satisfaction (Oliver 1999 and Suh and Yi 2006). Satisfaction was users' finite complex emotional response derived immediately from actual situation then soon decays into users' overall attitude (Oliver 1981). Attitude summarizing every post-use satisfaction then ends up with customer loyalty (Suh and Yi 2006).

H5: Satisfaction is positively associated with attitude

3.2 Continuous Intention

Intention is defined as degree of strength to perform particular behavior. Ajzen and Fisbein revealed intention behaviour could highly accurate predicted volitional actions of behavior (Ajzen and Fishbein 1980; Ajzen 1988). Base on Bhattcherjee's (2001) definition, this research defines continuous intention as continuous intending to use of a new technology of social computing, swarm, data mining system…etc.

Intention was the function of attitude (Ajzen 1988) attitude could explicitly predicted intention behaviour (Ajzen 1988). Attitude was a stable enduring affect to act the particular intention (Zmud and Price 2000), simultaneously, attitude was the key of repurchase (Donio et al. 2006). Intention of continuous was solely determined by personal attitude (Karahanna 1999). Hence, this research hypothesis 6th as

H6: Attitude is positively associated with Information System's (IS) continuous intention.

4   Research Analysis

This research took electronic survey via e-mail to collect data. The sample populations were individual users of enterprises system just went live within one to fourth years. The samples population included departments of production, finance, marketing, procurement, material control. Samples lists of implementation bases were provided by SAP and Oracle Taiwan branch offices. Researchers first phone through implementation list customers for asking willingness to accept research survey. Implement consultants also provide assistance to distribute survey form by email. Follow up by telephone immediately within one week after survey form distributed. Second time pushing for no response users four weeks after survey form scattered.

4.1   Data Collection

The revised investigation form was mailed to total 753 of ERP end user in organizations which ERP project go live within one to fourth years. Of the 753 surveys, 316 were returned. 21 of 316 observations are dropped because of missing data of incomplete questionnaires. A total of valid questionnaires 295, valid return rate was 39.2%. Demographic data about the respondents in the final sample are as below.

4.2   Research Model Test Results

First step was to test hypotheses signification for research model. Enhanced model as below Fig. 3, path coefficients of H1, H2, H3 are 0.7, 0.65, 0.29 (t value are 12.10, 9.25, 4.69 respectively at 0.001 levels). Hence H1 of expectation confirmation was positively associated with perceived usefulness of IS use. H 2 of expectation confirmation was positively related with satisfaction. H3 of perceived usefulness was positively associated with satisfaction are supported at significant level of 0.001. H4 path coefficient was 0.19 with t value 3.03 which means hypothesis 4th of perceived usefulness was positively associated with continue intention was supported at significant level of 0.01. H5, H6 was 0.85, 0.74 with t value are 13.30 and 6.92. H5 of satisfaction was positively associated

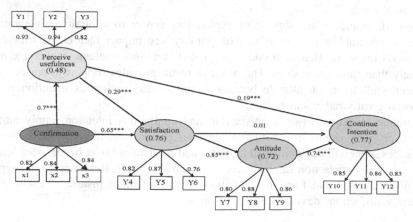

Fig. 3. Research result: the extended TAM model for attitude mediating effect

with affective attitude and H6 of affective attitude was positively associated with IS continuous intention are supported at significant level of 0.001.

5 Conclusion and Discussion

First, research results showed enhanced model was better than original model. Enhanced model own better model goodness-fit measures than original model, they are incremental chi-square per degree of freedom, RMSEA and explanatory power of continuous intention. (1) Explanatory power of continuous intention construct in enhanced model of 0.77 increased from original TAM of 0.62. The incremental of explanatory power was significant at $P < 0.01$. It implies that with affective attitude mediator added into TAM model can more preciously predict user continuous intention behaviour than original model did. (2) Enhanced model having better chi-square/d.f. model fit and better RMSEA than original TAM model. It showed enhanced model with affective attitude was better model than original.

Second, for the fully mediating effects of affective attitude test, research result showed path loading between satisfactions and continuous intention dramatically dropped when affective attitude was added in. The correlation between satisfaction and continuous intention was significantly dropped from original TAM of 0.47 to enhanced model at 0.01. Correlation dropped from significantly of 0.47 to insignificantly down to approach zero which means affective attitude work as a fully mediation variance between satisfaction and continuous intention. Research result implies affective attitude was one of the primary predictors to predict continuous intention rather satisfaction. So, affective attitude should be added into the model.

In management meaning, this study suggests for new technology of information system, manager shall focus on how to increase users' attitude toward overall new technology of information system. Attitude is an enduring emotion which implies commitment of employees toward system. Attitude is the users' commitment to new technology system which results to strong continuous intention of usage. With strongly attitude, large new technology system can be preferred and loved. With preferred new technology of information system, business performance of enterprise will be elevated by optimal usage.

Second, attitude gives significant explanatory power to continuous intention of usage, which implies attitude is one of primary key impact factors, contributes to continuous intention. Hence, attitude can predict continuous intention of usage more precisely than satisfaction does. The research result provides support to reasons why manager shall focus on attitude because it influences continuous intention of use behaviour greatly rather satisfaction.

Attitude mediates between satisfaction and continuous intention, imply attitude takes over every events of satisfaction. In management meaning, it means dissatisfaction deviation will be diminished into elevated positive attitude; hence, occasionally deviation of dissatisfaction can be cover by affective attitude. Research result suggests CIO of enterprise shall focus on elevating attitude of favor instead of multifarious trivial dissatisfactions deviation event handling.

References

Abdullah, M.B., Ali Abdallah, A., Nripendra, P.R., Hatice, K.: Consumer use of mobile banking (M-Banking) in Saudi Arabia: towards an integrated model. Int. J. Inf. Manag. **44**, 38–52 (2019)

Ajzen, I.: Attitudes. Personality and Behavior. The Dorsey Press, IL (1988)

Ajzen, I., Fishbein, M.: Understanding Attitudes and Predicting Social Behavior. Prentice-Hall, Englewood Cliffs (1980)

Bhattacherjee, A.: Understand information systems continuance: an confirmation model. MIS Q. **25**(3), 351–370 (2001)

Bitner, M.J.: Service capes: The Impact of Physical Surroundings on Customers and Employees. J. Mark. **56**(2), 57–71 (1992)

Bloch, P.H.: Seeking the ideal form: product design and consumer response. J. Mark. **59**(3), 16–29 (1995)

Donio, J., Massari, P., Passiante, G.: Customer satisfaction and loyalty in a digital environment: an empirical test. J. Consum. Mark. **23**, 445–457 (2006)

Hsu, M.H., Chiu, C.M., Ju, T.L.: Determinants of continued use of the WWW: an integration of two theoretical models. Ind. Manag. Data Syst. **104**(9), 766–775 (2004)

Karahanna, E.: Information technology adoption across time: a cross-sectional comparison of pre-adoption and post-adoption beliefs. MIS Q. **23**(2), 183–213 (1999)

Liao, C., Chen, J.L., Yen, D.C.: Theory of Planning Behavior (TPB) and customer satisfaction in the continued use of e-service: an integrated model. Comput. Hum. Behav. **23**, 2804–2822 (2007)

Lin, C.S., Wu, S., Tsai, R.J.: Integrating perceived playfulness into expectation confirmation model for web portal context. Inf. Manag. **42**, 683–693 (2005)

MacKenzie, S.B., Lutz, R.J., Belch, G.E.: The role of attitude toward the ad as a mediator of advertising effectiveness: a test of competing explanations. J. Mark. Res. (JMR) **23**, 130–143 (1986)

Mohammed-issa, R.J., Naseem, M.T.: Assessing the introduction of mobile banking in Jordan using technology acceptance model. Int. J. Interact. Mob. Technol. **4**(1), 14–21 (2010)

Negahaban, S.: Utilization of enterprise resource planning tools by small to medium size construction organizations: a decision-making model. PHD dissertation, University of Maryland USA (2008)

Oliver, R.L.: Whence consumer loyalty? J. Mark. **63**, 33–44 (1999)

Oliver, R.L.: Measurement and evaluation of satisfaction processes in retail settings. J. Retail. **57**(3), 25–48 (1981)

Spreng, R.A., MacKenzie, S.B., Olshavsky, R.W.: A re-examination of the determinants of consumer satisfaction. J. Mark. **60**(3), 15–32 (1996)

Suh, J.-C., Yi, Y.: When brand attitudes affect the customer satisfaction loyalty relation: the moderating role of product involvement. J. Consum. Psychol. **16**(2), 145–155 (2006)

Thomas, W.S.: Managing for return on investment – attributes for enterprise resource planning success and failure. Brave Bulletin, vol. 6. University of North Carolina at Pembroke (2004)

Tse, D.K., Wilton, P.C.: Models of consumer satisfaction formation: an extension. J. Mark. Res. **25**(2), 204–213 (1988)

Zmud, R.W., Price, M.F.: "Framing the Domains of IT Management: Projecting the Future Through the Past" Cincinnati. Pinnaflex Education Resource Inc., Ohio (2000)

Social Coalition-Based V2V Broadcasting Optimization Algorithm in VANETs

Xi Hu, Tao Wu[(✉)], and Yueqing Wang

Northeastern University at Qinhuangdao, Qinhuangdao 066004, Hebei, China
2495546760@qq.com

Abstract. V2V broadcasting is a data transmission mode covering a local area in vehicle ad-hoc networks (VANETs). It can reduce the channel competition in traditional cellular mobile networks by transferring transmission tasks to it. However, V2V broadcasting has the problems of data redundancy, serious conflicts, and resource waste. Therefore, this paper optimizes V2V broadcasting from the perspective of social relations based on the fact that the vehicle network just is the human network. We establish a probabilistic model for evaluating current relationship intensity with the encounter time as parameter, and introduces historical information to revise the current value for reducing occasionality. Vehicles with strong ties form cooperative broadcasting coalition. Considering the effectiveness of relay coverage, probabilistic relay broadcasting based on distance is adopted in the coalition. The simulation results show that the algorithm can not only ensure high reachability, but also further reduce data redundancy and transmission delay in open-field and urban environments respectively.

Keywords: VANETs · V2V broadcasting · Social relations ·
Probabilistic model · Coalition

1 Introduction

V2V broadcasting is a useful high-efficiency data transmission mode in VANETs. The construction and layout of vehicle network not only increases the service coverage of traditional cellular mobile network, but also helps to reduce the increasingly fierce resource competition of cellular mobile network. The communication method of VANETs is divided into V2I (Vehicle-to-Infrastructure) communication and V2V (Vehicle-to-Vehicle) communication.

Road traffic information service is one of the core applications of VANETs. It mainly uses broadcasting to cover local areas. Using V2V broadcasting can not only meet the requirements of the application, but also does not need to occupy cellular mobile network resources. However, V2V broadcasting uses distributed transmission, which causes problems such as large data redundancy, serious conflicts, and channel resources wasted [1, 2].

Different from the existing broadcast optimization scheme, we consider that the vehicular network just is the human network essentially with many characteristics and attributes of social networks. Therefore, this paper proposes a social coalition-based

Y. Tan et al. (Eds.): ICSI 2019, LNCS 11656, pp. 318–325, 2019.
https://doi.org/10.1007/978-3-030-26354-6_32

V2V broadcasting optimization (SCBO) algorithm in VANETs. It proposes a probability model to evaluate the relationship intensities among nodes. Furthermore, the historical encounter knowledge is introduced to correct the current relationship intensity to reduce the occasionality. On this basis, the vehicles that have strong relationship are selected to form a social coalition for collaborative communication. At the same time, in order to balance the effectiveness of broadcasting coverage, distance-based probability relay is adopted in the coalition.

The rest of the paper is structured as follows: Sect. 2 provides an overview of related work; Sect. 3 provides a detailed introduction to SCBO; Sect. 4 discusses and analyzes the performance of the algorithm; Sect. 5 concludes the full text.

2 Related Works

In view of the problems existing in the process of vehicle network broadcasting, many researchers have proposed different solutions. Depending on the method used to choose a broadcast relay, each scheme can be classified into various categories such as probabilistic-based broadcast, counter-based broadcast, density-based broadcast, distance-based broadcast and so on.

In the probabilistic-based broadcasting schemes [3], calculating forwarding probability or threshold based on a single network state parameter in VANETs. In [3], Wisitpongphan et al. proposed three kinds of vehicle network broadcasting schemes: p-persistence, slotted 1-persistence, and weighted p-persistence. In the process of vehicle network broadcasting, the fixed probability method lacks the adaptability to the changes of network environment, and can't improve the broadcasting performance very well.

In the density-based broadcasting schemes [4, 5], the forwarding behavior is adjusted according to the current node's neighbor density in VANETs. In dense networks, the probability of forwarding is smaller, otherwise the probability of forwarding is higher. In [4], Abdalla et al. proposed a probabilistic broadcast algorithm DP for vehicle network. The algorithm calculates the power of the maximum probability $P_{max} = 0.9$ according to the number of neighbor nodes, and determines the forwarding probability P of the current node.

In the distance-based broadcasting schemes [6, 7], the forwarding behavior is adjusted according to the distance between nodes in VANETs. There are two methods to measure the distance between nodes: one is based on position coordinates, the other is based on received signal energy. In [6], Khan et al. proposed a coverage-based probabilistic broadcast optimization algorithm, CDAPF. The CDAPF algorithm calculates the distance between the current node and the last hop node, and then obtains the additional coverage area of the current node relative to the last hop node. The larger the additional coverage area, the greater the forwarding probability. In [7], Hu et al. proposed an adaptive game model for broadcasting in VANETs. The algorithm calculates the forwarding probability according to the number of neighbor nodes and the distance between nodes.

In the count-based broadcasting algorithms [8–10], the forwarding behavior is adjusted according to the number of times it receives the same broadcast data from the last hop nodes. In [9], Meneguete et al. proposed an adaptive data transmission algorithm PREDAT. In this algorithm, the node calculates the forwarding delay time and probability according to the statistics of the same number of packets received.

3 Social Coalition-Based V2V Broadcasting Optimization (SCBO) Algorithm

3.1 Social Network Model for V2V Broadcasting

This paper describes the V2V broadcasting process as a social communication activity. Vehicles with closer relationship are more willing to cooperate as relay node with each other in data transmission.

Definition 1: V2V broadcasting social network G

$$G = (V(G), E(G), R(G)). \tag{1}$$

Where $V(G) = \{n_i | i = 1, 2, \ldots, k\}$ is the set of vehicles. $E(G)$ is the set of social relations among nodes. $R(G)$ is the set of relationship intensity.

3.2 Probability Model of Relationship Intensity

Let $t_{ij}(m)$ $(i \neq j \cap ij \Leftrightarrow ji)$ be the m-th meeting time of vehicles i and j, so the time interval $\tau_{ij}(m) = t_{ij}(m) - t_{ij}(m-1)$.

In VANETs, the encounter between vehicles can be expressed as the Poisson process [11, 12]. Let Δt be the meeting time interval of any two nodes, then the probability density function of Δt can be expressed as:

$$f(\Delta t) = \lambda e^{-\lambda \Delta t} \ (\Delta t \geq 0). \tag{2}$$

Where λ is the encounter frequency of vehicles i and j in unit time T.

Therefore, the probability distribution function of $\tau_{ij}(m)$ can be further expressed as:

$$F(\tau_{ij}(m)) = P(\Delta t \leq \tau_{ij}(m)) = \int_0^{\tau_{ij}(m)} \lambda e^{-\lambda \Delta t} = 1 - e^{-\lambda \tau_{ij}(m)} \ (\tau_{ij}(m) \geq 0). \tag{3}$$

where $\lambda = m/T$.

With Eq. (4), the relationship intensity $R_{ij}(m)$ of the m-th encounter between vehicle nodes i and j can be calculated by the following formula:

$$R_{ij}(m) = 1 - F(\tau_{ij}(m)) = e^{-\lambda \tau_{ij}(m)} \ (\tau_{ij}(m) \geq 0). \tag{4}$$

Then, the calculating process of relationship intensity R_{ij}^* of vehicle node i and j after meeting m times is as follows.

$$R_{ij}^* = \sum_{x=1}^{m} e^{-\lambda\left(T_{current} - \tau_{ij}(x)\right)}. \tag{5}$$

Where $T_{current}$ denotes the current time.

3.3 Establishment of Social Coalition

Any vehicle i has a social relationship index table L_i, which can be expressed as $L_i = list < id,\ t_{first},\ t_{last},\ R_{id}^*,\ cnt_{last}, cnt_{avg} >$. Here, id represents the identity of node which has a social relationship with node i. t_{first} and t_{last} represent the time of the first and last meeting of nodes i and id, respectively. R_{id}^* denotes the relationship intensity. cnt_{last} denotes the number of encounters. cnt_{avg} is the number of encounters per unit time.

Definition 2: Social coalition C_i of arbitrary node i.

$$C_i = \{id | R_{id}^* \geq R_{th} \text{ and } cnt_{avg} \geq cnt_{th}\}. \tag{6}$$

According to Definition 2, the update rules for setting C_i are as follows:

$$C_i^{new} = \begin{cases} C_i^{old} \cup \{id\} & \text{if } (id \notin C_i^{old}) \text{ and } (R_{id}^* \geq R_{th} \text{ and } cnt_{avg} \geq cnt_{th}) \\ C_i^{old} & \text{if } (id \in C_i^{old}) \text{ and } (R_{id}^* \geq R_{th} \text{ and } cnt_{avg} \geq cnt_{th}) \\ C_i^{old} - \{id\} & \text{if } (id \in C_i^{old}) \text{ and } (R_{id}^* < R_{th} \text{ and/or } cnt_{avg} < cnt_{th}) \end{cases} \tag{7}$$

3.4 Probabilistic Forwarding of Coalition Nodes

In order to maximize the coverage of relay broadcasting, the relay broadcasting probability $p_{j,i}$ will be set according to the distance between vehicles i and j.

$$p_{i,j} = \frac{d(n_i, n_j)}{R_{comm}}. \tag{8}$$

Where R_{comm} denotes the communication radius, and $d(n_i, n_j) = \sqrt{(X_i - X_j)^2 + (Y_i - Y_j)^2}$ is Cartesian distance between vehicles i and j.

3.5 SCBO Algorithm Description

The details of SCBO algorithm are shown in Fig. 1.

SCBO Algorithm
1.   Some nodes broadcast a message
2.   It's neighbors execute RecvBrodMsg fuction
3.   Function RecvBrodMsg
4.   If the Msg is broadcasted by itself then
5.   drops the Msg;
6.   Else
7.   executes ProessBroadMsg function;
8.   End if
9.   End Function
10.   Function ProcessBroadMsg
11.   If the Msg is new then
13.   Calculates R_{ij}^* with Eqn.(5);
14.   If $R_{id}^* \geq R_{th}$ and $cnt_{avg} \geq cnt_{th}$ then
15.   Join the social coalition C_i
15.   Calculates $P_{j,i}$ with Eqn.(8);
16.   Packet forwarding with a probability of $P_{j,i}$
17.   Else
18.   drops the Msg;
19.   End if
20.   Else
21.   drops the Msg;
22.   End if
22.   End Function

Fig. 1. SCBO algorithm description

4 Simulation Experiment and Analysis

This paper uses NS-2.35 + SUMO to simulate the proposed CABO algorithm in urban environment and the open-field environment (without road and traffic rules). Then the performance are compared with p-persistence [3] algorithm and GB [7] algorithm. The specific simulation parameters are set as shown in Table 1.

4.1 Performance Metrics

- Saved Rebroadcast (SRB): It is defined as the ratio of the number of nodes that receive packets without forwarding to the number of nodes receiving packets.
- Reachability: It is defined as the ratio of the number of nodes that received the broadcast packets to the total number of nodes in the network.
- End-to-end delay: It is defined as the average dissemination delay of packets from the source vehicle to the last receiver.

Table 1. Simulation parameters

Parameters	Value
Open-field environment size	800 m * 800 m
Urban traffic environment size	600 m * 700 m
The number of nodes	40–140
Transmission radius	250 m
Node moving speed	40 km/h–80 km/h
Data stream	CBR, 512 Bytes/Packet, 1 Packet/s
Simulation time	200 s
The value of λ	0.025
The value of R_{th}	0.8

4.2 Performance Analysis

Figure 2 shows the SRB with different node density in two scenarios. The SRB of p-persistence algorithm and GB algorithm are lower than SCBO algorithm in two scenarios. The SRB of SCBO algorithm fluctuates horizontally with the increase of the number of nodes. This is because each node has the same status in the data forwarding process. P-persistence scheme forwards packets with a fixed probability of 0.6, so it also shows a horizontal trend. In GB algorithm, as the number of neighbor nodes increases, the value of forwarding probability decreases, so SRB shows an upward trend.

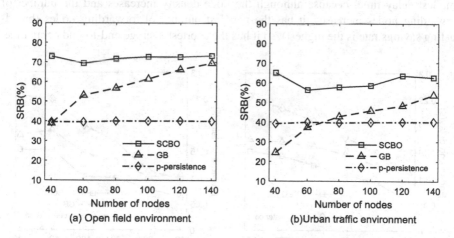

Fig. 2. The SRB in two scenarios with different node densities

Figure 3 shows the trend of achievable rate with different node density in different scenarios. The achievable rate of three broadcast algorithms increase with the increase of node density. At the same time, it can be seen that p-persistence algorithm and GB algorithm achieve higher achievable rate by increasing the number of broadcast forwarding nodes, which will lead to the increase of forwarding redundancy. While SCBO algorithm guarantees a high achievable rate, it significantly improves the saved rebroadcast rate.

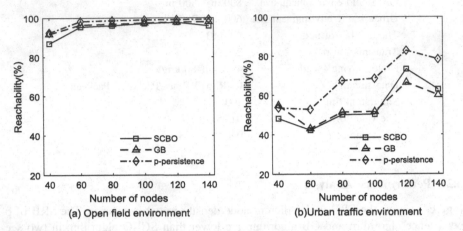

Fig. 3. Node reachability in two scenarios with different node densities

Figure 4 shows the trend of end-to-end delay with different node density in different scenarios. The average end-to-end delay times of the three algorithms increases slowly with the increase of the number of nodes. But the SCBO algorithm has the smallest delay time, because although the node density increases and the number of forwarding nodes increases, it has the smallest number of forwarding nodes (broadcasting savings rate is the highest), so it has the shortest average end-to-end delay time.

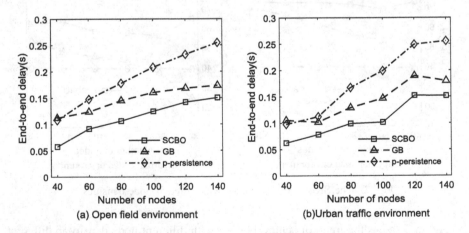

Fig. 4. End-to-end delay in two scenarios with different node densities

5   Conclusion

This paper proposes a social coalition-based V2V broadcasting optimization algorithm which focuses on the V2V broadcasting optimization from the perspective of social relations. It establishes a probability model for computing relationship intensity, and constructs a social coalition based on strong relationship. Furthermore, probability relay broadcasting based on distance is adopted in the coalition. The simulation results show that the SCBO algorithm can not only maintain a high achievable rate under different node densities, but also significantly improve the broadcasting saving rate and reduce the average end-to-end delay time.

Acknowledgement. The research is sponsored by the National Natural Science Foundation of China (Grant No. 61501102).

References

1. Basheer, H.S., Bassil, C.: A review of broadcasting safety data in V2V: weaknesses and requirements. Ad Hoc Netw. J. **2**(5), 13–25 (2017)
2. Chaqfeh, M., Lakas, A., Jawhar, I.: A survey on data dissemination in vehicular ad hoc networks. Veh. Commun. J. **11**(7), 214–225 (2014)
3. Tonguz, Z., Wisitpongphan, N., Bai, F., et al.: Broadcasting in VANET. In: 2007 Mobile Networking for Vehicular Environments. Proceeding of IEEE Anchorage, pp. 7–12 (2007)
4. Hanashi, A.M., Siddique, A., Awan, I., et al.: Performance evaluation of dynamic probabilistic broadcasting for flooding in mobile ad hoc networks. Simul. Model. Pract. Theory **17**(2), 364–375 (2008)
5. Wisitpong, N., Tonguz, O.K.: Broadcast storm mitigation techniques in vehicular ad hoc networks. IEEE Wirel. Commun. J. **14**(6), 84–94 (2007)
6. Khan, I.A., Javaid, A., Qian, H.L.: Coverage-based dynamically adjusted probabilistic forwarding for wireless mobile ad hoc networks. In: HeterSanet 2008 Proceeding of the 1st ACM International Workshop on Heterogeneous Sensor and Actor Networks, pp. 81–88 (2008)
7. Hu, X., Wu, T.: An adaptive game model for broadcasting in VANETs. In: Tan, Y., Shi, Y., Tang, Q. (eds.) ICSI 2018. LNCS, vol. 10941, pp. 58–67. Springer, Cham (2018). https://doi.org/10.1007/978-3-319-93815-8_7
8. Rayeni, M.S., Hafid, A., Sahu, P.K.: Dynamic spatial partition density-based emergency message dissemination in VANETs. Veh. Commun. J. **2**(4), 208–222 (2015)
9. Meneguete, R., Boukerche, A., Maia, G., et al.: A self-adaptive data dissemination solution for intelligent transportation systems. In: Proceeding of PE-WASUN 2014, pp. 69–76 (2014)
10. Chitra, M., Sathya, S.S.: Selective epidemic broadcast algorithm to suppress broadcast storm in vehicular ad hoc networks. Egypt. Inform. J. **19**(1), 1–9 (2017)
11. You, L., Xiao, L., Ting, Y.Y., et al.: Information-centric delay-tolerant mobile ad-hoc networks. In: Proceeding of Workshop on Infocom (2014)
12. Xinjuan, Z., Bo, X.: A traffic resource diffusion scheme in vehicular networks. In: Proceeding of 2009 International Forum on Information Technology and Applications. IEEE Computer Society (2009)

An Interpretable Recommendations Approach Based on User Preferences and Knowledge Graph

Yanru Zhong, Xiulai Song, Bing Yang[✉], Chaohao Jiang,
and Xiaonan Luo

Guangxi Key Laboratory of Intelligent Processing of Computer
Images and Graphic, Guilin University of Electronic Technology, Guilin, China
170058612@qq.com

Abstract. In recent years, how to accurately recommend and solve the opacity of the recommendation system has received more and more attention. Some researchers introduced some auxiliary information into the recommendation system, such as Knowledge Graph (KG). This method improves the accuracy of the recommendation, but there is still the problem of opacity of the recommendation system. In this paper, we propose a Knowledge-aware Path Model Based On User Preferences (KPUP), using knowledge map paths for interpretative recommendations. KPUP forms a preference distribution of users relative to candidates by exploring chain links in the KG. The KPUP can generate path representations by combining the semantics of entities and relationships. By using sequential dependencies in paths, we allow valid reasoning of paths to infer the interaction principle of user items and can be used to predict the final click probability (CTR). In addition, we set up a weighted pool operation to distinguish the contribution points of different paths to the preferences, so that the recommendations are better interpreted. We obtained two data sets, which reflected people's preferences for movies and books, and conducted a lot of experiments. Compared with the most advanced Baseline, our results are better.

Keywords: Recommender Systems · Knowledge Graph · Interpretability · User Preferences

1 Introduction

Previous studies have shown that introducing auxiliary data into the recommendation system can achieve better results such as social networks [1], context [2], user profiles, and project attributes [11]. In recent years, the KG has received increasing attention due to its comprehensive auxiliary data. It usually represents the semantic relation between entities in the form of a triple, such as (Back to the Future, isdercted, RobertZemeckis), it can accurately express the semantic information that users interact with items. By exploring the inherent connections in the KG, we find that the KG can also explain the prediction results of the recommendation system by analyzing the connectivity between users and projects. Figure 1 shows the role of the KG in generating recommendation results.

© Springer Nature Switzerland AG 2019
Y. Tan et al. (Eds.): ICSI 2019, LNCS 11656, pp. 326–337, 2019.
https://doi.org/10.1007/978-3-030-26354-6_33

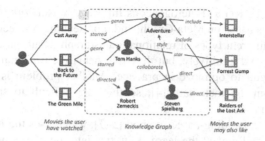

Fig. 1. Interaction between user and movie recommendation system.

As shown in Fig. 1, the user was linked to "Forrest Gump" because he had seen "Back to the Future" from the same director. This connectivity helps explain opaque user-item interactions through the information in the synthetic path [17], and reveals the user intent behind the interaction, providing interpretability to the recommendation system [18].

In order to solve the limitations of existing methods, we proposed KPUP, which is an end-to-end knowledge graph perception framework. KPUP is designed to predict click-through rates while explaining recommendations. Our method can distinguish different contributions from different paths. KPUP not only considers entities and relations to generate path representation, but also deduces user preferences based on the path. Specifically, we used the user interaction history as the seed set of KG, and then found the user preferences according to the path of KG link, and then extracted the limited path between user item pairs, and distinguish the contribution points of different paths to the recommended path. We conducted extensive experiments on two data sets to prove our method.

The main contributions of this paper are as follows:

(1) We provide interpretable recommendation methods to better mine users' interest and preference.
(2) We propose an end-to-end neural network model to assist the recommendation system by combining KG path representation, disseminating user preferences in KG and making interpretable recommendations.
(3) We used two real data sets for experimental verification, and the results proved the effectiveness of our model, which was more accurate than several state-of-the-art baselines.

2 Related Work

Previously, the solutions that integrate KG into the recommendations were broadly divided into embedded and path-based approaches. There are two types of existential perceptual recommendations:

One is the path-based approach [3, 4], which examines in detail the different linking patterns of items in KG to provide additional guidance for recommendations. For example, Personalized Entity Recommendation (PER) [3] and Meta-Graph Based

Recommendation take KG as Heterogeneous Information Network (HIN) [14], extract the potential features based on Meta-Graph, and represent the connection between users and new items of different types of relational paths/graphs. Path-based approaches use KG more naturally and intuitively, but they rely heavily on manually designed meta-paths that are difficult to optimize in practice. Another problem is that relations are often excluded from the meta-path [4], so they are difficult to specify the overall semantics of the path.

The other is an embedding-based method [5–7], which uses the KGE [8] algorithm to pre-process KG and embed the learned entities into the recommended framework. For example, the Deep Knowledge graph awareness Network (DKN) [6] embedded entities and words as different channels, and then designed a CNN framework to combine them together for news recommendation. Collaborative Knowledge base Embedding (CKE) [7] combines CF module with knowledge embedding, text embedding and project image embedding in a unified bayesian framework. Wang et al. [5] designed a deep self-encoder, which is used to embed emotional network, social network and celebrity recommendation file network.

3   KPUP

3.1   Background

User-item data is usually represented as a matrix in a basic recommendation system, let $u = \{u_1, u_2, ...\}$ and $v = \{v_1, v_2, ...\}$ represent the set of users and items, respectively. User-item interaction matrix $Y = \{y_{uv} | u \in U, v \in V\}$ is defined according to the implicit feedback of users:

$$y_{uv} = \begin{cases} 1, & f(u,v) \text{ is observed} \\ 0, & \text{otherwise} \end{cases} \tag{1}$$

where the value of 1 represents the implicit interaction between user u and item v. For example, in the case of movies, click, watch, browse and other actions, namely, the interaction exists. In many recommendation scenarios, entity items may be associated with one or more entities in the KG.

3.2   User Preference Propagation

The triples in KG clearly describe the relations properties of direct or indirect (that is, multi-step) items that should form one or more paths between a given user and item pairs [16]. We explore these paths to achieve comprehensive reasoning and understanding of recommendations. In KG, the path from user u to item v is formally defined as a sequence of entities and relations: $p = [e_1 \xrightarrow{r_1} e_2 \xrightarrow{r_2} \cdots \xrightarrow{r_{L-1}} e_L]$, where $e_1 = u$, $e_L = v$, (e_l, r_l, e_{l+1}) is the l-th triples in p, and L represents the number of triples in the path. In KG, each item v is related to another embedded item $v \in R^d$, where d is the embedded dimension. Item embedding can combine a popular ID [9], attribute [5], word pack [6] or item context information [2] based on an application scenario. Given the preference set F_u for embedded item v and user u, each triple $(h_i,\ r_i,\ t_i)$ in preference F_u assigns an association probability by comparing item v to the header entities h_i and relations r_i in the triple:

$$p_i = soft\max(v^T R_i h_i) = \frac{\exp(v^T R_i h_i)}{\Sigma_{(h,r,t)\in F_u} \exp(v^T Rh)} \qquad (2)$$

where $R_i \in R^{d\times d}$ and $h_i \in R^d$ represent relations R_i and head entity h_i respectively.

The correlation probability p_i can be regarded as the similarity between item v and entity h measured in the relations R_i space vector. Note that it is necessary to take the embedded matrix R_i into account when calculating the correlation between item v and entity h_i, because item-entity pairs may have different similarities through different relations. After obtaining the associated probability, we take the sum at the tail of F_u and weighted it with the corresponding associated probability to get the vector S_u:

$$S_u = \Sigma_{(h_i,r_i,t_i)\in F_u} p_i t_i \qquad (3)$$

where $t_i \in R^d$ is the embedded tail entity t_i. Vector S_u is regarded as the first target feedback of user u's click history and relevant item v, that is, to get the relevant path representation.

Given user u, target item i, and a set of links between u and i and path set $P = \{s_1, s_2, ..., s_N\}$, the overall goal is to link through the following evaluation:

$$Y_{ui} = f_\theta(u, i|P(u, i)) \qquad (4)$$

where f represents the underlying model of the parameter θ, and Y_{ui} represents the prediction score of user-item interaction. Different from the embedding-based approach, we can explain the rationality score of triple $\tau = (u, \text{interact}, i)$ inferred by connectivity $P(u, i)$.

3.3   Building Modeling

KUPU takes the user-item pair path based on user preferences as input and outputs a score that represents how the user interacts with the target item. It consists of three parts:

(1) the embedded layer contains three types of information: the entity, the entity classes, and the relations between the potential space of the next node;
(2) the LSTM layer, the element of its embedded coding, capture the combined semantic entities and relations;
(3) the pooling layer, will output the user and the target of end points of the multiple paths, according to the gradient to determine the path of the biggest contribution points.

We modeled KPUP, as shown in Fig. 2:

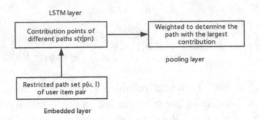

Fig. 2. Knowledge-aware path model

Embedded Layer. Given the path s_n of the user item, we divide the triples of the user item information (for example, characters and movies) into two independent embedded vectors, one is entity $e_l \in R^d$, the other is the relations between entities $e_l' \in R^d$, where d denote the size of embedding.

In a real scenario, there may be different semantics due to the different relations between the same linked entity and the entity pair, which may also have different semantics and may represent different intentions of the user. Multiple paths through the KG to the entity, for example, a user who saw terminal, "Jurassic Park", and braver heart through actor "Tom Hanks", director "Steven. Pielberg", and genre "War", can be linked to "Saving Private Ryan". Therefore, it is an important process to integrate the semantics of entity-relations into path representation learning. We represent entity e_i and relation r_i as embedded vectors $e_i \in R^d$ and $r_l \in R^d$, respectively. Therefore, the set of embedded datasets in path s_n is $(e_1, r_1, e_2, r_2, ..., r_{L-1}, e_L)$, which serves as the input of the embedded layer.

LSTM Layer. Using embedded sequences to describe the path, we can use the RNN model to study the sequence information and generate a single representation to encode its overall semantics. Among the various RNN methods, we use LSTM because LSTM can remember the long-term dependencies in the sequence.

In path step $l-1$, the LSTM layer outputs hidden state vector h_{l-1}, depletion subsequence $(e_1, r_1, e_2, r_2, ..., r_{L-1}, e_L)$. Meanwhile, we embed the current entity e_{l-1} and relation r_{l-1} as the input vector:

$$x_{l-1} = e_{l-1} \oplus e_{l-1}' \oplus r_{l-1} \tag{5}$$

where $\oplus$ is the connection operation. Notice that for the last entity e_l, an empty relations r_l is filled at the end of the path. Therefore, the input vector contains not only the sequence information, but also the semantic information of the entity and its relations with the next entity. Therefore, h_{l-1} and x_{l-1} are used to learn the hidden state of the next path step l, which is defined by the following equation:

$$
\begin{aligned}
z_l &= \tanh(Q_z x_l + Q_h h_{l-1} + b_z) \\
f_l &= \sigma(Q_f x_l + Q_h h_{l-1} + b_f) \\
i_l &= \sigma(Q_i x_l + Q_h h_{l-1} + b_i) \\
o_l &= \sigma(Q_o x_l + Q_h h_{l-1} + b_o) \\
c_l &= f_l \odot c_{l-1} + i_l \odot z_l \\
h_l &= o_l \odot \tanh(c_l)
\end{aligned}
\tag{6}
$$

where $c_l \in R^{d'}$, $z \in R^{d'}$ represent the unit (memory) state vector and the information transformation module respectively, and d is the number of hidden units. i_l, o_l and f_l represent the input gate, output gate, and forget gate, respectively. Q_z, Q_i, Q_f, $Q_o \in R^{d' \times 3d}$ and $Q_h \in R^{d' \times d'}$ is the mapping coefficient matrix, while b_z, b_i, b_f and Q_o are bias vectors. $\sigma(\cdot)$ is the activation function set to sigmoid, an $\odot$ represents the product of two vectors. Using memory state, the last state h_l can represent the entire path p_n. Build a representation of path p_n, our goal is to predict the reasonability of $T = (u,$ interact, $i)$. To this end, two completely connected layers are adopted to project the final state into the predicted score of the output, as follows:

$$
s(\tau_n) = Q_2^T \operatorname{ReLU}(Q_1^T p_n)
\tag{7}
$$

where Q_1 and Q_2 are the coefficient weights of the first and second layers respectively. For simplicity, the bias vector is omitted and the rectifier is used as the activation function.

Pooling Layer. Given a user-item entity pair, there is usually a set of paths in the knowledge graph that connect them. The prediction score is calculated by the LSTM layer, and let $S = \{s_1, s_2, ..., s_N\}$ be the prediction score of N paths, where each element is calculated according to formula (7). However, previous studies is only used to indicate that different paths contribute to different user preferences of the model, the final prediction is the average of all path scores [10], instead this method does not specify the importance of each path. Thus, to solve this problem, we designed a weighted pool operation to aggregate the scores of all paths. The pooling function here is defined as follows:

$$
V(s_1, s_2, \cdots, s_n) = \cos t \left[\sum_{n=1}^{N} \exp(\lambda s_n) \right]
\tag{8}
$$

where λ is the hyper-parameter to control each weight index and the final predicted score is:

$$Y_{ui} = sigmoid(V(s_1, s_2, \cdots, s_N)) \tag{9}$$

such a pool can distinguish the importance of the path, which is determined by the gradient:

$$\frac{\partial v}{\partial s_n} = \frac{\exp(\lambda s_n)}{\lambda \sum_{k'} \exp(\lambda s'_n)} \tag{10}$$

where λ is the hyper-parameter, it is proportional to the fraction of each path in the back propagation step. In addition, the pool function gives more flexibility to the final prediction. In particular, when $\lambda \rightarrow \infty$ is set, the maximum pooling function may degrade. However, it can reduce the average pooling by setting $\lambda \rightarrow 0$.

4 Experiment

4.1 Datasets

We experimented with our method using the following datasets, film and book. The statistics of two datasets are summarized in Table 1.

Table 1. Statistics of our datasets

	Dataset	MovieLens-1M	Book-Crossing
User-item interaction	#User	6,036	17,860
	#Items	2,445	14,967
	#Interaction	753,772	139,746
Knowledge graph	#Entities	9,586	32,727
	#Relation-Types	9	11
	#Triplets	862,333	1,125192

Movie: MovieLens-1M provides user-item interaction datasets. In the part of KG, that contains ancillary information about the movie, such as type, actor and director. Book-Crossing: in addition to interactive data for user-items, the data set contains descriptions of books by authors, styles, publishers, and more.

According to previous research results [10, 12, 13], we process datasets: Because of movies and books are explicit feedback data, we convert them to implicit feedback, If a user reviews a movie or interacts with a book, we set the user-movie or user-book pair to the positive feedback observed (data indicate that the user rating item movielens-1m is a threshold for a rating of 4, while books have no threshold setting due to their rarity), with a target value of 1, otherwise it is set to 0. For MovieLens-1M and Book-Crossing, we first include "movie" or "book" from the entire KG relations name, and select a subset of triples with confidence greater than 0.9. Given the stator KG, we collect the names of all valid movies/books by matching them with the tail entities of (film.head, film.name, tail) or (book.head, book.name, tail) triples. We set items that do not match or have more than one matching entity to be excluded, match the id to the head and tail of all KG triples, select all well-matched triples from the child KG, and use these triples as preferences and generate a path representation.

4.2 Baseline

CKE [7]. Combining CF with structured knowledge, textual knowledge and visual knowledge in a unified framework for recommendation. In this article, we implemented CKE as CF enhanced version of structural knowledge module.

DKN [6]. Entity embedding and word embedding were used as multiple channels for combined CTR prediction in CNN. In this article, we use the title of the movie/book as text input for the DKN.

FMG [14]. This is one of the most advanced meta-graph based methods, which pre-defined various types of meta-graph and recommends matrix decomposition for each meta-graph similarity matrix.

NFM [15]. This method is an advanced factorization model, which regards historical items as user characteristics. In this article, we used a hidden layer compared to NFM.

4.3 Experimental Settings

Experimental Evaluation: We used two evaluation protocols to evaluate the performance of top-K recommendation and preference ranking respectively:

- **top@K**: Evaluate whether related items are retrieved in the first K positions of the recommendation list.
- **pn@K**: Evaluate the positive correlation terms and negative pole terms of the top K terms.

We report the average metrics at $K = \{1, 2, ..., 15\}$ of all instances in the test set.

In KPUP, in both the movie and book data sets, we set the first feedback target generated by the user history combined with the knowledge graph path as the user's preference. In order to better represent the experimental effect, we did not have any pre-trained parameters. The learning rate was adjusted at $\{0.001, 0.002, 0.01, 0.02\}$ in the L_2 regularization coefficient adjusted at $\{10^{-5}, 10^{-4}, 10^{-3}, 10^{-2}\}$. Other parameters of our proposed model are set as follows: batch size is 256, embedding size of relations and entity type is 32, embedding size of entity value is 64, and unit number of LSTM is 256.

For each dataset, we built the training set, validation set and test set according to the datasets of user interaction history in a ratio of 6:2:2. For each positive user-item interaction pair in the training set, we used a negative sampling strategy to pair it with four negative items that the user did not interact with. In the test phase, the ratio of positive interaction to negative interaction was set as 1:100.

4.4 Case Study

To visually show the propagation of path preference in KPUP, we then extracted a user. Here we show an example of a movie recommendation task.

We randomly selected a user with ID u4825 at MovieLens-1M and selected "Shakespeare in Love" from her interactions. Then, extract all the qualified paths of the connected user-item pairs and display in Fig. 3, we have several findings.

Fig. 3. Case studies

Collaborative filtering is a key rule for recommending "Shakespeare in Love" to users, as the interaction of other users (such as u940 and u5448) involves two paths. In particular, the path containing u5448 provides a high contribution score of 0.356 to infer user interest.

Through the comprehensive analysis of these three paths, we find that different paths describe the user-item connectivity from different perspectives, which can be used as evidence for why items are suitable for users. This shows that KPRN can extend user interest along the KG path. Such as "Shakespeare's love" is recommended because you've seen the same actor Tom Wilkinson in rush hour or seen the "Titanic". This case demonstrates KPUP's ability to provide information interpretation.

4.5 Result

Results of all methods in CTR prediction are shown in Table 2, top@K and pn@K of interpretable recommendations are shown in Fig. 4(a), (b) on MovieLens-1M and Fig. 4 (c), (d) on Book-Crossing, respectively. Figure 5(a), (b) show the influence on top@K and pn@K with different hyper-parameters in MovieLens-1M. A few things to note:

CKE performs relatively poorly compared to other baselines, probably because we have only available structured knowledge and no visual or textual input. Compared with other baselines, DKN performed the worst in terms of recommendations in these two data sets. This is because of the titles of films and books are too short and vague to provide useful information. FMG performed poorly in both datasets. This indicates that the meta-graph based approach relies heavily on predefined meta-graph based patterns, may introduce remote entities, and does not fully explore the connectivity of user items. The performance of NFM is better than that of CKE. This makes sense because NFM essentially enhances the proximity of secondary user items by treating the items rated as user features, while MF only considers primary user item connections.

Table 2. The result of AUC and ACC in CTR prediction

Model	MoviesLens-1M		Book-Crossing	
	AUC	ACC	AUC	ACC
KPUP	0.924	0.847	0.732	0.671
CKE	0.796	0.733	0.674	0.635
DKN	0.665	0.589	0.621	0.598
FMG	0.712	0.667	0.623	0.588
NFM	0.892	0.812	0.685	0.639

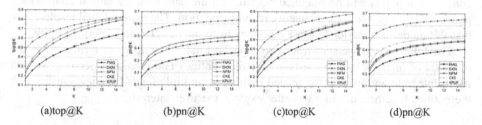

(a)top@K   (b)pn@K   (c)top@K   (d)pn@K

Fig. 4. Top-K recommendation performance between all the methods on MovieLens-1M and Book-Crossing datasets top@K and pn@K.

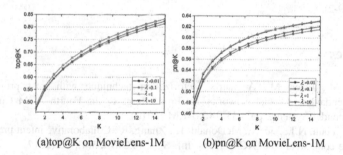

(a)top@K on MovieLens-1M   (b)pn@K on MovieLens-1M

Fig. 5. Performance comparison of KPRN λ

KPUP in these two data sets, KPUP performance is significantly better than CKE and other baselines of top@k and pn@K, AUC and ACC, achieved the best performance, is the best of all methods. Specifically, the performance of KPUP is better than the baseline. AUC recommended by movies and books is improved by 21.2% and 11.1%, and ACC by 26% and 8.3%, respectively, compared with the worst baseline. The path is used to make interpretable recommendations for user preferences, and KPUP can explicitly explore the connectivity of user-items. CKE only KG to guide the representation learning of the project. This demonstrates the importance of utilizing the entities and relations of KG. As can be seen from Fig. 4, KPUP's top@K and pn@K are higher than other baselines, showing the strong ability of ranking user preferences.

5 Conclusion

In this paper, we propose an interpretable recommendation model KPUP for users, which integrates the auxiliary information knowledge graph into the recommendation system. KPUP overcomes the limitations of existing recommendation methods based on embedding and path by introducing user preference propagation. We use user preferences to construct paths as additional user-item connections, by combining semantics of entity and relations to represent multiple paths to the recommended entity. By using LSTM on the path, we can capture the sequential dependencies of the elements on the path and get the contribution points to the user's preferred path. The contribution points will be weighted pooled, and the path with the largest contribution points will be selected for explanatory recommendation. The experimental results show that the model is superior to other baselines in terms of CTR and interpretability.

For future work, we start from two aspects. First, we will try to further study the methods of interaction characteristics between entities and relations. Second, we will try to integrate and expand the related entities in multiple fields (movies, music), link the entities together, in order to better explore the user interests.

Acknowledgments. The authors would like to acknowledge the financial support by the National Natural Science Foundation of China (61562016), and by Guangxi Colleges and Universities Key Laboratory of Intelligent Processing of Computer Images and Graphics (No. GIIP1805) and by Guangxi Science and Technology Plan Project (AD18216004, AA18118039-2).

References

1. Jamali, M., Ester, M.: A matrix factorization technique with trust propagation for recommendation in social networks. In: Proceedings of the Fourth ACM Conference on Recommender Systems, pp. 135–142. ACM (2010)
2. Sun, Y., Yuan, N.J., Xie, X., McDonald, K., Zhang, R.: Collaborative intent prediction with real-time contextual data. ACM Trans. Inf. Syst. (TOIS) **35**(4), 30 (2017)
3. Yu, X., et al.: Personalized entity recommendation: a heterogeneous information network approach. In: Proceedings of the 7th ACM International Conference on Web Search and Data Mining, pp. 283–292. ACM (2014)
4. Hu, B., Shi, C., Zhao, W.X., Yu, P.S.: Leveraging meta-path based context for top-n recommendation with a neural co-attention model. In: Proceedings of the 24th ACM SIGKDD International Conference on Knowledge Discovery & Data Mining, pp. 1531–1540. ACM (2018)
5. Wang, H., Zhang, F., Hou, M., Xie, X., Guo, M., Liu, Q.: Shine: signed heterogeneous information network embedding for sentiment link prediction. In: Proceedings of the Eleventh ACM International Conference on Web Search and Data Mining, pp. 592–600. ACM (2018)
6. Wang, H., Zhang, F., Xie, X., Guo, M.: DKN: deep knowledge-aware network for news recommendation. In: Proceedings of the 2018 World Wide Web Conference on World Wide Web, pp. 1835–1844. International World Wide Web Conferences Steering Committee (2018)

7. Zhang, F., Yuan, N.J., Lian, D., Xie, X., Ma, W.Y.: Collaborative knowledge base embedding for recommender systems. In: Proceedings of the 22nd ACM SIGKDD International Conference on Knowledge Discovery and Data Mining, pp. 353–362. ACM (2016)
8. Wang, Q., Mao, Z., Wang, B., Guo, L.: Knowledge graph embedding: a survey of approaches and applications. IEEE Trans. Knowl. Data Eng. **29**(12), 2724–2743 (2017)
9. Koren, Y.: Factorization meets the neighborhood: a multifaceted collaborative filtering model. In: Proceedings of the 14th ACM SIGKDD International Conference on Knowledge Discovery and Data Mining, pp. 426–434. ACM (2008)
10. Huang, J., Zhao, W.X., Dou, H., Wen, J.R., Chang, E.Y.: Improving sequential recommendation with knowledge-enhanced memory networks. In: The 41st International ACM SIGIR Conference on Research & Development in Information Retrieval, pp. 505–514. ACM (2018)
11. Bayer, I., He, X., Kanagal, B., Rendle, S.: A generic coordinate descent framework for learning from implicit feedback. In: Proceedings of the 26th International Conference on World Wide Web, pp. 1341–1350. International World Wide Web Conferences Steering Committee (2017)
12. He, X., Liao, L., Zhang, H., Nie, L., Hu, X., Chua, T.S.: Neural collaborative filtering. In: Proceedings of the 26th International Conference on World Wide Web, pp. 173–182. International World Wide Web Conferences Steering Committee (2017)
13. Sun, Z., Yang, J., Zhang, J., Bozzon, A., Huang, L.K., Xu, C.: Recurrent knowledge graph embedding for effective recommendation. In: Proceedings of the 12th ACM Conference on Recommender Systems, pp. 297–305. ACM (2018)
14. Zhao, H., Yao, Q., Li, J., Song, Y., Lee, D.L.: Meta-graph based recommendation fusion over heterogeneous information networks. In: Proceedings of the 23rd ACM SIGKDD International Conference on Knowledge Discovery and Data Mining, pp. 635–644. ACM (2017)
15. He, X., Chua, T.S.: Neural factorization machines for sparse predictive analytics. In: Proceedings of the 40th International ACM SIGIR Conference on Research and Development in Information Retrieval, pp. 355–364. ACM (2017)
16. Wang, H., et al.: RippleNet: propagating user preferences on the knowledge graph for recommender systems. In: Proceedings of the 27th ACM International Conference on Information and Knowledge Management, pp. 417–426. ACM (2018)
17. Lian, J., Zhou, X., Zhang, F., Chen, Z., Xie, X., Sun, G.: xDeepFM: combining explicit and implicit feature interactions for recommender systems. In: Proceedings of the 24th ACM SIGKDD International Conference on Knowledge Discovery & Data Mining, pp. 1754–1763. ACM (2018)
18. Costa, F., Ouyang, S., Dolog, P., Lawlor, A.: Automatic generation of natural language explanations. In: Proceedings of the 23rd International Conference on Intelligent User Interfaces Companion, p. 57. ACM (2018)

WSIA: Web Ontological Search Engine Based on Smart Agents Applied to Scientific Articles

Paola Patricia Ariza-Colpas[1(✉)], Marlon Alberto Piñeres-Melo[2],
Wilson Nieto-Bernal[2], and Roberto Morales-Ortega[1]

[1] Department of Computer Science and Electronic,
Universidad de la Costa CUC, Barranquilla, Colombia
{parizal, rmorales}@cuc.edu.co
[2] Department of System Engineering, Universidad del Norte,
Barranquilla, Colombia
{pineresm, wnieto}@uninorte.edu.co

Abstract. The Semantic Web proposed by the W3C (Word Wide Web Consortium), aims to make the automation of the information contained in the current web through semantic processing based on ontologies that define what must be the rules used for the representation knowledge. This article resulting from the research project "Model for the representation of knowledge based on Web ontologies and intelligent search agents, if required: Scientific articles WSIA" proposes an architecture for finding information through intelligent agents and ontologies Web of scientific articles. This paper shows the architecture, implementation and comparing these with traditional applications.

Keywords: Semantic Web · Web Ontologies · Intelligent Agents · WSIA

1 Introduction

In the current era of knowledge, research has been established as an essential aspect in the search for answers to different phenomena of everyday life, the evidences of these investigations are clearly visible being reflected in scientific articles [1, 2]. The use of scientific articles to show the results of research has made it possible for the academic community to access and know the existing production in different areas of knowledge. Therefore, it is necessary that when conducting a search for information about a particular topic, the result of this provides what the user really needs [3]. Currently, the content displayed on the Internet is immeasurable and the use of technologies such as HTML is absolutely essential for viewing contents in a browser. But before this it should be noted that the use of this language brings as a disadvantage a poor semantic representation of the data [4, 5]. This leads to the current Web pages providing syntax instead of being added the semantics [6, 7].

Based on these ideas it is necessary to specify that the structure of the current web makes this objective extremely difficult, because it is structured through the use of hyperlinks, in which users navigate from one page to another, addressed by search engines. but finally the machines do not understand the meaning of this. That is why the same author of the website Tim Berners-Lee, proposes the incursion of the

Y. Tan et al. (Eds.): ICSI 2019, LNCS 11656, pp. 338–347, 2019.
https://doi.org/10.1007/978-3-030-26354-6_34

Semantic Web, which adds meaning to the Web, also modifying the structure of the content available on the WWW [8, 9]. In contrast to the chaos and disorder of the current web, it proposes a scheme of classification, modification of the structure and annotation of the resources in a semantic way and understandable by the machines. In Fig. 1, note the schema of the Semantic Web [10].

The semantic web, is based on the general characteristics in terms of accessibility that achieved the success of the current web, but adds, emanating from the field of artificial intelligence, ontologies, necessary for the resolution of difficulties such as those raised above [11, 12]. A Web Ontology represents a hierarchy of concepts, through attributes and relationships, as the purpose of the creation of so-called semantic networks [13]. With the creation of ontologies, it is structured of classes and defined relationships of a domain of knowledge. The purpose of the raid of the semantic web is the conformation of nodes that are typified by means of classes and relationships defined in ontologies, which not only allows access to content, but also adds functionality and procedures to describe web services [14, 15]. This research article is organized as follows, in the first instance some basic concepts necessary for the understanding of the research proposal are defined. In the second instance, the proposed architecture for the solution to the problem is described and ultimately the resulting Web application and the conclusions of the proposal are discriminated.

2 Ontologies Applied to the Search of Articles

There are many applications or Web search engines whose main objective is to search for information without any discrimination [16, 17]. However, it is necessary to specify that when performing these searches on scientific type articles, the results that these usually do not satisfy those expected by the user. In this way, this research topic arises, which has as specific contributions [18–20]: present an architecture to improve the results of the searches of scientific articles in Web ontologies based on Intelligent Agents [21], encourage the use of free software for the representation of the ontology and development of the proposed application [22], make a comparison when implementing the architecture with a solution developed under the traditional scheme, making relational databases and the programming language PHP [24].

3 Basic Concepts

To enter to specify very specific aspects of the architecture, it is worth mentioning some basic and relevant concepts for a good understanding of the essential parts that make up this research proposal, which are: Ontology, Reasoning and Intelligent Agent.

3.1 Web Ontologies

Ontologies have their general origin in Artificial Intelligence [25, 26]. According to Gruber: "An ontology is a formal and explicit specification of a shared conceptualization, this is best understood as follows. **Formal:** refers to the fact that the ontology must be readable by a computer, excluding natural language [27], **explicit:** means that the concepts that are used and their limitations are explicitly defined [28], **conceptualization:** refers to the identification of the most relevant concepts of a world phenomenon [29], **shared:** it means that an ontology captures a consensus of knowledge, that is, knowledge does not come from a single individual but is accepted by a group [30, 31]." Ontologies can be represented by different languages, namely: RDF (Resource Description Framework), RDF Schema, XML (Extensible Markup Language), XML Schema, OWL (Ontology Web Language).

3.2   Reasoner

The main objective of the reasoners, is to make inferences about the Web Ontology, for the specific case of this research Jena Semantic Web Framework was used. Jena is a Java framework, designed exclusively for the programming of applications that support the Semantic Web and is open source. It is an API (Application Programming Interface) [32], which allows working with ontologies that are framed in the languages [33]: OWL and RDF Schema, additionally allows the processing of queries of type SPARQL (Query Language for RDF), has inference engines and connectors to external motors. In such a way that it helps to establish the different queries that have to be made to the Web Ontology, with the objective of interacting with this representation of knowledge [34]. Protegé was used in this research, which is an open source editor and at the same time it is a knowledge acquisition system and is made in Java using Swing, developed by a whole community of approximately 10,000 users.

3.3   Intelligent Agents

The incursion of the Intelligent agents within the proposal, acquires a primordial role due to the fact that it becomes its differentiating factor in Web 3.0. It can be understood as intelligent agent, [35, 36] "an entity capable of perceiving its environment, process such perceptions and respond or act in their environment in a rational manner, that is, in a correct manner and tending to maximize an expected result". In his article Is There and Intelligent Agent in Your Future? [37, 38] Hendler reveals what the main characteristics of an intelligent agent should be.

In the first instance, an intelligent agent must be communicative, since he must have the ability to understand what the real needs of the user are, because without this quality it is impossible to perform efficiently [39, 40]. In the second instance it must be capable, because it must develop the faculty not only to show information but also to infer. In the third instance, it must be autonomous, that is, it must have the capacity to make decisions on its own, through rules established in advance [41, 42]. Ultimately, it must be adaptable, coupled with different preferences of users in terms of visualization, sources of information, must be able to learn from the environment.

4 Proposed Architecture for a Semantic Web Searcher Based on Intelligent Agents

Result of this research process is proposed the following architecture, called WSIA (Web Semantic Intelligent Agent), which is composed of six general layers namely. (See Fig. 1).

Fig. 1. WSIA general architecture.

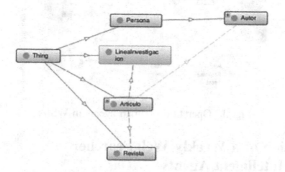

Fig. 2. General outline of the web ontology created in Protegé

In the first layer of the architecture, the general scheme of the Web ontology was defined, which is shown in Fig. 2. Here we can see the classes proposed for solving the problem, taking into account the relationships that exist between each of them. For example: the authors are a subclass of the person class, scientific articles are written by authors and belong to a line of research, journals publish articles that are made by people and they are ascribed to a line research. The methodology used for the construction of the ontology, was to identify the relevant concepts of the domain of the problem and define the existing relationships between them, in order to represent the area of knowledge of the scientific articles.

In this research the scientific articles are discriminated in three areas of knowledge: Health, Basic Engineering and Applied Engineering, taken from the journal WORLD ACADEMY OF SCIENCE, ENGINEERING AND TECHNOLOGY ISSUE 63 MARCH 2018. In the second layer of architecture, it was used the software Protegé to be able to carry out the general scheme of the ontology proposed and in this way to be able to use the Jena reasoner and verify the construction of it. It was used to perform queries to the SPARQL ontologies, which is an RDF query language, a prime factor of the Web Application, to show the results of the queries that are required by the user. In the third, fourth and fifth layer was used JADE, a Java API, whose main objective is to provide a platform of agents required for the creation and designation of the general rules to be developed by each of the intelligent agents in the search of the information on scientific articles. The following graph shows the general form of the operation of the agents within this architecture.

A mobile agent differs from common intelligent agents by its ability to mobilize through different nodes of the network, can perfectly implement persistence, communication and collaboration. The main characteristic of these agents is not only the mobilization in the computer of its owner, but also in different servers.

In this research, the main function of intelligent agents is cloning and reproducing, thus allowing obtaining the search that the user really needs, as shown in Fig. 3.

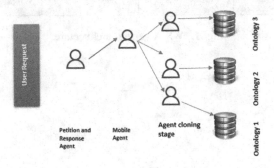

Fig. 3. Operation of smart agents in WSIA.

5 Construction of a Weekly Web Searcher Based on Intelligent Agents

The architecture proposed above brings as a consequence the creation of a Web application that allows the search through the interaction of intelligent agents in different ontologies. As shown in Fig. 4, the user enters the specific information from

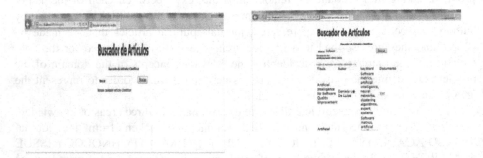

Fig. 4. Semantic Web search engine based on smart agents in execution

which they wish to obtain a scientific article that matches the search string, internally the application will send this request to a request and response agent who will later distribute this search in the intelligent agents that will be cloned to enter the proposed ontology for this case of investigative study. It is necessary to specify that this architecture can be applied for n ontologies. The result is a set of scientific articles that agree with the search performed by the user.

A parallel Web application was developed for this solution using PHP and MySql, keeping the traditional Web development scheme. The results thrown by this were contracted by those issued by the ontological search engine based on intelligent search agents. It should be noted that both solutions were deployed in local environments, with a configuration of servers with the technical requirements that are named below (Table 1):

Table 1. Basic configuration of the servers needed to perform the test and memory requirements

Characteristics required for operation adequate of the applications	Traditional search engine (PHP MySql)	WSIA
Operative System	Windows	Windows
Server	Apache	Tomcat
Memory	2 GB	2 GB

Results of these comparisons were analyzed two indispensable variables for this investigation, which were: The response time and the concordance of the searches made. Regarding the response time, the difference was not very significant as can be seen in Table 2 and Fig. 5.

Table 2. Tests carried out general applications and smart agents.

Query response time of the applications	Traditional search engine (PHP MySql)	WSIA
	0,0056 seg	0,0036 seg

However, the concordance of the searches carried out, marks a relevant aspect in this investigation, because it allows to glimpse the real differences of substance. For example, the following search string was entered to corroborate the existing efficiency between the aforementioned solutions: "Show me the articles written by Marlon Piñeres", the results were measured on a scale of 1 to 5, taking into account the conventions shown in Table 3, obtaining the results shown in Table 4.

Therefore, it is to be appreciated, that although it is true that an application built in a traditional way, for that matter specific to this example with a MySQL database and PHP can compete depending on the response time to WSIA, it significantly exceeds it in terms of intelligence in the results shown in congruence with what the user really requires.

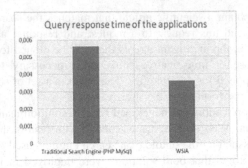

Fig. 5. Performance of standard applications vs WSIA.

Table 3. Matching conventions of searches carried out

Convention	Description
1	The search is not consistent
2	The search result is acceptable
3	The result of the search is good
4	The result of the search is very good
5	The result of the search is excellent

Table 4. Concordance of the searches carried out

Level of coherence of the results of the applications	Traditional search engine (PHP MySql)	WSIA
	2	4

6 Conclusions

As a result of this research process, it can be appreciated that using the Web Ontologies, Reasoners and Intelligent Search Agents, the traditional ways of searching the Web can be improved. That is why an architecture was proposed which served as the basis for the construction of an ontological search engine of WSIA scientific articles (Web Semantic Intelligent Agent), making use of free software, which facilitated its development.

Through the application of black box testing techniques, it was possible to determine that the operation of this application as a function of the response time and concordance of the searches carried out, turned out to be quite competitive when contracted with traditional implementation schemes of Web applications. Undoubtedly, this statement is based primarily on the inclusion of intelligent agents, which allow to increase in a circumstantial way the coherence in the results issued by this.

With the implementation of this solution an improvement of the search by sense is achieved in the case of study of scientific articles, which allows for more agile searches based on the requirements or keywords defined by the user. The use of Web ontologies allows you to create a structure of knowledge and meaning in the searches thus achieving that the user can find what he was really looking for.

As for future work, as a result of the analysis of this research proposal, we can appreciate the possible application of the proposed architecture, to achieve efficient searches in companies of the public sector such as: city halls, governorates, public notaries, among others.

References

1. Dyachenko, Y., Nenkov, N., Petrova, M., Skarga-Bandurova, I., Soloviov, O.: Approaches to cognitive architecture of autonomous intelligent agent. Biol. Inspired Cogn. Archit. **26**, 130–135 (2018)
2. Fougères, A.J., Ostrosi, E.: Intelligent agents for feature modelling in computer aided design. J. Comput. Des. Eng. **5**(1), 19–40 (2018)
3. Snezhin, A., Prostokishin, V., Vaskan, I.: ISC–the technology for behaviors planning of the intelligent agent. Procedia Comput. Sci. **145**, 418–422 (2018)
4. Pawlak, M., Poniszewska-Marańda, A., Kryvinska, N.: Towards the intelligent agents for blockchain e-voting system. Procedia Comput. Sci. **141**, 239–246 (2018)
5. Palechor, M., Enrique, F., De La Hoz Manotas, A.K., De La Hoz Franco, E., Ariza Colpas, P.P.: Feature selection, learning metrics and dimension reduction in training and classification processes in intrusion detection systems (2015)
6. Drakaki, M., Gören, H.G., Tzionas, P.: An intelligent multi-agent based decision support system for refugee settlement siting. Int. J. Disaster Risk Reduction **31**, 576–588 (2018)
7. Lin, L., Jiantian, C., Guan, L., Dong, Z., Chen, H., Xiao, M.: Fault location and isolation for distribution network with DGs based on intelligent multi-agent system. Energy Procedia **145**, 234–239 (2018)
8. Shvetsov, A.: Models of neuro-fuzzy agents in intelligent environments. Procedia Comput. Sci. **103**, 135–141 (2017)
9. Gelaim, T.Â., Hofer, V.L., Marchi, J., Silveira, R.A.: Sigon: a multi-context system framework for intelligent agents. Expert Syst. Appl. **119**, 51–60 (2019)
10. Mendoza-Palechor, F.E., Ariza-Colpas, P.P., Sepulveda-Ojeda, J.A., De-la-HozManotas, A., Piñeres Melo, M.: Fertility analysis method based on supervised and unsupervised data mining techniques (2016)
11. Coulter, R., Pan, L.: Intelligent agents defending for an IoT world: a review. Comput. Secur. **73**, 439–458 (2018)
12. Nassiri-Mofakham, F.: How does an intelligent agent infer and translate? Comput. Hum. Behav. **38**, 196–200 (2014)
13. Kamara-Esteban, O., Azkune, G., Pijoan, A., Borges, C.E., Alonso-Vicario, A., Lópezde-Ipiña, D.: MASSHA: an agent-based approach for human activity simulation in intelligent environments. Pervasive Mob. Comput. **40**, 279–300 (2017)
14. Ötting, S.K., Maier, G.W.: The importance of procedural justice in Human-Machine Interactions: intelligent systems as new decision agents in organizations. Comput. Hum. Behav. **89**, 27–39 (2018)

15. Palechor, F.M., De la Hoz Manotas, A., Colpas, P.A., Ojeda, J.S., Ortega, R.M., Melo, M.P.: Cardiovascular disease analysis using supervised and unsupervised data mining techniques. JSW **12**(2), 81–90 (2017)
16. Panov, A.I.: Behavior planning of intelligent agent with sign world model. Biol. Inspired Cogn. Archit. **19**, 21–31 (2017)
17. Zuccolotto, M., Fasanotti, L., Cavalieri, S., Pereira, C.E.: Artificial immune intelligent maintenance system–diagnostic agents. IFAC Proc. Volumes **47**(3), 7116–7121 (2014)
18. Haynes, S.R., Cohen, M.A., Ritter, F.E.: Designs for explaining intelligent agents. Int. J. Hum. Comput. Stud. **67**(1), 90–110 (2009)
19. Yang, G., Chen, Y., Huang, J.P.: The highly intelligent virtual agents for modeling financial markets. Phys. A **443**, 98–108 (2016)
20. Jimeno-gonzalez, K., Ariza-colpas, P., Piñeres-melo, M.: Gobierno de TI en Pymes Colombianas. ¿Mito o Realidad?
21. Chemchem, A., Drias, H.: From data mining to knowledge mining: application to intelligent agents. Expert Syst. Appl. **42**(3), 1436–1445 (2015)
22. Correa, J.C.: The behavioral interaction of road users in traffic: an example of the potential of intelligent agent-based simulations in psychology. Revista Latinoamericana de Psicología **48** (3), 201–208 (2016)
23. Asgari, Z., Rahimian, F.P.: Advanced virtual reality applications and intelligent agents for construction process optimisation and defect prevention. Procedia Eng. **196**, 1130–1137 (2017)
24. Șoavă, G., Sitnikov, C., Dănciulescu, D.: Optimizing quality of a system based on intelligent agents for e-learning. Procedia Econ. Finan. **16**, 47–55 (2014)
25. Calabria-Sarmiento, J.C., et al.: Software applications to health sector: a systematic review of literature (2018)
26. Chao, C.Y., Chang, T.C., Wu, H.C., Lin, Y.S., Chen, P.C.: The interrelationship between intelligent agents' characteristics and users' intention in a search engine by making beliefs and perceived risks mediators. Comput. Hum. Behav. **64**, 117–125 (2016)
27. Basterretxea, K., Martínez, M.V., Del Campo, I., Echanobe, J.: A fault tolerant single-chip intelligent agent with feature extraction capability. Appl. Soft Comput. **22**, 358–371 (2014)
28. Valckenaers, P., Hadeli, H., Germain, B.S., Verstraete, P., Van Belle, J., Van Brussel, H.: From intelligent agents to intelligent beings. In: Mařík, V., Vyatkin, V., Colombo, A.W. (eds.) HoloMAS 2007. LNCS, vol. 4659, pp. 17–26. Springer, Heidelberg (2007). https://doi.org/10.1007/978-3-540-74481-8_3
29. Vidoni, M.C., Vecchietti, A.R.: An intelligent agent for ERP's data structure analysis based on ANSI/ISA-95 standard. Comput. Ind. **73**, 39–50 (2015)
30. De-La-Hoz-Franco, E., Ariza-Colpas, P., Quero, J.M., Espinilla, M.: Sensor-based datasets for human activity recognition–a systematic review of literature. IEEE Access **6**, 59192–59210 (2018)
31. Kruger, G.H., Shih, A.J., Hattingh, D.G., van Niekerk, T.I.: Intelligent machine agent architecture for adaptive control optimization of manufacturing processes. Adv. Eng. Inform. **25**(4), 783–796 (2011)
32. Sidner, C.L.: Engagement, emotions, and relationships: on building intelligent agents. In: Emotions, Technology, Design, and Learning, pp. 273–294. Academic Press (2016)
33. Warkentin, M., Sugumaran, V., Sainsbury, R.: The role of intelligent agents and data mining in electronic partnership management. Expert Syst. Appl. **39**(18), 13277–13288 (2012)
34. Dam, H.K., Ghose, A.: Supporting change impact analysis for intelligent agent systems. Sci. Comput. Program. **78**(9), 1728–1750 (2013)
35. Guerrero, H., Polo, S., Ariza, J.M.R.P.: Trabajo colaborativo como estrategia didáctica para el desarrollo del pensamiento crítico. Opción **34**(86), 959–986 (2018)

36. Liang, W.Y., Huang, C.C., Tseng, T.L.B., Lin, Y.C., Tseng, J.: The evaluation of intelligent agent performance—an example of B2C e-commerce negotiation. Comput. Stand. Interfaces **34**(5), 439–446 (2012)
37. McShane, M., Beale, S., Nirenburg, S., Jarrell, B., Fantry, G.: Inconsistency as a diagnostic tool in a society of intelligent agents. Artif. Intell. Med. **55**(3), 137–148 (2012)
38. Walsh, S.M., Baechle, D.M.: The confluence of intelligent agents and materials to enable protection of humans in extreme and dangerous environments. In: Robotic Systems and Autonomous Platforms, pp. 523–546. Woodhead Publishing (2019)
39. López, V.F., Medina, S.L., de Paz, J.F.: Taranis: neural networks and intelligent agents in the early warning against floods. Expert Syst. Appl. **39**(11), 10031–10037 (2012)
40. Lopez-Rodriguez, I., Hernández-Tejera, M., Hernandez-Cabrera, J.: Regulation of the buyers' distribution in management systems based on simultaneous auctions and intelligent agents. Expert Syst. Appl. **42**(21), 8014–8026 (2015)
41. Echeverri-Ocampo, I., Urina-Triana, M., Patricia Ariza, P., Mantilla, M.: El trabajo colaborativo entre ingenieros y personal de la salud para el desarrollo de proyectos en salud digital: una visión al futuro para lograr tener éxito (2018)
42. Ariza, P., Pineres, M., Santiago, L., Mercado, N., De la Hoz, A.: Implementation of MOPROSOFT level I and II in software development companies in the Colombian Caribbean, a commitment to the software product quality region. In: 2014 IEEE Central America and Panama Convention (CONCAPAN XXXIV), pp. 1–5. IEEE November 2014

Service Quality and Energy Management

Record Management in the Cloud: Service Quality and Service Level Agreement

Youngkon Lee[1](✉) and Ukhyun Lee[2](✉)

[1] Business Administration Department, Korea Polytechnic University,
2121 Jeongwangdong, Siheung, Korea
Yklee777@kpu.ac.kr
[2] School of IT Convergence Engineering, Shinhan University,
233-1 Sangpae dong, Dongducheon, Korea
uhlee@shinhan.ac.kr

Abstract. Recently, many companies or organizations are introducing cloud services for managing digital records. Cloud services can dramatically reduce the cost of archiving and managing digital records, and provide a foundation for resilient management of digital records, depending on the business environment. Many companies and organizations outsource management of digital records to the cloud. Generally, companies sign SLA contracts when outsourcing computing systems to the cloud. This means that they will pay for the usage of the service while expecting cloud service more or less quantitative level. Customers who request cloud record management services want to be assured that their records are kept in trust in the cloud while meeting records requirements. The cloud record management service provider wants to know which quality items or criteria associated with records should be used to manage records. To establish a cloud record management service SLA, customers and service providers must be aware of each other's interrelationships, make a clear statement of their requirements and expectations, and agree on them. Because cloud services pay for service usage and satisfaction, the SLA must be defined for the purpose so that the customer and service provider can provide services that are mutually satisfactory. This paper describes the requirements for ensuring the quality of cloud record management services and the quality items and classification schemes and key indicators and values required for establishing SLAs.

Keywords: Cloud services · SLA · Records management · Quality factors · Digital records

1 Introduction

As the spread of the record management utilizing cloud services, there is a growing interest of stakeholders on the quality of the digital record management based on cloud services. According to a lot of companies and organizations outsource their IT systems because of cost and ease of use in the cloud as well as their digital records.

Generally, companies sign SLA contracts when outsourcing computing systems to the cloud. This means that they will pay for the usage of the service while expecting cloud service more or less quantitative level.

© Springer Nature Switzerland AG 2019
Y. Tan et al. (Eds.): ICSI 2019, LNCS 11656, pp. 351–360, 2019.
https://doi.org/10.1007/978-3-030-26354-6_35

The SLA items or values that a company enters into when outsourcing hardware or software to the cloud can vary depending on the service to be provided or the business needs. However, the cloud service provider can present to the companies that are going to enter into an SLA contract for the type of service they can provide, the quality item, and the quality level that they can provide. Most SLA items are limited to general computing content such as availability, performance, and security of computing resources. When outsourcing digital records management to cloud services, additional SLA item definitions are needed.

Customers who request cloud record management services want to be assured that their records are kept in trust in the cloud while meeting records requirements. The cloud record management service provider wants to know which quality items or criteria associated with records should be used to manage records. In other words, it is necessary to understand and agree on the quality and level of records management quality between cloud record management service customer and provider.

Service Level Agreement (SLA) in cloud record management service can be defined as a detailed agreement to quantify the level of cloud record management services and to evaluate and compensate for service performance to ensure service between the service provider and the customer. The customer will evaluate the service quality according to the evaluation items specified in the SLA, and pay the service fee according to the evaluated service level.

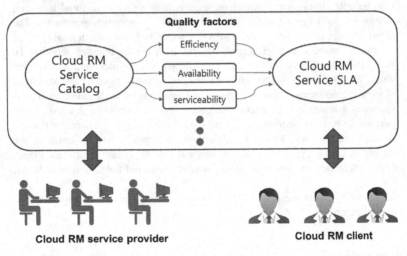

Fig. 1. Model for SLA and quality factors on cloud RM service

To establish a cloud record management service SLA, customers and service providers must understand each other's requirements, make a clear statement of their requirements and expectations, and agree on them. Because cloud services pay for service usage and satisfaction, the SLA must be defined for the purpose so that the customer and service provider can provide services that are mutually satisfactory. In order to make an SLA, it is necessary to classify and define the cloud service catalog and the quality of services, and the reference value of the quality. The cloud service catalog is a functional specification of services provided by a cloud service provider (see Fig. 1).

Cloud service quality is classified into nonfunctional and quantifiable quality and functional quality. Non-functional quality is quality that can be quantified and expressed numerically, such as response time or the number of concurrent transactions. Functional quality could be measured by the presence or absence of features or capabilities provided by cloud service providers, such as security or interoperability. In particular, the cloud record management service should include in the functional quality whether or not the cloud service can guarantee the characteristics of the record.

This paper describes the requirements for ensuring the quality of the cloud record management service and the quality items and the classification system and the key indicators and values necessary for establishing the SLA with the results obtained through the project cases.

2   Related Studies

2.1   Cloud SLA Studies

To spread and accelerate the use of cloud services, it is important to ensure quality that meets the tenant's requirements. To this end, an analysis should be made of the quality of the services currently provided or to be provided in the future. However, the quality requirements and attributes of the service can vary depending on the service object or delivery model of cloud computing such as IaaS, PaaS, SaaS [1]. In addition, the quality attributes provided by cloud service providers are measured by different criteria and the units of calculation are different [2, 3].

Cross-cutting based quality metric and SLA model for cloud service brokerage [4] presents the result of analyzing cross-cutting quality metric by type of cloud service. It proposed a meta model of VSLA (Variable SLA) as an extended SLA model to guarantee and improve quality. Although this model specifically analyzed the quality of the cloud service target, it did not provide a link analysis for the target quality metric.

Cloud standardization forum summarized quality items and SLA standard system for cloud SLA [5]. IaaS, SaaS, PaaS, and quality items classified by service are summarized and presented in standard form. In addition, there are a number of articles that present SLA elements by analyzing quality items for each service target. E. Badidi proposed SLA-based service broker model for SaaS provisioning [6]. H. He proposed an SLA-based cache optimization model for PaaS [7], and Ayadi proposed an existing ISMS-based SLA approach for the cloud [8]. The above methods can be considered as SLA model for each cloud service layer. Some studies have been applied to the cloud by modifying the existing SLA model. M. Alhamed proposed a conceptual SLA framework for the cloud [9], and K. Stamou proposed a new SLA graph model for the cloud data model [10]. Youngmin Ahn et al. Proposed a new SLA model based on a variable quality item [11], and S. Hussain proposed a SLA concept framework in a cloud-based smart grid model [12]. In this paper, quality item elements for cloud record management are analyzed for each service layer and distinguished from previous papers in terms of providing SLA model from the perspective of service provider integration.

2.2 Cloud Record Management (RM) Usecases

The cloud record management service is classified into three types according to the type of cloud service used in the record management as shown in Fig. 2. The first is when records management is performed by utilizing the IaaS infrastructure service. In this case, the customer (the record management entity) utilizes the cloud infrastructure service to perform the record management by himself. The software and platform required for record management are either developed by the customer or purchased in package form and distributed to IaaS for use. In addition to the infrastructure provided by the cloud, customers have full responsibility for record management. Customers and infrastructure service providers will have SLA agreements to use infrastructure services. The IaaS service provider presents all the service items and characteristics that can be provided in the form of a service catalog. The quality items for the SLA agreement between the customer and the IaaS service provider are infrastructure availability, reconfiguration, performance, security, and preservation and availability of functions.

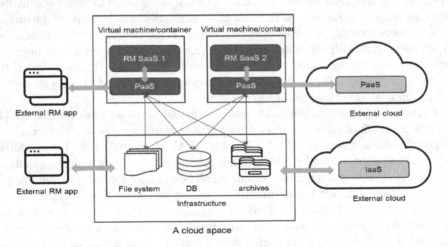

Fig. 2. Usecases of cloud RM

The second is when a customer builds his own application using the cloud platform services. In this case, the customer directly performs the record management through the application that he has established. The customer enters into SLA contract with a platform service provider for use of platform service in order to use platform service of stable and required quality. In general, cloud platform services are implemented in IaaS, and therefore SLA contracts are concluded including quality factors that take into account the platform characteristics in the cloud infrastructure. For example, container scalability, security, application management capabilities, and DB query processing speed.

3   Requirements and Structure of SLA for Cloud RM

Cloud services must be able to accommodate the different requirements of multiple users and as a result have a very complex structure. Cloud services must be capable of delivering a wide variety of services, and cloud service users can demand so many different levels of quality. Therefore, cloud service SLAs must have a pre-defined critical, core, and formal quality metric that can lead to an agreement between users and cloud service providers.

Depending on the type of cloud service they use, the content of the SLA differs from the cloud service provider that is the target of the SLA contract. A SaaS service provider may be a customer of a PaaS service provider or an IaaS service provider. In this case, the SaaS provider may enter into an SLA contract with the PaaS provider or the IaaS service provider. A PaaS service provider can be a customer of an IaaS service provider, in which case an SLA contract can be signed between the PaaS service provider and the IaaS service provider.

Each cloud service provider may enter into an Operation Level Agreement (OLA) with the internal organization to maintain the service level specified in the SLA (See Fig. 3). Cloud service providers can provide reliable services to service users through agreements on operational levels with computing resource managers or internal providers. An IaaS service provider may enter into an "Underpinning Contract" contract with an external maintenance provider. External maintenance companies include software or hardware, computing environments or network vendors, and UCs are essential for IaaS service providers to provide cloud services above a certain level.

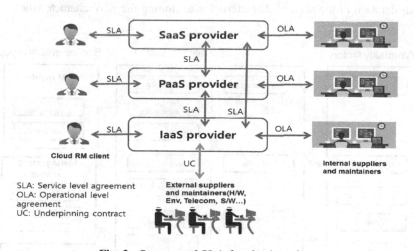

Fig. 3. Structure of SLA for cloud services

In order to structure the cloud computing SLA, the level of internal OLA operation and the level of external maintenance UC contract should be managed more than the level of SLA service provided to the end user. In SLA-OLA-UC structure, OLA quality level should be higher than SLA quality level and UC quality level should be higher than OLA quality level. If there is an OLA or UC contract level that does not meet the SLA quality level, the level of SLA service provided to the end customer falls into a structural contradiction that cannot be guaranteed. Therefore, the SLA structure of the cloud service should always be provided at a level where the quality index in the sub structure exceeds the quality index in the upper structure.

4 Classification of Cloud Service Quality Factors

ISO 9126 specifies the quality characteristics of the software. Software quality depends on the platform and hardware on which the software runs. The quality characteristics of cloud services are provided in the form of software based on hardware and platform, and thus have a very similar aspect to software quality characteristics. In this technical report, the quality characteristics are classified based on the software quality characteristics as set forth in ISO 9126, and a classification of quality characteristics is set by adding service quality characteristics. The cloud service has features that are provided as services rather than objects, and the on-premise-based software quality characteristics are excluded from the cloud service quality characteristics. In addition, the quality characteristics are organized by adding service provisionability.

The quality characteristics are primarily based on the characteristics of the cloud service, among the detailed characteristics, to select the quality characteristics. Figure 4 shows the characteristics of the cloud service in relation to the software quality characteristics. In order to derive the quality characteristics of the cloud service, the sub characteristics of the above software quality characteristics are considered and reflected in consideration of the service characteristics excluding the S/W characteristics.

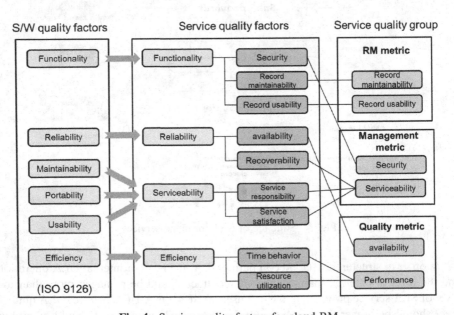

Fig. 4. Service quality factors for cloud RM

In addition to the selected characteristics, general characteristics for service provision were added to the serviceability (serviceability), and the service characteristics and service satisfaction were classified into subordinate groups. In terms of functionality, preservation and usability of digital records are classified as sub-characteristics. The quality characteristics are divided into quality metric group, operation metric group and digital record management metric group to derive metrics again. The quality group and sub-characteristics are shown in Table 1.

Table 1. Quality group and sub-characteristics

Quality group	Contents	Sub-characteristics
Quality metric group	Quantitative metrics that can be provided to cloud service providers	Availability, time responsiveness, resource efficiency
Management metric group	Types of administrative metrics that can be provided to cloud service administrators	Security, resilience, service processability, service satisfaction
Digital records management metric group	Types of digital record management metrics that can be provided to cloud service administrators	Digital record preservability, long-term preservability, usability, audit trailability, service dependency, integrity in deliver, format transformability, ease of migration

4.1 Quality Factors in IaaS

IaaS is a service that provides IT infrastructure resources (server, storage, network, etc.), minimizing the manual work of system administrators and being processed by automated processes. These automation processes include techniques that can minimize operator intervention and provide defined services in a short time. The service provided to the customer should be managed by the defined criteria (SLA), and the customer should be provided with a service catalog containing the service definition and service contents so that the customer can charge the same amount as the usage amount.

Most infrastructure services are provided based on virtualization technology, and the service catalog is an item that is presented to the user before the service application and must include all the contents of the service. The basic contents to be included in the service catalog are a description of the service, a procedure of using the service, a time required, or an SLA and a price for performing the service.

Details of the provided service catalog (basic service item, supplementary service item) should be presented. In particular, since it is necessary to provide a catalog in the form of a business service without consultation or coordination itself, it is necessary to specify and provide basic service provision units and additional service types to a range that the user can select. In addition, the unit cost of the services provided and billing methods for billing should be defined. In particular, when providing a billing method based on usage amount, the user should be provided with detailed billing method according to usage amount.

4.2 Quality Factors in PaaS

PaaS services provide development and testing tools, DBMSs, middleware, and APIs for application development, and provide infrastructure and software environments that can provide services by running the developed applications. PaaS services should provide a development and test environment that can support the entire software development lifecycle and have license management capabilities for the software they provide.

The PaaS service catalog items should be defined as a detail. The service catalog shall be presented to the user before the service application and shall include all contents of the service. The service catalog should describe the name of the service, the description of the service, the procedure of use, and the subject. In addition, detail items (basic service items, supplementary service items) of the catalog of services to be provided should be presented. In particular, since it is necessary to provide a catalog in the form of a business service without consultation or coordination itself, it is necessary to specify and provide basic service provision units and additional service types to a range that the user can select.

4.3 Quality Factors in SaaS

The service provided should be managed by defined criteria (SLA, Policy), and the service catalog should be designed so that it can charge the usage fee. The SaaS service catalog is provided by all types of applications required by the enterprise.

To manage the service level of the service provided, an SLA containing the individual metrics should be presented, packaged including the SLA level, measurement method, and performance evaluation (including discount rate), and provided to enable the customer to select the SLA level if necessary. In the case of SaaS services, various applications and software are provided including sub-infrastructures, so details of the sub-elements are excluded and services that are evaluated based on the availability of services and applications are provided. The service quality indicators of software type services are as shown in Table 2.

Table 2. Quality factors and value range in SaaS

Division		Contents	Value range
Quality metric group	Performance	The amount of time a service is available without platform service interruption due to an infrastructure failure or problem Indicated as a percentage of the defined time (up time)	0.1 s–5 s
	Availability	Time the service is available without interruption of the applications and software provided	99.5%–99.9999%

(*continued*)

Table 2. (*continued*)

Division		Contents	Value range
		Indicated as a percentage of the defined time (Up Time)	
Management metric group	Security	Indicated by the security level of the service providing system consisting of the level of confidentiality, i.e. OS, firewall, intrusion detection system, etc., so that only legitimate users can access the platform	Security class Is there compliance with existing security system such as ISMS?
	Serviceability	• Can be image data backed up? • Backup cycle and availability • Is backup data delivered when the service is stopped? • Is the breakdown time reported? • Is data encryption supported? • Is secure channel is supported? • Service delivery time • Workload Optimization Time	Yes/No D/W/M. Yes/No Yes/No Yes/No, Hour/Day Yes/No Yes/No (Minute)/(Hour) (Minute)/(Hour)
RM metric group	Record maintainability	• Electronic record preservation • Long-term preservability • Audit Trailability • Service non-dependency: independent of PaaS or IaaS	Yes/No Yes/No Yes/No Yes/No
	Record usability	• Usability: access/search should be convenient • Interoperability: records must be available in different clouds • Format responsiveness: records must be available for some conversion of digital record format • Relevance: records must be readable and usable even if transferred. • Disposal: records should be disposed with all distributed files	Yes/No Yes/No Yes/No Yes/No Yes/No

5 Conclusion and Contemplation

In this paper, we analyze the quality items and SLA that should be urgently addressed in order to solve the problem of record management quality, which is the main concern of companies applying digital cloud for cloud. We have not yet applied a lot of clouds to the records management area, because users think that the cloud does not solve the quality degradation and management opacity that can occur in records management yet. In this paper, we propose an alternative method to solve the problem of record management quality that can occur when applying record management to the cloud through quality item definition, SLA item and index value setting. Users can ensure the quality of cloud digital record services based on their SLAs and can be used as a foundation for building overall governance mechanisms for cloud service providers, organizations and businesses.

References

1. Na, J.: Qualitative study on service features for cloud computing. J. Digit. Contents Soc. **12** (3), 319–327 (2011)
2. Qiu, M.M., Zhou, Y., Wang, C.: Systematic analysis of public cloud service level agreements and related business values. In: Proceedings of International Conference on Services Computing, pp. 729–736, June 2013
3. Wu, C., Zhu, Y., Pan, S.: The SLA evaluation model for cloud computing. In: Proceedings of International Conference on Computer, Networks and Communication Engineering, pp. 331–334
4. Ahn, Y., Park, J., Choi, B.: Cross-cutting based quality metric and SLA model for mediating cloud service. In: Proceedings of International Conference on Information Society, pp. 61–66, June 2013
5. Quality Factors for Cloud Computing SLA. CCForum, December 2010
6. Badidi, E.: A cloud service broker for SLA-based SaaS provisioning. In: Proceedings of International Conference on Information Society, pp. 61–66, June 2013
7. He, H., Ma, Z., Chen, H., Shao, W.: Towards an SLA-Driven cache adjustment approach for applications on PaaS. In: Proceedings of the Asia-Pacific Symposium on Internetware, pp. 11–20, October 2013
8. Ayadi, I., Simoni, N., Aubonnet, T.: SLA approach for Cloud as a Service. In: Proceedings of International Conference on Cloud Computing, pp. 966–967. IEEE Computer Society, June 2013
9. Alhamad, M., Dillon, T., Chang, E.: Conceptual SLA framework for cloud computing. In: Proceedings of International Conference on Digital Ecosystems and Technologies, pp. 606–610, April 2010
10. Stamou, K., Kantere, V., Morin, J.H., Geogiou, M.: A SLA graph model for data services. In: Proceeding of International Workshop on Cloud Data Management, pp. 27–34, October 2013
11. Ahn, Y., Park, J., Yeom, G.: Service analysis model based on variation for cloud service mediation. Korea Computer Convention, June 2014
12. Hussain, S., Gustavsson, R., Saleem, A., Nordstrom, L.: A SLA conceptual framework for monitoring QoS in smart grid. In: Proceedings of IEEE Grenoble on PowerTech, pp. 1–6, June 2013

Recovering Scale in Monocular DSO Using Multi-sensor Data

Shan Fang, Yanhong Luo, Jianru Huo$^{(\boxtimes)}$, Yipu Zeng,
and Zhimin Song

Northeastern University, Shenyang, China
1642156713@qq.com, 1127791687@qq.com

Abstract. Monocular visual odometry like DSO (Direct Sparse Odometry) or visual SLAM can be used for UAV navigation. But the scale of DSO is set more or less arbitrarily during its initialization, because the absolute scale is unobservable by using a single-camera. Therefore, the map reconstructed by DSO and the pose estimated by DSO can't be used directly. In order to recover the scale, firstly, we use IMU, GPS and ultrasonic data and Kalman filter algorithm to calculate the position and pose of UAV. Particularly, we improve the Kalman filtering algorithm instead of using the original algorithm. After the calculation, we get the position and pose of UAV with real scale, and then estimate the proportion between DSO's scale and real scale by least square method. Finally, using this proportion to correct the scale of point cloud, we can get the point cloud map with real scale which can be used for UAV navigation in the future work.

Keywords: DSO · UAV · Visual odometry · Kalman filter · Least square method

1 Introduction

With the development of visual SLAM (simultaneous localization and mapping) and visual odometry, autonomous flight navigation of UAV using visual sensors has become a major research hotspot. Usually UAVs are equipped with a single camera, so monocular visual odometry or SLAM algorithms [1] are used widely. About the scale uncertainty of monocular visual odometry or SLAM, there are many ways to recover. The simplest way is to use stereo vision [2] like binocular camera; it doesn't have the problem of scale uncertainty because the baseline between two cameras is known. But it's not an economical and convenient choice to change the camera on the UAV. The University of Science and Technology of Hong Kong proposed VINS-Mono which is a real-time monocular SLAM by using a tightly coupled and nonlinear optimization-based method to fuse IMU data [3, 4]. Although it successfully applied in autonomous navigation of UAV, it is complicated and it requires a lot of computing power. In another category of scale recovery, cameras are at a fixed height above the ground [5–7]. The local scale of the map can be corrected by detecting the ground plane. But this method will limit the maneuverability of UAV when used on drones.

In this paper, AR. Drone 2.0 quad-rotor UAV of Parrot Company in France is used as the experimental platform. The forward-looking camera, ultrasonic altimeter module,

© Springer Nature Switzerland AG 2019
Y. Tan et al. (Eds.): ICSI 2019, LNCS 11656, pp. 361–369, 2019.
https://doi.org/10.1007/978-3-030-26354-6_36

inertial unit (IMU) and GPS are used to recover the scale. Our main work is divided into four parts. In the first part, we use the DSO to reconstruct the three-dimensional map of the flight environment, so that we can perceive the obstacle information in front of the UAV. In the second part, we use IMU, ultrasound and GPS to calculate the attitude and position of UAV, and then use the calculated position to recover the scale of DSO. In the last part, we use AR. Drone 2.0 quad-rotor UAV to verify the feasibility of our scale recovery method and obtain good results.

2   DSO: Direct Sparse Odometry

DSO (Direct Sparse Odometry) is a monocular visual odometry algorithm proposed by Technical University of Munich in 2016 [8, 9], it can reconstruct semi-dense three-dimensional map which can be used to navigate the UAVs in simple environments. DSO uses direct method. The direct method relies on the assumption of invariant gray level [10]: the gray level of a pixel in the same space is fixed in each frame image. It calculates the motion of the camera based on the pixel information of the image, and optimizes the motion of the camera by minimizing the photometric error. Unlike feature-based (indirect) methods, it does not rely on keypoint detectors or descriptors, so it can naturally sample pixels from across all image regions that have intensity gradient, including edges or objects without obvious texture.

What's more, DSO creatively introduces photometric calibration [11]. In the direct method, the accuracy of the brightness value will affect the accuracy and stability of the algorithm because the estimation of pose is based on the brightness value of the image. Therefore, DSO introduces the concept of photometric calibration. It uses the fine camera imaging model to calibrate the photometric parameters in the imaging process, and these parameters will be used to correct the brightness value of images (Fig. 1).

Fig. 1. Localizing and reconstructing in the real environment by using DSO, the green line is the trajectory of the camera which is equipped on the UAV.

3   Pose Estimation Based on Multi-sensor Fusion and Scale Recovery

3.1   Description of the Coordinate System

The motion and position of an object are meaningful only in a relative sense. Before establishing the mathematical model, the reference coordinate system of space should be determined firstly, and then the attitude and position parameters of the airframe in space should be determined. Commonly used in Four-rotor UAV models are airframe coordinate system and navigation coordinate system [12].

For the definition of the UAV navigation coordinate system, the origin of coordinates is defined as the starting point of the UAV motion as shown in Fig. 2. The positive east direction of the origin is the coordinate system x-axis, the north-north direction of the origin is the coordinate system y-axis, and the origin is in the opposite direction of gravity. The coordinate system is the z-axis. The above coordinate system is also called the NEU coordinate system [13].

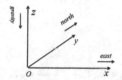

Fig. 2. UAV navigation coordinate system

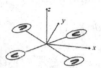

Fig. 3. UAV body coordinate system

The body coordinate system is fixed on the body of the drone. As shown in Fig. 3, the head of the drone is oriented to the x-axis, the vertical and the plane of the drone are the z-axis, and the y-axis is perpendicular to the x-axis and Z axis.

3.2   EKF-Based UAV Attitude Estimation

The UAV attitude information fusion system is a nonlinear system [14], and its discrete time state model (state equation and measurement equation) is as follows:

$$X_k = f(X_{k-1}) + W_{k-1}$$
$$Z_k = H_k X_k + V_k \tag{1}$$

Where, $X_k = [\gamma_k \quad \theta_k \quad \psi_k]^T$ is the state vector, which is three attitude angles of the UAV at time k in the navigation coordinate system and $Z_k = [z_{\gamma k} \quad z_{\theta k} \quad z_{\psi k}]$, calculated by accelerometer and magnetometer in IMU, is three attitude angles of UAV in the navigation coordinate system at time k. The nonlinear function $f(X_{k-1})$ in Eq. (1) is expanded as follows [15]:

$$\gamma_k = \gamma_{k-1} + w_{xk}T_s + \frac{\sin\gamma_{k-1}\sin\theta_{k-1}}{\cos\theta_{k-1}}w_{yk} + \frac{\cos\gamma_{k-1}\sin\theta_{k-1}}{\cos\theta_{k-1}}w_{zk}T_s$$

$$\theta_k = \theta_{k-1} + \cos\gamma_{k-1}w_{yk}T_s - \sin\gamma_{k-1}w_{zk}T_s$$

$$\psi_k = \psi_{k-1} + \frac{\sin\gamma_{k-1}}{\cos\theta_{k-1}}w_{yk}T_s + \frac{\cos\gamma_{k-1}}{\cos\theta_{k-1}}w_{zk}T_s$$

$w_{bk} = [\,w_{xk} \quad w_{yk} \quad w_{zk}\,]$ is the three-axis angular velocity in the body coordinate system output at the time k. T_s is the sampling period. Linearize the nonlinear relationship in Eq. (1):

$$X_k = \Phi_{k/k-1}X_{k-1} + W_{k-1}$$
$$Z_k = H_kX_k + V_k \tag{2}$$

In the formula (2),

$$\Phi_{k/k-1} = \frac{\partial f(X_{k-1})}{\partial X_{k-1}}$$

$$= \begin{bmatrix} 1 + \frac{\cos\gamma_{k-1}\sin\theta_{k-1}}{\cos\theta_{k-1}}w_{yk}T_s - \frac{\sin\gamma_{k-1}\sin\theta_{k-1}}{\cos\theta_{k-1}}w_{zk}T_s & \frac{\sin\gamma_{k-1}}{\cos^2\theta_{k-1}}w_{yk}T_s + \frac{\cos\gamma_{k-1}}{\cos^2\theta_{k-1}}w_{zk}T_s & 0 \\ -\sin\gamma_{k-1}w_{yk}T_s - \cos\gamma_{k-1}w_{zk}wT_s & 1 & 0 \\ \frac{\cos\gamma_{k-1}}{\cos\theta_{k-1}}w_{yk}T_s - \frac{\sin\gamma_{k-1}}{\cos\theta_{k-1}}w_{zk}T_s & \frac{\sin\gamma_{k-1}\sin\theta_{k-1}}{\cos^2\theta_{k-1}}w_{yk}T_s + \frac{\cos\gamma_{k-1}\sin\theta_{k-1}}{\cos^2\theta_{k-1}}w_{zk}T_s & 1 \end{bmatrix}$$

Finally, the Kalman filter is applied to the Eq. (2) to obtain the attitude angle filter estimation value of the time. The specific process is as follows:

$$\widehat{X}_{k/k-1} = A_{k/k-1}\widehat{X}_{k-1} \tag{3}$$

$$P_{k/k-1} = \Phi_{k/k-1}P_{k-1}\Phi_{k/k-1}^T + Q \tag{4}$$

$$v_k = P_{k/k-1}H_k^T[H_kP_{k/k-1}H_k^T + R]^{-1} \tag{5}$$

$$\widehat{X} = \widehat{X}_{k/k-1} + v_k[Z_k - H_k\widehat{X}_{k/k-1}] \tag{6}$$

$$P_k = [I - v_kH_k]P_{k/k-1} \tag{7}$$

3.3 Based on Improved KF Drone Position Estimation

Because the height error calculated by using GPS information is very large [16], and the horizontal position calculated is relatively accurate, so when we calculate the horizontal position of unmanned aerial vehicle (UAV), we use GPS to calculate the horizontal position, while the height calculated by using high-precision ultrasound. The UAV horizontal position information fusion system is a nonlinear system, and its discrete time state model (state equation and measurement equation) is as follows:

$$Z_k = HX_k + V_k$$
$$X_k = \Phi X_{k-1} + Bu_{k-1} + \Gamma W_{k-1}$$

(8)

Expansion of formula (8) is expressed as follows:

$$
\begin{bmatrix} S_{xk} \\ S_{yk} \\ ve_{xk} \\ ve_{yk} \end{bmatrix} = \begin{bmatrix} 1 & 0 & T_s & 0 \\ 0 & 1 & 0 & T_s \\ 0 & 0 & 1 & 0 \\ 0 & 0 & 0 & 1 \end{bmatrix} \begin{bmatrix} S_{xk-1} \\ S_{yk-1} \\ ve_{xk-1} \\ ve_{yk-1} \end{bmatrix} + \begin{bmatrix} \frac{T_s^2}{2} & 0 \\ 0 & \frac{T_s^2}{2} \\ T_s & 0 \\ 0 & T_s \end{bmatrix} \left(\begin{bmatrix} \dot{v}_{xk-1} \\ \dot{v}_{yk-1} \end{bmatrix} + \begin{bmatrix} W_{xk-1} \\ W_{yk-1} \end{bmatrix} \right)
$$

$$
\begin{bmatrix} S_{gxk} \\ S_{gyk} \end{bmatrix} = \begin{bmatrix} 1 & 0 & 0 & 0 \\ 0 & 1 & 0 & 0 \end{bmatrix} \begin{bmatrix} S_{xk} \\ S_{yk} \\ ve_{xk} \\ ve_{yk} \end{bmatrix} + \begin{bmatrix} V_{xk} \\ V_{yk} \end{bmatrix}
$$

where (S_{xk}, S_{yk}) is the horizontal coordinate position of the drone at time k in the navigation coordinate system. (ve_x, ve_y) is the speed of the horizontal plane for the time drone in the navigation coordinate system. $(\dot{v}_{kx}, \dot{v}_{ky})$ is the acceleration of the horizontal plane of the UAV in the navigation coordinate system, and it can be calculated by the attitude angle calculated by formula (6) and the output information of accelerometer in IMU. The specific solution method is detailed in [17]. T_s is the fusion period, W_k is the dimensional system noise vector, its statistical properties of variance are completely determined by the statistical properties, which can be measured by multiple experiments, and therefore the noise driving matrix is $\Gamma = B$. (S_{gxk}, S_{gyk}) is the horizontal coordinate of UAV calculated directly from GPS in navigation coordinate system. The specific solution method is detailed in [18]. V_k is a system noise vector.

Because GPS is a device with good long-term static performance, its short-term response speed is poor. The final result of Kalman filter is to minimize the variance of each fusion result. Because of the slow response of GPS, the calculated value is easy to remain unchanged for a long time, so it is easier to occupy a larger proportion in the fusion process. Obviously, such a result is not what we want. The solution is not to let the one-step state prediction mean square error matrix not iterate with each filter, so that the constant matrix is determined at the beginning of the filter:

$$P_{k/k-1} = \Phi P_{k-1} \Phi^T + \Gamma \hat{Q}_{k-1} \Gamma^T = \Phi P_0 \Phi^T + \Gamma \hat{Q} \Gamma^T = P$$

(9)

This filter gain will also be a constant matrix:

$$K = \frac{PH^T}{HPH^T + \hat{R}}$$

(10)

Φ, Γ, $\widehat{Q}$ and H are both constant matrices, so that the effect of the one-step prediction from the state will not be less and less. The final Kalman filter algorithm is as follows:

$$P_{k/k-1} = \Phi P_0 \Phi^T + \Gamma \widehat{Q} \Gamma^T = P$$

$$K = \frac{PH^T}{HPH^T + \widehat{R}}$$

$$\widehat{X}_{k/k-1} = \Phi \widehat{X}_{k-1} + Bu_{k-1} \tag{11}$$

$$v_k = Z_k - H\widehat{X}_{k/k-1}$$

$$\widehat{X}_k = \widehat{X}_{k/k-1} + Kv_k$$

3.4   Correcting the Scale of Point Cloud

The position and point cloud estimated by the monocular visual odometry have problems such as coordinate rotation translation and scale scaling. In order to navigate the done, we need to use the real-scale point cloud map estimated by visual odometry under the NEU coordinate system. We believe that the position in the NEU coordinate system obtained by the fusion of IMU, GPS and ultrasound is estimated as the position estimate at the true scale. Moreover, for the same motion process, we believe that the position estimation in the NEU coordinate system obtained by IMU, GPS and ultrasonic fusion has a linear relationship with the visual odometry position estimation. The point cloud and position estimated by visual odometry are in the same coordinate system, so we use the position estimation obtained by IMU, GPS and ultrasonic information fusion to restore the scale position and attitude of the point cloud map estimated by visual odometry in the NEU coordinate system. The position obtained by the fusion of IMU and accelerometer is estimated as the position estimate under the real scale, and the position estimation scale obtained by the monocular visual odometry is problematic.

We want to use the least squares method to find such a matrix A and vector b such that $y = Ax + b$; where $y = (y_1, y_2, y_3)$ is the position estimate obtained by the fusion of IMU, GPS and ultrasonic information; $x = (x_1, x_2, x_3)$ is the position estimate obtained by the monocular visual odometry.

The following is the process of restoring monocular visual odometry by least squares method.

Collect m sets of data: $D = \{(x_1, y_1), (x_2, y_2), (x_3, y_3), \cdots, (x_m, y_m)\}$

Where $x_k = (x_{k1}, x_{k2}, x_{k3})$ is the position estimate obtained by the monocular visual odometry at time k, $y_k = (y_{k1}, y_{k2}, y_{k3})$ is the position estimate obtained by the fusion of IMU, GPS and ultrasonic at time k.

Trying to find such a matrix A and vector b enables $y = Ax + b$ to best fit the relationship between y and x. Incorporate vector b into matrix $A' = (A, b)$ and then rewrite x, y in data set D to the following format:

$$X = \begin{bmatrix} x_1 \\ x_2 \\ x_3 \\ \vdots \\ x_m \end{bmatrix} = \begin{bmatrix} x_{11} & x_{12} & x_{13} & 1 \\ x_{21} & x_{22} & x_{23} & 1 \\ x_{31} & x_{32} & x_{33} & 1 \\ \vdots & \vdots & \vdots & \vdots \\ x_{m1} & x_{m2} & x_{m3} & 1 \end{bmatrix} \qquad Y = \begin{bmatrix} y_1 \\ y_2 \\ y_3 \\ \vdots \\ y_m \end{bmatrix} = \begin{bmatrix} y_{11} & y_{12} & y_{13} \\ y_{21} & y_{22} & y_{23} \\ y_{31} & y_{32} & y_{33} \\ \vdots & \vdots & \vdots \\ y_{m1} & y_{m2} & y_{m3} \end{bmatrix}$$

Then the fitting target is expressed as

$$y = A'x \tag{12}$$

According to the principle of the second most multiplication, results obtained by least squares is as follow:

$$A' = (X^T X)^{-1} X^T y \tag{13}$$

The final Λ is the scale matrix for the conversion from original point cloud to the real-scale point cloud.

4 Experimental Results

In Fig. 4, the blue line is the motion trajectory estimated by DSO before scale recovery, and the red line is the motion trajectory obtained by the fusion of IMU, GPS and ultrasound.

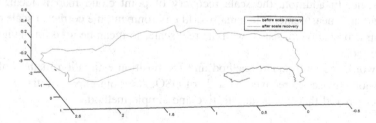

Fig. 4. Motion trajectory (red line) estimation based on multi-sensor fusion and motion trajectory (blue line) estimation based on DSO. (Color figure online)

From Fig. 4, we can see that the trajectory estimated by DSO in the same motion process are only different in scale from those estimated by multi-sensor fusion. This also verifies the validity of our previous assumptions and ensures that the future work is meaningful.

The two images of Fig. 5 are point cloud map of the same scene before scale recovery and after scale recovery, and the width of each unit grid in the two maps is 1 m. The scale before recovery is obviously smaller than the real scale of the world. After our measurement of the actual scene, the scale of the point cloud is basically consistent with the size of the real object. Through the above experimental analysis, we believe that we have basically completed the scale recovery of monocular visual odometry.

Fig. 5. The left image is point cloud map without recovering scale and the right is point cloud map after scale recovery

5   Conclusion

Through the verification of the experimental results, we conclude that the position estimation results based on the improved Kalman filter are accurate. In position calculation, the discreteness of the data obtained by improved Kalman filter is obviously better than that before, which lays a foundation for the accuracy of the next step of scale recovery.

By comparing DSO location estimation with multi-sensor fusion location estimation, we confirm the corresponding relationship between DSO location estimation and multi-sensor fusion location estimation, and the feasibility of least squares method to recover scale. In addition, the scale recovery of point cloud map is ideal. By our experiment and measurements in a real-world environment, the corrected scale of point cloud map is basically consistent with the real scale, so it can be used for navigation in the future work.

In a word, the least square method and the position estimation method of multi-sensor fusion are used to recover the scale of DSO. After our experimental verification, it has been proved that this is an effective and simple method.

Acknowledgment.   This work was supported in part by the National Natural Science Foundation of China (61433004, 61703289).

References

1. Liu, H.M., Zhang, G.F., Bao, H.J.: A survey of monocular simultaneous localization and mapping. J. Comput.-Aided Des. Comput. Graph. **29**(6), 855–868 (2016)

2. Wang, R., Schwörer, M., Cremers, D.: Stereo DSO: large-scale direct sparse visual odometry with stereo cameras. In: International Conference on Computer Vision (ICCV) (2017)
3. Qin, T., Li, P.L., Yang, Z.F., Shen, S.J.: VINS-Mono: a robust and versatile monocular visual-inertial state estimator. IEEE Trans. Rob. **34**(4), 1004–1020 (2018)
4. Qin, T., Shen, S.J.: Online temporal calibration for monocular visual-inertial systems. In: IEEE/RSJ International Conference on Intelligent Robots and Systems (IROS 2018) (2018)
5. Scaramuzza, D., Fraundorfer, F., Pollefeys, M., Siegwart, R.: Absolute scale in structure from motion from a single vehicle mounted camera by exploiting nonholonomic constraints. In: Proceedings of the 12th IEEE International Conference on Computer Vision, pp. 1413–1419 (2009)
6. Kitt, B., Geiger, A., Lategahn, H.: Visual odometry based on stereo image sequences with RANSAC-based outlier rejection scheme. In: Proceedings of the Intelligent Vehicles Symposium III, pp. 486–492 (2010)
7. Geiger, A., Ziegler, J., Stiller, C.: StereoScan: dense 3D reconstruction in real-time. In: Proceedings of the IEEE Intelligent Vehicles Symposium IV, pp. 963–968 (2011)
8. von Stumberg, L., Usenko, V., Cremers, D.: Direct sparse visual-inertial odometry using dynamic marginalization. In: International Conference on Robotics and Automation (ICRA) (2018)
9. Engel, J., Koltun, V., Cremers, D.: Direct sparse odometry. IEEE Trans. Pattern Anal. Mach. Intell. **40**(3), 611–625 (2018)
10. Gao, X., Zhang, T., Liu, Y., Yan, Q.R.: 14 Lectures of Visual SLAM: From Theory to Practice. Publishing House of Electronics Industry, Beijing (2017)
11. Engel, J., Usenko, V., Cremers, D.: A photometrically calibrated benchmark for monocular visual odometry (2016)
12. Zhe, X.: Design and implementation of four-rotor UAV control system. Nanjing University of Technology (2017)
13. Boxin, Z.: Research on the UAV localization based on the low-cost and micro sensors. National University of Defense Technology (2016)
14. Pan, Z.: Motion estimation of four-rotor vehicle based on multi-sensor fusion. China University of Science and Technology (2014)
15. Zhang, X.: Research on attitude and navigation information fusion algorithms for multi-rotor UAV. University of Chinese Academy of Sciences (2015)
16. Chende, F., Qinyun, L.: Design and implementation of integrated navigation scheme based on MEMS-IMU/GPS/GPRS. Sig. Process Syst. **22**(5), 24–28 (2016)
17. Chi, X.W.: Research on MES-IMU/GPS integrated attitude measurement system for miniature UAV. Harbin Engineering University (2016)
18. Zhong, L.Q.: Conversion method and accuracy analysis of WGS-84 coordinate system to local coordinate system. Urban Reconnaissance, pp. 109–111 (2016)

Energy Management Strategy (EMS) for Hybrid Electric Vehicles Based on Safe Experimentation Dynamics (SED)

Muhammad Ikram bin Mohd Rashid[✉], Hamdan Daniyal,
and Mohd Ashraf Ahmad

Faculty of Electrical and Electronic Engineering, University Malaysia Pahang,
Pekan, Pahang, Malaysia
{Mikram,Hamdan,Mashraf}@ump.edu.my

Abstract. This paper addresses optimization for hybrid electric vehicle (HEV) by using a single agent method to optimize the power losses and fuel consumption under a specific driving cycle base on Safe Experimentation Dynamics (SED) method. For optimization process, four gain are added in four main parts of the HEV system. Those main parts are engine, motor, generator and battery. These four gain are controlled the output for each components to give the minimum power losses. The design method is applied to free model of HEV by using Simulink/MATLAB software while M-File/MATLAB is used to apply the Safe Experimentation Dynamics (SED) method. The result from design method achieved minimum reduction of power losses and fuel consumption compared to original system. Thus, the comparison of the simulation results shown that the algorithm approach provides better performance.

Keywords: HEV · Safe Experimentation Dynamics (SED) ·
Energy Management Strategy (EMS)

1 Introduction

Hybrid electric vehicles (HEV) is introduce to help user reduce their daily cost when using vehicle as fuel consumption can be minimize with help of electric system. This is because HEV is using hybrid of two sources which are Internal Combustion Engine (ICE) and an electric generator as alternate energy source. ICE consume fuel (petrol/diesel) to generate energy to move the vehicle while electric motor use electricity that generate by generator. HEV give a minimum fuel consumption as the electric motor used to move the vehicle from the rest and ICE support the vehicle when it start to accelerate. This fuel economic give an advantage to HEV compare to ICE vehicle. Energy Management Strategy (EMS) is a method to optimize the split usage between electric motor and fuel in order to give the best optimization of the fuel consumption. The main function of the EMS is power management. Automotive and communication control make a joint research that focusing on fuel consumption optimization [1]. Many approach has been proposed to optimize the fuel consumption

© Springer Nature Switzerland AG 2019
Y. Tan et al. (Eds.): ICSI 2019, LNCS 11656, pp. 370–377, 2019.
https://doi.org/10.1007/978-3-030-26354-6_37

which are consider many aspects in HEV model based on the method as optimal control and input control.

There are some aspect that can be optimize in HEV model. One of them is optimize the power usage in four main components in HEV which are ICE, generator, motor and battery. Most HEV research is focusing on optimization using advanced control algorithms which lead to minimization of the energy circulation loss [2]. The power usage can be optimize by reducing the power losses in those component to give a high performance to HEV.

One of method that can used to optimize the HEV model is using Safe Experimentation Dynamics (SED). This method is one of Game Theory group method. This type of Game Theory has potential applications in a number of areas relevant to statistical modelling and control [3]. Thus, this method can be most suitable for this project.

As conclusion, EMS is needed to improve the development of HEV in future for a better performance to compute with others type of vehicles. This optimization is important to give more advantage to the HEV model.

2 Free Model of HEV

A simple hybrid electric vehicle model is chosen due to its simplicity and practicality. The model is taken from MATLAB library archive to be apply in the simulation. This model consist of functioning circuit that will be able to produce output such as vehicle velocity, power loss, and etc. It is also made up from electrical and physical part. Hybrid Electric Vehicles (HEVs) consist of two power sources, that is, (1) Internal Combustion Engine (ICE) and (2) battery [4]. The block diagram of the simple HEV model as below (Fig. 1):

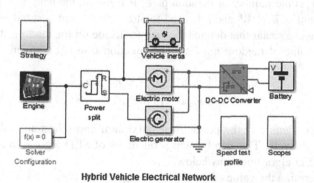

Hybrid Vehicle Electrical Network

Fig. 1. HEV models MATLAB Simulink

In order to tune our output which are power loss and fuel consumption, there are four parameter that are being tune which are the engine, electric generator, electric motor, and battery. There are one gain that are being place inside each of the four parameter. Before the tuning is done, the initial output is being taken. The power loss and power graph is the being recorded so it will be compare to the final result.

Gain is being used. L, H, Y, and U gain is placed inside the four parameter and been given initial value of 1. With this initial value, first simulation will be run and the output will be recorded. Then using Simulated Annealing Algorithm, new number will be generated and replace the initial value. Thus new output performance will be produce.

3 Methodology

In this section, it is presented how to implement the design into the HEV system. Combination of Simulink and M-File in MATLAB software is used. The Simulink used to for HEV model while M-File used to optimize the gains in the Simulink based on SED method. SED algorithm is as below:

There is a optimization problem;

$$\min_{p \in R^n} f(p) \tag{1}$$

Where the objective function is represented by $f : Rn -> R$ and $p^* \in R^n$ is the design variable. The optimal solution $p^* \in R^n$ of optimization problem in (1) is obtain by repetitively updating the design parameter using the SED algorithm.

The SED algorithm updates the values of design parameter for each iteration to achieve $p^* \in R^n$. The update law is:

$$p_i(k+1) = h(\bar{p}_i - K_g r_2), \tag{2}$$

where $k = 0, 1,$ is the number of iteration $p_i \in R$ is the ith element of $p \in R^n, \bar{p}_i \in R^n$ is the ith element of $\bar{p} \in R^n$ and $\bar{p}$ is used to store the current best value of the design parameters, Kg is a scalar that defined the size to decide on the random steps on $p_i \in R$ and $r_2 \in R$ is value of random number. The function h in (2) is given as follows,

$$h(\cdot) = \begin{cases} p_{\max}, & \bar{p}_i - K_g r_2 > p_{\max} \\ p_{\min}, & \bar{p}_i - K_g r_2 < p_{\min} \end{cases}, \tag{3}$$

where of *Pmax, Pmin,* are the pre-defined maximum and minimum values of design parameter respectively. The step by step procedures of SED algorithm are as follows:

Step for SED algorithm is as below:

Step 1:   Determine the value of *Pmax, Pmin, Kg* and E. Then set $k = 0$ and the initial condition of the parameter is set as $p(0)$ and the objective function will be $f(p$ (0)). Therefore as default $\bar{p} = p(0)$ and $\bar{f} = f(p(0))$

Note that E is a scalar that define the probability to use a new random setting of p. Variable f is used to store the current best value of the objective function

Step 2:   If the value of $f(\boldsymbol{p}(k)) < \bar{f}$, execute $\boldsymbol{p} = \boldsymbol{p}(k)$ and $\bar{f} = f(\boldsymbol{p}(k))$. Otherwise
proceed to step 3.

Step 3:   Generate random number r_1. If $r_1 < E$, generate second number r_2 and obtain
the value for $p_i(k + 1)$ by using the update law (2). Otherwise $p_i(k+1) = \bar{p}_i$

Note that, $r_1 \in R$ is value of random number which is chosen by uniformly distribute
between 0 and 1, while r_2 is between *Pmin* and *Pmax*

Step 4:   Obtain the objective function $f(p_i(k + 1))$

Step 5:   If the pre-stated termination condition is satisfied, the algorithm terminates
with the solution $\boldsymbol{p}^* := arg$

$$\min_{p \in \{(0), p(1), \Box, p(k+1)\}} f(\boldsymbol{p}) \tag{4}$$

Otherwise, set $k = k + 1$ and continue to step 2.

The pre-stated termination condition is based on the designated maximum number
of iteration, *kmax*.

Algorithm of SED is implement in M-file (Matlab) to generate the value for
parameters for each iteration while running. The value will sent to Simulink (Matlab)
block diagram of HEV where the parameters are placed. M-file also used to call the
HEV in Simulink to run over and over again according to iteration until it reach
maximum iteration. So, the value or four parameter will change continuously and give
a different output value of power losses. The four parameters is as below (Table 1):

Table 1. Gain added name and parameter

Gain name	Parameter
L	Electric motor
Y	Internal combustion engine
U	Battery
H	Electric generator

Figures below show place of each gain that have been added (Figs. 2, 3, 4 and 5):

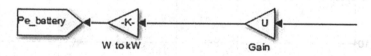

Fig. 2. Gain in battery

Fig. 3. Gain in motor

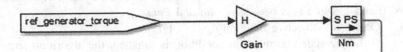

Fig. 4. Gain in generator

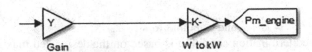

Fig. 5. Gain in engine

4   Result

In this section, we discuss about the value of parameters that most suitable to use for this free model HEV. There are many value that we get from the iterations that we have done. Each of value that came out is generated by SED algorithm that we implement in coding (m-file Matlab). Each of the parameter give a different value for each iteration to minimize the power losses. After we get the lowest value of power loss, the analysis is

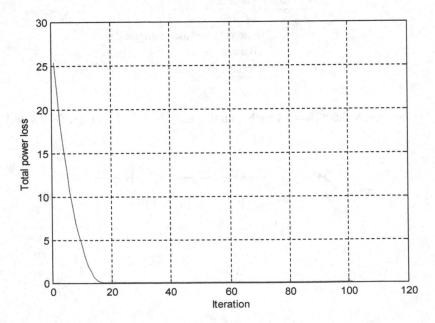

Fig. 6. Response of objective function using SED

taking place as to determine the gain values. SED-based method may be extended to a more complicated situation as long as the objective function can be measured [6]. Also, comparison between the original and the optimize model for the analysis part. Tables below show value for all gains (L, Y, H and U) and power losses (Ploss) (Fig. 6, Tables 2 and 3).

Finally, a comparative assessment between the proposed scheme and power loss problem is presented [7].

Table 2. Gains value for each iteration

Gain iteration		Y	L	H	U
1st	x(1)	0.8134	0.8134	0.8134	1.1866
	x(50)	1.2764	0.1480	0.4138	0.8754
2nd	x(1)	0.8134	1.1866	0.8134	1.1866
	x(50)	1.1464	−0.0961	1.1692	0.8824
3rd	x(1)	0.8134	0.8134	1.1866	1.1866
	x(50)	1.3188	1.9521	−0.0932	1.5265
4th	x(1)	0.8134	0.8134	0.8134	1.1866
	x(50)	1.1227	−0.1245	0.4087	1.1515
5th	x(1)	1.1866	0.8134	0.8134	1.1866
	x(50)	1.1004	0.1666	0.9755	1.1474
6th	x(1)	0.8134	1.1866	1.1866	1.1866
	x(50)	1.9611	0.1621	1.0608	1.1473
7th	x(1)	0.8134	1.1866	0.8134	1.1866
	x(50)	0.5298	−0.1032	1.2758	1.1541
8th	x(1)	1.1866	0.8134	1.1866	0.8134
	x(50)	1.5232	0.1594	1.0878	0.8821
9th	x(1)	1.1866	0.8134	0.8134	1.1866
	x(50)	0.5478	0.1552	0.8911	0.8750
10th	x(1)	1.1866	0.8134	0.8134	0.8134
	x(50)	0.3190	0.1472	0.6851	0.8792

Table 3. Value of power loss for each iteration

Iteration	Power loss
1st	0.1983
2nd	0.1860
3rd	0.2282
4th	0.1753
5th	0.1634
6th	0.1779
7th	0.1581
8th	0.1407
9th	0.1721
10th	0.1673

5 Discussion

In this section, we will discuss about the result we get. Based on table in result above, the lowest power loss that we get at 8th iteration with 0.1407 while the worst is 0.2282 at 3rd iteration. By comparing with the original model which is 852.7655 value of power losses, this deduction is quite large margin between them. As we determine the lowest power loss, we obtain the gain value for each of parameter. All the value for gain parameter is shown in table below (Table 4).

Table 4. Recommend gain value for parameter

Gain parameter	Value
Internal combustion engine	1.5232
Electric motor	0.1594
Electric generator	1.0878
Battery	0.8821

For more information about the different between the optimize model and the original model, table below show the comparison (Table 5).

Table 5. Comparison between graph of original and optimize HEV model

Model Graph	Original model	Optimize model
Power loss		
Power		
Shaft speed		

Since the shaft speed is maintain as the same, it is mean that both of model moving at the same speed and reducing the power consumption and power loss by the HEV model.

6 Conclusion

This paper has presented optimization of a free model HEV by using simultaneous perturbation stochastic approximation method to reduce power loss as a cost function. This project work properly and a minimize power loss value as the output that can give advantage to HEV users. SED is an efficient gradient-free Game Theory algorithm that has performed well on a variety of complex optimization problems [5]. The technologies of HEV can be develop further more in the future to compete in automotive industry. As the result is positive for development, this project can be consider as successful and the innovation apply to the HEV is suitable. Since this is a free model HEV, there are many aspect that can be optimize for future uses.

Acknowledgement. This research study is supported by Ministry of Higher Education Malaysia (MoHE) and Universiti Malaysia Pahang under Fundamental Research Grant Scheme FRGS/1/2017/TK04/UMP/03/1 or RDU 170129.

References

1. Ahmad, M.A., Azuma, S.I., Baba, I., Sugie, T.: Switching controller design for hybrid electric vehicles. SICE J. **7**(5), 273–282 (2014)
2. Wang, Q., Frank, A.A.: Plug-in HEV with CVT: configuration, control, and its concurrent multi-objective optimization by evolutionary algorithm. Int. J. Automot. Technol. **15**(1), 103–115 (2014)
3. Abdul Shukor, N.S., Ahmad, M.A., Zaidi, M., Tumari, M.: Data-driven PID tuning based on safe experimentation dynamics for control of liquid slosh. In: 8th IEEE Control and System Graduate Research Colloquium (ICSGRC 2017), Shah Alam, Malaysia, 4–5 August 2017, pp. 1–5 (2017)
4. Panday, A., Bansal, H.O.: A review of optimal energy management strategies for hybrid electric vehicle. Int. J. Veh. Technol. **2014**, 1–19 (2014)
5. Prokhorov, D.: Toyota Prius HEV neurocontrol. In: Proceedings of International Joint Conference on Neural Networks (2007)
6. Ahmad, M.A., Baba, I., Azuma, S.I., Sugie, T.: Model free tuning of variable state of charge target of hybrid electric vehicles. The International Federation of Automatic Control (2013)
7. Spall, J.C.: An overview of simultaneous perturbation method for efficient optimization. John Hopkins APL Tech. Digest **19**(4), 482–492 (1998)

Serial Interface Converter of Micromechanical Sensors to a Parallel Interface

Eugene V. Larkin and Maxim A. Antonov[(✉)]

Tula State University, Tula 300012, Russia
elarkin@mail.ru, max0594@yandex.ru

Abstract. The necessity of converting a serial interface into a parallel interface, when entering data into the Von-Neumann computer, as a result of the poling procedure, is shown. An algorithm for the operation of the interface converter has been proposed, and it has been shown that the use of serial interface conversion of multiple sensors into a parallel interface, with the ability to access each sensor separately, has greater speed than accessing each sensor separately through a serial interface. The possible technical implementation of the proposed algorithm on the FPGA is shown.

Keywords: Serial interface · Parallel interface · Algorithm · Time delays · Gyroscope · Mobile robot · FPGA

1 Introduction

Mobile robots (MR), moving across rough terrain are widely used in various fields of human activity, such as ecology, geology, after man-made disasters.

The movement of a mobile robot (MR) over rough terrain is accompanied by the occurrence of transverse oscillations of the platform with the target equipment placed on it [1], as a result, the accuracy of the tasks performed by the MR is reduced. Therefore, it is necessary to stabilize the spatial orientation of the platform, for which a subsystem for stabilizing the spatial orientation of the platform is introduced into the MR control system.

The system of stabilization of spatial orientation includes an onboard computer, a gyroscope and executive drives that provide the angular mechanical movement of the platform relative to the swinging base. The frequency and amplitude of the natural oscillations of the platform depend on the coefficients of the characteristic polynomial transfer function, describing the movement of the platform relative to the base.

The use of the Von Neumann computer for controlling leads implies, firstly, the discretization of information from the gyroscope, and secondly, the time delay in data processing associated with the sequential interpretation of control algorithm operators. Moreover, the sampling intervals must meet the requirements of the theorem from samples [2, 3], and the data processing time must provide the required performance indicators of the control [2, 3], in particular, to ensure the stability of the stabilization system as a whole.

© Springer Nature Switzerland AG 2019
Y. Tan et al. (Eds.): ICSI 2019, LNCS 11656, pp. 378–386, 2019.
https://doi.org/10.1007/978-3-030-26354-6_38

At present, micromechanical gyroscopes are widely used to measure the spatial orientation of the platform relative to the base, which perform the functions [4]:

the actual measurement of the angles of pitch, roll and course;
discretization of measurement information and its conversion into a digital code;
the conversion of a digital code into a form defined by the data exchange protocol between the computer and the micromechanical device;
physical data transmission over communication lines.

Each of these functions is associated with the corresponding delays in data processing, which must be taken into account when managing the platform. Therefore, it is necessary to develop an engineering solution for the structure of the data entry and processing system, which determines the importance and relevance of this work.

2 Interfaces to Access Measurement Data

Consider the data entry and processing cycle by the spatial orientation stabilization system using a typical three-axis gyroscope [4] connected to the onboard Von Neumann computer MR via the SPI [5] interface, and the time intervals are formed, shown in Fig. 1.

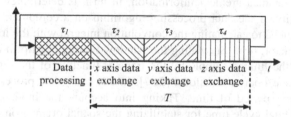

Fig. 1. Time intervals formed during the cycle of stabilization of the spatial orientation of the platform

The connection of a three-axis gyroscope to Von Neumann computers via a standard SPI interface has a drawback: when polling measurement data along three axes, the time interval T of data input, including time intervals $\tau2$, $\tau3$ and $\tau4$. As a result, there is a queue of access to the measurement data.

Based on the communication protocol that requires the SPI interface, time slots can be calculated τ_2, τ_3 and τ_4. A typical three-axis gyroscope has 6 internal registers, each of which includes 8 bits, two registers per coordinate. Therefore, the time interval T consists of six data packets, each of which, in turn, consists of two parts: the control part, the format of which is shown in Table 1, and the part containing measurement data, the format of which is shown in Table 2.

R/W - the bit responsible for the operation with data, when R/W = 1, data is read from the register with the address written in ADR [5: 0], if R/W = 0, the data is written into the register with the address recorded in ADR [5: 0];

Table 1. Control data packet format.

R/W	M/S	ADR5	ADR4	ADR3	ADR2	ADR1	ADR0

Table 2. The measurement data packet format.

DO7	DO6	DO5	DO4	DO3	DO2	DO1	DO0

M/S - bit responsible for data exchange: if M/S = 1 exchange in the format of two bytes, if M/S = 0 exchange in the format of one byte;

ADR7 - 0 - address of the data register, which is access.

DO7 - 0 - the data bits stored in the register from which reading occurred.

Thus, each of the time intervals τ_2, τ_3 and τ_4 includes 24 clock pulses. Consequently, the time interval T of data input to the Von Neumann computer takes 72 clock pulses. Considering that the maximum clock frequency for the SPI [4, 5] interface is 10 MHz, 7,2 µs is spent for data input into the Von Neumann computer.

The allowable sampling period is determined by the impulse response of the mechanical part of the MR [1].

In the considered case, the sampling period τ_s is made up of the time interval for processing data τ_1 and the time interval for entering measurement information T. The processing time for measurement information, in turn, is determined by the computational complexity of the data processing algorithm on a computer. As a rule, data processing is reduced to calculating the convolution integral with the impulse response of the [6, 7] regulator, or in calculating the window Fourier transform and multiplying the spectrum of the limited sample by the transfer function of the regulator and calculating the inverse Fourier transform [2, 7]. In any case, data processing on a computer takes a long period of time. Taking into account the input of measurement information, the total cycle time for stabilizing the spatial orientation of the MP platform may not fit into the requirements of the Sampling theorem $\tau_1 + T \leq \tau_s$ [2, 8]. In addition, when condition $\tau_1 + T \cong \tau_s$ is satisfied, a so-called occurrence occurs at discretization. "Moire effect" [7, 8], which changes the parameters for controlling the position of the platform relative to the base.

In addition, the data processing time interval is a random variable [9]. This means that with the data entry method shown in Fig. 1, a poling noise [9] occurs.

3 The Concept of Building Converter a Serial Interface to Parallel Interface

To improve the temporal characteristics of the input of measurement information into the Von Neumann computer and to exclude the random factor, it is proposed:

to separate the processes of polling the internal registers of the triaxial gyroscope and the process of data input into the computer;

enter a buffer device between the triaxial gyroscope and Von Neumann computer, which will allow the gyroscope internal rengers to be polled autonomously, without the participation of a computer, and save the measurement information until the need for it appears from the computer;
input measurement information into the Von Neumann type computer via a parallel interface, which will shorten the actual input procedure.

The generation of the access queue to the measurement data stored in the internal registers of the triaxial gyroscope is explained in Fig. 2(a). An explanation of the exclusion of the access queue to the measurement data stored in the internal registers of the triaxial gyroscope using the buffer device is shown in Fig. 2(b).

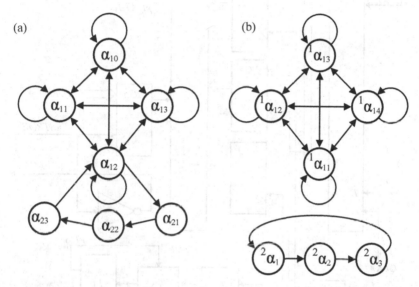

Fig. 2. Graphs illustrating the implementation of the cycle of stabilization of the spatial orientation of the MP platform using the standard SPI interface (a) and using the device for converting serial interface to parallel (b).

In Fig. 2(a) operators α_{12} are the operator of the algorithm responsible for entering data into a von Neumann type computer, operator α_{21} is the operator polling the first internal register of a triaxial gyroscope, operator α_{22} is the operator of polling the second internal register of a triaxial gyroscope, operator α_{23} is the operator of polling the third internal register triaxial gyroscope operators α_{10}, α_{11}, α_{13} are other operators of the algorithm.

Figure 2(b) shows the 2-parallel semi-Markov process [10–12], in which the operator $^1\alpha_{11}$ is responsible for actually entering data into the Von Neumann computer, the operators $^1\alpha_{12} \div {}^1\alpha_{14}$ other operators of the abstract data processing algorithm, and the operators $^2\alpha_1 \div {}^2\alpha_3$ - The polling operators of the first, second, and third internal registers of the triaxial gyroscope, respectively.

4   Block of Conversion of Serial Interface to a Parallel Interface

The device for converting serial interface to parallel one is implemented on the FPGA, since their operation is associated with the ability to perform several actions in parallel, which is necessary in the case under consideration.

The block diagram of the interface converter consists of the Moore state machine (Fig. 3(b)), that allows to control part of the block diagram, that shown in Fig. 3(a).

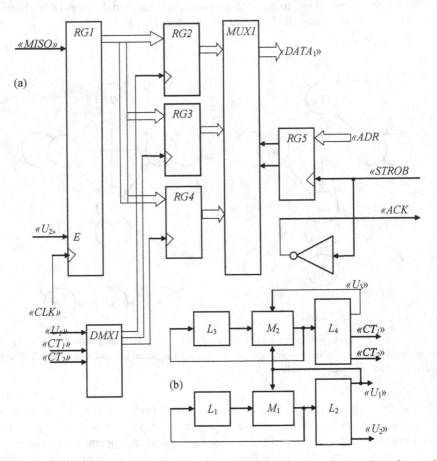

Fig. 3. The device for converting serial interface to parallel interface, that consists of controlled part (a) and control Moore state machine (b).

Let's give a description of Moore's automaton shown in Fig. 3(b).
The logical function L_1 is described by the expression

$$L_1 = <M_1> +1, \tag{1}$$

where $<M_1>$ - the contents of the memory; + - arithmetic plus.
The logical function L_3 is described by the expression

$$L_3 = <M_2> +1, \tag{2}$$

where $<M_2>$ - the contents of the memory; + - arithmetic plus.
Logical function L_2, is a vector, the components of the vector are:

$$U_1 = \overline{M_{1,0}} \wedge \overline{M_{1,1}} \wedge M_{1,2} \wedge M_{1,3} \wedge M_{1,4}, \tag{3}$$

where $M_{1,0} - M_{1,4}$- respectively bits from zero to fourth.

$$U_2 = M_{1,0} \vee M_{1,1}, \tag{4}$$

where $M_{1,0} - M_{1,1}$- respectively zero and first bits.
The logical function mosi is described by the expression

$$MOSI = \overline{M_{1,0} \vee M_{1,1}} \wedge (\overline{M_{1,3} \vee M_{1,2}} \vee \overline{M_{1,4} \vee M_{1,3}} \vee \overline{M_{1,4} \vee M_{1,2}} \vee \\ \vee M_{1,4} \wedge M_{1,3} \wedge M_{1,2} \wedge CT_2 \vee M_{1,4} \wedge M_{1,3} \wedge M_{1,2} \wedge CT_3) , \tag{5}$$

where $M_{1,0} - M_{1,4}$- respectively bits from zero to fourth.
The system operates as follows.

1. Presetting the counter of n packages: $n: = 1$;
2. Presetting the counter m bits: $m: = 1$;
3. If $m < 24$, then $m: = m + 1$; otherwise, go to step 4;
4. If $n < 3$, then $n: = n + 1$ and go to step 2, otherwise go to step 1.

The interface convertor circuit works as follows. The serial data is received by the shift register $RG1$, to the control input of which the signal $U2$ is received to enable the reception of serial data formed on the $MISO$ line accompanied by the clock signal CLK. Parallel storage registers $RG2 - RG4$ are connected to the output of the shift register $RG1$, each of which has its own address, determined by the bits $CT1 - CT2$ of the package counter. The $U1$ signal for completing a two-byte receive cycle is demultiplexed by the $DMX1$ demultiplexer and goes to the clock input of one of the parallel registers $RG2$ storage - $RG4$, with the corresponding code, $CT1 - CT2$.

The measurement data stored in the $RG2 - RG4$ registers is accessed via the universal parallel interface having the data bus $DATA1$, the ADR address bus and the $STROBE$ and ACK control lines.

If it is necessary to access one of the $RG2 - RG4$ registers, the computer on the ADR bus of the address generates the address of the register that is to be accessed. $MUX2$ data, receive acknowledgment ACK signal. Thus, the output of the parallel storage register that is being accessed is connected to the data bus $DATA1$. Exposed to the $DATA1$ bus data is recorded in the Von Neumann computer.

The implemented device for converting a serial interface to a parallel interface allows to:

shorten the procedure of data input to the Von Neumann computer, by using a faster operation of inputting measurement data on the parallel interface;
sampling the data entered into the Von Neumann computer in accordance with the requirements of the sampling theorem [2, 3, 7];
minimize poling noise [9] that occurs during the operation of the Von Neumann computer.

5   Experiment

To confirm the above considerations that data input to the Von Neumann computer as a result of poling procedure is less fast, and the time interval τ_1 (Fig. 1) data processing time is random, a direct experiment was conducted.

During the experiment, the subsystem of stabilization of spatial orientation of the platform MP was used, which includes:

a triaxial gyroscope L3G4200D;
a device for converting a serial interface into a parallel interface implemented on FPGA Altera, MAX II family;
a Von Neumann computer Raspberry pi 3 b+, performing the input and processing of measurement data.

To confirm the relevance of the method proposed in this article, it is proposed to analyze the "competition" of two processes [10–12]:

the process of filling the buffer registers $RG2$ - $RG4$ from of the device for converting a serial interface into a parallel interface;
the process of emptying the buffer registers $RG2$ - $RG4$ by Von Neumann computer, which processes the measurement data on the spatial position of the platform MR.

In Fig. 4 shows a screenshot of the digital oscilloscope UTD2102CEX screen, where the process of emptying the buffer registers $RG2$ - $RG4$ Von Neumann computer displays 1st channel, and the process of filling the buffer registers $RG2$ - $RG4$ with a device for converting a serial interface into a parallel interface is displayed by 2nd channel.

To estimate the time interval between updates of the measurement data in the buffer registers $RG2$ - $RG4$, the time is measured between two samples. To measure the time interval, the function of "cursor measurements" is enabled.

According to the results of the experiment we can draw the following conclusions:

the time interval τ_S between samples for filling the buffer registers $RG2$ - $RG4$ is stable and equal to 8.6 μs (the capabilities of the FPGA debug board do not allow to obtain a higher frequency, improvements are required debug board);
the time interval τ_1 of data processing is random and longer than time interval τ_S of the sampling rate.

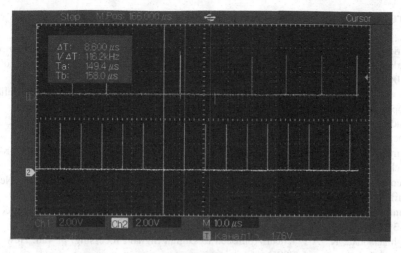

Fig. 4. The oscillogram of the experiment

6   Conclusion

So, to control the MR, which moves over rough terrain, it is necessary to stabilize the spatial orientation of the platform with the target equipment.

The article notes that in order to correctly manage objects, it is necessary to take into account the requirements of the sampling theorem on sampling time intervals and minimize the time required for the actual data input to the Von Neumann computer. Therefore, in the present scientific research the emphasis is placed on the fact that when building digital control systems for MR it is important to consider the control cycle as a data entry process and data processing process. The time delays arising from the execution of the data processing process are related to its computational complexity, and the time delays of the actual data entry process in the Von Neumann computer are related to the specificity of the interfaces used.

This article proposes a block diagram of a device that allows you to convert a serial interface into a parallel interface. Using this device in the path of the MP measuring system allows you to take into account the requirements of the sampling theorem and minimize the time of actual data input to the Von Neumann computer.

An experiment that confirms the performance of the proposed device for converting a serial interface into a parallel interface and the proposed method of data entry as a whole.

The research was carried out within the state assignment of the Ministry of Education and Science of Russian Federation (No 2.3121.2017/PCH).

References

1. Larkin, E., Antonov, M., Privalov, A.: The tricycle mobile robot movement simulation. In: Larkin, E.V., Antonov, M.A., Privalov, A.N. (eds.) MATEC Web of Conferences, vol. 220, p. 06001 (2018)
2. Lyons, R.G.: Understanding Digital Signal Processing, 2nd edn., p. 665. Prentice Hall/PTR, Upper Saddle River (2004)
3. Madisetti, V.K.: The Digital Signal Processing Handbook, vol. 3 Set, p. 2394. CRC Press, Boca Raton (2009)
4. Armenise, M.N., Ciminelli, C., Dell'Olio, F., Passaro, V.M.N.: Advances in Gyroscope Technologies, p. 117. Springer, Heidelberg (2010)
5. Frenzel, L.: Handbook of Serial Communications Interfaces, 1st edn., p. 340. Newnes, Burlington (2015)
6. Bandyopadhyay, M.N.: Introduction to Signals and Systems and Digital Signal Processing, p. 396. PHI Learning Pvt. Ltd., New Delhi (2005)
7. Padmanabhan, K.: A Practical Approach to Digital Signal Processing, p. 428. New Delhi, New Age International (2006)
8. Holdsworth, B., Woods, C.: Digital Logic Design, 4th edn., p. 519. Elsevier, Amsterdam (2002)
9. Larkin, E.V., Kotov, V.V., Kotova, N.A., Antonov, M.A.: Data buffering in mobile robot control systems. In: PUBLIN Conference Proceedings of 2018 4th International Conference on Control, Automation and Robotics (ICCAR 2018), Auckland, New Zealand, pp. 50–54 (2018)
10. Larkin, E., Ivutin, A.: «Concurrency» in M-L-parallel semi-Markov process. In: MATEC Web Conferences, vol. 108, pp. 1–5, May 2017
11. Larkin, E.V., Ivutin, A.N., Kotov, V.V., Privalov, A.N.: Simulation of Relay-Races. Bulletin of the South Ural State University. Series: Mathematical Modelling, Programming and Computer Software, vol. 9, no. 4, pp. 117–128 (2016)
12. Larkin, E.V., Lutskov, Yu.I., Ivutin, A.N., Novikov, A.S.: Simulation of concurrent process with Petri-Markov nets. Life Sci. J. 11(11), 506–511 (2014)

The Location Privacy Preserving Scheme Based on Hilbert Curve for Indoor LBS

Yanru Zhong, Ting Wang, Caijun Gan$^{(\boxtimes)}$, and Xiaonan Luo

Guangxi Key Laboratory of Intelligent Processing of Computer Images and Graphic,
Guilin University of Electronic Technology, Guilin 541004, China
64530223@qq.com

Abstract. Location-based service (LBS) brings great benefits to individuals and society, but it also exist serious threat to users' privacy, because LBS supplier may leak users' location-related information. It is important to protect users' privacy while providing LBS. However, current privacy protection and location recommendation service have the problem of timeliness. To address the problem, a location privacy preserving scheme based on Hilbert curve for LBS is proposed. Firstly, a Hilbert curve is generated from given parameters for coordinate transformation to correspond to Hilbert coordinates. Secondly, the points of users are transmitted to the location service provider (LSP) through the randomly generated point of the fog server without using such methods as K anonymous, which satisfy the demand. Then the user's point of interest (POI) could be obtained by the weighted KNN algorithm of LSP. Finally, the user's POI would be transmitted back to the client. Simulation results show that the proposed scheme provide location privacy with timeliness.

Keywords: Hilbert curve · WKNN · Location privacy ·
Point of interest

1 Introduction

With the development of wireless communication technology and mobile positioning technology, LBS is increasingly popular and to be one of the most promising services for mobile users. LBS involve user's location and location related date provided by mobile devices. Its' information and entertainment [10] services provide by LBS, typical applications include map applications (such as Google Maps), point of interest retrieval (such as Around Me), coupons or discounts available (such as Group On).

This work was supported in part by Guangxi Colleges and Universities Key Laboratory of Intelligent Processing of Computer Images and Graphics (No. GIIP1805) and Innovation Project of Guangxi Graduate Education (No. YCSW2018140), and Guangxi Science and Technology Plan Project (AD18216004£AA18118039-2).

Y. Tan et al. (Eds.): ICSI 2019, LNCS 11656, pp. 387–399, 2019.
https://doi.org/10.1007/978-3-030-26354-6_39

However, the true location information of users will be disclosed to the service provider. Therefore, privacy protection [2,18] has become an increasingly important issue, which has aroused widespread concern in industry and academia. In 2003, Beresford proposed the concept of location privacy [20], which started the first research on LBS privacy protection. Since then, LBS privacy protection has become a research hot spot in the field of information technology. Many famous international conferences and journals have published a large number of LBS privacy [9]. Over the past years, many promising approaches have been proposed concerning preserving location privacy. Dividing them into three main types: (1) User-based privacy protection method [12]; (2) Privacy protection based on transmission process [13]; (3) LBS based privacy protection [4,11]. User-based privacy protection means that an attacker lure a user to click on a dangerous link to reveal the user's privacy; or one user can be compromise to get other user's privacy information. In the face of the attack of the transmission process, mainly using encryption algorithms to resist. In this paper, we mainly concern about the last one type of privacy preservation. There are many LBS-based privacy protection methods, such as K-anonymity, mix zone, path confusion, dummy-Q, cache clock [11].

Privacy protection mainly play a part in two aspects: query privacy and location privacy. Example issues of query privacy include:

- A user can not be identified (i.e., Unanonymity) by a malicious LBS provider.
- A user's interest and/or habit cannot be inferred from LBS query contents, among others.

Location privacy refers to users' private information, directly related to their locations, as well as other private information that can be inferred from the location information. Example issues of location information and location privacy include:

- A user cannot be accurately located.
- User's interest and/or habit cannot be inferred from the location information contained in LBS queries, among others.

Our work is protecting location privacy while enjoying location-based-service. Recently the location privacy mainly divided into two structures: Trusted Third Party (TTP)-free scheme [3,5,14] and TTP based scheme [15,17]. They all need trusted servers, and privacy leaks occur when the servers are not trusted. In this paper, we propose the Hilbert Location Privacy Preserving (HLPP) scheme for indoor localization environment, in which location privacy is guaranteed without needing any fully trusted entities. The K-anonymity technique is that the number of records in each equivalent group is k, that is, when an attacker against big data carries out a link attack, an attack on any record is also associated with another $k - 1$ record in the equivalent group. This feature prevents an attacker from determining records associated with a particular user, thereby protecting the privacy of the user. Although k-anonymous [1] could be more suitable for centralized structure, some researchers have proposed some methods to implement it in distributed structure. However, since there are no unreasonable points in the room, we use the method of generating pseudo-nodes randomly, which reduces the computation and feedback time, and satisfy the demand of timeliness. And the location of the invisible area containing the anonymous set and the location of any non-query user are sent to the LBS provider HilCloak [7]. Based on Hilbert curve, firstly rotates the entire space by an angle, and establishes a Hilbert curve with the key H in the rotated space. The key is known only to the user and the trusted entity. In the query preparation phase, the entity converts each POI to a Hilbert value $H(p_i)$ and then uploads them to the server. When the user q is querying, it submits $H(q)$ to the server, and the server returns the Hilbert value closest to $H(q)$. HilCloak can guarantee the privacy of users in any location, but only guarantees the privacy of one query. And the weighted KNN [6,8,16,19] algorithm is used for location-based POI recommendation. It can satisfy the claim of timeliness.

Without the Hilbert Curve Coefficients, the attacker cannot have any knowledge about a user's real location. We make the following contribution in this paper:

(1) Since the encryption method of aggregate encryption without any trusted devices.
(2) It provides users with location services while protecting the location privacy of users.
(3) The experimental results also show that the proposed scheme preserves location privacy at low computational.

The remainder of this paper is organized as follows: Sect. 2 introduces the proposed scheme. Simulation results are demonstrated in Sect. 3. Finally, we conclude the paper in Sect. 4.

2   Location Privacy Preserving Scheme Based on Hilbert Curve

In this section, the method of location privacy preserving based on Hilbert curve will be introduced (see Fig. 1). Firstly, the coordinate position of the user is obtained by indoor localization technology. According to the parameters set by Hilbert function, the coordinate position of the user is transformed into the corresponding Hilbert coordinate. Secondly, the user's Hilbert coordinates and ID, requests are sent to the fog server for anonymity. Then the fog server sends the anonymous user information mixed pseudo-information to LSP. The LSP can decode the actual coordinates of the user according to Hilbert parameters and recommend the service. LSP sends the reference point mixed pseudo reference point to the fog server, and the fog server picks out the user's reference point and feeds it back to the user. In view of the shortcomings of the prior art, the problem solved in the paper through an improved privacy protection structure to protect the user's privacy while accurately obtaining POI information.

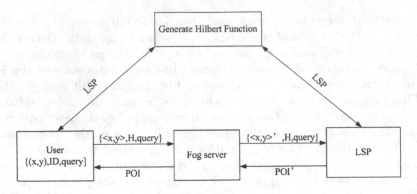

Fig. 1. The construction of LPPS

In order to solve the technical problem, a privacy protection method of indoor location based on Hilbert is proposed in this paper, which includes four parts: user end, fog server, location service provider and Hilbert curve generator. Fog server is an extension of cloud computing. And fog server is not composed of powerful servers but computers with weaker performance and more dispersed functions. On the client side, the locations are transmitted to LSP according to the location point information feedback from the location device. In this process, the fog server, the transmission process, LSP may all be attacked to cause the information disclosure. In order to protect the privacy of the transmission process from being leaked, we use Hilbert curve to convert the user's 2D coordinate information into the corresponding relative position on the Hilbert curve with setting Set Transform Parameter (STP). It produces a Hilbert curve with a different starting point, order, direction, and size. The user's information are not be distinguished timely when the attacker does not know the exact parameters of these Hilbert curves. This protects the fog server from attacker and protects the user's privacy during transmission.

Step 1 Location Transformation. Convert user coordinates to Hilbert coordinates at the client end and produce a Hilbert value. All the information would be sent to the fog server.

Step 2 Randomize. Multiple pseudo Hilbert coordinates and Hilbert values are randomly generated on the fog server side, and all points are sent to the LSP.

Step 3 WKNN. Recommend with POI on the location server side, through the WKNN algorithm, calculate the point of POI, sending these POI to the fog server.

Step 4 Results Transformation. Pick out the user's POI from all POI', separate the user's POI from the fog server side and send the correct POI to the user.

2.1 User Real Coordinates Are Converted to Corresponding Hilbert Coordinates

The client obtains its own precise position information coordinates from the indoor positioning device. The user receives the Hilbert parameter sent by the Hilbert function generator when the user needs to query an interest point of a certain type of store or the like around the user. According to the real coordinates of the client side, Hilbert parameters are converted to Hilbert relative coordinates and Hilbert value H on the client side.

$$STP = \{N, (x_0, y_0), \sigma, \Theta\}. \tag{1}$$

In STP, N represents the Hilbert order; σ respect direction; (x_0, y_0) is the starting point of Hilbert curve; Θ respect the scale of Hilbert Curve.

$$H(i) = h(< x_i, y_i >). \tag{2}$$

Where $H(i)$ represents the transformation of 2D coordinate points into 1D Hilbert values, and h is the transformation function, in which the input value of the function is relative Hilbert coordinates.

$$< x_i, y_i >= \lfloor \frac{(x_i, y_i) - (x_0, y_0)}{L} \rfloor. \tag{3}$$

Where L denotes the length of each Hilbert curve lattice and the real coordinates of the lattice corresponding to the lower left corner of Hilbert (x_0, y_0) with respect to the Hilbert characteristic $< 0, 0 >$. It translates the real coordinate (x_i, y_i) into $< x_i, y_i >$, corresponding to Hilbert curve. And generate the Hilbert value of the resulting Hilbert curve, determined from the lattice on the generated Hilbert curve. For example, the transformation result of Hilbert value, 55, can

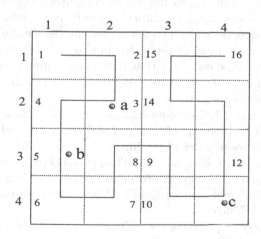

Fig. 2. Second order Hilbert curve

be gotten through third order Hilbert curve from the real coordinate (5, 2). At the same time, the function generator transmits the Hilbert STP to LSP, so that the real location coordinates can be obtained by parsing at the location server side.

As you can see in Fig. 2, if each Hilbert line is equal to 1, the upper-left corner is the starting point, and the starting point is $< 1, 1 >$. Then if the x-axis real coordinate of a are greater than or equal to 2 and less than 3, and the coordinate value of y axis of a is greater than or equal to or less than 3, the Hilbert coordinate corresponding to point a is $< 2, 2 >$. As can be seen from the graph, if the x-axis real coordinate value of b is greater than or equal to 2 and less than 3, and the y-axis coordinate of b is greater than or equal to 4 less than 5, the Hilbert coordinate corresponding to point b is $< 1, 3 >$. Similarly, if the x and y coordinate range of c are greater than or equal to 4 less than 5, the Hilbert coordinate corresponding to c point is $< 4, 4 >$. In other words, the corresponding Hilbert coordinates of a, b and c respectively are $< 2, 2 >$, $< 1, 3 >$, $< 4, 4 >$. (x_c, y_c) can be supposed to be the start point of Hilbert curve. Compensation coordinate is $(x_u, y_u)'$. $< x_u, y_u >$ corresponding to the real coordinate $(x_u, y_u)'$ in Hilbert curve. (x_0, y_0) show the real coordinate $(0, 0)$ of Hilbert curve. The following figuration represents the realizing of Hilbert transformation:

$$(x_c, y_c) = L^* < x_u, y_u > +(x_0, y_0) . \tag{4}$$

$$(x_u, y_u)' = (x_u, y_u) - (x_c, y_c) . \tag{5}$$

2.2   Randomly Generate Pseudo Hilbert Values and Coordinates

Fog computing in fog servers is not composed of powerful servers, but consists of weaker and more decentralized functional computers. Fog server accepts relative Hilbert coordinates $< x, y >$, Hilbert value H, query information from the client over the wireless network. The fog server can reduce the probability that the user is found by the random generated analog Hilbert's relative coordinate equivalent. A certain amount of relative Hilbert coordinates and Hilbert values are reached, and the fog server sends this information to LSP, due to there are rarely unreasonable points in the room.

First of all, it product Hilbert coordinates. L represent the length of each cell, which can be got from the scale of factor Θ and the number of grid cells in 1D. We suppose the real coordinates of the initial point are $(0, 0)$, the order is 2, and the direction is random, L is equal to 1. Then it can be conclude that the range of x and y with random Hilbert coordinates, $[0, 2^N - 1]$. When the parameter values of STP are different, the range of it that can be used to produce random Hilbert coordinates changes.

Then, the fog service products the Hilbert value randomly. In order to make the Hilbert value and Hilbert coordinate obtained by random generation more realistic, we select the random value that does not meet the requirements by following the normal distribution.

Step 1 Calculate the average value (u) of n random variables H.

Step 2 Sort n random variables and calculate the difference (dx) between two adjacent numbers.

Step 3 Calculate the second number and the n-th number:

$$z[i] = \frac{x[i] - u}{dx}.$$

(6)

Step 4 Calculate $\max\{z[i]\}$ and $\min\{z[i]\}$, divide the range $[\min, \max]$ into n fragment, Count the number of elements belonging to the first I interval $(z[j])$.

$$z[j] <= \min + \frac{\max - \min}{n} * i.$$

(7)

Step 5 Set $\min + \frac{\max - \min}{n} * i$ to be x-axis, and num$[i]$ to be y-axis, determining whether this one point is in a straight line.

Step 6 Select the random value that does not meet the requirements.

2.3   Weighted KNN (WKNN) Algorithm

The weighted K-nearest-neighbor is a classification technique based on the majority voting of neighbors. The set of the K-nearest training points must be determined by calculating the weighted distances between the test point and each training point. And the concept of KNN: if most of the k most similar (that is, nearest neighbor) samples of a sample in a feature space belong to a class, then the sample also belongs to this class.

Algorithm 1. Algorithm Weighted KNN Algorithm

Input: users' location

1. : For $i=0$ to M do
2. : Calculate distance: $dis = \sqrt{(x - x_i)^2 - (y - y_i)^2}$
3. : End for
4. : Sorting the distances of M points by KNN
5. : Calculate: $w_i = ae^{-\frac{(x - dis)^2}{2c^2}}$
6. : $p_i = \frac{w_i}{\Sigma_{j=1}^M w_j}$
7. : The probability that the prediction result is the same as the label of the n-th data
8. : select the first K entries

Output: K POI

2.4   Send the POI Belong to the User Back to the Client

According to the user's Hilbert parameters, LSP decodes the information and obtains the real coordinates of these points. According to the WKNN algorithm, the POI search is carried out, and the POI of these points are obtained. However, what we get here is an imprecise location recommendation service. Picking out the user's POI from all POI, and separate the user's POI from the fog server side and send the correct POI to the user.

3   Simulation and Performance Analysis

In this section, we will provide the security analysis for the LPPS scheme and the analysis of performance.

3.1   Security Analysis

The purpose of our analysis is to explain how LPPS protects the privacy of users. Here are a few examples of how LPPS protects the privacy of users.

Case 1 On the client side, it is generally the user's initiative to click on the suspicious link or to become an attacker to pose a threat to the privacy of the user himself or other users.

Case 2 And in the transmission process, because only the LSP and the client have the correct Hilbert parameters, even if the attacker intercepts the information, it will take a long time to decipher, so the attacker cannot obtain the privacy of the user's location.

Case 3 When the attacker attacks the location server provider, although the location server can obtain the real location including N confusion points and users, the attacker still cannot obtain the recommendation information that belongs to the user. So the attacker is unable to identify the location recommendations that belong to the real user.

4   The Performance of Simulation

This part mainly analyzes the performance of simulation experiments. It mainly includes two aspects, the effect of POI recommendation with number of users and Hilbert Transformation. Figure 3 shows the randomly generated 700 sample points. When the decoded user points and other points are transmitted to the LSP, the POI of the crowd points is obtained by the WKNN algorithm. Figure 4 is an example of putting in a randomly generated point and using the WKNN and KNN algorithm to get POI respectively. It can be concluded that WKNN is more likely to rule out some extreme endpoints than KNN form Fig. 4. Although the complexity of algorithm and time of WKNN is higher than that of KNN, WKNN is more sensitive than KNN when dealing with extreme endpoint, and can avoid the influence of extreme point on the result. Since the WKNN algorithm uses the weight to be transformed with the Gaussian function, the weight assigned to the neighbor is up to 1, and the weight decreases as the distance increases, and the weight decreases by 0 when the distance increases to a certain distance. Figure 5 The figure above shows the change in the time required for the WKNN and KNN methods to complete with the increase of POI points. From the above figure, we can see that when the number of POI is small, the KNN algorithm is faster, but with the increase of the number of POI points, the speed of WKNN algorithm shows the advantage of low growth speed. Therefore, the WKNN algorithm used in this paper has a good time-effectiveness.

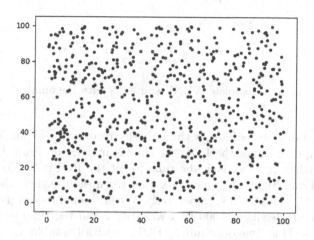

Fig. 3. LSP sample point (WKNN)

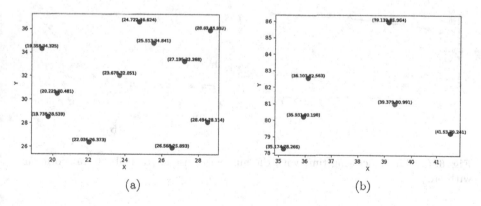

(a)   (b)

Fig. 4. (a) A random point and its POI (WKNN); (b) Another random point and its POI (KNN)

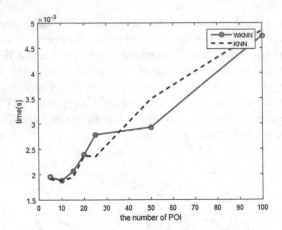

Fig. 5. Time to complete WKNN and KNN with the number of POI

As more and more points go through the recommended algorithm to get the POI, computer to get the POI, the time is increasing. From Fig. 6(a), you can see that when the user is 5, the time to get the POI is 0.255 s and 0.351 s, respectively. From Fig. 6(a), you can see that when the user is 5, the time to get the POI is 0.255 s and 0.351 s, respectively. When the number of users increased to 16, the time to feedback 1000 POI was 0.42 s, and the time to feedback 500 POI was 0.31 s. This time of acquiring POI is basically stable.

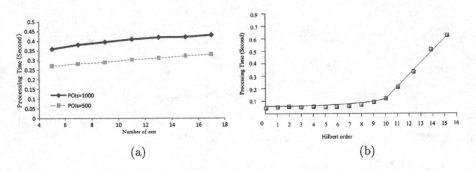

Fig. 6. (a) The processing time with the number of users; (b) Hilbert transform time with order

Figure 6(b) shows the transformation coordinates as the Hilbert coordinate and the Hilbert's worth of feedback as the Hilbert factor changes. From the user end to the fog server side, the algorithm is complicated to $O(N^2)$ due to the pseudo-Hilbert coordinates generated by random simulation. It is not difficult to see from the graph that when the Hilbert order is less than 10, the feedback time is basically stable within 0.1 s. When the Hilbert order exceeds 10, the feedback time would increases exponentially. In order to take into account the timeliness of privacy protection, we have found that the Hilbert function within 10th order can meet the requirements of both safety and timeliness. The greatest advantage of this method is that it does not require any trusted server side to ensure that the location will not be disclosed while the user acquires the location service. Next, we analyze the security of each point:

(1) In the fog server part. The data transferred to the fog server is encrypted by Hilbert transformation, and the pseudo Hilbert feature is confused on the fog server side. When the attacker attacks the fog server side, it takes a long time to decode and distinguish real user locations. However, the user has completed the POI reception in short period, so on the fog service and the attacker cannot get the real data of the user in time.

(2) In LSP part. The confused point is transmitted to the LSP terminal, and according to Hilbert coefficient, each point is decoded, but because the confusion point is generated randomly, this makes it more difficult for the attacker to distinguish the real user point, even if the attacker acquires all the information of the LSP. It is impossible to distinguish the real information of the user in time, which can protect the privacy of the user and prevent the user from being tracked.

(3) In the process of transmission, because there are many parameters of Hilbert encryption, it takes a long time for attacker to decode and cannot track the user's location in time.

5   Conclusion

This paper mainly studies a kind of privacy protection method for indoor location and the system recommended by the POI. Here's the Hilbert transform in the encryption privacy protection method, ensures that the privacy of the user's location is protected during transmission. On the one hand, the weighted KNN algorithm is used to implement the location-based POI recommendation. Compared with KNN, WKNN is more stable when dealing with extreme points. It can meet the timeliness requirement of the recommended system. On the other hand, the fog server side uses the method of randomly generating pseudo Hilbert coordinates to reduce the complexity of the algorithm and meet the requirements of timeliness in privacy protection too. The experiment shows that the transformation time of Hilbert coordinate is related to Hilbert order. We will get the best Hilbert order by further experiments. And it will not only further improve the experimental system, but also improve the feedback time while protecting the privacy of the user's location.

References

1. Casino, F., Domingo-Ferrer, J., Patsakis, C., Puig, D., Solanas, A.: A k-anonymous approach to privacy preserving collaborative filtering. J. Comput. Syst. Sci. **81**(6), 1000–1011 (2015)

2. Chen, H., Lou, W.: On protecting end-to-end location privacy against local eaves-dropper in wireless sensor networks. Pervasive Mob. Comput. **16**, 36–50 (2015)
3. Chow, C.Y., Mokbel, M.F., Liu, X.: A peer-to-peer spatial cloaking algorithm for anonymous location-based service. In: Proceedings of the 14th Annual ACM International Symposium on Advances in Geographic Information Systems, pp. 171–178. ACM (2006)
4. Gedik, B., Liu, L.: Location privacy in mobile systems: a personalized anonymiza-tion model. In: 25th IEEE International Conference on Distributed Computing Systems (ICDCS 2005), pp. 620–629. IEEE (2005)
5. Ghinita, G., Kalnis, P., Skiadopoulos, S.: MOBIHIDE: a mobilea peer-to-peer system for anonymous location-based queries. In: Papadias, D., Zhang, D., Kollios, G. (eds.) SSTD 2007. LNCS, vol. 4605, pp. 221–238. Springer, Heidelberg (2007). https://doi.org/10.1007/978-3-540-73540-3_13
6. Hongliang, T., Zhihong, Q., Liang, X., et al.: Discrete degree WKNN location fingerprinting algorithm based on Wi-Fi. J. Harbin Inst. Technol. **49**(5), 94–99 (2017)
7. Khoshgozaran, A., Shahabi, C.: Blind evaluation of nearest neighbor queries using space transformation to preserve location privacy. In: Papadias, D., Zhang, D., Kollios, G. (eds.) SSTD 2007. LNCS, vol. 4605, pp. 239–257. Springer, Heidelberg (2007). https://doi.org/10.1007/978-3-540-73540-3_14
8. Liu, W., Fu, X., Deng, Z., Xu, L., Jiao, J.: Smallest enclosing circle-based finger-print clustering and modified-WKNN matching algorithm for indoor positioning. In: 2016 International Conference on Indoor Positioning and Indoor Navigation (IPIN), pp. 1–6. IEEE (2016)
9. Liu, Y., Li, Z., Guo, W., Chaoxia, W.: Privacy-preserving multi-keywor ranked search over encrypted big data [keywor read keyword] (2015)
10. Lu, R., Lin, X., Liang, X., Shen, X.: A dynamic privacy-preserving key management scheme for location-based services in VANETs. IEEE Trans. Intell. Transp. Syst. **13**(1), 127–139 (2012)
11. Meyerowitz, J., Roy Choudhury, R.: Hiding stars with fireworks: location privacy through camouflage. In: Proceedings of the 15th Annual International Conference on Mobile Computing and Networking, pp. 345–356. ACM (2009)
12. Pan, X., Xu, J., Meng, X.: Protecting location privacy against location-dependent attacks in mobile services. IEEE Trans. Knowl. Data Eng. **24**(8), 1506–1519 (2012)
13. Panda, M.: Performance analysis of encryption algorithms for security. In: 2016 International Conference on Signal Processing, Communication, Power and Embedded System (SCOPES), pp. 278–284. IEEE (2016)
14. Pingley, A., Yu, W., Zhang, N., Fu, X., Zhao, W.: Cap: a context-aware privacy protection system for location-based services. In: 2009 29th IEEE International Conference on Distributed Computing Systems, pp. 49–57. IEEE (2009)
15. Pingley, A., Zhang, N., Fu, X., Choi, H.A., Subramaniam, S., Zhao, W.: Protection of query privacy for continuous location based services. In: 2011 Proceedings IEEE INFOCOM, pp. 1710–1718. IEEE (2011)
16. Thilina, K.M., Choi, K.W., Saquib, N., Hossain, E.: Pattern classification tech-niques for cooperative spectrum sensing in cognitive radio networks: SVM and W-KNN approaches. In: 2012 IEEE Global Communications Conference (GLOBE-COM), pp. 1260–1265. IEEE (2012)
17. Vu, K., Zheng, R., Gao, J.: Efficient algorithms for k-anonymous location privacy in participatory sensing. In: 2012 Proceedings IEEE INFOCOM, pp. 2399–2407. IEEE (2012)

18. Wernke, M., Skvortsov, P., Dürr, F., Rothermel, K.: A classification of location privacy attacks and approaches. Pers. Ubiquit. Comput. **18**(1), 163–175 (2014)
19. Yen, L., Yan, C.H., Renu, S., Belay, A., Lin, H.P., Ye, Y.S.: A modified WKNN indoor Wi-Fi localization method with differential coordinates. In: 2017 International Conference on Applied System Innovation (ICASI), pp. 1822–1824. IEEE (2017)
20. Yiu, M.L., Jensen, C.S., Huang, X., Lu, H.: SpaceTwist: managing the trade-offs among location privacy, query performance, and query accuracy in mobile services. In: 2008 IEEE 24th International Conference on Data Engineering, pp. 366–375. IEEE (2008)

SSwWS: Structural Model of Information Architecture

Marlon Alberto Piñeres-Melo[1], Paola Patricia Ariza-Colpas[2(✉)],
Wilson Nieto-Bernal[1], and Roberto Morales-Ortega[2]

[1] Department of System Engineering, Universidad del Norte, Colombia,
Barranquilla, Colombia
{pineresm, wnieto}@uninorte.edu.co
[2] Department of Computer Science and Electronic, Universidad de la Costa,
CUC, Barranquilla, Colombia
{parizal, rmorales}@cuc.edu.co

Abstract. The Web Technologies allow a representation of a domain of knowledge. This facilitates the conversion of an explicit and tacit knowledge to the possibility of adding knowledge to the Web for automatic processing by the computer. For this reason, it has been designed to be an architecture known as SSwWS (Search Semantic with Web Services) or Search Semantic Web Services, to show how to extend the functionality of the Web search and semantic raised by Berners-Lee, on the meta-references, defined in a Web ontology, so that a user on the Internet can find the answers to their questions through Web services in a simple and fast.

Keywords: SSwWS architecture · Metadata · XML · XML schema ·
RDF schema · OWL · Ontology · Web semantic web · Reasoners

1 Introduction

This article develops a structural model of an information architecture known as: "SSwWS", which allows integrating, interoperating and applying the technologies recommended by w3c, in order to have a Web ontology that makes it easier to search for information objects such as articles and projects related to jobs. Degree of university students, which through an application based on Web Services facilitates a knowledge management strategy, facilitating the storage, distribution, sharing and intermediation of this explicit knowledge present in the documents, in this case product of the application of theoretical knowledge and the provision of new knowledge. Currently, the content displayed on the Internet is immeasurable and the use of technologies such as HTML is absolutely essential for viewing contents in a browser. But before this it should be noted that the use of this language brings as a disadvantage a poor semantic representation of the data [1]. This leads to the current Web pages providing syntax instead of being added the semantics [2].

The current Web is an extraordinary economic means for accessing explicit knowledge, services, entertainment, commerce and electronic business, among others. For this the technologies that make it possible have had a great evolution to ensure the ease of use, to the point of linking databases with these applications and the creation of algorithms for content recovery [3]. However, the amount of information that can be found on the Internet has become incalculable, which means that search engines are forced to change the way in which this information is retrieved. This paper intends to carry out qualitative and theoretical research processes in order to model and design an information architecture that, supported on the Semantic Web, allows information to be leaked and for queries to be understandable. by computers and humans, thus allowing the extensibility of the current Web. It is for this reason that the w3c has proposed new technologies that facilitate the incorporation of semantics to Web pages such as the Resource Description Framework (RDF) and its extension, such as the Resource Description Framework Schema (RDF-S) and Ontology Web Language. (OWL) allowing through this to model present knowledge [4].

The implementation of the architecture is consolidated in an application that uses Web Services, to facilitate automate processes in the Web developed in a Web environment, using the following development tools: Java, Eclipse version 3.4.1, Apache Tomcat 6.0 and Protégé-OWL 4 and making use of the JENA and PELLET libraries that allow the reasoning of the Web Ontology [5].

2   The Information Architecture SSwWS

The architecture presented below emerges as an innovative solution for semantic searches using Web Services (see Fig. 1).

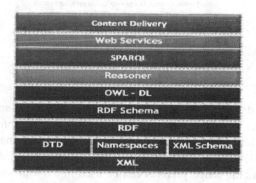

Fig. 1. Proposed architecture SSwWS

2.1   XML and Namespace in SSwWS for the Representation of the Ontological Structure

This labeling language is basic for the exchange of a variety of data and was developed by W3C (World Wide Web Consortium), bringing together a family of technologies such as XLink, XPath, XLST, XPointer, XQuery, among others. It can be said that it is the syntactic base of the future Web known as the Semantic Web, because it facilitates us to define a set of extensible marks, where it can be customized based on a knowledge domain, which helps to distinguish the content of the presentation that can be written in XLS (eXtensible Stylesheet Language), validated by Document Type Definitions (DTD) and/or XML Schema for the definition of data types of the respective metadata [7]. We can represent its syntax in the following way: see Fig. 2. Every XML document must have the following structure:

<? xml version = "1.0" encoding = "ISO-8859-1" standalone = "yes"?>

Currently there is version 1.1, 1.0 is used because it is very general. The header can have two optional attributes, the first is encoding, which determines the type of encoding the document will contain, very important for the interpretation of the characters. The most used for the text in Spanish are UTF-8 and ISO-8859-1. The second attribute is standalone (its values are yes or no), which indicates whether an external document is needed, such as DTD or XML Schema [8, 9].

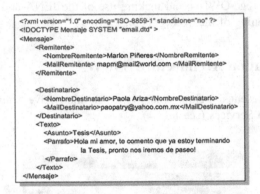

```
<?xml version="1.0" encoding="ISO-8859-1" standalone="no" ?>
<!DOCTYPE Mensaje SYSTEM "email.dtd" >
<Mensaje>
    <Remitente>
        <NombreRemitente>Marlon Piñeres</NombreRemitente>
        <MailRemitente> mapm@mail2world.com </MailRemitente>
    </Remitente>

    <Destinatario>
        <NombreDestinatario>Paola Ariza</NombreDestinatario>
        <MailDestinatario>paopatry@yahoo.com.mx</MailDestinatario>
    </Destinatario>
    <Texto>
        <Asunto>Tesis</Asunto>
        <Parrafo>Hola mi amor, te comento que ya estoy terminando
                 la Tesis, pronto nos iremos de paseo!
        </Parrafo>
    </Texto>
</Mensaje>
```

Fig. 2. Representation of XML

In the world of data, it is possible to find that the name and surname of a person refers to a client and simultaneously to a vendor, this can be considered a problem, much riskier when they appear on the Web, because it can cause name collisions. This can be avoided by defining a unique name within a Namespaces, for example: in the case of the client and the seller, prefixes can be used in the following way: see Fig. 3. This will allow us to have several vocabularies in the same XML document, to facilitate the exchange of information. In XML a Namespaces consists of a set of names that provides a mechanism by which the names of the elements and attributes can be designated for each desired use, based on suitable prefixes [10], to mix different vocabularies in a single XML document, define univocally each XML tag and finally provide universal names that go beyond the documents that contain them, for example: the elements of the XHTML Namespaces are body, table, center, h3, etc. [11]. And its URI name is: http://www.w3.org/1999/xhtml to declare a Namespaces a reserved attribute, a prefix and a URI is taken into account, for example: see Fig. 4. In general, we would have: xmlns: prefix = <<URI>> supported in the w3c recommendation.

```
<cliente:nombre>Pepito</cliente:nombre>
<cliente:apellido>Peréz</cliente:apellido>
<vendedor:nombre>Pepito</vendedor:nombre>
<vendedor:apellido>Peréz</vendedor:apellido>
```

xmlns:xhtml=http://www.w3.org/1999/
xhtml

Fig. 3. Grouping labels by namespaces   **Fig. 4.** Representation of a namespaces

2.2   DTD for the Definition of Types of Documents and XML SCHEMA in SSwWS

The DTD restricts to describe the structure and syntax of the XML or SGML document. The purpose of this is to have well-formed documents. It should be noted that an XML document is valid if its content matches its definition of elements and attributes of the document, using DTD [12]. A DTD is declared in an XML document through DOCTYPE (See: Fig. 5).

```
<?xml version="1.0" encoding="ISO-8859-1" ?>

<!ELEMENT Mensaje (Remitente, Destinatario, Texto)">
    <!ELEMENT Remitente (NombreRemitente, MailRemitente)>
        <!ELEMENT NombreRemitente (#PCDATA)>
        <!ELEMENT MailRemitente  (#PCDATA)>

    <!ELEMENT Destinatario (NombreDestinatario, MailDestinatario)>
        <!ELEMENT NombreDestinatario (#PCDATA)>
        <!ELEMENT MailDestinatario  (#PCDATA)>

    <!ELEMENT Texto (Asunto, Parrafo)>
        <!ELEMENT Asunto (#PCDATA)>
        <!ELEMENT Parrafo (#PCDATA)>
```

Fig. 5. Representation of a DTD

XML Schema allows you to incorporate XML documents, a set of restrictions to define the elements of the XML document, how they will be organized, what their attributes will be and their respective types of data that they can have in the XML document. In Fig. 6, you can see an example of the XML Schema. It must be borne in mind that until now these mentioned technologies are facilitating grammar, but not semantics, it should also be noted that XML is independent of the platform, as proposed by the architecture-led models (MDA).

```
<?xml version="1.0" encoding="UTF-8"?>
<xs:schema xmlns:xs="http://www.w3.org/2001/XMLSchema">
<xs:element name="Mensaje">
    <xs:complexType>
        <xs:sequence>
            <xs:element ref="Remitente" minOccurs="1" maxOccurs="1"></xs:element>
            <xs:element ref="Destinatario" minOccurs="1" maxOccurs="1"></xs:element>
            <xs:element ref="Texto" minOccurs="1" maxOccurs="1"></xs:element>
        </xs:sequence>
    </xs:complexType>
</xs:element>
    <xs:element name="Remitente">
        <xs:complexType>
            <xs:sequence>
                <xs:element ref="NombreRemitente" minOccurs="1" maxOccurs="1"></xs:element>
                <xs:element ref="MailRemitente" minOccurs="1" maxOccurs="1"></xs:element>
            </xs:sequence>
        </xs:complexType>
    </xs:element>
    <xs:element name="NombreRemitente" type="xs:string"></xs:element>
    <xs:element name="MailRemitente" type="xs:string"></xs:element>
    <xs:element name="Destinatario">
        <xs:complexType>
            <xs:sequence>
                <xs:element ref="NombreDestinatario" minOccurs="1" maxOccurs="1"></xs:element>
                <xs:element ref="MailDestinatario" minOccurs="1" maxOccurs="1"></xs:element>
            </xs:sequence>
        </xs:complexType>
    </xs:element>
    <xs:element name="NombreDestinatario" type="xs:string"></xs:element>
    <xs:element name="MailDestinatario" type="xs:string"></xs:element>
    <xs:element name="Texto">
        <xs:complexType>
            <xs:sequence>
                <xs:element ref="Asunto" minOccurs="1" maxOccurs="1"></xs:element>
                <xs:element ref="Parrafo" minOccurs="1" maxOccurs="1"></xs:element>
            </xs:sequence>
        </xs:complexType>
    </xs:element>
    <xs:element name="Asunto" type="xs:string"></xs:element>
    <xs:element name="Parrafo" type="xs:string"></xs:element>
</xs:schema>
```

Fig. 6. Representation of XML schema

2.3 RDF and RDF in SCHEMA in SSwWS

Resource description framework [13], developed by w3c, based on the idea of converting the declarations of resources with the form of Subject - Predicate - Object. Its syntax is based on XML. **Subject:** is what is being described, i.e. the resource, for example the URI http://www.w3.org/Icons/WWW/ w3c_main returns the logo of the W3C in PNG or GIF format. **Predicate:** is the property or relationship that you want to establish about the resource. Take into account that the properties can be defined and used independently of the classes [14]. **Object:** is the value of the property or the other resource with which the relationship is maintained. It can be a literal or an Object. The literal includes a specific data and the object refers to another subject.

Figure 7 is interpreted as: the object is the value of the predicate for the subject.

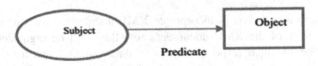

Fig. 7. RDF graph

It can also be represented by the following table:

Table 1. RDF Matrix

Resource (Subject)	http://www.uac.edu.co/marlon/tesis.pdf
Properties (Predicate)	Author
Sentences (Object)	"Marlon Piñeres"

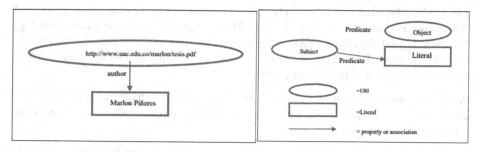

Fig. 8. Example RDF graph   **Fig. 9.** Notation for RDF graphs

The interpretation of Table 1 is: Marlon Piñeres is the creator (author) of the resource http://www.uac.edu.co/marlon/tesis.pdf. This definition can also be visualized in the form of a graph, taking into account that the arcs are the predicate, the subject is represented by means of circular nodes and the rectangular nodes correspond to the value of the object [15]. The graphical notation for the graphs of RDF can be summarized by the following graph [16]: See Fig. 9.

RDF Schema [17] consists of a vocabulary description language RDF defining classes, objects, properties, relations between classes and properties, domain restrictions and range over properties, inheritance between classes and Hierarchy of properties. This vocabulary is used, because RDF does not indicate that what is going to be described is a specific type or class of resources. It is for this reason that RDF Schema extends RDF by taking into account a broad vocabulary with a variety of additional meanings [18]. The XML and XML Schema technologies provide syntactic control, whereas in RDF and RDFS it provides semantic control, that is, XML certifies that the metadata is used correctly, while RDF certifies that, for example, in an assertion where the subject is of citizenship and the predicate is name, the object is the name of an individual and not the model of a car (Fig. 8).

2.4   OWL-DL and REASONER in SSwWS

The language of Web Ontologies, it is used to capture knowledge of a domain of interest. OWL-DL allows you to add vocabulary for the description of classes and properties as the cardinality between classes, equality between classes [19], characteristics of the properties like symmetry, relationships between classes such as disjunction, primitives describes the concepts of a domain and the existing relationship between these concepts [20], based on RDF and RDF Schema. In other words, it is used to provide more vocabulary to describe classes and properties taking into account relationships between classes and characteristics of properties. This language of Web Ontologies, is derived from DAML+OIL (Darpa Agent Markup Language+Ontology Inference Layer) providing maximum expressivity, conserving computationality and resolubility. OWL-DL [21] is so named because of the correspondence it has with the Logic of description (Description Logics).

Pellet: It consists of an open reasoner Java source, created to make inferences about an OWL-DL ontology [22] It also provides an API to consult, validate and check the coherence of ontologies [23].

Jena 2: Jena is a Java FrameWork to build applications of the Semantic Web [24], providing a programming environment for technologies such as RDF, RDFS, OWL, SPARQL, including inference rules. Currently it has been developed until the second version. These reasoners can be combine to make inferences about the ontology, which will allow the recovery of contents using a query language called SPARQL [25].

2.5   SPARQL and Services in SSwWS

Protocol and RDF Query Language [26], defines a language for recovery for RDF/RDFS, used by the Reasoner API to do consultations in the Web Ontology (See Fig. 10).

```
PREFIX pj:<http://www.semanticweb.org/ontologies/2008/10/tesis-uac-sist.owl#>
SELECT ?ta ?est ?sd{
  ?s pj:proyFechaEntrega ?sd.
  ?s pj:ProyEstudiante ?tt.
  ?s pj:proyTitulo ?ta.
  ?tt pj:prsNombre ?est.
}
```

Fig. 10. Sparql query

Nowadays, when we talk about develop Web products to build applications that provide the possibility of carrying out transactions, online shopping systems, display corporate information, among others, which leads to having a Web oriented to the visualization of data. In this layer will facilitate automate the processes carried out by the Web, allowing Web applications, in addition to what is mentioned in the previous paragraph, to perform transactions without human intervention [27]. This model is based on Service Oriented Architectures, also known as SOA, which encapsulate services to make them available to the network and these (Web Services) in turn, have a set of methods used to be used by other applications through the Remote Procedure Call (RPC) [28].

3   Result of the Proposed Architecture (SSwWS)

The product developed as pilot test, is used to make related semantic searches with degree projects of the program Systems Engineering of the Autonomous University of the Caribbean, in which allows to make available and facilitate the sharing of explicit

knowledge, facilitating good knowledge management with respect to the projects that
they make the candidate students to be systems engineers. The Website contemplates
two systems of searches: a general and an advanced. In the general search the user can
write any phrase in the form of a question, for example: "Show me the projects in
which participated henry burgos " (see Fig. 11).

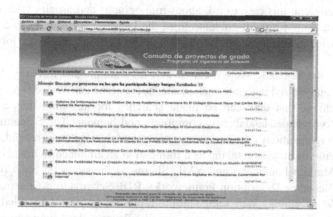

Fig. 11. Search results with SSwWS

Regarding the query advanced, this will be used to make a more specific search,
such as the number of minutes of a project, the beneficiary of the project or a person
involved in the project, such as the technical advisor, methodological advisor, Director,
Coordinator, participating jury or project developers. For example, if we want to search
by record number, we would do the following (see Fig. 12):

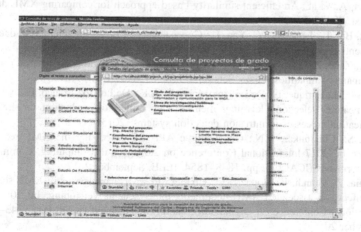

Fig. 12. Advanced search results with SSwWS

4 Conclusions

With the development of this research we could see the importance of the Semantic Web and demonstrate, as through integration of a set of technologies that conform to the w3c, you can design an architecture that allow effective searches, based on meanings and the most important for the community of engineers, and is to apply this set of knowledge, in this case to ask about monographs and articles related to degree projects the students who will graduate from the Universidad Autonoma del Caribe to support knowledge management, allowing any person has access to jobs made by these.

Thanks to the Semantic Web, it can search for a simple and fast way. For this it is necessary to analyze and integrate each of the layers of the call Web 3.0 proposed by its author, to achieve that they can be made searches for meaning, thus allowing the information to be understandable by computers and humans. The Semantic Web will facilitate the organizations have the information available, ordered, related, indexed by means of the use of metadata, taking as a foundation an architecture based on the XML (Extensible Markup Language) and XML Shema as the syntactic basis of the future Web, RDF (Resource Description Framework), RDF Schema to give semantics to the Web and OWL (Ontology Web Language) to represent an area of knowledge, finally a demonstration where by means of a reasoner like Pellet or Jena, you can make logical inferences over said domain of knowledge represented by means of a ontology.

Acknowledgment. To the Universidad del Norte and the Universidad Autonoma del Caribe for the support provided in the development of this work.

References

1. Oliveira, A., et al.: An efficient similarity-based approach for comparing XML documents. Inf. Syst. **78**, 40–57 (2018)
2. Ma, Z., Bai, L., Ishikawa, Y., Yan, L.: Consistencies of fuzzy spatiotemporal data in XML documents. Fuzzy Sets Syst. **343**, 97–125 (2018)
3. Ma, Z., Zhao, Z., Yan, L.: Heterogeneous fuzzy XML data integration based on structural and semantic similarities. Fuzzy Sets Syst. **351**, 64–89 (2018)
4. Palechor, M., Enrique, F., De La Hoz Manotas, A.K., De La Hoz Franco, E., Ariza Colpas, P.P.: Feature selection, learning metrics and dimension reduction in training and classification processes in intrusion detection systems (2015)
5. Pawar, S., Chiplunkar, N.N.: Open source APIs for processing the XML result of web services. In: 2017 International Conference on Advances in Computing, Communications and Informatics (ICACCI), pp. 1848–1854. IEEE, September 2017
6. Brahmia, Z., Grandi, F., Bouaziz, R.: Changes to XML namespaces in XML schemas and their effects on associated XML documents under schema versioning. In: 2016 Eleventh International Conference on Digital Information Management (ICDIM), pp. 43–50. IEEE, September 2016

7. Mendoza-Palechor, F.E., Ariza-Colpas, P.P., Sepulveda-Ojeda, J.A., De-la-HozManotas, A., Piñeres Melo, M.: Fertility analysis method based on supervised and unsupervised data mining techniques (2016)

8. Ciobanu, G., Horne, R., Sassone, V.: A descriptive type foundation for RDF schema. J. Logical Algebraic Methods Program. **85**(5), 681–706 (2016)

9. Kejriwal, M., Miranker, D.P.: An unsupervised instance matcher for schema free RDF data. Web Semant. Sci. Serv. Agents World Wide Web **35**, 102–123 (2015)

10. Palechor, F.M., De la Hoz Manotas, A., Colpas, P.A., Ojeda, J.S., Ortega, R.M., Melo, M.P.: Cardiovascular disease analysis using supervised and unsupervised data mining techniques. JSW **12**(2), 81–90 (2017)

11. Barati, M., Bai, Q., Liu, Q.: Mining semantic association rules from RDF data. Knowl.-Based Syst. **133**, 183–196 (2017)

12. Tong, Q.: Mapping object-oriented database models into RDF(S). IEEE Access **6**, 47125–47130 (2018)

13. Jimeno-Gonzalez, K., Ariza-Colpas, P., Piñeres-Melo, M.: Gobierno de TI en Pymes Colombianas, Mito o Realidad (2017)

14. Hilal, M., Schuetz, C.G., Schrefl, M.: Superimposed multidimensional schemas for RDF data analysis. In: 2017 IEEE 14th International Scientific Conference on Informatics, pp. 104–110. IEEE, November 2017

15. Bouhamoum, R., Kellou-Menouer, K., Lopes, S., Kedad, Z.: Scaling up schema discovery for RDF datasets. In: 2018 IEEE 34th International Conference on Data Engineering Workshops (ICDEW), pp. 84–89. IEEE, April 2018

16. Calabria-Sarmiento, J.C., et al.: Software applications to health sector: a systematic review of literature (2018)

17. Bayoudhi, L., Sassi, N., Jaziri, W.: A hybrid storage strategy to manage the evolution of an OWL 2 DL domain ontology. Procedia Comput. Sci. **112**, 574–583 (2017)

18. Lu, W., Qin, Y., Liu, X., Huang, M., Zhou, L., Jiang, X.: Enriching the semantics of variational geometric constraint data with ontology. Comput. Aided Des. **63**, 72–85 (2015)

19. Zheleznyakov, D., Kharlamov, E., Nutt, W., Calvanese, D.: On expansion and contraction of DL-Lite knowledge bases. J. Web Semant. **57**, 100484 (2019)

20. De-La-Hoz-Franco, E., Ariza-Colpas, P., Quero, J.M., Espinilla, M.: Sensor based datasets for human activity recognition–a systematic review of literature. IEEE Access **6**, 59192–59210 (2018)

21. Abadi, A., Ben-Azza, H., Sekkat, S.: Improving integrated product design using SWRL rules expression and ontology-based reasoning. Procedia Comput. Sci. **127**, 416–425 (2018)

22. Boustil, A., Maamri, R., Sahnoon, Z.: An OWL DL ontology based on classification of web services into communities. In: 2014 4th International Symposium on ISKO-Maghreb: Concepts and Tools for knowledge Management (ISKO-Maghreb), pp. 1–8. IEEE, November 2014

23. Altowayan, A.A., Tao, L.: Simplified approach for representing partwhole relations in OWL-DL ontologies. In: 2015 IEEE 17th International Conference on High Performance Computing and Communications (HPCC), 2015 IEEE 7th International Symposium on Cyberspace Safety and Security (CSS), 2015 IEEE 12th International Conference on Embedded Software and Systems (ICESS), pp. 1399–1405. IEEE, August 2015

24. Pani, S., Mishra, J.: Building semantics of E-agriculture in India: semantics in e-agriculture. In: 2015 International Conference on Man and Machine Interfacing (MAMI), pp. 1–4. IEEE, December 2015

25. Guerrero, H., Polo, S., Ariza, J.M.R.P.: Trabajo colaborativo como estrategiadidáctica para el desarrollo del pensamiento crítico. Opción **34**(86), 959–986 (2018)
26. Boustil, A., Maamri, R., Sahnoon, Z.: A semantic selection strategy for composite Web services based on conforming objects. In: 2016 International Conference on Information Technology for Organizations Development (IT4OD), pp. 1–6. IEEE, March 2016
27. Echeverri-Ocampo, I., Urina-Triana, M., Patricia Ariza, P., Mantilla, M.: El trabajo colaborativo entre ingenieros y personal de la salud para el desarrollo de proyectos en salud digital: una visión al futuro para lograr tener éxito (2018)
28. Ariza, P., Pineres, M., Santiago, L., Mercado, N., De la Hoz, A.: Implementation of moprosoft level I and II in software development companies in the Colombian Caribbean, a commitment to the software product quality region. In 2014 IEEE Central America and Panama Convention (CONCAPAN XXXIV), pp. 1–5. IEEE, November 2014

Author Index